Concavity and Optimization in Microeconomics

PAUL MADDEN

Concavity and Optimization in Microeconomics

Basil Blackwell

First published 1986

Basil Blackwell Ltd
108 Cowley Road, Oxford OX4 1JF, UK

Basil Blackwell Inc.
432 Park Avenue South, Suite 1505,
New York, NY 10016, USA

British Library Cataloguing in Publication Data

Madden, Paul
Concavity and optimization in microeconomics.
1. Economics, Mathematical
2. Mathematical optimization
I. Title
515 QA402.5

ISBN 0-631-14192-8

Library of Congress Cataloging-in-Publication Data

Madden, Paul
Concavity and optimization in microeconomics.

Bibliography: p.
Includes index.
1. Microeconomics. 2. Concave functions.
3. Mathematical optimization. 4. Economics, Mathematical.
I. Title
HB172.M3 1986 338.5′01′519 85-22217
ISBN 0-631-14192-8

Typeset by Unicus Graphics Ltd, Horsham
Printed in Great Britain by T.J. Press Ltd, Padstow

To My Parents

Contents

Preface

Recently the so-called 'duality' methods have become fashionable propagators of the major theoretical results in microeconomic theory and have also provided a stimulus to empirical work in this area. The term 'duality' is not totally precise in encompassing all such methods, which correspond more generally to applications of various aspects of convex and concave analysis to optimization and microeconomics. The objective of this book is to provide an exposition of this material which is accessible to students of economics with a mathematical propensity, from second-year undergraduate level upwards. The book effectively presumes some knowledge of calculus and matrix algebra up to a level which might reasonably be attained in a first-year undergraduate 'mathematics for economists' course.

In terms of style, the book aims to be formal but leisurely. The mathematics is developed at some length, prior to applications to consumer theory and the theory of the firm. Chapters 1–9 are devoted to the mathematics of convex sets, concave functions, concave programming and homogeneous functions and chapters 10–12 derive the basic comparative statics results of microeconomics. Chapters 13–20 then generalize and extend the material of the first 12 chapters with respect to the mathematics and the economics. With an eye to audience accessibility, differentiability assumptions are employed in many cases where they could have been dispensed with; for instance, subgradients do not appear until chapter 19, and then only briefly. Each chapter concludes with some exercises. References and bibliographical notes for all chapters are found at the end of the book.

The material of chapters 1–12 has been the basis for 20 lectures to the Mathematical Economics I course at Manchester. This is a second-year undergraduate course, following a first-year 'mathematics for economists' course which satisfies the presumptions on calculus and matrix algebra mentioned earlier. Chapters 13–20 have been taught to the ensuing third-year course, Mathematical Economics II. Various parts of the book have been used in the graduate Mathematical Economics course for the M.A. in Econometrics. Although the book contains proofs of most theorems, these are by no means necessary for a working knowledge of its material: for instance, in our Mathematical Economics I course the emphasis has been very much on the understanding of the use of the theorems in examples, rather than on proofs.

As a course text, the book is aimed primarily at mathematical economics and microeconomics courses. In addition it hopes to provide at least useful back-up to courses in applied econometrics and less technically oriented microeconomics.

I acknowledge, with great pleasure, the help of my colleague Chris Birchenhall who has taught me, either explicitly or by prompting, much of the material which follows, and who has read and commented on much of the manuscript. In general the Department of Econometrics and Social Statistics at Manchester has provided a most happy and stimulating environment during the preamble to, and the writing of, this book. Roger Hartley of the Department of Decision Theory at Manchester has been a most helpful source of discussion and guidance on convexity/concavity in general. Peter Lambert of the University of York kindly agreed to read the entire manuscript and I am very grateful for his extensive and careful comments, which, alongside correspondence from A. Mas-Colell, have saved me from a number of embarrassments. My intellectual debt to the people cited in the bibliographical notes is, of course, immense. Naturally, I remain responsible for all errors and shortcomings.

I acknowledge, with regret, that my handwritten manuscript has not been ideally legible and I am therefore particularly grateful to Jean Ashton, Linda Cooper, Clare Dyson, Angela Jones and Marie Waite for their good humour and efficiency in typing. Good humour and efficiency have also been characteristics of the representatives of the publishers whom I have dealt with so far, namely Sue Corbett and Rene Olivieri.

Very special thanks to my wife, Anne, for her love and encouragement, particularly during the 18 months since I committed myself to the writing of this book. After about 12 of those 18 months our first child, David, was born, and provided the most happy environment for completion of the book.

1 Convex sets

1.1 Introduction

Convex sets appear frequently throughout this book although they are not the main theme. Nonetheless, it is probably best to acquire some familiarity with the concept straight away. To begin we define some no doubt familiar terminology for sets in general, and then eventually introduce the idea of a convex set.

A *set* is a collection of objects. The set of books in a library, the set of people on earth, the set of positive integers are all sets in this general sense. If S denotes a set then an object which belongs to S is called an *element* of S. If x is an element of S we write $x \in S$, alternatively read as 'x belongs to S' or 'x is in S'. If we remove some (possibly none, possibly all) elements from S we end up with another set T, say; T is then said to be a *subset* of S, written $T \subset S$ (or $S \supset T$) and alternatively read as 'T is contained in S' or simply 'T is in S'. If we were to remove all elements from S then T would contain no elements; such a set is called an empty set and written $\emptyset$. Notice that $\emptyset \subset S$ for any set S. A set S is *finite* if it has a finite number of elements; otherwise it is infinite. The *intersection* of two sets, V and W say, written $V \cap W$, is the set whose elements belong to *both* V and W. V and W are said to be *disjoint* if $V \cap W = \emptyset$; i.e. if they have no elements in common. The *union* of two sets V and W, written $V \cup W$ is the set whose elements belong to V *or* W *or both*. Finally, two symbols which we use frequently are '$\forall$' which means 'for all' and '$\exists$' which means 'there exists'.

Examples illustrating these definitions will emerge shortly.

1.2 Subsets of R

Throughout this book the letter R will be used to denote a very important set, the set of all real numbers. Many of the sets which interest us will be subsets of R, found by removing some (maybe none, maybe all) elements from R. For instance $\emptyset$ and R itself are both subsets of R. Some further examples are

$$S_1 = \{x \in R \mid 0 \leqslant x \leqslant 1\}.$$

This means that S_1 is the set of real numbers in R which lie between (and including) 0 and 1. Generally, in order to define a set, we place a description of the elements of the set within curly brackets.

$$S_2 = \{x \in R \mid -1 \leqslant x \leqslant 1\}$$
$$S_3 = \{x \in R \mid -1 < x < 1\}$$
$$S_4 = \{x \in R \mid 2 < x < 3\}$$
$$S_5 = \{x \in R \mid 0 \leqslant x \leqslant 1 \quad \text{or} \quad 2 < x < 3\}$$
$$S_6 = \{x \in R \mid x = 1 \quad \text{or} \quad x = 2 \quad \text{or} \quad x = 3\}$$
$$S_7 = \{x \in R \mid x \geqslant 0\}$$
$$S_8 = \{x \in R \mid x > 0\}.$$

All these sets are subsets of R and all except S_6 are infinite sets. S_6 is finite and we sometimes describe finite sets merely by listing their elements within curly brackets. For instance $\{1,2,3\}$ is an alternative description of S_6. Most of the sets in this book, however, are infinite.

To illustrate the earlier definitions notice that: $S_1 \subset S_2, S_3 \cap S_4 = \emptyset$ (so S_3 and S_4 are disjoint), $S_1 \cap S_2 = S_1$ and $S_1 \cup S_4 = S_5$.

S_7 is the set of all non-negative real numbers and since this set occurs frequently we give it a special symbol, namely R_+. Similarly, S_8 is the set of strictly positive real numbers and we denote it by R_{++}. The negative analogues are $R_- = \{x \in R \mid x \leqslant 0\}$ and $R_{--} = \{x \in R \mid x < 0\}$.

Subsets of R can be depicted visually by drawing a horizontal line to depict R itself, so that points on the line correspond to the elements of R, and by imposing indicators of the subset in question. For instance S_1–S_8 are depicted in fig. 1.1 in this manner, where a rounded arrow-head means that the end of the line indicated is not included.

The symbol '$+\infty$', read as plus infinity, is defined by: $\forall x \in R$, $x < +\infty$. Similarly, $\forall x \in R$, $x > -\infty$. In this book $+\infty$ and $-\infty$ are not regarded as real numbers; they do not belong to R.

A set $S \subset R$ is *bounded* if there is a positive real number, M say, such that: $\forall x \in S$, $-M < x < +M$. In the above examples $M = 4$ suffices to show that S_1–S_6 are bounded. There is no such number for S_7 and S_8 and these sets (like R itself) are not bounded.

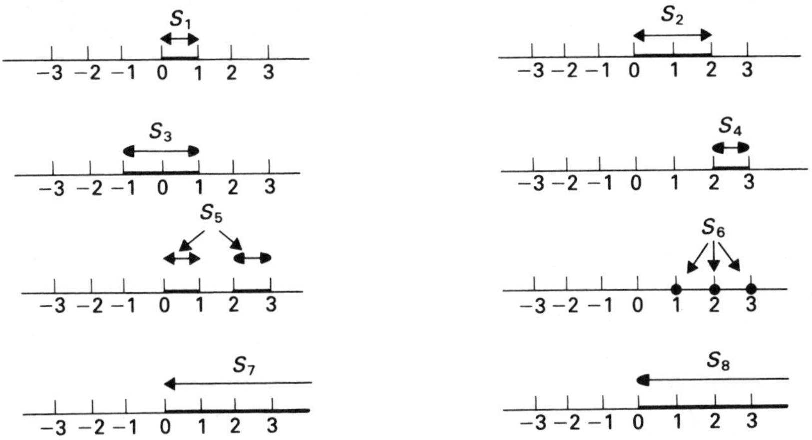

Figure 1.1

There is some shorthand notation for certain subsets of R which we use freely in what follows. When $a \leqslant b$, we write

$[a, b]$	for $\{x \in R \mid a \leqslant x \leqslant b\}$	(1.1)
(a, b)	for $\{x \in R \mid a < x < b\}$	(1.2)
$[a, b)$	for $\{x \in R \mid a \leqslant x < b\}$	(1.3)
$(a, b]$	for $\{x \in R \mid a < x \leqslant b\}$	(1.4)
$[a, +\infty)$	for $\{x \in R \mid a \geqslant x\}$	(1.5)
$(-\infty, b]$	for $\{x \in R \mid x \geqslant b\}$	(1.6)
$(a, +\infty)$	for $\{x \in R \mid x > a\}$	(1.7)
$(-\infty, b)$	for $\{x \in R \mid x < b\}$	(1.8)
$(-\infty, +\infty)$	for R itself	(1.9)

A subset of R corresponding to any of these forms is termed an *interval* of R. Notice that the visual representation of any interval will be a *connected* line. In our examples, S_1–S_4, S_7 and S_8 are intervals; $S_1 = [0, 1]$, $S_2 = [0, 2]$, $S_3 = (-1, +1)$, $S_4 = (2, 3)$, $S_7 = [0, +\infty)$, $S_8 = (0, +\infty)$. S_5 and S_6 are not intervals.

1.3 Convex subsets of R

Suppose $S \subset R$ and suppose $x^1, x^2 \in S$ where $x^1 \leqslant x^2$. The set $[x^1, x^2]$ is then the set of real numbers between and including x^1 and x^2, or, visually, the set of points on the line joining x^1 to x^2. Now it may or may not be that $[x^1, x^2] \subset S$. However, if it *is* the case that, *for all* $x^1, x^2 \in S$ where $x^1 \leqslant x^2$ we have $[x^1, x^2] \subset S$ then we say that S is a convex set.

Definition 1.1 A set $S \subset R$ is *convex* if and only if

$$[x^1, x^2] \subset S \quad \forall x^1, x^2 \in S \text{ where } x^1 \leqslant x^2$$

Visually this merely says that a set in R is convex if and only if, *for every pair of points in the set, the line joining these points lies entirely in the set.* The set S_5 before, for instance, is *not* convex since (e.g.) the line joining $x^1 = \frac{1}{2}$ to $x^2 = \frac{5}{2}$ does not lie entirely within S_5 although $\frac{1}{2}, \frac{5}{2} \in S_5$. Similarly, S_6 is not convex. However, it is easy to see that S_1–S_4 and S_7, S_8 are all convex sets. It should be clear that a set $S \subset R$ is convex if and only its visual representation is a *connected* line. In other words $S \subset R$ is convex if and only if it is an *interval* of R of one of the forms (1.1)–(1.9). So in the one-dimensional setting of R identification of convex sets is very simple; merely check whether the set is an interval. However, matters are not always quite so simple in higher dimensions and a useful alternative statement to definition 1.1 emerges by noticing that the line joining x^1 to x^2 can be represented as:

$$\{x \in R | x = \lambda x^1 + (1-\lambda) x^2 \quad \text{where } \lambda \in [0, 1]\}$$

To see why, consider $x = \lambda x^1 + (1-\lambda) x^2$ where $\lambda \in [0, 1]$. When $\lambda = 1$, $x = x^1$; when $\lambda = 0$, $x = x^2$; when $\lambda = \frac{1}{2}$, x is the arithmetic mean of x^1 and x^2; and so on. As λ varies between 1 and 0, x as defined here varies between x^1 and x^2 and takes on all intermediate values as λ varies between 1 and 0. Such points are given a special name. If x^1, $x^2 \in R$ and $\lambda \in [0, 1]$ then $x = \lambda x^1 + (1-\lambda) x^2$ is said to be a *convex combination* of x^1 and x^2. What we require for convexity of $S \subset R$ is that all convex combinations of all pairs of points in S are also in S. Hence we define set convexity alternatively and equivalently by:

Definition 1.2 A set $S \subset R$ is *convex* if and only if

$$\lambda x^1 + (1-\lambda) x^2 \in S \quad \forall \lambda \in [0, 1] \text{ and } \forall x^1, x^2 \in S$$

We argued earlier that convexity or otherwise of subsets of R is a trivial and geometrically obvious matter. However, we can now (and will have to later) check our geometric intuition by verifying definition 1.2. For instance consider a set of the form $[a, b]$. We want to show that $[a, b]$ is a convex set using definition 1.2. So choose any $x^1, x^2 \in [a, b]$, any $\lambda \in [0, 1]$ and consider $x = \lambda x^1 + (1-\lambda)x^2$. Since $x^1, x^2 \in [a, b]$

$$a \leqslant x^1 \leqslant b \tag{1.10}$$

$$a \leqslant x^2 \leqslant b \tag{1.11}$$

Multiplying (1.10) by λ, (1.11) by $(1-\lambda)$ and adding gives

$$a \leqslant \lambda x^1 + (1-\lambda)x^2 \leqslant b$$

So $\lambda x^1 + (1-\lambda)x^2 \in [a, b]$ also, $\forall x^1, x^2 \in [a, b]$ and $\forall \lambda \in [0, 1]$. Hence $[a, b]$ is confirmed as a convex set.

1.4 Subsets of R^n

We now move to higher dimensions. The *Cartesian product* of two sets A_1 and A_2, written $A_1 \times A_2$, is the set of all *ordered pairs* (x_1, x_2) such that $x_1 \in A_1$ and $x_2 \in A_2$. Of particular importance is the Cartesian product $R \times R = \{(x_1, x_2) | x_1 \in R, x_2 \in R\}$ and for shorthand we denote this set R^2; R^2 is simply the set of all ordered pairs of real numbers. Elements of R^2 can be depicted visually as points in a plane in the usual fashion. Here are some examples of subsets of R^2 and a visual representation in fig. 1.2.

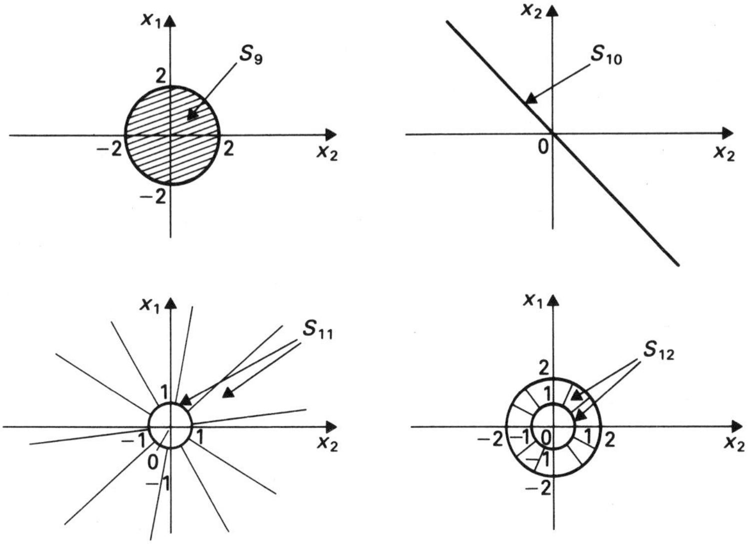

Figure 1.2

$$S_9 = \{(x_1, x_2) \in R^2 | x_1^2 + x_2^2 < 4\}$$
$$S_{10} = \{(x_1, x_2) \in R^2 | x_1 + x_2 = 0\}$$
$$S_{11} = \{(x_1, x_2) \in R^2 | x_1^2 + x_2^2 \geqslant 1\}$$
$$S_{12} = \{(x_1, x_2) \in R^2 | 1 < x_1^2 + x_2^2 \leqslant 4\}$$

All these sets are infinite subsets of R^2. Notice that $S_9 \cap S_{11} = S_{12}$ and $S_9 \cup S_{11} = R^2$. Notice also that the circumference of the circle in S_9 and the inner circle in S_{12} do not belong in these sets.

Moving on, the Cartesian product of n sets, $A_1, A_2, \ldots, A_n$, written $A_1 \times A_2 \times \ldots \times A_n$ is the set of ordered n-tuples $(x_1, \ldots, x_n)$ such that $x_i \in A_i$, $i = 1, \ldots, n$. We write R^n for the Cartesian product of R with itself n times; so $R^n = \{(x_1, \ldots, x_n) | x_i \in R, i = 1, \ldots, n\}$ and is the set of ordered n-tuples of real numbers. When $n > 1$ we often shorten the notation by writing the vectors $\mathbf{x}$ for $(x_1, \ldots, x_n)$. Most of the sets of interest in this book are subsets of R^n, for some n. Some further examples are

$$S_{13} = \{\mathbf{x} \in R^3 | x_1 + x_2 + x_3 = 0\}$$
$$S_{14} = \{\mathbf{x} \in R^3 | x_1^2 + x_2^2 + x_3^2 < 1\}$$
$$S_{15} = \left\{\mathbf{x} \in R^n | \sum_{i=1}^{n} x_i = 1\right\}$$
$$S_{16} = \left\{\mathbf{x} \in R^n | \sum_{i=1}^{n} x_i^2 \geqslant 1\right\}$$

These are all infinite subsets of R^n with $n = 3$ in the first two and n unspecified in the others. Visual representation of subsets of R^3 is possible but requires three-dimensional diagrams which are difficult to convey in the plane of the page; we do not attempt such sketches. However, if we did so attempt, S_{13} would correspond to a plane in R^3 while S_{14} would be the inside of a sphere. For $n > 3$ a visual representation is not possible.

Finally, a set $S \subset R^n$ is *bounded* if there is a positive real number M such that

$$\forall \mathbf{x} \in S \text{ and } \forall i \quad -M < x_i < +M$$

For instance $M = 3$ is sufficient to show that S_9 and S_{12} are bounded. $M = 2$ (in fact $M = 1$) ensures that S_{14} is bounded (since $\mathbf{x} \in S_{14}$ implies $x_i \in (0, 1)$). However, S_{10}, S_{11}, S_{13}, S_{15} and S_{16} are not bounded.

1.5 Convex subsets of R^n

A convex set in R^n can be envisaged in the same way as $n=1$; $S\subset R^n$ is convex if and only if the line joining any two points in the set lies entirely within the set. To formalize this notion, if $\lambda \in [0, 1]$ and if $\mathbf{x}^1$ and $\mathbf{x}^2$ are two points in R^n then $\mathbf{x} = \lambda\mathbf{x}^1 + (1-\lambda)\mathbf{x}^2$ is said to be a convex combination of $\mathbf{x}^1$ and $\mathbf{x}^2$; writing out the vector $\mathbf{x}$ term by term gives $x_i = \lambda x_i^1 + (1-\lambda)x_i^2$, $i=1, \ldots, n$. Figure 1.3 illustrates such an $\mathbf{x}$ when $n=2$ and $\lambda=\frac{1}{2}$. Clearly $\mathbf{x}$ is the mid-point of the line joining $\mathbf{x}^1$ to $\mathbf{x}^2$. Moreover as λ varies between 1 and 0, $\mathbf{x}$ maps out the entire line joining $\mathbf{x}^1$ to $\mathbf{x}^2$. In general, and as earlier when $n = 1$, the convex combinations of $\mathbf{x}^1$ and $\mathbf{x}^2$ represent the points on the line joining $\mathbf{x}^1$ to $\mathbf{x}^2$. So for $S\subset R^n$ to be convex we require that all convex combinations of all pairs of points in S are also in S:

Definition 1.3 A set $S\subset R^n$ is *convex* if and only if

$$\lambda\mathbf{x}^1 + (1-\lambda)\mathbf{x}^2 \in S \quad \forall\lambda \in [0, 1], \forall\mathbf{x}^1, \mathbf{x}^2 \in S$$

By inspection of fig. 1.2 we see that S_9 and S_{10} are convex sets while S_{11} and S_{12} are not convex (since for instance the points $(1, 0)$, $(-1, 0)$ belong to both sets but the line joining these points does not lie entirely within either set). More formal demonstration of set convexity requires us to show that definition 1.3 is satisfied. Consider for instance S_{15}. We have to show that $\lambda\mathbf{x}^1 + (1-\lambda)\mathbf{x}^2 \in S_{15}$ for any $\lambda \in [0, 1]$ and for any $\mathbf{x}^1, \mathbf{x}^2 \in S_{15}$. So let $\mathbf{x}^1, \mathbf{x}^2 \in S_{15}$; then

$$\sum_{i=1}^{n} x_i^1 = 1 \quad \text{and} \quad \sum_{i=1}^{n} x_i^2 = 1$$

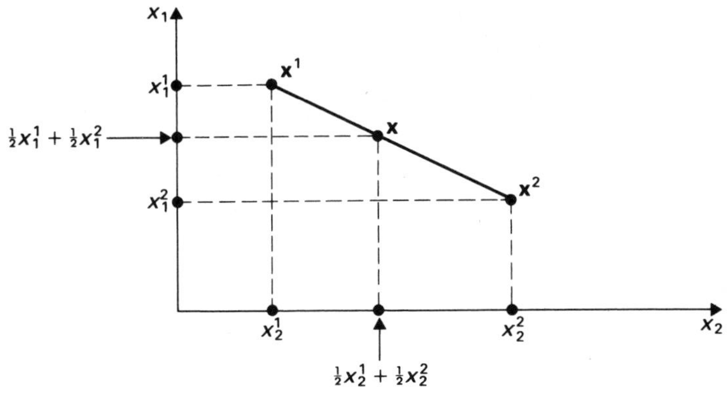

Figure 1.3

Let $\lambda \in [0, 1]$, multiply the first equation by λ, the second by $(1-\lambda)$ and add, giving

$$\lambda \sum_{i=1}^{n} x_i^1 + (1-\lambda) \sum_{i=1}^{n} x_i^2 = \lambda + (1-\lambda) = 1$$

So

$$\sum_{i=1}^{n} [\lambda x_i^1 + (1-\lambda) x_i^2] = 1$$

which means $\lambda \mathbf{x}^1 + (1-\lambda)\mathbf{x}^2 \in S_{15}$. Hence, if $\mathbf{x}^1, \mathbf{x}^2 \in S_{15}$ and if $\lambda \in [0, 1]$ then $\lambda \mathbf{x}^1 + (1-\lambda)\mathbf{x}^2 \in S_{15}$ also and S_{15} is indeed a convex set.

In fact S_9, S_{10}, S_{13}, S_{14} and S_{15} are all convex sets while S_{11}, S_{12} and S_{16} are not convex. However, the reader will find that demonstration of definition 1.3 for S_9 or S_{14} is rather more difficult (but possible) than for S_{15} above (or for S_{10}, S_{13} which are like S_{15}). The reader should not worry about this. We shall be reporting various theorems involving convex sets, and usually when we want later to show that a set is convex we will be able to invoke one or more of these theorems. This will establish the desired result and save us from working through definition 1.3. We start this particular ball rolling with the following rather obvious result:

Theorem 1.1 If A_1 and A_2 are two convex sets in R^n then $A_1 \cap A_2$ is also convex.

Proof Let $\mathbf{x}^1, \mathbf{x}^2 \in A_1 \cap A_2$. Then $\mathbf{x}^1, \mathbf{x}^2 \in A_1$ and $\mathbf{x}^1, \mathbf{x}^2 \in A_2$. Since A_1 and A_2 are convex it follows that $\mathbf{x} \in A_1$ *and* $\mathbf{x} \in A_2$ where

$$\mathbf{x} = \lambda \mathbf{x}^1 + (1-\lambda)\mathbf{x}^2 \quad \text{and} \quad \lambda \in [0, 1]$$

Hence $\mathbf{x} \in A_1 \cap A_2$. Since this is true for any $\mathbf{x}^1, \mathbf{x}^2 \in A_1 \cap A_2$ and any $\lambda \in [0, 1]$, $A_1 \cap A_2$ is indeed convex. *Q.E.D.*

In fact if $A_1, A_2, A_3, \ldots$ are an infinite collection of convex sets then $\cap_{i=1}^{\infty} A_i$ is also convex: the intersection of any number of convex sets is also convex. This is useful. However, we should note that the same is *not* true for unions of convex sets. S_1 and S_4 earlier were convex; but $S_5 = S_1 \cup S_4$ is not convex. Unions of convex sets are not in general convex.

1.6 Hyperplanes

An important family of subsets of R^n are *hyperplanes*.

Definition 1.4 A set $H \subset R^n$ is a *hyperplane* if and only if it can be described as

$$H = \left\{ \mathbf{x} \in R^n \mid \sum_{i=1}^{n} \alpha_i x_i = \beta \right\}$$

for some $(\alpha_1, \ldots, \alpha_n) \in R^n$ where $\alpha_i \neq 0$ some i and for some $\beta \in R$.

When $n = 1$, H contains the single point (β/α). When $n = 2$ a hyperplane is a straight line with equation $\alpha_1 x_1 + \alpha_2 x_2 = \beta$, where $\alpha_1 \neq 0$, or $\alpha_2 \neq 0$, while for $n = 3$ it is a plane $\alpha_1 x_1 + \alpha_2 x_2 + \alpha_3 x_3 = \beta$, α_1 or α_2 or α_3 not zero. For instance S_{10} is a hyperplane in R^2, S_{13} is a hyperplane in R^3 and S_{15} is a hyperplane in R^n. When $n = 2$ and if $\alpha_1 = 0$, H becomes $\{\mathbf{x} \in R^2 \mid x_2 = (\beta/\alpha_2)\}$. In the usual visual representation (x_1 measured vertically, x_2 horizontally) H then corresponds to a *vertical* line in R^2. On the other hand if $\alpha_1 \neq 0$ then H corresponds to a non-vertical line. This motivates a general definition needed in the next chapter (but not here) namely: H satisfying definition 1.4 is said to be a non-vertical hyperplane if and only if $\alpha_1 \neq 0$.

Generally, if rather loosely, a hyperplane in R^n 'splits' R^n into two parts: those points on or 'above' the hyperplane and those on or 'below' the hyperplane. Associated with H we define

$$H^+ = \left\{ \mathbf{x} \in R^n \mid \sum_{i=1}^{n} \alpha_i x_i \geqslant \beta \right\}$$

and

$$H^- = \left\{ \mathbf{x} \in R^n \mid \sum_{i=1}^{n} \alpha_i x_i \leqslant \beta \right\}.$$

Notice $H^+ \cup H^- = R^n$ and $H^+ \cap H^- = H$, giving sense to the 'split' idea. H^+ and H^- are then called *half-spaces* associated with H. It is straightforward to show that hyperplanes and their associated half-spaces are always *convex sets*: the technique used to show the convexity of S_{15} earlier can be easily adapted by the reader to prove this.

Theorem 1.2 A hyperplane $H \subset R^n$ and its associated half-spaces H^+ and H^- are always convex sets.

The major importance of hyperplanes stems from some celebrated theorems about (general) convex sets. We now state and explain, but do not prove, one of these results. Since it is visually entirely plausible, the omission is not too disastrous.

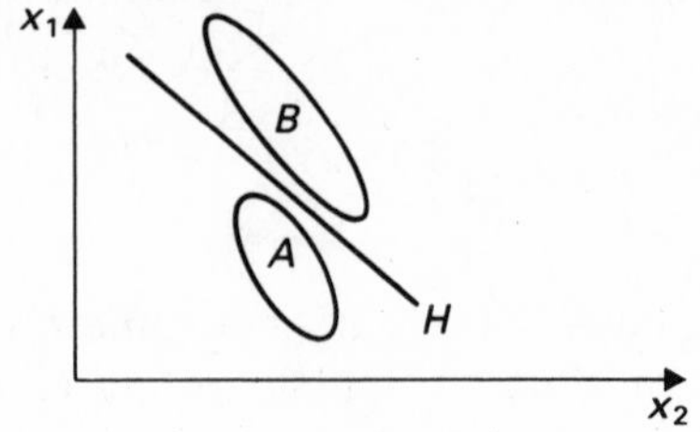

Figure 1.4

Theorem 1.3 The separating hyperplane theorem. If A and B are two disjoint convex sets in R^n then there is a hyperplane $H \subset R^n$ such that $A \subset H^+$ and $B \subset H^-$.

Figure 1.4 illustrates two disjoint convex sets in R^2, A and B. The theorem tells us that there exists a line (hyperplane in R^2) such that A lies entirely on one side of the line and B lies entirely on the other side of the line. H in fig. 1.4 has this property that it separates A from B. The reader can easily visualize that this separation of A and B is not in general possible if A and B are not disjoint or if either is not convex. In the case $n = 1$, the theorem is trivially true.

Exercise 1

1. Find whether the following sets are (i) convex, (ii) finite, (iii) bounded:

   (a) $T_1 = \{x \in R | x^2 + 5x + 6 = 0\}$
   (b) $T_2 = \{\mathbf{x} \in R^2 | x_1 \leqslant x_2^4\}$
   (c) $T_3 = \{\mathbf{x} \in R^2 | x_1 \leqslant 1\}$
   (d) $T_2 \cap T_3$
   (e) $T_2 \cup T_3$

2. Show that a hyperplane is convex; that is, show that $H \subset R^n$ is convex where $H = \{\mathbf{x} \in R^n | \Sigma_{i=1}^n \alpha_i x_i = \beta\}$ where $\alpha_i \neq 0$ some i.
3. On a line representing R indicate the meaning of the separating hyperplane theorem with $n = 1$.
4. Suppose X and Y are two convex subsets of R^n. The sum of X and Y denoted $Z = X + Y$ is defined by

$$Z = \{\mathbf{z} \in R^n | \mathbf{z} = \mathbf{x} + \mathbf{y} \text{ some } \mathbf{x} \in X, \text{ some } \mathbf{y} \in Y\}$$

   Prove that Z is convex.

2 Concave functions of one variable on R

2.1 Introduction

We start by recapping certain ideas regarding functions of one variable including their graphs, continuity and differentiability. The reader who finds this brief revision inadequate is referred to the Bibliography for further reading. In section 2.2, and in the one variable setting, we introduce the central concept of this book, concave functions.

A function of one variable is a rule or mapping, f say, which associates with every point of some subset of R, known as the *domain* of f, a unique point in R. In this chapter we are interested only in the case where the domain is the entire set R; such functions are functions of one variable on R. We write $f:R \to R$ to indicate that f associates (maps) points in the domain R with (or into) points in R. To describe such a function fully we have to describe the mapping rule. Let $f(x)$ denote the (unique) point in R 'mapped into' by the rule f from $x \in R$; $f(x)$ is known as the *value* of f at x or the image of x under f. The *range* of f is the set of all possible values of f; i.e. the range of $f = \{y \in R \mid y = f(x), \text{ some } x \in R\}$. To complete the description of f we need to define $f(x)$. For instance

$$f:R \to R \quad \text{where } f(x) = 4x + 1 \tag{2.1}$$

Here the rule is to map any point $x \in R$ into the point $4x + 1$, also in R; to each $x \in R$ this rule associates a unique point in R, namely $f(x) = 4x + 1$, and so (2.1) does indeed describe a function.

For functions of one variable there is a familiar and useful visual representation. This is the graph of f which we denote G_f and it is the following subset of R^2:

$$G_f = \{(y, x) \in R^2 \mid y = f(x)\}$$

Equivalently G_f is the set of all ordered pairs of the form $(f(x), x)$ for $x \in R$. We assume that the reader is familiar with sketching graphs. For instance fig. 2.1 shows the graph of (2.1).

If $a,b \in R$ then a *linear* (sometimes called affine when $b \neq 0$) function on R is of the form

$$f:R \to R \quad \text{where } f(x) = ax + b$$

The graph of such a function is $G_f = \{(y, x) \in R^2 | y = ax + b\} = \{(y, x) \in R^2 | y - ax = b\}$. This is a hyperplane in R^2 (i.e. a straight line) with $\alpha_1 = 1$, $\alpha_2 = -a$ and $\beta = b$ in the notation of chapter 1. Since $\alpha_1 \neq 0$, G_f is a non-vertical line. In fact any non-vertical line in R^2 is the graph of some linear function on R. The number a measures the slope of the line.

A more general class of functions on R is the class of *polynomial* functions:

$$f:R \to R \quad \text{where } f(x) = a_0 + a_1 x + a_2 x^2 + \ldots + a_n x^n$$

where n is a positive integer and $a_i \in R$, $i = 0, 1, \ldots, n$. If $a_i \neq 0$ for some $n \geqslant 2$ the associated graphs are non-linear and we speak of a non-linear function. If $a_2 \neq 0$ but $a_i = 0$, $i > 2$ the polynomial is a *quadratic* function; if $a_3 \neq 0$ but $a_i = 0$, $i > 3$ we have a cubic function; and so on. The graphs of a few non-linear polynomial functions are shown in fig. 2.2. For shorthand we describe these functions merely by defining $f(x)$, it being understood that the domain is R.

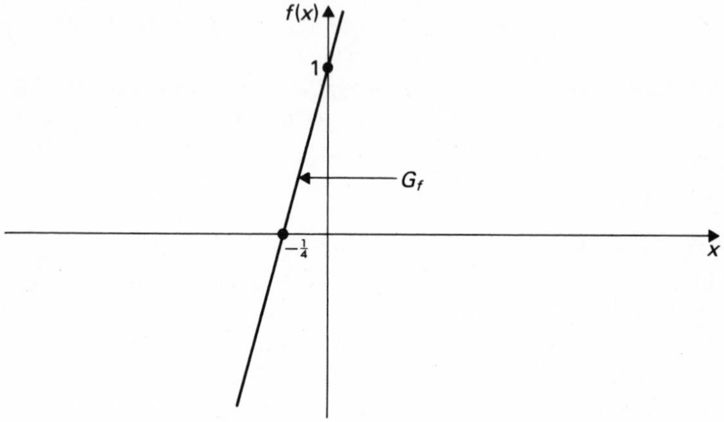

Figure 2.1

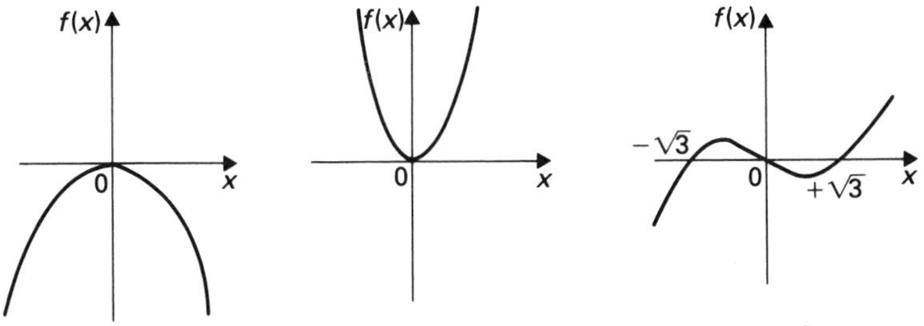

Figure 2.2

A function $f:R \to R$ is said to be continuous if $\lim_{x \to x^*} f(x) = f(x^*)$, $\forall x^* \in R$. Visually and very loosely a continuous function has a 'connected graph' in the sense that you can sketch the graph without taking your pen off the paper! An example of a function which is not continuous (when $x^* = 0$) is

$$f:R \to R \quad \text{where } f(x) = \begin{cases} 0 & \text{if } x \geqslant 0 \\ 1 & \text{if } x < 0 \end{cases}$$

However all polynomial functions are continuous as are sums, products and ratios (provided the denominator is never zero) of continuous functions.

A function $f:R \to R$ is said to be differentiable if $\forall x^* \in R$ there is a unique real number $f'(x^*)$ such that

$$\lim_{\Delta x \to 0} \frac{f(x^* + \Delta x) - f(x^*)}{\Delta x} = f'(x^*)$$

$f'(x^*)$ is the *first derivative* of f at x^* or the *gradient* of f at x^*. For differentiable functions there is a unique tangent line to the graph at any point and the equation of this line at $(f(x^*), x^*)$ on the graph is

$$y = f(x^*) + (x - x^*)f'(x^*) \tag{2.2}$$

Figure 2.3 illustrates such a tangent line and its equation for an unspecified differentiable function. The tangent line is the graph of a linear function and must be non-vertical; so, visually, differentiable functions are characterized by a *unique*, *non-vertical tangent* line at every point of the graph.

A differentiable function must be continuous, but continuous functions need not be differentiable. Figure 2.4 sketches graphs of

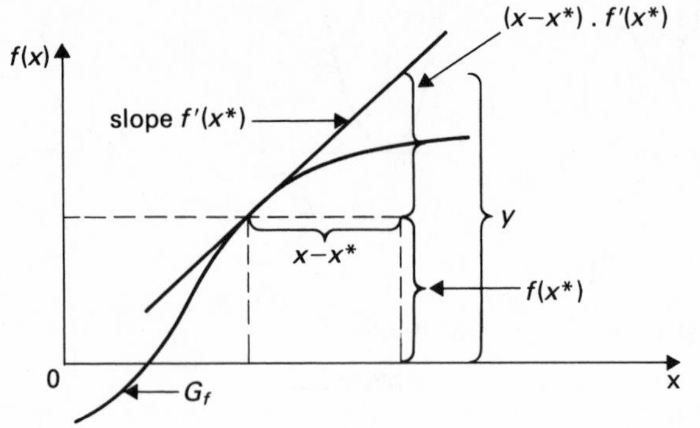

Figure 2.3

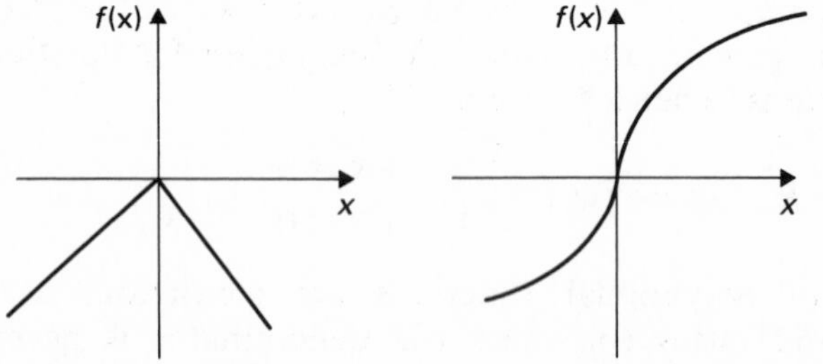

(i) $f(x) = -|x|$

(ii) $f(x) = \begin{cases} +x^{\frac{1}{3}} \text{ if } x = 0 \\ -(-x)^{\frac{1}{3}} \text{ if } x = 0 \end{cases}$

Figure 2.4

two functions which are continuous but not differentiable (when $x^* = 0$). In fig. 2.4(i) differentiability fails at the origin since there are multiple tangent lines to the graph there; the limit defining $f'(x^*)$ would not be unique. In fig. 2.4(ii) the tangent line at the origin becomes vertical and the corresponding limit would not be finite.

For differentiable functions the first derivative defines a new function, the first derivative function $f':R \to R$ with values $f'(x)$. If this function is continuous, f is said to be *continuously differentiable*: for shorthand we they say 'f is C^1'. If the first derivative function is differentiable then *its* first derivative is denoted $f''(x)$ and is the *second derivative* of f; we then say f is *twice differentiable.* The second derivative then defines yet another function $f'':R \to R$ with values $f''(x)$ and if this is continuous we say f is *twice con-*

tinuously differentiable or 'f is C^2' for short; and so on, if you wish, to third and higher derivatives.

Notice that 'f is C^2' $\Rightarrow$ 'f is twice differentiable' $\Rightarrow$ 'f is C^1' $\Rightarrow$ 'f is differentiable' $\Rightarrow$ 'f is continuous' but these implications do not reverse in general.

Polynomial functions are certainly C^2; in fact they can be continuously differentiated any number of times. Moreover sums, products and ratios (provided the denominator is never zero) of functions with the same differentiability property also possess this property; e.g. sums of C^2 functions are C^2.

We assume the reader is completely familiar with the mechanics of finding derivatives including the product, quotient and function of a function rules for differentiation. For instance the first and second derivatives of the functions in fig. 2.2 are:

(i) $f(x) = -x^2$, $f'(x) = -2x$, $f''(x) = -2$

(ii) $f(x) = x^4$, $f'(x) = 4x^3$, $f''(x) = 12x^2$

(iii) $f(x) = x^3 - 3x$, $f'(x) = 3x^2 - 3$, $f''(x) = 6x$

we make much use of differentiability assumptions in the development of concave functions shortly. However we shall overlook the subtle distinctions between C^1 and differentiability, and between C^2 and twice differentiability in what follows and always assume C^1 or C^2. In fact it can be shown that for concave functions C^1 is the same as differentiability. However some results using the C^2 assumption in what follows can be refined to twice differentiability. We ignore these refinements.

2.2 Concave functions of one variable on *R*

If we draw the graph of a function $f:R \to R$ we may (or may not) find that this graph possesses the following geometric feature:

(GF) The straight line joining any two points on the graph lies entirely on or below the graph.

In fig. 2.5 we have reproduced the graphs of six earlier examples and joined two arbitrary points (A and B) on each graph by a line. By varying A and B we see that (GF) is a feature of (a), (b) and (e) but (GF) is not a feature of (c), (d) or (f). Notice in particular (case (a)) that any straight-line graph will possess (GF) since, trivially, the straight line joining any two points on a line lies entirely *on* the

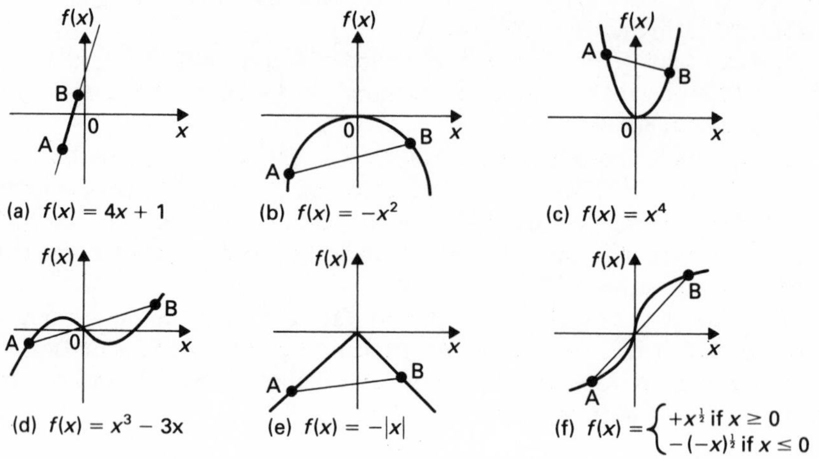

Figure 2.5

line. The concept of a concave function evolves from (GF). Indeed we can define:

A function of one variable is concave if and only if its graph possesses the geometric feature (GF).

So the functions in (a), (b) and (e) of fig. 2.5 are concave functions while those in (c), (d) and (f) are not concave. Notice in particular that *any* linear function will be concave since the graph is a straight line.

We proceed to give a more formal version of the above geometric definition of concavity. In fig. 2.6 the graph of an unspecified concave function is shown and two points, A$(=(f(x^1), x^1))$ and B$(=(f(x^2), x^2))$, have been joined by a straight line. The point C on the line joining A to B is a convex combination of A and B and has co-ordinates

$$(\lambda f(x^1)+(1-\lambda)f(x^2), \lambda x^1+(1-\lambda)x^2) \quad \text{for some } \lambda \in [0,1]$$

Moving vertically up from C we hit the graph itself at D whose co-ordinates will be

$$(f[\lambda x^1+(1-\lambda)x^2], \lambda x^1+(1-\lambda)x^2)$$

The property of 'the line AB lying on or below the graph' requires that the vertical co-ordinates of C be less than or equal to that of D; that is

$$\lambda f(x^1)+(1-\lambda)f(x^2) \leqslant f[\lambda x^1+(1-\lambda)x^2]$$

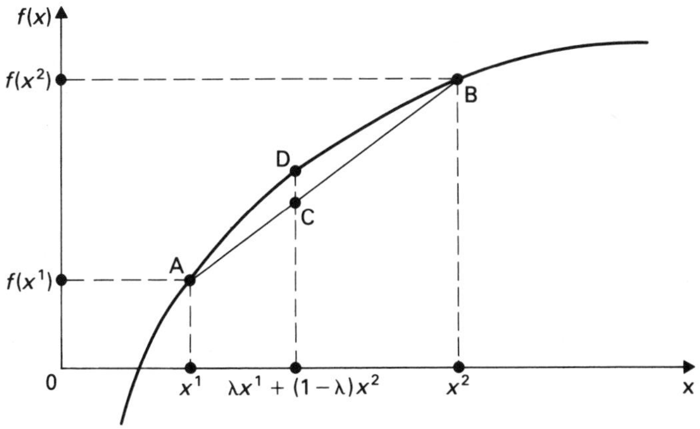

Figure 2.6

For the *entire* line AB to lie below the graph requires this inequality for all C between A and B, i.e. for all $\lambda \in [0,1]$. Moreover for concavity we need all this for all A, B or for every x^1, x^2. Hence:

Definition 2.1 $f: R \to R$ is concave if and only if

$$f[\lambda x^1 + (1-\lambda)\,x^2] \geqslant \lambda f(x^1) + (1-\lambda)\,f(x^2) \qquad \forall \lambda \in [0, 1], \forall x^1, x^2$$

This is the precise definition of the concept of concavity for a one variable function on R. The concept plays a major role in the theory of maximization which we begin to study in the next chapter. First we see how definition 2.1 is used to identify concavity of a specific function.

Example 2.1 Consider $f(x) = -x^2$. The graph of this function was shown earlier. By 'inspection' we see that the function is concave. To be more precise we now demonstrate this using definition 2.1. We need to show

$$f[\lambda x^1 + (1-\lambda)\,x^2] \geqslant \lambda f(x^1) + (1-\lambda)\,f(x^2) \qquad \forall \lambda \in [0, 1], \forall x^1, x^2$$

or, equivalently

$$-[\lambda x^1 + (1-\lambda)\,x^2]^2 \geqslant -\lambda(x^1)^2 - (1-\lambda)\,(x^2)^2 \qquad \forall \lambda \in [0, 1], \forall x^1, x^2$$

or

$$-\lambda^2(x^1)^2-(1-\lambda)^2(x^2)^2-2\lambda(1-\lambda)\,x^1x^2$$
$$\geqslant -\lambda(x^1)^2-(1-\lambda)(x^2)^2 \qquad \forall\lambda\in[0,1],\ \forall x^1,x^2$$

or

$$(x^1)^2(\lambda-\lambda^2)+(x^2)^2(\lambda-\lambda^2)-2x^1x^2(\lambda-\lambda^2)\geqslant 0$$
$$\forall\lambda\in[0,1],\ \forall x^1,x^2$$

or

$$(\lambda-\lambda^2)(x^1-x^2)^2\geqslant 0 \qquad \forall\lambda\in[0,1],\ \forall x^1,x^2$$

But if $\lambda\in[0,1]$ then $\lambda-\lambda^2=\lambda(1-\lambda)\geqslant 0$; also $(x^1-x^2)^2\geqslant 0$, $\forall x^1,x^2$. So indeed $(\lambda-\lambda^2)(x^1-x^2)^2\geqslant 0$, $\forall\lambda\in[0,1]$, $\forall x^1,x^2$ and hence f is a concave function.

This demonstration is rather tortuous even though f itself is a very simple function. Indeed showing directly in the above fashion that a function is concave becomes very cumbersome for anything other than the simplest functions. Fortunately, at least for differentiable functions, there are easier ways of identifying concavity, evolving from what we call the derivative characterizations of concavity.

2.3 Alternative definitions of concavity; the first derivative characterization

The definition of concavity did not explicitly impose restrictions on the continuity or differentiability of the function. In fact it can be shown that;

Theorem 2.1 If $f{:}R\rightarrow R$ is concave then f is continuous. A proof of this is omitted. See bibliographical notes for references.

However it does not follow that concave functions must be differentiable. For instance $f(x)=-|x|$ whose graph was shown in fig. 2.5(e) is concave but not differentiable (when $x^*=0$). So the assumption that f is concave and differentiable (or C^1) is more powerful than mere concavity.

Consider then for a moment the graphs of those functions we have met so far which are concave and C^1; these are found in fig. 2.5(a) and (b). Since they are C^1 there is a unique tangent line at each point of the graph. A moment's thought will confirm that these two graphs possess a new geometric feature.

(New GF) At any point of the graph, the tangent line to the graph at that point lies entirely on or above the graph.

Using the tangent line formula (2.2) this translates into the statement

$$f(x^*) + (x - x^*) f'(x^*) \geqslant f(x) \quad \forall x, x^*$$

Our reasoning has suggested that for C^1 functions, if f is concave then this inequality must hold. The reader should consider the reverse implication; namely, if the tangent line to the graph at any point lies entirely on or above the graph, does it follow that the function is concave? Indeed it does and we have the following fundamental result:

Theorem 2.2 Suppose $f: R \rightarrow R$ is C^1. Then f is concave if and only if;

$$f(x^*) + (x - x^*) f'(x^*) \geqslant f(x) \quad \forall x, x^*$$

Proof 'if' Suppose $f(x^*) + (x - x^*) f'(x^*) \geqslant f(x)$, $\forall x, x^*$. We have to show that this implies

$$f[\lambda x^* + (1 - \lambda) x] \geqslant \lambda f(x^*) + (1 - \lambda) f(x) \qquad \forall \lambda \in [0, 1], \forall x, x^*$$

To do this choose any x, x^* and any $\lambda \in [0, 1]$ and for notational convenience let $\hat{x} = \lambda x^* + (1 - \lambda) x$. From our initial supposition it follows that

$$f(\hat{x}) + (x^* - \hat{x}) f'(\hat{x}) \geqslant f(x^*) \tag{2.3}$$

and

$$f(\hat{x}) + (x - \hat{x}) f'(\hat{x}) \geqslant f(x) \tag{2.4}$$

Multiplying (2.3) by λ ad (2.4) by $(1 - \lambda)$ and adding gives, since $\lambda \in [0, 1]$,

$$f(\hat{x}) + f'(\hat{x}) [\lambda x^* + (1 - \lambda) x - \hat{x}] \geqslant \lambda f(x^*) + (1 - \lambda) f(x)$$

But $\hat{x} = \lambda x^* + (1 - \lambda) x$ and so the square bracket in the last inequality is zero. Hence

$$f(\hat{x}) = f[\lambda x^* + (1 - \lambda) x] \geqslant \lambda f(x^*) + (1 - \lambda) f(x)$$

Since this is true for any x, x^* and any $\lambda \in [0, 1]$ it follows that f is concave.

'only if' Now suppose f is concave. We have to show that this implies

$$f(x^*) + (x - x^*)f'(x^*) \geqslant f(x) \quad \forall x, x^*$$

If $x = x^*$ this implication follows trivially since $f(x^*) = f(x^*)$! So suppose $x \neq x^*$. Since f is concave

$$f[\lambda x + (1-\lambda)x^*] \geqslant \lambda f(x) + (1-\lambda)f(x^*) \qquad \forall \lambda \in [0,1], \forall x, x^*$$

or, equivalently, rearranging

$$f[x^* + \lambda(x - x^*)] - f(x^*) \geqslant \lambda[f(x) - f(x^*)] \qquad \forall \lambda \in [0,1], \forall x, x^*$$

Assuming $\lambda \neq 0$ we may divide and get

$$(x - x^*)\frac{f[x^* + \lambda(x - x^*)] - f(x^*)}{\lambda(x - x^*)} \geqslant f(x) - f(x^*) \qquad \forall \lambda \in [0,1], \forall x, x^* \tag{2.5}$$

On the left-hand side we have a term

$$\frac{f[x^* + \lambda(x - x^*)] - f(x^*)}{\lambda(x - x^*)}$$

Writing $\Delta x = \lambda(x - x^*)$, this term takes on the more familiar form

$$\frac{f(x^* + \Delta x) - f(x^*)}{\Delta x} \qquad \text{(see fig. 2.7)}$$

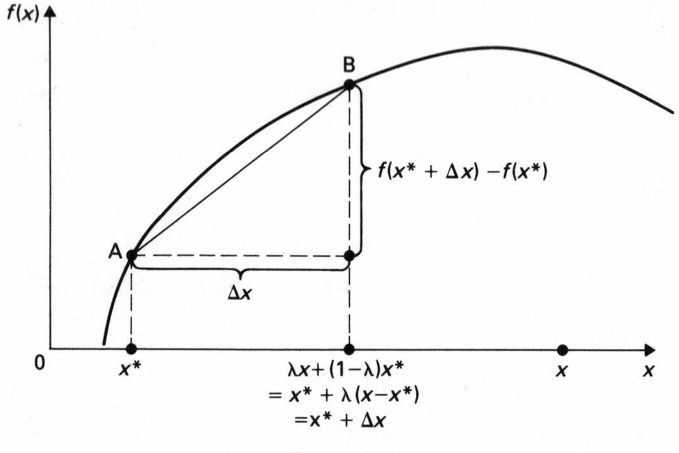

Figure 2.7

You see in fig. 2.7 that this ratio measures the slope of the chord AB. Now if we let $\lambda \to 0$, keeping x, x^* fixed, then $\Delta x \to 0$ and

$$\lim_{\lambda \to 0} \frac{f[x^* + \lambda(x - x^*)] - f(x^*)}{\lambda(x - x^*)} = \lim_{\Delta x \to 0} \frac{f(x^* + \Delta x) - f(x^*)}{\Delta x}$$

The right-hand side is definitely familiar; it is exactly $f'(x^*)$.

Returning to (2.5), this weak inequality holds for all $\lambda > 0$ and so must continue to hold in the limit as $\lambda \to 0$. Hence

$$(x - x^*) f'(x^*) \geqslant f(x) - f(x^*) \quad \forall x, x^*$$

or

$$f(x^*) + (x - x^*) f'(x^*) \geqslant f(x) \quad \forall x, x^* \qquad \textit{Q.E.D.}$$

Since this is an 'if and only if' result, we could use the inequality of theorem 2.2 as the defining characteristic of concavity for C^1 functions. Such equivalent, alternative statements are referred to as 'characterizations', and since that of theorem 2.2 involves the first derivative, it is known as the first derivative characterization of concavity.

One consequence of theorem 2.2 is that we may now think of C^1 concave functions as being generated by the geometric property of 'the tangent to the graph of the function at any point lies entirely on or above the graph': this is often useful. We could also use theorem 2.2 to identify concavity of a given C^1 function. For instance, returning to example 2.1 we need to show

$$f(x^*) + (x - x^*) f'(x^*) \geqslant f(x) \quad \forall x, x^*$$

or

$$-(x^*)^2 - (x - x^*)\, 2x^* \geqslant -x^2 \quad \forall x, x^*$$

or

$$-(x^*)^2 - 2xx^* + 2(x^*)^2 + x^2 \geqslant 0 \quad \forall x, x^*$$

or

$$(x^* - x)^2 \geqslant 0 \quad \forall x, x^*$$

But this last inequality is certainly true; hence from theorem 2.2, f is concave (which we knew anyway!).

For C^2 functions, the second derivative characterization of the next section provides an easier way of identifying concavity, however. In fact the most important role for theorem 2.2 lies in its application to maximization problems which we do not come to until the next chapter. For the time being the reader may wish to ponder (briefly or otherwise) the following consequence of theorem 2.2; if f is C^1 and concave and if $f'(x^*)=0$ then $f(x^*)\geqslant f(x)$, $\forall x$.

Finally let us remind the reader that there is no significance attached to the use of the notation 'x^*' in theorem 2.2. The theorem is true for any pair of x values; for instance the inequality could be equivalently written

$$f(x)+(x^*-x)f'(x)\geqslant f(x^*) \quad \forall x, x^*$$

2.4 The second derivative characterization

The second derivative characterization of concave functions, like the first, has an obvious geometric meaning and origin. To see this look once again at the graphs of the concave (and C^2) functions in fig. 2.5(a) and (b). In each case you will observe that the slope of the graph diminishes (or to be precise, does not increase) as x increases; that is, $f''(x)\leqslant 0$ everywhere. This suggests; for C^2 functions if f is concave then $f''(x)\leqslant 0$, $\forall x$. This is indeed the case. Furthermore, the 'reverse' implication is also true giving us the second derivative characterization.

Theorem 2.3 Suppose $f{:}R\rightarrow R$ is C^2. Then f is concave if and only if $f''(x)\leqslant 0$, $\forall x$.

Proof 'if' Suppose $f''(x)\leqslant 0$, $\forall x$. We need to show that this implies that f is concave and we shall do this by establishing the inequality of theorem 2.2 which we now know to be equivalent to concavity. Consider the tangent line to G_f at the point $(f(x^*),x^*)$. Above x the height of this tangent line is

$$y=f(x^*)+(x-x^*)f'(x^*)$$

Consider now how this height changes if we *fix* x and let x^* vary. Differentiating the above expression with respect to x^* (x fixed) we get

$$\frac{dy}{dx^*}=f'(x^*)-f'(x^*)+(x-x^*)f''(x^*)$$

$$=(x-x^*)f''(x^*)\begin{cases}\geqslant 0 & \text{if } x\leqslant x^*\\ =0 & \text{if } x=x^*\\ \leqslant 0 & \text{if } x\geqslant x^*\end{cases} \qquad (2.6)$$

since $f''(x^*)\leqslant 0$.

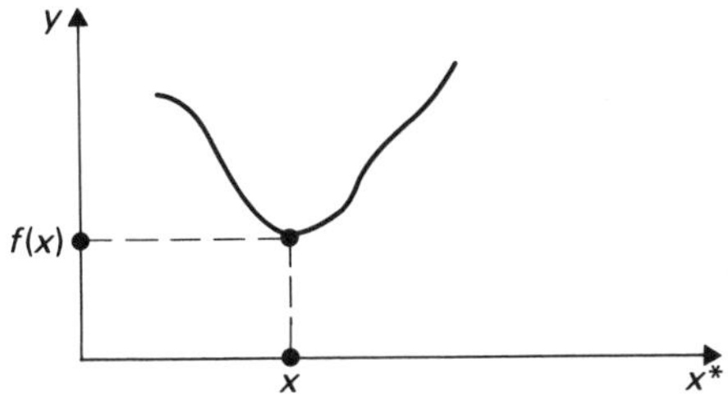

Figure 2.8

Now if x^* equals the fixed x we get $y = f(x^*) = f(x)$. For x^* larger than x, y is non-decreasing with x^* from (2.6), and y is non-increasing with x^* for $x^* < x$. Figure 2.8 summarizes this behaviour of y as x^* varies with x fixed. In particular, it follows that $y \geqslant f(x)$ everywhere, or

$$f(x^*) + (x - x^*)f'(x^*) \geqslant f(x) \quad \forall x^* \tag{2.7}$$

The choice of x was arbitrary; so (2.7) is true $\forall x$ as well, and it follows from theorem 2.2 that f is concave.

'only if' Suppose f is concave: we need to show that this implies $f''(x) \leqslant 0$. Since f is concave we have from theorem 2.2

$$f(x^*) + (x - x^*)f'(x^*) \geqslant f(x) \quad \forall x, x^*$$

and

$$f(x) + (x^* - x)f'(x) \geqslant f(x^*) \quad \forall x, x^*$$

Adding these inequalities gives

$$(x - x^*)\,[f'(x^*) - f'(x)] \geqslant 0 \quad \forall x, x^*$$

Hence $x > x^*$ implies $f'(x^*) \geqslant f'(x)$. This means that the first derivative of f never goes up as x increases. Since f is C^2 this means $f''(x) \leqslant 0$, $\forall x$. *Q.E.D.*

So we now have a third way of thinking about (C^2) concave functions of one variable; they are quite simply those functions whose second derivative is non-positive everywhere. This provides a very easy way of identifying whether a given C^2 function is concave or not.

Examples 2.2
(a) $f(x) = -x^2$ (for the third time!); $f'(x) = -2x$, $f''(x) = -2 \leqslant 0$, $\forall x$. So f is concave (again).

(b) $f(x) = ax + b$; $f'(x) = a$, $f''(x) = 0 \leqslant 0$, $\forall x$ and f is concave; any linear function is concave (again).

(c) $f(x) = x^3 - 3x$; $f'(x) = 3x^2 - 3$, $f''(x) = 6x$ which is positive for $x > 0$ and negative for $x < 0$. Hence f is not concave.

(d) $f(x) = ax^2 + bx + c$ where $a < 0$; $f'(x) = 2ax + b$, $f''(x) = 2a < 0$, $\forall x$ since $a < 0$. So any quadratic function with negative coefficient on x^2 is a concave function (e.g. (a), for the fourth time).

(e) $f(x) = -x^n$ where n is an even integer and $n \geqslant 2$; $f'(x) = -nx^{n-1}$, $f''(x) = -n(n-1)\,x^{n-2}$. Since n is even, $x^{n-2} \geqslant 0$, $\forall x$ and since $n \geqslant 2$, $n(n-1) \geqslant 0$. Hence $f''(x) \leqslant 0$, $\forall x$ and f is concave (e.g. (a) . . .).

(f) $f(x) = -e^{-rx}$; $f'(x) = re^{-rx}$, $f''(x) = -r^2e^{-rx}$. Now $e^{-rx} > 0$, $\forall x$ and $r^2 \geqslant 0$. Hence $f''(x) \leqslant 0$, $\forall x$ and f is concave.

2.5 Convex functions of one variable on *R*

It is now time to turn all our previous arguments upside-down, more or less literally. Suppose, for instance, that $f: R \to R$ is concave and consider the function $-f: R \to R$ with values $-f(x)$. Clearly the graph of $-f$ turns that of f upside-down and so will have the property that 'the line joining any two points of the graph lies entirely *on or above* the graph'. Such functions are known as convex functions. This is an entirely different concept from that of a convex *set*, and you should be clear at the outset that this is so despite the (unfortunately) similar terminology.

We can produce an exact analogue of our concavity story for convex functions simply by reversing signs in earlier arguments. For instance from definition 2.1:

(1) $f: R \to R$ is a convex function if and only if

$$f[\lambda x^1 + (1-\lambda)\,x^2] \leqslant \lambda f(x^1) + (1-\lambda)\,f(x^2)$$

$$\forall \lambda \in [0, 1], \ \forall x^1, x^2$$

Such functions must be continuous and their derivative characterizations are

(2) Suppose $f: R \to R$ is C^1. Then f is a convex function if and only if

$$f(x^*) + (x - x^*)\,f'(x^*) \leqslant f(x) \quad \forall x, x^*$$

(3) Suppose $f:R \to R$ is C^2. Then f is a convex function if and only if

$$f''(x) \geqslant 0 \quad \forall x.$$

Examples 2.3

(a) $f(x) = x^4; f'(x) = 4x^3, f''(x) = 12x^2 \geqslant 0$, $\forall x$ and f is convex.

(b) $f(x) = ax + b; f''(x) = 0 \geqslant 0$, $\forall x$ and f is convex. So any linear function is *both* convex and concave.

(c) $f(x) = ax^2 + bx + c$ where $a > 0$; $f''(x) = a \geqslant 0$, $\forall x$ and f is convex.

(d) $f(x) = x^n$ where n is an even integer and $n \geqslant 2$; $f''(x) = n(n-1)\,x^{n-2} \geqslant 0$, $\forall x$. So f is convex (e.g. (a)).

2.6 Hypographs and epigraphs; another characterization

So far we have described the concepts of a concave function and a convex function and we have found useful characterizations of such functions under differentiability assumptions. In fact there is yet another characterization of concave (and convex) functions; this does not require differentiability (like the original definition) and is in terms of the convexity of certain *sets* associated with the graphs of functions.

For $f:R \to R$ the hypograph of f, HG_f is

$$HG_f = \{(y, x) \in R^2 \mid y \leqslant f(x) \quad \text{some } x \in R\}$$

and the epigraph of f, EG_f is

$$EG_f = \{(y, x) \in R^2 \mid y \geqslant f(x) \quad \text{some } x \in R\}$$

Visually the hypograph of f is the set of points in R^2 which lie *on or below* the graph of f while the epigraph is the set of points on or above the graph. For instance fig. 2.9 illustrates HG_f and EG_f for the concave function $f(x) = -x^2$. Clearly from fig. 2.9 the hypograph (but not the epigraph) is a convex set in this case. Going back to fig. 2.5(a) and (e) the reader will see that the hypographs of those concave functions are also convex sets. In fact:

Theorem 2.4 $f:R \to R$ is a concave function if and only if the hypograph of f is a convex set.

Proof '*if*' Suppose HG_f is a convex set and choose any $x^1, x^2 \in R$; let $f(x^1) = y^1$ and $f(x^2) = y^2$. Then $(y^1, x^1) \in HG_f$ and $(y^2, x^2) \in HG_f$.

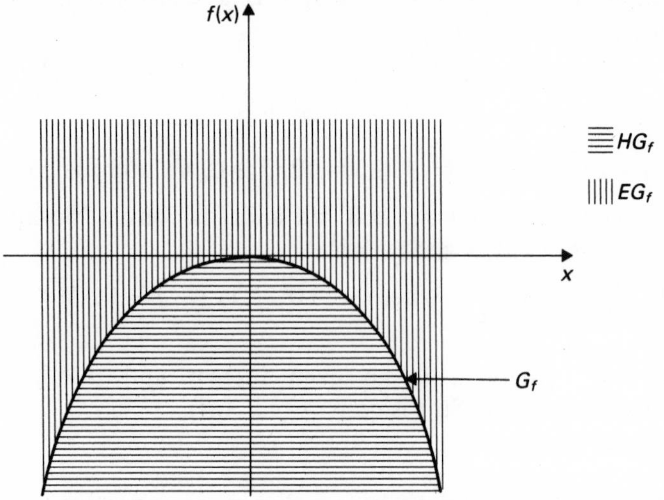

Figure 2.9

Since HG_f is a convex set, we have

$$(\lambda y^1 + (1-\lambda)\,y^2, \lambda x^1 + (1-\lambda)\,x^2) \in HG_f \qquad \forall \lambda \in [0, 1]$$

That is

$$f[\lambda x^1 + (1-\lambda)\,x^2] \geqslant \lambda y^1 + (1-\lambda)\,y^2$$
$$= \lambda f(x^1) + (1-\lambda)\,f(x^2) \qquad \forall \lambda \in [0, 1]$$

Since this is true for any x^1, x^2 it follows that f is concave.

'only if' Suppose f is concave and let $(y^1, x^1) \in HG_f$ and $(y^2, x^2) \in HG_f$; that is

$$f(x^1) \geqslant y^1 \quad \text{and} \quad f(x^2) \geqslant y^2$$

Multiplying the first inequality by λ, the second by $(1-\lambda)$ and adding, gives, if $\lambda \in [0, 1]$,

$$\lambda f(x^1) + (1-\lambda)\,f(x^2) \geqslant \lambda y^1 + (1-\lambda)\,y^2 \qquad \forall \lambda \in [0, 1]$$

But since f is concave

$$f[\lambda x^1 + (1-\lambda)\,x^2] \geqslant \lambda f(x^1) + (1-\lambda)\,f(x^2) \qquad \forall \lambda \in [0, 1]$$

Hence

$$f[\lambda x^1 + (1-\lambda) x^2] \geqslant \lambda y^1 + (1-\lambda) y^2$$
$$\forall \lambda \in [0, 1]$$

This tells us that $(\lambda y^1 + (1-\lambda) y^2, \lambda x^1 + (1-\lambda) x^2) \in HG_f$, $\forall \lambda \in [0, 1]$. Since this is true for any (y^1, x^1), $(y^2, x^2) \in HG_f$ it follows that HG_f is a convex set. *Q.E.D.*

The expected analogue of this for convex functions (see, e.g., fig. 2.5(c)), is:

> $f: R \to R$ is a convex function if and only if the *epigraph* of f is a convex set.

From the mathematician's viewpoint theorem 2.4 is central to the development of concave functions since the most general development of these functions does not use calculus or assume differentiability; indeed theorem 2.4 is often stated as the definition of a concave function, definition 2.1 emerging as a consequence. In this book the approach will be heavily calculus-oriented and theorems 2.2 and 2.3 are the central results used in what follows. Theorem 2.4 is of some use here, however, and it does provide useful and further 'visual' information about concave functions. For our purposes even more useful visual information is provided by the next section.

2.7 Contours and upper and lower contour sets

Consider $f: R \to R$ and suppose that y is in the range of f; i.e. there is at least one $x \in R$ with $f(x) = y$. The contour of f for the value y, written $C_f(y)$ is the complete *set* of $x \in R$ at which the value of f equals y; i.e.

$$C_f(y) = \{x \in R \mid f(x) = y\}$$

Notice that $C_f(y)$ is a subset of R whereas G_f is a subset of R^2. In fact the big pay-off to the concepts of this section comes later when we look at functions of two variables; there the graph is a subset of R^3 and is not easily drawn while contours are subsets of R^2 and are easily 'sketchable'. We introduce the concepts now, however, to pave the way for the later discussion.

To illustrate, consider the function of one variable $f(x) = -x^2$. The range is $(-\infty, 0]$. For $y \in (-\infty, 0]$, $C_f(y) = \{x \in R \mid -x^2 = y\} = \{x \in R \mid x^2 = -y\} = \{+\sqrt{-y}, -\sqrt{-y}\}$. For instance $C_f(-1) = \{+1, -1\}$.

An associated concept is *the upper contour set of f for the value y*, written $UC_f(y)$ and defined by

$$UC_f(y) = \{x \in R \mid f(x) \geqslant y\}$$

where y is in the range of f. $UC_f(y)$ is the set of $x \in R$ where the value of f is *at least* y. For instance when $f(x) = -x^2$, for $y \in (-\infty, 0]$, $UC_f(y) = \{x \in R \mid -x^2 \leqslant y\} = \{x \in R \mid x^2 \leqslant -y\} = [-\sqrt{-y}, +\sqrt{-y}]$; e.g. $UC_f(-1) = [-1, +1]$. Figure 2.10 illustrates $C_f(-1)$ and $UC_f(-1)$ for this example. Of course, f in this example is a concave function; and each $UC_f(y)$ is an interval of R and hence a convex set. The reader may wish to ponder the nature of upper contour sets for our other examples of concave functions. The following will not then be a surprise:

Theorem 2.5 If $f: R \to R$ is a concave function then $UC_f(y)$ is a convex set for all y in the range of f.

Proof Let $x^1, x^2 \in UC_f(y)$, where y is in the range of f. We need to show that $\lambda x^1 + (1-\lambda)x^2 \in UC_f(y)$, $\forall \lambda \in [0, 1]$. Since $x^1, x^2 \in UC_f(y)$

$$f(x^1) \geqslant y \quad \text{and} \quad f(x^2) \geqslant y$$

Multiplying the first inequality by λ and the second by $(1-\lambda)$ where $\lambda \in [0, 1]$ and adding gives

$$\lambda f(x^1) + (1-\lambda) f(x^2) \geqslant y$$

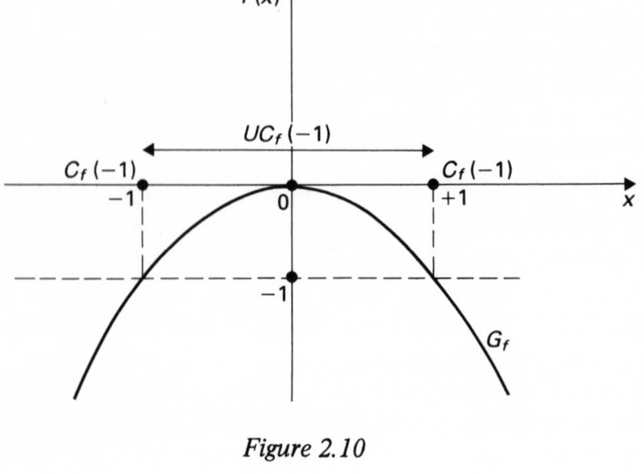

Figure 2.10

Since f is concave

$$f[\lambda x^1 + (1-\lambda)x^2] \geqslant \lambda f(x^1) + (1-\lambda)f(x^2) \geqslant y$$

and $\lambda x^1 + (1-\lambda)x^2 \in UC_f(y)$ also. Since this is true $\forall\lambda \in [0, 1]$ and for any $x^1, x^2 \in UC_f(y)$, $UC_f(y)$ is a convex set. *Q.E.D.*

It is *most important* to stress that the implication in theorem 2.5 goes only 'one way' in general. That is, it is *not* true in general that *if* f has convex upper contour sets *then* f is concave. For instance consider $f(x) = x^3$. The range is R and $UC_f(y) = \{x \in R | x^3 \geqslant y\} = \{x \in R | x \geqslant y^{1/3}\} = [y^{1/3}, +\infty)$. So the upper contour sets are intervals of R and so convex sets but the function is *not* concave. Hence the class of functions which have convex upper contour sets includes, but is larger than, the class of concave functions; they are known as *quasi-concave* functions and are a major theme later in the book. For instance $f(x) = x^3$ is quasi-concave but not concave. But more on this in due course.

The convex function analogue of theorem 2.5 involves the *lower* contour set of f for the value y, $LC_f(y) = \{x \in R | f(x) \leqslant y\}$, where y is in the range of f. Not surprisingly we get: if $f: R \to R$ is a convex function then $LC_f(y)$ is a convex set, for all y in the range of f. Again the implication does not reverse; quasi-convex functions are defined by convexity of $LC_f(y)$.

2.8 Strict concavity and convexity

Referring back to the graphs of concave functions sketched in fig. 2.5(a), (b) and (e), the reader may have already noticed a difference between the second of these and the other two; namely, in (b) the line joining any two points on the graph lies (apart from its endpoints) *entirely below* the graph, whereas in (a) and (e) this line, for some pairs of points, lies *on* the graph. All three cases satisfy the definition of concavity of course, since this requires only that such lines lie on *or* below the graph. However, in a sense, (b) possesses a 'stronger' concavity property than the other two. To be precise, we define:

Definition 2.2 $f: R \to R$ is strictly concave if and only if

$$f[\lambda x^1 + (1-\lambda)x^2] > \lambda f(x^1) + (1-\lambda)f(x^2)$$

$$\forall\lambda \in (0, 1),\ \forall x^1, x^2 \quad \text{with } x^1 \neq x^2$$

The differences between this and definition 2.1 are that '$>$' replaces '$\geqslant$', '$\lambda \in (0, 1)$' replaces '$\lambda \in [0, 1]$' and '$\forall x^1, x^2$ with $x^1 \neq x^2$'

replaces '$\forall x^1, x^2$'. The first change captures the notion of 'the line lying *below* the graph' and the other changes exclude the end-points of the line which obviously must lie on the graph. Visually, strictly concave functions are those concave functions whose graph contains no straight line sections; strictly concave functions must be concave but not vice-versa.

You may expect that we should obtain first and second derivative characterizations of strict concavity similar to those for concavity with '$>$' replacing '$\geqslant$'. This is nearly the case. One half of the expected second derivative characterization fails to materialize, but the first derivative characterization appears as anticipated.

Theorem 2.6 Suppose $f:R \to R$ is C^1. Then f is strictly concave if and only if

$$f(x^*) + (x - x^*)f'(x^*) > f(x) \quad \forall x, x^* \quad \text{where } x \neq x^*$$

Proof 'if' The proof follows exactly that of the 'if' part of theorem 2.2, changing '$\geqslant$' to '$>$', '$\lambda \in [0, 1]$' to '$\lambda \in (0, 1)$' and adding on the restriction '$x \neq x^*$'.

'only if' Suppose f is strictly concave; then, in particular f is concave and from theorem 2.2

$$f(x^*) + (x - x^*)f'(x^*) \geqslant f(x) \quad \forall x, x^* \tag{2.8}$$

Suppose $x \neq x^*$ and suppose we have equality then in (2.8). This means that the point $(f(x), x)$ lies *on* the tangent line to G_f at $(f(x^*), x^*)$. Let $\hat{x} = \lambda x + (1 - \lambda)x^*$ where $\lambda \in (0, 1)$, so that $\hat{x} - x^* = \lambda(x - x^*)$. From strict concavity

$$f(\hat{x}) > \lambda f(x) + (1 - \lambda)f(x^*)$$

Substituting the presumed equality in (2.8), for $f(x)$ gives

$$f(\hat{x}) > \lambda[f(x^*) + (x - x^*)f'(x^*)] + (1 - \lambda)f(x^*)$$

and so

$$f(\hat{x}) > f(x^*) + (x - x^*)f'(x^*)$$

This means $\hat{x}$ lies *above* the tangent line to G_f at $(f(x^*), x^*)$ and contradicts (2.8). Hence when $x \neq x^*$ we cannot have equality in (2.8). *Q.E.D.*

Turning to the second derivative characterization, consider the function $f(x) = -x^4$ whose graph is that of fig. 2.5(c) inverted. By inspection we see that f is strictly concave; a rigorous check can be made by demonstrating the inequality of theorem 2.6. However, its second derivative is $f''(x) = -12x^2$. Certainly $f''(x) \leqslant 0$, $\forall x$; but it is not the case, as we were anticipating, that $f''(x) < 0$, $\forall x$ since $f''(0) = 0$. So it is *not* true in general that; if f is C^2 and strictly concave then $f''(x) < 0$, $\forall x$. Of course it will be true that $f''(x) \leqslant 0$, $\forall x$ since f is C^2 and concave; but the expected strict inequality does not follow.

However, it is true that strictly negative second derivatives everywhere *imply* strict concavity.

Theorem 2.7 Suppose $f: R \to R$ is C^2. If $f''(x) < 0$, $\forall x$ then f is strictly concave.

Proof Suppose $f''(x) < 0$, $\forall x$. As in the 'if' proof for theorem 2.3 consider again

$$\frac{dy}{dx^*} = (x - x^*) f''(x^*)$$

We can now conclude that for $x^* > x$, y is *strictly increasing* with x^* and for $x^* < x$, y is *strictly decreasing* with x^*. Hence, $\forall x \neq x^*$ we have $y > f(x)$, or

$$f(x^*) + (x - x^*) f'(x^*) > f(x) \quad \forall x, x^* \quad \text{where } x \neq x^*$$

From theorem 2.6, f is then strictly concave. *Q.E.D.*

The first derivative characterization allows us to conclude that C^1 strictly concave functions are those functions whose tangent lines to their graphs lie entirely above the graph except at the point of tangency. Theorem 2.7 is not a characterization (i.e. it is not an 'if and only if' statement); but it does give sufficient conditions and provides an easy way of identifying strict concavity for C^2 functions.

Finally, inverting the story, strictly convex functions are defined by

$$f[\lambda x^1 + (1 - \lambda) x^2] < \lambda f(x^1) + (1 - \lambda) f(x^2)$$
$$\forall \lambda \in (0, 1), \forall x^1, x^2 \quad \text{where } x^1 \neq x^2$$

The first derivative characterization of such C^1 functions is

$$f(x^*) + (x - x^*) f'(x^*) < f(x) \quad \forall x, x^* \quad \text{where } x \neq x^*$$

And a sufficient condition for strict convexity of C^2 functions is $f''(x) > 0$, $\forall x$.

Examples 2.4

(a) $f(x) = ax^2 + bx + c$; $f''(x) = 2a > 0$, $\forall x$ if $a > 0$ and vice-versa if $a < 0$. So f is strictly convex if $a > 0$ and strictly concave if $a < 0$.

(b) $f(x) = -e^{-rx}$; $f''(x) = -r^2 e^{-rx} < 0$, $\forall x$ if $r \neq 0$. So f is strictly concave if $r \neq 0$.

Exercise 2

1. By demonstrating the equality '$f[\lambda x^1 + (1-\lambda)x^2] = \lambda f(x^1) + (1-\lambda) f(x^2)$, $\forall \lambda \in [0,1]$, $\forall x^1, x^2$', show that any linear function $f: R \to R$ where $f(x) = ax + b$ is both a concave function and a convex function.
2. Show that any linear function as in question 1 above is concave and convex by demonstrating the validity of the first derivative characterization of both concave and convex functions for such a function.
3. Supposing $f: R \to R$ is C^1, show that f is convex if and only if

$$f(x^*) + (x - x^*) f'(x^*) \leqslant f(x) \quad \forall x, x^*.$$

4. Using the second derivative characterization of concave and convex functions, evaluate whether the following C^2 functions $f: R \to R$ are (i) concave, (ii) convex, (iii) both, (iv) neither:

(a) $f(x) = \sin x$
(b) $f(x) = e^x$
(c) $f(x) = e^{x^2}$
(d) $f(x) = x^2(2-x)^2$
(e) $f(x) = ax + b$
(f) $f(x) = -x^2 - e^{-x}$

5. Using definition 2.1 and the equivalent convex function definition, prove the following:

(a) $f: R \to R$ is concave if $f(x) = g(x) + h(x)$ where $g: R \to R$ and $h: R \to R$ are concave functions.
(b) The same as (a) except that 'convex' replaces 'concave' throughout.
(c) $f: R \to R$ is concave if $f(x) = kg(x)$ where $k > 0$ and $g: R \to R$ is concave; what happens to f if g is concave but $k < 0$?
(d) $f: R \to R$ is concave if $f(x) = \Sigma_{i=1}^{m} k_i g_i(x)$ where $k_i > 0$, $i = 1, \ldots, m$ and $g_i: R \to R$ are all concave, $i = 1, \ldots, m$.
(e) The same as (d) except that 'convex' replaces 'concave' throughout.

6. Prove that:

(a) $f: R \to R$ is a convex function if and only if the epigraph of f is a convex set.

(b) If $f: R \to R$ is a convex function then the lower contour sets of f are all convex sets. Give an example showing that the sense of the implication in the last sentence does not reverse in general.

7. Repeat question 4 above replacing 'concave' and 'convex' with 'strictly concave' and 'strictly convex' respectively.
8. Prove by induction on m that $f: R \to R$ is concave if and only if

$$f(\lambda_1 x^1 + \lambda_2 x^2 \ldots + \lambda_m x^m)$$
$$\geqslant \lambda_1 f(x^1) + \lambda_2 f(x^2) + \ldots + \lambda_m f(x^m)$$

for all $x^1, \ldots, x^m \in R$ and for all $\lambda_1, \ldots, \lambda_m$ where

$$\sum_{i=1}^{m} \lambda_i = 1 \quad \text{and} \quad \lambda_i \geqslant 0, \quad i = 1, \ldots, m.$$

3 Maxima of functions of one variable on R

3.1 Introduction

In this chapter we start to bring out the role of concavity in theory of maximization. It is only a beginning since we continue to restrict attention to the one-variable case with domain R. However, like the subject matter of chapter 2, once we have mastered this case the generalizations become relatively straightforward.

So, given $f:R \to R$ the problem we are interested in is

$$\text{maximize } f(x) \tag{3.1}$$

usually abbreviated to 'max $f(x)$'. We are also interested in minimization problems and deal with those later.

To solve problem (3.1) requires us to find a value of x, x^* say, at which the largest possible value of f occurs.

Definition 3.1 x^* is a *solution* to the problem (3.1) if and only if $f(x^*) \geqslant f(x)$, $\forall x \in R$; we then say x^* is a *global maximum* of f and $f(x^*)$ is the *optimal value* for (3.1).

The primary objective of this chapter is to develop some procedures for finding solutions, and hence optimal values for the problem (3.1). Ideally we would like to have a set of necessary and sufficient ('if and only if') conditions defining or characterizing solutions to (3.1). Thus we want a set of conditions such that:

(a) if x^* is a solution to (3.1) then these conditions are satisfied by x^* (necessary), and
(b) if x^* satisfies these conditions, then x^* is a solution to (3.1) (sufficient).

This is the objective.

Before embarking on this quest a word about terminology is in order. We have introduced the adjective 'global' in definition 3.1 to distinguish from the concept of a 'local maximum'. The reader will no doubt have studied the latter concept elsewhere, and we do so here much later in the book. However, the primary focus of our maximization discussion throughout will be on global concepts.

Finally our approach will be calculus-orientated and we make differentiability assumptions about f as is convenient.

3.2 Characterizing global maxima

First recall a familiar necessary condition for x^* to be a global maximum of the C^1 function, $f: R \rightarrow R$. Specifically, if x^* is a global maximum of f, then it must be that $f'(x^*) = 0$. For if x^* is a global maximum of f and $f'(x^*) \neq 0$ then either $f'(x^*) > 0$ or $f'(x^*) < 0$. In the former case the graph of f is upward-sloping and $f(x) > f(x^*)$ for x 'just to the right' of x^*; so x^* cannot be a global maximum. Similarly, $f(x) > f(x^*)$ for x just to the left of x^* when $f'(x^*) < 0$ and again x^* is not a global maximum. So it must be that $f'(x^*) = 0$ at a global maximum. Visually if x^* is a global maximum of f then the tangent line to the graph of f at $(f(x^*), x^*)$ must be horizontal. Such points where $f'(x^*) = 0$ are called *stationary points* of f. In other words then a necessary condition for x^* to be a global maximum of f is that x^* be a stationary point of f. However, as you will also recall, stationarity at x^* is certainly not sufficient to ensure that x^* is a global maximum of f. For example $f(x) = x^2$ has a stationary point at $x^* = 0$ which is in fact a global *minimum*; $f(x) = x^3$ has a stationary point at $x^* = 0$ which is *point of inflexion*; $f(x) = x^3 - 3x$ has a stationary point at $x^* = -1$ which is a *local* maximum (but not global). So it is certainly *not* the case that stationarity at x^* implies that x^* is a global maximum, in general.

Suppose, however (and unlike the three examples above), that we restrict attention to *concave functions*. In particular suppose x^* is a stationary point of the C^1, concave function, $f: R \rightarrow R$. Then the tangent line to the graph of f at $(f(x^*), x^*)$ is horizontal with height $f(x^*)$ (see fig. 3.1). But we know from the first derivative characterization of concave functions that the tangent line at any point lies entirely on or above the graph. Hence the height of the tangent line in fig. 3.1 (viz. $f(x^*)$) is at least as large as the height of the graph at *any* other point, x (viz. $f(x)$). Hence $f(x^*) \geqslant f(x)$, $\forall x$ and x^* must be a global maximum of f.

To put it more concisely: if f is C^1 and concave then

$$f(x^*) + (x - x^*) f'(x^*) \geqslant f(x) \quad \forall x, x^*$$

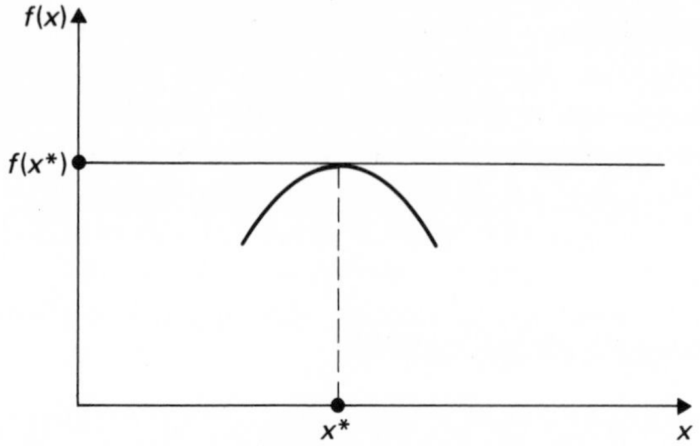

Figure 3.1

So if $f'(x^*) = 0$

$$f(x^*) \geqslant f(x) \ \forall x$$

and x^* is a global maximum of f.

For C^1 concave functions stationarity is necessary *and* sufficient for a global maximum; stationarity *characterizes* the global maxima of such functions. We thus have

Theorem 3.1 Suppose $f: R \to R$ is C^1 and concave. Then x^* is a global maximum of f if and only if $f'(x^*) = 0$.

This gives us a simple procedure for finding global maxima. Simply check that f is concave and find its stationarity points. Of course this is of no help if f is not concave; but often in economics the assumption of concavity is defensible. Even when this is not so, concavity is often assumed anyway, exactly because of theorems like 3.1.

Examples 3.1

(a) $f(x) = -x^2$; $f'(x) = -2x = 0 \Leftrightarrow x^* = 0$. f is concave (see chapter 2). So $x^* = 0$ is the global maximum of f with optimal value 0.

(b) $f(x) = -x^n$ where n is an even integer and $n \geqslant 2$; $f'(x) = -nx^{n-1} = 0 \Leftrightarrow x^* = 0$. f is concave (see chapter 2). So $x^* = 0$ is the global maximum with optimal value 0.

(c) $f(x) = ax^2 + bx + c$ where $a < 0$; $f'(x) = 2ax + b = 0 \Leftrightarrow x^* = -(b/2a)$. f is concave (chapter 2). So $x^* = -(b/2a)$ is the global maximum with optimal value

$$f\left(-\frac{b}{2a}\right) = -\frac{b^2}{4a} + c$$

3.3 Global minima

We turn things upside-down again. The problem now is: $\min f(x)$. Again stationarity is a necessary condition for x^* to be a solution to this problem (i.e. $f(x^*) \leqslant f(x)$, $\forall x \in R$), also referred to as a global minimum and $f(x^*)$ is the optimal value for this minimization problem. The reader will not be surprised to hear that, if we restrict attention to (C^1) convex functions, stationarity is a sufficient condition also; for if f is C^1 and convex

$$f(x^*) + (x - x^*) f'(x^*) \leqslant f(x) \quad \forall x, x^*$$

And if $f'(x^*) = 0$, it follows that

$$f(x^*) \leqslant f(x) \quad \forall x$$

and x^* is a global minimum.

So to find global minima; check the (C^1) function is convex and find its stationary point.

Examples 3.2
(a) $f(x) = x^n$ where n is an even integer and $n \geqslant 2$. $f'(x) = nx^{n-1} = 0 \Leftrightarrow x^* = 0$. f is convex (chapter 2) and so $x^* = 0$ is the global minimum with optimal value 0.

(b) $f(x) = e^x - x$. $f'(x) = e^x - 1 = 0 \Leftrightarrow e^x = 1 \Leftrightarrow x^* = 0$. $f''(x) = e^x > 0$, $\forall x$ and f is (strictly) convex. So $x^* = 0$ is the global minimum with optimal value 1.

3.4 The number of global maxima

How many global maxima can a concave function possess? Throughout examples 3.1 there was exactly one global maximum; putting it differently, there was a unique solution to each of those maximization problems. Such uniqueness need not always occur.

Examples 3.3 Consider $f: R \to R$ where

$$f(x) = \begin{cases} -x^4 & \text{if} \quad x \leqslant 0 \\ 0 & \text{if} \quad x \in [0, 1] \\ -(x-1)^4 & \text{if} \quad x \geqslant 1 \end{cases}$$

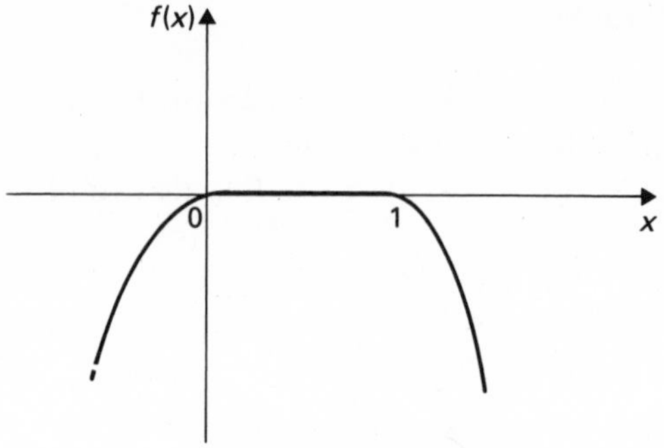

Figure 3.2

The graph of this function is shown in fig. 3.2. f is in fact C^2 and

$$f''(x) = \begin{cases} -12x^2 & \text{if} \quad x \leqslant 0 \\ 0 & \text{if} \quad x \in [0, 1] \\ -12(x-1)^2 & \text{if} \quad x \geqslant 0 \end{cases} \leqslant 0, \forall x$$

So f is concave; notice that f is not strictly concave. In addition $f'(x) = 0 \Leftrightarrow x^* \in [0, 1]$. So every member of the set $[0, 1]$ is a global maximum of f. The optimal value is the same at all these solutions, namely 0.

In this example there is an infinite number of global maxima, namely the convex subset of R, $[0, 1]$. Of course the value of f at all these maxima must be the same; otherwise they would not all be global maxima. In other words the optimal value of f is unique (always) but the global maxima need not be so.

In fact the particular type of multiple solutions seen in example 3.3 is typical. To be precise: if x^1 and x^2 are two global maxima of the concave function $f: R \to R$ then any convex combination of x^1 and x^2 is also a global maximum. To see why, let x^1 and x^2 be two (different) global maxima of f. Then $f(x^1) = f(x^2) \geqslant f(x)$, $\forall x$. But since f is concave

$$f[\lambda x^1 + (1-\lambda) x^2] \geqslant \lambda f(x^1) + (1-\lambda) f(x^2) \quad \forall \lambda \in [0, 1]$$

Hence

$$f[\lambda x^1 + (1-\lambda) x^2] \geqslant f(x^1) = f(x^2) \geqslant f(x) \quad \forall x, \forall \lambda \in [0, 1]$$

and so any convex combination of x^1 and x^2 is also a global maximum.

So if there is more than one global maximum of a concave function there must be an infinite number, corresponding to an interval or convex subset of R. Such non-uniqueness is sometimes inconvenient in economics. We can now see that the assumption of strict concavity would avoid this inconvenience.

Theorem 3.2 A strictly concave function $f:R \to R$ cannot possess more than one global maximum.

Proof Suppose the statement is false and x^1, x^2 are two different ($x^1 \neq x^2$) global maxima of the strictly concave function f. Then $f(x^1) = f(x^2)$ and

$$f[\lambda x^1 + (1-\lambda)x^2] > \lambda f(x^1) + (1-\lambda) f(x^2) \quad \forall \lambda \in (0, 1)$$

Hence

$$f[\lambda x^1 + (1-\lambda)x^2] > f(x^1) = f(x^2) \quad \forall \lambda \in (0, 1)$$

and x^1, x^2 are not global maxima, a contradiction. The statement cannot be false therefore. *Q.E.D.*

Exactly analogously we find that if a convex function has more than one global minimum then there must be an infinite number of such minima, corresponding to a convex subset of R; and a strictly convex function cannot possess more than one global minimum.

Unfortunately, we have not yet completely answered the original question regarding the number of maxima possessed by concave functions. There is also the possibility that a concave (or strictly concave) function may possess no global maximum (no stationary point).

Examples 3.4
(a) $f(x) = ax + b$, $a \neq 0$. This linear function is concave but $f'(x) = a \neq 0$, $\forall x$. So f has no stationary point and hence f has no global maximum.

(b) $f(x) = -e^{-x}$. Here $f''(x) = -e^{-x} < 0$, $\forall x$, and f is strictly concave. But $f'(x) = e^{-x} > 0$, $\forall x$, f has no stationary point and so f has no global maximum.

The complete answer to the original question is then:

(1) if f is concave its set of global maxima is either empty, or is a single point, or is an infinite convex set;
(2) if f is strictly concave its set of global maxima is either empty or consists of a single point.

For convex functions the same statements are true with minima replacing maxima.

Despite all this it is worthwhile to finish by stressing again that stationarity *characterizes* the global maxima of C^1 concave functions on R; if there are no stationary points there are no global maxima and vice-versa; if there is one stationary point there is one global maximum and vice-versa. And so on and analogously for the convex case.

Exercise 3

1. (a) The following C^2 functions $f:R \to R$ are all either concave or convex or both. Find which are concave and which are convex:

   (i) $f(x) = 7 + 12x - 3x^2$
   (ii) $f(x) = ax + b$
   (iii) $f(x) = x^4 - 4x + 17$
   (iv) $f(x) = x - e^x$
   (v) $f(x) = x^4 + 2x^2 + 1$
   (vi) $f(x) = 2x^4 - 8x^2 + 3$

   (b) Find the stationary points of the functions in (a) and hence the global maxima and minima of these functions and the corresponding optimal values.

2. (a) Prove that if $f:R \to R$ is a convex function then the set of global minima of f is a convex set.

   (b) Prove that if $f:R \to R$ is a strictly convex function then f has at most one global minimum.

4 Concave functions of n variables on R^n

4.1 Introduction

This chapter generalizes to the case of n variables the arguments of chapters 2 and 3. First we recap some preliminaries regarding functions of n variables; then we introduce concavity. As in chapter 2, the reader with little background in the preliminaries is referred to the bibliographical notes for further reading.

A function of n variables is a rule f which maps each point of some subset D of R^n into a unique point in R. We write $f:D \to R$ to denote this, and D is the *domain* of f. Throughout this chapter we assume $D = R^n$ and our functions $f:R^n \to R$ are n variable functions on R^n. To describe such functions we specify $f(\mathbf{x})$ for each $\mathbf{x} \in R^n$ where $f(\mathbf{x})$ denotes the unique point in R mapped into from $\mathbf{x} \in R^n$; $f(\mathbf{x})$ is the *value* of f at $\mathbf{x}$ or the image of $\mathbf{x}$ under f and the *range* of f is $\{y \in R \mid y = f(\mathbf{x}), \text{ some } \mathbf{x} \in R^n\}$. The graph of f is now a subset of R^{n+1};

$$G_f = \{(y, \mathbf{x}) \in R^{n+1} \mid y = f(\mathbf{x}), \mathbf{x} \in R^n\}$$

A linear function on R^n is of the form

$$f:R^n \to R \quad \text{where } f(\mathbf{x}) = \sum_{i=1}^{n} a_i x_i + b$$

where $b \in R$, $(a_1, \ldots, a_n) \in R^n$. The graph of such a function is

$$G_f = \left\{(y, \mathbf{x}) \in R^{n+1} \mid y = \sum_{i=1}^{n} a_i x_i + b\right\}$$

This is a non-vertical hyperplane in R^{n+1}.

Some other sets associated with any function $f:R^n \to R$ are:

(1) The *contour of* f *for the value* y (in the range of f)

$$C_f(y) = \{\mathbf{x} \in R^n \mid f(\mathbf{x}) = y\}$$

(2) The *upper contour set of* f *for the value* y (in the range of f)

$$UC_f(y) = \{\mathbf{x} \in R^n \mid f(\mathbf{x}) \geqslant y\}$$

(3) The *lower contour set of* f *for the value* y (in the range of f)

$$LC_f(y) = \{\mathbf{x} \in R^n \mid f(\mathbf{x}) \leqslant y\}.$$

For linear functions on R^n, $C_f(y)$ will be a hyperplane in R^n (not necessarily non-vertical, e.g. $f:R^n \to R$ where $f(\mathbf{x}) = x_2$) and $UC_f(y), LC_f(y)$ will be the associated half-spaces. Generally contours (and the associated upper and lower sets) are subsets of R^n while G_f is a subset of R^{n+1}. Since we are now interested in the case $n > 1$, visual representation of G_f is only available when $n = 2$ and then with difficulty since it is a subset of R^3. However, when $n = 2$ contour sets can be represented visually as they are subsets of R^2. In what follows we make liberal use of contours (etc.) as a visual aid for the two-variable case. For example consider

$$f:R^2 \to R \quad \text{where } f(\mathbf{x}) = x_1 + x_2$$

The domain is R^2, the range is R and the contour for $y \in R$ is

$$C_f(y) = \{\mathbf{x} \in R^2 \mid x_1 + x_2 = y\}$$

Figure 4.1 sketches $C_f(0)$ and $C_f(1)$. $UC_f(0)$ is the set of points on or above $C_f(0)$ in fig. 4.1 while $LC_f(0)$ is the set of points on or

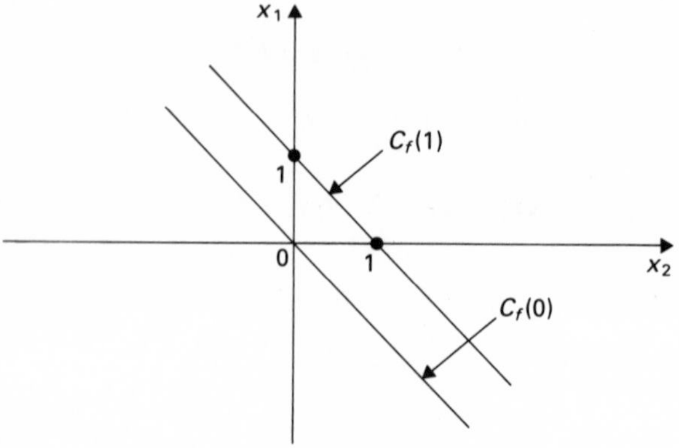

Figure 4.1

below $C_f(0)$; similarly for $UC_f(1)$, $LC_f(1)$. Along $C_f(0)$ the value of f is everywhere 0; along $C_f(1)$ the value of f is always 1. By sketching selected contours you can get an adequate representation in two dimensions of how the graph behaves in three dimensions. Of course cartographers use exactly this device for indicating heights above sea level in two-dimensional maps. Economists use contour 'sketches' or 'maps' liberally. As we discuss in detail in chapters 10–12, an indifference curve is a contour of a utility function, while an isoquant is a contour of a production function.

A couple of examples of non-linear functions of two variables are:

(a) $f:R^2 \to R$ where $f(x_1, x_2) = x_1^2 + x_2^2$
(b) $f:R^2 \to R$ where $f(x_1, x_2) = x_1 x_2$

Figure 4.2 sketches a few contours of these functions. In case (a) $UC_f(1)$ is the points on or outside the circle $C_f(1)$ while $LC_f(1)$ is on or inside the circle; similarly for $UC_f(4)$, $LC_f(4)$. Notice that $C_f(0) = \{\mathbf{x} \in R^2 | x_1^2 + x_2^2 = 0\} = \{(0, 0)\}$ and this contour is a single point (the origin). Of course $(0, 0)$ is the unique global minimum of f (since $x_i^2 \geqslant 0$, $\forall x_i \in R$ and $x_i^2 > 0$ if $x_i \neq 0$) and so is the only point where f attains the value 0. Generally contours degenerate to a unique point at either a unique global minimum or a unique global maximum (the trough of the valley, the peak of the mountain). For (b) $UC_f(1)$ consists of the points on or above the top branch and on or below the bottom branch of the rectangular hyperbola $C_f(1)$; and so on. There is no global maximum or minimum for (b). Notice $C_f(0) = \{\mathbf{x} \in R^2 | x_1 = 0 \text{ or } x_2 = 0\}$ and is the axes of (b).

A function $f:R^n \to R$ is *continuous* if $\lim_{\mathbf{x} \to \mathbf{x}^*} f(\mathbf{x}) = f(\mathbf{x}^*)$, $\forall \mathbf{x}^*$. For $n = 2$ this means visually and loosely that the graph of f is an 'unbroken surface' in R^3. We do not engage in a detailed discussion

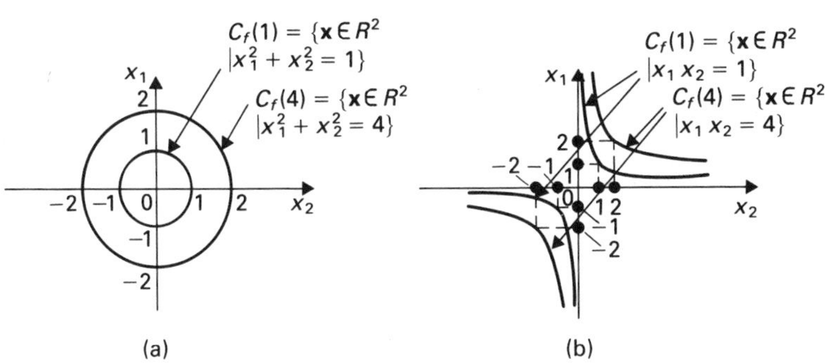

Figure 4.2

of continuity in this book. The following assertion will be useful at various stages. Suppose $f:R^n \to R$ is such that $f(\mathbf{x})$ is composed of sums, products or ratios (provided the denominator is never zero) of continuous functions of the single variables x_i on R for $i=1,\ldots,n$. Then f is continuous on R^n. For instance in example (b) before (fig. 4.2(b)), x_1 and x_2 are continuous on R; hence x_1x_2 is continuous on R^2. Similarly the other (two) two-variable functions earlier are continuous.

The partial derivative of f with respect to x_i at $\mathbf{x}^*$, denoted $f'_i(\mathbf{x}^*)$ exists if there is a unique real number $f'_i(\mathbf{x}^*)$ such that

$$\lim_{\Delta x_i \to 0} \frac{f[x_1^*,\ldots,x_{i-1}^*, x_i^* + \Delta x_i, x_{i+1}^*,\ldots,x_n^*] - f(\mathbf{x}^*)}{\Delta x_i}$$

$$= f'_i(\mathbf{x}^*)$$

If $f'_i(\mathbf{x}^*)$ exists for all $\mathbf{x}^* \in R^n$ and for all i and if the n partial derivative functions:

$$f'_i : R^n \to R \quad \text{with values } f'_i(\mathbf{x})$$

are continuous then f is *continuously differentiable* or f is C^1.

If f is C^1 then there is a unique non-vertical tangent hyperplane to the graph of f at every point. The equation defining this hyperplane tangent to G_f at $(f(\mathbf{x}^*), \mathbf{x}^*)$ is

$$y = f(x^*) + (x_1 - x_1^*) f'_1(\mathbf{x}^*)$$

$$+ (x_2 - x_2^*) f'_2(x^*) + \ldots + (x_n - x_n^*) f'_n(\mathbf{x}^*)$$

$$= f(x^*) + \sum_{i=1}^{n} (x_i - x_i^*) f'_i(\mathbf{x}^*)$$

When $n = 2$ the graph of a C^1 function will be a 'smooth' surface in R^3 in the sense that there is a unique (non-vertical) tangent plane to G_f at each point.

If the n partial derivative functions are themselves C^1 (as well as continuous) then their own partial derivatives are the second partial derivatives of f. Formally, the *second partial derivative* of f with respect to x_i and then x_j at $\mathbf{x}^*$, denoted $f''_{ij}(\mathbf{x}^*)$, exists if there is a unique real number $f''_{ij}(\mathbf{x}^*)$ such that,

$$\lim_{\Delta x_j \to 0} \frac{f'_i[x_1^*,\ldots,x_{j-1}^*, x_j^* + \Delta x_j, x_{j+1}^*,\ldots,x_n^*] - f'_i(\mathbf{x}^*)}{\Delta x_j}$$

$$= f''_{ij}(\mathbf{x}^*)$$

If $f''_{ij}(\mathbf{x}^*)$ exists for all $\mathbf{x}^* \in R^n$ and for all i, j and if the n^2 second partial derivative functions

$$f''_{ij}: R^n \to R \quad \text{with values } f''_{ij}(\mathbf{x})$$

are continuous then f is *twice continuously differentiable* or f is C^2.

An important and well-known theorem in mathematics is Young's Theorem; if f is C^2 then $\forall \mathbf{x}$, $f''_{ij}(\mathbf{x}) = f''_{ji}(\mathbf{x})$. That is, the order of differentiation does not matter.

It is very convenient to 'stack' the n first partial derivatives in a column vector. We write

$$\mathbf{f}'(\mathbf{x}) = \begin{bmatrix} f'_1(\mathbf{x}) \\ f'_2(\mathbf{x}) \\ \vdots \\ f'_n(\mathbf{x}) \end{bmatrix}$$

Similarly the n^2 second partial derivatives are stacked into an $n \times n$ matrix, known as the Hessian of f and defined by:

$$\mathbf{f}''(\mathbf{x}) = \begin{bmatrix} f''_{11}(\mathbf{x}) & f''_{12}(\mathbf{x}) \ldots f''_{1n}(\mathbf{x}) \\ f''_{21}(\mathbf{x}) & f''_{22}(\mathbf{x}) \ldots f''_{2n}(\mathbf{x}) \\ \cdots & \cdots \\ f''_{n1}(\mathbf{x}) & f''_{n2}(\mathbf{x}) \ldots f''_{nn}(\mathbf{x}) \end{bmatrix}$$

If f is C^2 then from Young's theorem the Hessian of f is a *symmetric* matrix.

A function will be C^1 (or C^2) if it is composed of sums, products and ratios (provided the denominator is never zero) of C^1 (or C^2) functions on R of the single variables x_i, $i = 1, \ldots, n$, just as with continuity. Accordingly the three earlier examples are all C^2 (and hence C^1). We assume the reader is familiar with the rules of partial differentiation. For instance the column vector $\mathbf{f}'(\mathbf{x})$ and the matrix $\mathbf{f}''(\mathbf{x})$ for the earlier examples are as follows:

(1) $f(x_1, x_2) = x_1 + x_2$ implies $f'_1(\mathbf{x}) = 1$, $f'_2(\mathbf{x}) = 1$, $f''_{ij}(\mathbf{x}) = 0$, $\forall i, j$. So

$$\mathbf{f}'(\mathbf{x}) = \begin{bmatrix} 1 \\ 1 \end{bmatrix}, \quad \mathbf{f}''(\mathbf{x}) = \begin{bmatrix} 0 & 0 \\ 0 & 0 \end{bmatrix}$$

(2) $f(x_1, x_2) = x_1^2 + x_2^2$ implies $f'_1(\mathbf{x}) = 2x_1$, $f'_2(\mathbf{x}) = 2x_2$, $f''_{12}(\mathbf{x}) = 0 = f''_{21}(\mathbf{x})$, $f''_{11}(\mathbf{x}) = 2 = f''_{22}(\mathbf{x})$. So

$$\mathbf{f}'(\mathbf{x}) = \begin{bmatrix} 2x_1 \\ 2x_2 \end{bmatrix}, \quad \mathbf{f}''(\mathbf{x}) = \begin{bmatrix} 2 & 0 \\ 0 & 2 \end{bmatrix}$$

(3) $f(x_1, x_2) = x_1 x_2$ implies $f_1'(\mathbf{x}) = x_2$, $f_2'(\mathbf{x}) = x_1$, $f_{12}''(\mathbf{x}) = 1 = f_{21}''(\mathbf{x})$ and $f_{11}''(\mathbf{x}) = 0 = f_{22}''(\mathbf{x})$. Hence

$$\mathbf{f}'(\mathbf{x}) = \begin{bmatrix} x_2 \\ x_1 \end{bmatrix}, \quad \mathbf{f}''(\mathbf{x}) = \begin{bmatrix} 0 & 1 \\ 1 & 0 \end{bmatrix}$$

4.2 Concave functions of n variables on R^n

Almost everything in chapters 2 and 3 has a very straightforward and obvious generalization to the context of n variable functions on R^n. Only the derivative discussion becomes slightly more complicated than earlier.

Definition 4.1 $f: R^n \to R$ is concave if and only if

$$f[\lambda \mathbf{x}^1 + (1-\lambda)\mathbf{x}^2] \geqslant \lambda f(\mathbf{x}^1) + (1-\lambda) f(\mathbf{x}^2) \qquad \forall \lambda \in [0, 1], \forall \mathbf{x}^1, \mathbf{x}^2$$

For strictly concave functions the defining inequality is

$$f[\lambda \mathbf{x}^1 + (1-\lambda)\mathbf{x}^2] > \lambda f(\mathbf{x}^1) + (1-\lambda) f(\mathbf{x}^2) \qquad \forall \lambda \in (0, 1), \forall \mathbf{x}^1, \mathbf{x}^2 \text{ with } \mathbf{x}^1 \neq \mathbf{x}^2$$

and for convex and strictly convex functions we merely reverse the inequality sign in the corresponding concave definition.

As in chapter 2, definition 4.1 requires that the line joining any two points on the graph lies entirely on or below the graph (e.g. a surface in R^3 like an 'inverted bowl').

Theorem 4.1 Suppose $f: R^n \to R$ is a concave function. Then f is continuous. A proof of this is omitted; see bibliographical notes. The next two theorems are proved at the end of this chapter.

Theorem 4.2 Suppose $f: R^n \to R$ is a C^1 function. Then f is concave if and only if

$$f(\mathbf{x}^*) + (\mathbf{x} - \mathbf{x}^*)\,\mathbf{f}'(\mathbf{x}^*) \geqslant f(\mathbf{x}) \quad \forall \mathbf{x}, \mathbf{x}^*$$

Our notation is such that this looks just like the one-variable result. Notice, however, that now $(\mathbf{x} - \mathbf{x}^*)\,\mathbf{f}'(x^*)$ is the product of a row and column vector. Writing it out in full

$$(\mathbf{x} - \mathbf{x}^*)\,\mathbf{f}'(\mathbf{x}^*) = \sum_{i=1}^{n} (x_i - x_i^*) f_i'(\mathbf{x}^*)$$

and the inequality in theorem 4.4 is

$$f(\mathbf{x}^*) + \sum_{i=1}^{n} (x_i - x_i^*) f_i'(\mathbf{x}^*) \geqslant f(\mathbf{x}) \quad \forall \mathbf{x}, \mathbf{x}^*$$

For $n = 2$ theorem 4.2 says that a function of two variables is concave if and only if the tangent plane to its graph ($\subset R^3$) at any point lies entirely on or above the graph (e.g. the inverted bowl again). See the earlier formula for tangent hyperplanes to graphs of C^1 functions.

The strictly concave analogue of theorem 4.2 replaces the inequality with:

$$f(\mathbf{x}^*) + (\mathbf{x} - \mathbf{x}^*)\,\mathbf{f}'(\mathbf{x}^*) > f(\mathbf{x}) \quad \forall \mathbf{x}, \mathbf{x}^*, \mathbf{x} \neq \mathbf{x}^*$$

and for convex and strictly convex the sense of the inequality in theorem 4.2 and above is reversed.

Theorem 4.3 Suppose $f: R^n \to R$ is a C^2 function. Then f is concave if and only if $\mathbf{f}''(\mathbf{x})$ is negative semi-definite, $\forall \mathbf{x}$.

For $n = 1$ the corresponding result required the second derivative $f''(x)$ to be less than or equal to 0 everywhere. The generalization now requires *the Hessian matrix* $\mathbf{f}''(\mathbf{x})$ *to be negative semi-definite everywhere.* When $n = 2$ this matrix is:

$$\mathbf{f}''(\mathbf{x}) = \begin{bmatrix} f_{11}''(\mathbf{x}) & f_{12}''(\mathbf{x}) \\ f_{21}''(\mathbf{x}) & f_{22}''(\mathbf{x}) \end{bmatrix}$$

Such a matrix is negative semi-definite if and only if

(i) $f_{11}''(\mathbf{x}) \leqslant 0$ and $f_{22}''(\mathbf{x}) \leqslant 0$, and

(ii) $\det \mathbf{f}''(\mathbf{x}) = f_{11}''(\mathbf{x}) f_{22}''(\mathbf{x}) - f_{12}''(\mathbf{x}) f_{21}''(\mathbf{x}) \geqslant 0$.

Generally the $n \times n$ matrix $\mathbf{f}''(\mathbf{x})$ is negative semi-definite if and only if its principal minors of order k $(= 1, \ldots, n)$ are all 0 or of sign $(-1)^k$ (see section 4.5 for a fuller discussion).

This gives us a mechanical procedure for testing the concavity of C^2 functions. For instance a two-variable function is concave if and only if (i) and (ii) are satisfied $\forall \mathbf{x}$. Examples follow shortly.

For strictly concave functions we get, instead of the statement in theorem 4.3: *if* $\mathbf{f}''(\mathbf{x})$ is negative definite $\forall x$ *then* f is strictly concave. So, analogous to chapters 2 and 4, negative definite Hessians are sufficient (but not necessary) for strict concavity. Sufficient conditions for negative definiteness are (i) and (ii) with strict replacing weak inequalities, with a similar change for the general case.

The convex function analogue of theorem 4.3 merely replaces 'negative semi-definite' with 'positive semi-definite'. When $n = 2$ this requires:

(iii) $f''_{11}(\mathbf{x}) \geqslant 0, \quad f''_{22}(\mathbf{x}) \geqslant 0$

(iv) $\det \mathbf{f}''(\mathbf{x}) \geqslant 0$

Generally positive semi-definiteness of $\mathbf{f}''(\mathbf{x})$ requires *all* principal minors of every order to be non-negative.

Finally a sufficient (but not necessary) condition for f to be strictly convex is that $\mathbf{f}''(\mathbf{x})$ be positive definite, and a sufficient condition for positive definiteness is that all principal minors be strictly positive.

Examples 4.1

(1) $f: R^2 \to R$ where $f(\mathbf{x}) = x_1^2 + x_2^2$. From the introduction

$$\mathbf{f}''(\mathbf{x}) = \begin{bmatrix} 2 & 0 \\ 0 & 2 \end{bmatrix}$$

(i) $2, 2 \geqslant 0$ and (ii) $4 \geqslant 0$. So the Hessian is positive semi-definite (p.s.d.) $\forall x$ and f is *convex*. In fact (i) $2, 2 > 0$ and (ii) $4 > 0$; the Hessian is positive definite (p.d.) $\forall \mathbf{x}$ and f is *strictly convex*.

(2) $f: R^3 \to R$ where $f(\mathbf{x}) = -x_1^2 - 4x_2^2 - 2x_3^2$. The Hessian is

$$\mathbf{f}''(\mathbf{x}) = \begin{bmatrix} -2 & 0 & 0 \\ 0 & -8 & 0 \\ 0 & 0 & -4 \end{bmatrix}$$

(i) $-2, -8, -4 < 0$

(ii) $\begin{vmatrix} -2 & 0 \\ 0 & -8 \end{vmatrix} = 16 > 0, \begin{vmatrix} -8 & 0 \\ 0 & -4 \end{vmatrix} = 32 > 0,$

$\begin{vmatrix} -2 & 0 \\ 0 & -4 \end{vmatrix} = 8 > 0.$

(iii) $\det \mathbf{f}''(\mathbf{x}) = (-2)(32) = -64$

So minors alternate in sign beginning negative: none are zero and so $\mathbf{f}''(\mathbf{x})$ is n.d. $\forall \mathbf{x} \in R^3$; f is *strictly concave*.

(3) $f:R^2 \to R$ where $f(\mathbf{x}) = x_1 x_2$. From before

$$\mathbf{f}''(\mathbf{x}) = \begin{bmatrix} 0 & 1 \\ 1 & 0 \end{bmatrix}$$

det $\mathbf{f}''(\mathbf{x}) = -1$ so $\mathbf{f}''(\mathbf{x})$ is *neither* p.s.d. *nor* n.s.d. Hence f is *neither concave nor convex.*

Turning to the discussion of maxima we write our problem as:

$$\max f(\mathbf{x})$$

where $f:R^n \to R$ is a function of n variables. A *solution* to this problem is a *global maximum* of f; i.e. $\mathbf{x}^*$ such that $f(\mathbf{x}^*) \geqslant f(\mathbf{x})$, $\forall \mathbf{x}$. Then $f(\mathbf{x}^*)$ is the *optimal value* of f.

Assuming f is C^1, a *stationary point* of f is $\mathbf{x}^*$ where $\mathbf{f}'(\mathbf{x}^*) = 0$. Notice this is a vector equation now, requiring $f_i'(\mathbf{x}^*) = 0, i = 1, \ldots, n$. A probably familiar *necessary* condition for x^* to be a global max of f is that x^* be a stationary point; if x^* is a global max the tangent (hyper)plane to the graph at $(f(\mathbf{x}^*), x^*)$ must be horizontal, namely $y = f(x^*)$. As you should by now expect if f is also concave, then stationarity at $\mathbf{x}^*$ is *sufficient* for a global max. For suppose f is C^1 and concave. From theorem 4.2

$$f(\mathbf{x}^*) + (\mathbf{x} - \mathbf{x}^*)\, \mathbf{f}'(\mathbf{x}^*) \geqslant f(x) \quad \forall x, x^*$$

If $\mathbf{f}'(\mathbf{x}^*) = 0$ we have

$$f(\mathbf{x}^*) \geqslant f(\mathbf{x}) \quad \forall x$$

and $\mathbf{x}^*$ is therefore a global maximum of f. Hence:

Theorem 4.4 Suppose $f:R^n \to R$ is a C^1 concave function. Then $\mathbf{x}^*$ is a global maximum of f if and only if $\mathbf{f}'(\mathbf{x}^*) = 0$.

So for C^1, concave functions, on R^n, stationarity characterizes the global maxima of f. And for C^1 convex functions the analogue of theorem 4.4 tells us that stationarity characterizes the global *minima* of f.

Concave (convex) functions, of n variables on R^n may have 0, 1 or an infinite number of global maxima (minima). If the last possibility occurs then the set of maxima (minima) is a convex subset of R^n. Moreover, the last possibility cannot occur if the function is strictly concave (convex). These assertions are proved easily by generalizing the arguments of chapter 2.

Examples 4.2 These are a repeat of examples 4.1

(a) $\mathbf{f}'(\mathbf{x}) = \begin{bmatrix} 2x_1 \\ 2x_2 \end{bmatrix} = \begin{bmatrix} 0 \\ 0 \end{bmatrix}$

if and only if $\mathbf{x}^* = (0, 0)$; $\mathbf{x}^* = (0, 0)$ is the unique stationary point; f is convex. So $(0, 0)$ is the unique *global minimum* with optimal value $f(0, 0) = 0$.

(b) $\mathbf{f}'(\mathbf{x}) = \begin{bmatrix} -2x_1 \\ -8x_2 \\ -4x_3 \end{bmatrix} = \begin{bmatrix} 0 \\ 0 \\ 0 \end{bmatrix}$

if and only if $\mathbf{x}^* = (0, 0, 0)$; f is concave. So $\mathbf{x}^* = (0, 0, 0)$ is the unique *global maximum* with optimal value $f(0, 0, 0) = 0$.

(c) $\mathbf{f}'(\mathbf{x}) = \begin{bmatrix} x_2 \\ x_1 \end{bmatrix} = \begin{bmatrix} 0 \\ 0 \end{bmatrix}$

if and only if $\mathbf{x}^* = (0, 0)$. However, f is neither concave nor convex, so we can make *no inference* from our theorems about this stationary point.

4.3 Contours of concave functions

The following result provides valuable information about the nature of contours of concave functions of n variables.

Theorem 4.5 If $f: R^n \to R$ is a concave function then $UC_f(y)$ is a convex set, for all y in the range of f.

The proof requires only trivial amendments to that of theorem 2.5. Let us stress again that the implication in theorem 4.5 does not reverse: quasi-concave functions are functions with convex upper contour sets and are a larger class of functions than concave functions.

Visually, when $n = 2$ theorem 4.5 tells us that the set of points on one side or the other of a contour of a concave function is a convex set (depending which side is the upper contour set). Since the two-dimensional case occurs frequently in what follows some amplification of this remark is in order. You may for instance expect that if $f: R^2 \to R$ is a C^1 function then the contours of f are 'nice smooth' curves in R^2. In fig. 4.2(b) you see that this is not true in general since $C_f(0)$ is then the axes of R^2. However, when $f_1'(\mathbf{x}^*) \neq 0$ (not true at the origin in fig. 4.2(b)) it can be shown (using the implicit function theorem—see chapter 17) that the contour $C_f(y)$

where $y = f(\mathbf{x}^*)$ will be a 'nice smooth' curve going through $\mathbf{x}^*$, at least for $\mathbf{x}$ close to $\mathbf{x}^*$. To be more precise there will be a one-variable C^1 function $h(x_2)$ such that

$$f(x_1, x_2) = y \quad \text{if and only if } x_1 = h(x_2)$$

at least for $\mathbf{x}$ close to $\mathbf{x}^*$, where $y = f(\mathbf{x}^*)$. $x_1 = h(x_2)$ is then the equation of this contour for $\mathbf{x}$ close to $\mathbf{x}^*$ and its slope at $\mathbf{x}^*$, $h'(x_2^*)$ is found by implicit differentiation, as follows. We know

$$f[h(x_2), x_2] = y, x_2 \text{ close to } x_2^*$$

Differentiating with respect to x_2 gives

$$f_1'[h(x_2), x_2]\, h'(x_2) + f_2'[h(x_2), x_2] = 0$$

When $x_2 = x_2^*$, $h(x_2) = x_1^*$ and we get

$$h'(x_2^*) = -\frac{f_2'(\mathbf{x}^*)}{f_1'(\mathbf{x}^*)} \quad \text{since } f_1'(\mathbf{x}^*) \neq 0$$

Summarizing, if $f_1'(\mathbf{x}^*) \neq 0$ then at least near $\mathbf{x}^*$ the contour of f 'through $\mathbf{x}^*$' (i.e. for the value $y = f(\mathbf{x}^*)$) is a 'nice smooth' curve (i.e. the graph of a C^1 function) with slope given by the above formula. For instance if $f_1'(\mathbf{x}^*)$ and $f_2'(\mathbf{x}^*)$ have the same sign then the contour through $\mathbf{x}^*$ is a downward-sloping curve (near $\mathbf{x}^*$) and upward-sloping if the partials have opposite sign. Moreover, if $f_1'(\mathbf{x}^*) > 0$ and $f_2'(\mathbf{x}^*) > 0$ *everywhere* the upper contour set will then be the set of points on or above the contour which will be downward sloping throughout. If f is in addition concave these upper contour sets must be convex, giving a typical contour map as shown in fig. 4.3.

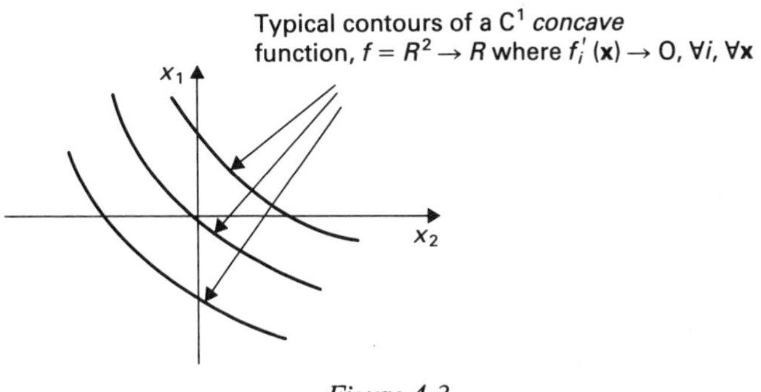

Figure 4.3

The reader is invited to consider the nature of the typical contour map when f is C^1 and concave but, everywhere: (i) $f_1'(\mathbf{x}) < 0, f_2'(\mathbf{x}) < 0$; (ii) $f_1'(\mathbf{x}) < 0, f_2'(\mathbf{x}) > 0$; and (iii) $f_1'(\mathbf{x}) > 0, f_2'(\mathbf{x}) < 0$.

For convex functions the analogue of theorem 4.5 is that *lower* contour sets are convex sets. For instance if $f:R^2 \rightarrow R$ is C^1 and convex and $f_1'(\mathbf{x}) > 0$, $f_2'(x) > 0$ everywhere then a typical contour map is shown in fig. 4.4.

Finally we mention the hypograph (epigraph) characterization of concave (convex) functions. The hypograph HG_f and epigraph, EG_f of $f:R^n \rightarrow R$ are,

$$HG_f = \{(y, \mathbf{x}) \in R^{n+1} | y \leqslant f(\mathbf{x})\}$$

$$EG_f = \{(y, \mathbf{x}) \in R^{n+1} | y \geqslant f(\mathbf{x})\}$$

Like G_f these are subsets in R^{n+1} and are not much use visually when $n > 1$. However, by trivial amendments to theorem 2.4 we get:

$f:R^n \rightarrow R$ is concave if and only if HG_f is a convex set;

and

$f:R^n \rightarrow R$ is convex if and only if EG_f is a convex set.

4.4 A proof of theorems 4.2 and 4.3

The strategy of proof is to reduce the n-variable result to a one-variable statement with the following:

Lemma 4.1 Consider a function of n variables, $f:R^n \rightarrow R$. For any pair $\mathbf{x}^1$, $\mathbf{x}^2$ define $\phi:R \rightarrow R$ by

$$\phi(\lambda) = f[\lambda \mathbf{x}^1 + (1 - \lambda)\mathbf{x}^2]$$

Then f is concave if and only if ϕ is concave $\forall \mathbf{x}^1, \mathbf{x}^2$.

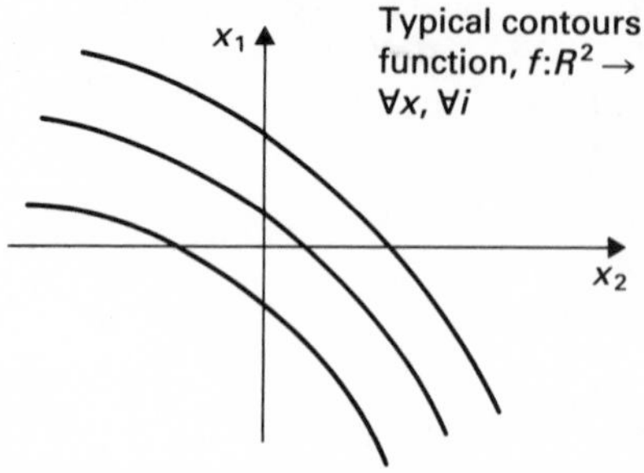

Figure 4.4

Proof '*if*' Suppose ϕ is concave $\forall \mathbf{x}^1, \mathbf{x}^2$. Then $\forall \mathbf{x}^1, \mathbf{x}^2$ and $\forall \lambda \in [0, 1]$.

$$\phi(\lambda) = \phi(\lambda \times 1 + (1-\lambda) \times 0)$$
$$\geqslant \lambda\phi(1) + (1-\lambda)\,\phi(0))$$

since ϕ is concave. But

$$\phi(\lambda) = f(\lambda \mathbf{x}^1 + (1-\lambda)\,\mathbf{x}^2),\ \phi(1) = f(\mathbf{x}^1) \text{ and } \phi(0) = f(\mathbf{x}^2).$$

Hence

$$f[\lambda \mathbf{x}^1 + (1-\lambda)\,\mathbf{x}^2] \geqslant \lambda f(\mathbf{x}^1) + (1-\lambda)\,f(\mathbf{x}^2) \qquad \forall \lambda \in [0, 1] \text{ and } \forall \mathbf{x}^1, \mathbf{x}^2$$

Hence f is concave.

'*only if*' Suppose f is concave. $\forall \mathbf{x}^1, \mathbf{x}^2$ we have to show that for any $\lambda_1, \lambda_2 \in R$ and for any $\lambda \in [0, 1]$,

$$\phi(\lambda\lambda_1 + (1-\lambda)\,\lambda_2) \geqslant \lambda\phi(\lambda_1) + (1-\lambda)\,\phi(\lambda_2)$$

For short write $\mathbf{y}^1 = \lambda_1 \mathbf{x}^1 + (1-\lambda_1)\,\mathbf{x}^2$ and $\mathbf{y}^2 = \lambda_2 \mathbf{x}^1 + (1-\lambda_2)\,\mathbf{x}^2$: then $\phi(\lambda_1) = f(\mathbf{y}^1)$ and $\phi(\lambda_2) = f(\mathbf{y}^2)$. Writing $t = \lambda\lambda_1 + (1-\lambda)\,\lambda_2$,

$$\phi(\lambda\lambda_1 + (1-\lambda)\,\lambda_2) = f[t\mathbf{x}^1 + (1-t)\,\mathbf{x}^2]$$

But

$$\begin{aligned} t\mathbf{x}^1 + (1-t)\,\mathbf{x}^2 &= [\lambda\lambda_1 + (1-\lambda)\,\lambda_2]\,\mathbf{x}^1 \\ &\quad + [1 - \lambda\lambda_1 - (1-\lambda)\,\lambda_2]\,\mathbf{x}^2 \\ &= \lambda\lambda_1\mathbf{x}^1 + \lambda_2\mathbf{x}^1 - \lambda\lambda_2\mathbf{x}^1 + \mathbf{x}^2 \\ &\quad - \lambda\lambda_1\mathbf{x}^2 - \lambda_2\mathbf{x}^2 + \lambda\lambda_2\mathbf{x}^2 \end{aligned}$$

(after rearranging)

$$\begin{aligned} &= \lambda[\lambda_1\mathbf{x}^1 + (1-\lambda_1)\,\mathbf{x}^2] \\ &\quad + (1-\lambda)\,[\lambda_2\mathbf{x}^1 + (1-\lambda_2)\,\mathbf{x}^2] \\ &= \lambda\mathbf{y}^1 + (1-\lambda)\,\mathbf{y}^2 \end{aligned}$$

So what we have to show becomes

$$f[\lambda\mathbf{y}^1 + (1-\lambda)\,\mathbf{y}^2] \geqslant \lambda f(\mathbf{y}^1) + (1-\lambda)\,f(\mathbf{y}^2).$$

But this must be true since f is concave. *Q.E.D.*

It is now a straightforward matter to apply the results of chapter 2 to ϕ and the desired characterizations will follow.

Proof of theorem 4.2 Under the assumption of the theorem ϕ defined in lemma 4.1 will be C^1. Suppose f is concave: then ϕ is concave and

$$\phi(\lambda^*) + (\lambda - \lambda^*)\,\phi'(\lambda^*) \geqslant \phi(\lambda) \quad \forall\lambda, \lambda^*$$

Now $\phi'(\lambda^*) = \Sigma\,(x_i^1 - x_i^2)\,f_i'(\lambda^*\mathbf{x}^1 + (1-\lambda^*)\,\mathbf{x}^2)$. With $\lambda^* = 0$, $\lambda = 1$ we get $\phi(\lambda^*) = f(\mathbf{x}^2)$, $\phi(\lambda) = f(\mathbf{x}^1)$ and $\phi'(\lambda^*) = (\mathbf{x}^1 - \mathbf{x}^2)\,\mathbf{f}'(\mathbf{x}^2)$. Hence

$$f(\mathbf{x}^2) + (\mathbf{x}^1 - \mathbf{x}^2)\,\mathbf{f}'(\mathbf{x}^2) \geqslant f(\mathbf{x}^1)$$

as required. Conversely suppose $f(\mathbf{x}^2) + (\mathbf{x}^1 - \mathbf{x}^2)\,\mathbf{f}'(\mathbf{x}^2) \geqslant f(\mathbf{x}^1)$, $\forall\mathbf{x}^1, \mathbf{x}^2$. This is also true replacing $\mathbf{x}^1$ with $\lambda\mathbf{x}^1 + (1-\lambda)\,\mathbf{x}^2$ and $\mathbf{x}^2$ with $\lambda^*\mathbf{x}^1 + (1-\lambda^*)\,\mathbf{x}^2$, for any $\lambda, \lambda^* \in R$. Hence

$$f[\lambda^*\mathbf{x}^1 + (1-\lambda^*)\,\mathbf{x}^2] + (\lambda - \lambda^*)(\mathbf{x}^1 - \mathbf{x}^2)\,\mathbf{f}'[\lambda^*\mathbf{x}^1 + \\ + (1-\lambda^*)\,\mathbf{x}^2] \geqslant f[\lambda\mathbf{x}^1 + (1-\lambda)\,\mathbf{x}^2] \\ \forall x^1, x^2, \forall\lambda, \lambda^*$$

i.e.

$$\phi(\lambda^*) + (\lambda - \lambda^*)\,\phi'(\lambda^*) \geqslant \phi(\lambda) \quad \forall\lambda, \lambda^*$$

So ϕ is concave and f is concave. *Q.E.D.*

Proof of theorem 4.3 ϕ will also be C^2. Suppose f is concave; then ϕ is concave and $\phi''(\lambda) \leqslant 0$, $\forall\lambda$. Hence

$$\phi''(\lambda) = \sum_{i=1}^{n}\sum_{j=1}^{n}(x_i^1 - x_i^2)(x_j^1 - x_j^2)\,f_{ij}''(\lambda\mathbf{x}^1 + (1-\lambda)\,\mathbf{x}^2) \\ \leqslant 0 \quad \forall\lambda, \forall\mathbf{x}^1, \mathbf{x}^2$$

Let $\mathbf{x} \in R^n$ and let $\mathbf{z} \in R^n$. Then for $k > 0$, $\mathbf{x}^1, \mathbf{x}^2 \in R^n$ where $\mathbf{x}^1 = \mathbf{x} + k\mathbf{z}$ and $\mathbf{x}^2 = \mathbf{x} - k\mathbf{z}$; moreover $\mathbf{x}^1 - x^2 = 2k\mathbf{z}$ and $\mathbf{x} = \frac{1}{2}\mathbf{x}^1 + \frac{1}{2}x^2$. Hence from $\phi''(\lambda) \leqslant 0$ we get, for any $\mathbf{x} \in R^n$ and $\mathbf{z} \in R^n$:

$$\sum_{i=1}^{n}\sum_{j=1}^{n} z_i z_j\, f_{ij}''(\mathbf{x}) \leqslant 0$$

This means $\mathbf{f}''(\mathbf{x})$ is negative semi-definite, $\forall\mathbf{x}$.

Conversely suppose $\Sigma\Sigma z_i z_j f_{ij}''(\mathbf{x}) \leqslant 0$, $\forall z \in R^n$ and $\forall\mathbf{x} \in R^n$. Choose any $\mathbf{x}^1, \mathbf{x}^2 \in R^n$ and any $\lambda \in R$ and let $\mathbf{x} = \lambda\mathbf{x}^1 + (1-\lambda)\,\mathbf{x}^2$ and $\mathbf{z} = \mathbf{x}^1 - \mathbf{x}^2$. Then $\mathbf{x} \in R^n$, $\mathbf{z} \in R^n$ and it follows that $\phi''(\lambda) \leqslant 0$, $\forall\lambda, \forall\mathbf{x}^1, \mathbf{x}^2$. Hence f is concave. *Q.E.D.*

4.5 Definite matrices: a brief introduction

Let $\mathbf{z}$ denote an n-dimensional column vector

$$\begin{bmatrix} z_1 \\ z_n \end{bmatrix}$$

and let $\mathbf{z}^T$ denote the transpose of $\mathbf{z}$, the row vector $(z_1 \ldots z_n)$. If

$$\mathbf{A} = \begin{bmatrix} a_{11} \ldots a_{1n} \\ a_{n1} \ldots a_{nn} \end{bmatrix}$$

is an $n \times n$ matrix then $\mathbf{A}$ is said to be

(i) negative semi-definite if and only if $\mathbf{z}^T\mathbf{A}\mathbf{z} \leqslant 0$, for all $\mathbf{z}$;
(ii) negative definite if and only if $\mathbf{z}^T\mathbf{A}\mathbf{z} < 0$, for all $\mathbf{z} \neq 0$;
(iii) positive semi-definite if and only if $\mathbf{z}^T\mathbf{A}\mathbf{z} > 0$, for all $\mathbf{z}$;
(iv) positive definite if and only if $\mathbf{z}^T\mathbf{A}\mathbf{z} > 0$, for all $\mathbf{z} \neq 0$.

$\mathbf{z}^T\mathbf{A}\mathbf{z}$ is a scalar, quadratic function of $z_1, \ldots, z_n$. Checking the above definitions by direct evaluation of the sign of this quadratic form for all relevant $\mathbf{z}$ is feasible only in simple cases. Fortunately, two types of theorem are available which characterize definiteness in terms of the properties of $\mathbf{A}$. One type is associated with the 'eigenvalues' of $\mathbf{A}$ and we do not use this here. The other is in terms of principal minors of $\mathbf{A}$. A kth-order ($k = 1, \ldots, n$) principal minor of $\mathbf{A}$ is the determinant of the matrix found by deleting any n–k rows and the same columns of $\mathbf{A}$. For instance when $n = 2$,

$$\mathbf{A} = \begin{bmatrix} a_{11} & a_{12} \\ a_{21} & a_{22} \end{bmatrix}$$

and the 1st-order principal minors are

(1) a_{11}, a_{22}

while the 2nd-order principal minor is

(2) $\begin{vmatrix} a_{11} & a_{12} \\ a_{21} & a_{22} \end{vmatrix}$

When $n = 3$ the 1st-order principal minors of $\mathbf{A}$ are

(3) a_{11}, a_{22}, a_{33}

the 2nd-order principal minors are

(4) $$\begin{vmatrix} a_{11} & a_{12} \\ a_{21} & a_{22} \end{vmatrix}, \begin{vmatrix} a_{11} & a_{13} \\ a_{31} & a_{33} \end{vmatrix}, \begin{vmatrix} a_{22} & a_{23} \\ a_{32} & a_{33} \end{vmatrix}$$

while the 3rd-order principal minor is

(5) $$\begin{vmatrix} a_{11} & a_{12} & a_{13} \\ a_{21} & a_{22} & a_{23} \\ a_{31} & a_{32} & a_{33} \end{vmatrix} = \det \mathbf{A}$$

And so on for $n = 4, 5 \ldots$. Notice that the 1st-order principal minors are always the leading diagonal elements of **A** $(a_{11}, a_{22}, \ldots, a_{nn})$, while the nth-order principal minor is always det **A**.

In this book all matrices of interest are Hessians of C^2 functions and so symmetric ($a_{ij} = a_{ji}$, $\forall ij$).

The crucial results (without proof) are as follows:

The $n \times n$ symmetric matrix **A** is negative semi-definite if and only if, for $k = 1, \ldots, n$, the kth-order principal minors of **A** are all of sign $(-1)^k$ or 0.

The $n \times n$ symmetric matrix **A** is positive semi-definite if and only if the kth-order principal minors of **A** are all non-negative.

For instance for negative semi-definiteness in the case $n = 2$ we need

(1) $a_{11} \leqslant 0, a_{22} \leqslant 0$

(2) $$\begin{vmatrix} a_{11} & a_{12} \\ a_{21} & a_{22} \end{vmatrix} \geqslant 0$$

And when $n = 3$ negative semi-definiteness requires

(3) $a_{11} \leqslant 0, a_{22} \leqslant 0, a_{33} \leqslant 0$

(4) $$\begin{vmatrix} a_{11} & a_{12} \\ a_{21} & a_{22} \end{vmatrix} \geqslant 0, \begin{vmatrix} a_{11} & a_{13} \\ a_{31} & a_{33} \end{vmatrix} \geqslant 0, \begin{vmatrix} a_{22} & a_{23} \\ a_{32} & a_{33} \end{vmatrix} \geqslant 0$$

(5) $$\begin{vmatrix} a_{11} & a_{12} & a_{13} \\ a_{21} & a_{22} & a_{23} \\ a_{31} & a_{32} & a_{33} \end{vmatrix} \leqslant 0$$

and so on.

For negative and positive definiteness the results are:

If for $k = 1, \ldots, n$ the kth-order principal minors of the $n \times n$ symmetric matrix **A** are all of sign $(-1)^k$ then **A** is negative definite.

If for $k = 1, \ldots, n$, the kth-order principal minors of the $n \times n$ symmetric matrix $\mathbf{A}$ are all strictly positve then $\mathbf{A}$ is positive definite.

Thus if the weak inequalities required for semi-definiteness are made strict, we have sufficient (but not necessary) conditions for definiteness. However, these sufficient conditions are more than is needed, strictly speaking, since we can get away with testing the sign of only one of the kth-order minors for each k in the definite case (but not for semi-definiteness). To be precise: the kth-order *leading* principal minor of $\mathbf{A}$ is the determinant found by deleting the *last* k rows and columns from $\mathbf{A}$. For instance when $n = 3$ the kth-order leading principal minors are:

$$\mathrm{k} = 1 \quad a_{11}$$

$$\mathrm{k} = 2 \quad \begin{vmatrix} a_{11} & a_{12} \\ a_{21} & a_{22} \end{vmatrix}$$

$$\mathrm{k} = 3 \quad \begin{vmatrix} a_{11} & a_{12} & a_{13} \\ a_{21} & a_{22} & a_{23} \\ a_{31} & a_{32} & a_{33} \end{vmatrix}$$

And we have:

If for $k = 1, \ldots, n$ the kth-order *leading* principal minor of the $n \times n$ symmetric matrix of $\mathbf{A}$ has sign $(-1)^k$ then $\mathbf{A}$ is negative definite.

If for $k = 1, \ldots, n$ the kth-order leading principal minor of the $n \times n$ symmetric matrix $\mathbf{A}$ is strictly positive then $\mathbf{A}$ is positive definite.

We do not proceed further with this refinement, however.

Examples

$$\begin{bmatrix} 2 & 1 \\ 1 & 2 \end{bmatrix} \quad \begin{matrix} \text{1st-order} & 2, 2 > 0 \\ \text{2nd-order} & 4 - 1 = 3 > 0 \end{matrix} \Bigg\} \Rightarrow \text{p.d.}$$

$$\begin{bmatrix} 2 & -1 \\ -1 & 2 \end{bmatrix} \quad \begin{matrix} \text{1st-order} & 2, 2 > 0 \\ \text{2nd-order} & 4 - 1 = 3 \geqslant 0 \end{matrix} \Bigg\} \Rightarrow \text{p.d.}$$

$$\begin{bmatrix} 2 & 2 \\ 2 & 2 \end{bmatrix} \quad \begin{matrix} \text{1st-order} & 2, 2 > 0 \\ \text{2nd-order} & 4 - 4 = 0 \geqslant 0 \end{matrix} \Bigg\} \Rightarrow \text{p.s.d.}$$

$$\begin{bmatrix} 0 & -1 & 3 \\ -1 & 0 & 2 \\ 3 & 2 & 0 \end{bmatrix} \quad \begin{matrix} \text{1st-order} & 0, 0, 0 \\ \text{2nd-order} & \begin{vmatrix} 0 & -1 \\ -1 & 0 \end{vmatrix} = -1 \Rightarrow \text{not definite} \end{matrix}$$

$$\begin{bmatrix} -3 & 0 & 0 \\ 0 & 0 & 0 \\ 0 & 0 & -1 \end{bmatrix} \quad \begin{array}{ll} \text{1st-order} & -3, 0, -1 \leqslant 0 \\ \text{2nd-order} & \begin{vmatrix} -3 & 0 \\ 0 & 0 \end{vmatrix} = \begin{vmatrix} -3 & 0 \\ 0 & -1 \end{vmatrix} = \begin{vmatrix} 0 & 0 \\ 0 & -1 \end{vmatrix} = 0 \\ \text{3rd-order} & \begin{vmatrix} -3 & 0 & 0 \\ 0 & 0 & 0 \\ 0 & 0 & -1 \end{vmatrix} = 0 \end{array}$$

So 1st-order $\leqslant 0$; 2nd-order $\geqslant 0$; 3rd-order $\leqslant 0 \Rightarrow$ n.s.d.

Notice that if $\mathbf{A}$ is a *diagonal* matrix (that is for all $i \neq j$, $a_{ij} = 0$) then $\mathbf{A}$ is

(a) n.s.d. if and only if $a_{ii} \leqslant 0, i = 1, \ldots, n$
(b) n.d. if and only if $a_{ii} < 0, i = 1, \ldots, n$
(c) p.s.d. if and only if $a_{ii} \geqslant 0, i = 1, \ldots, n$
(d) p.d. if and only if $a_{ii} > 0, i = 1, \ldots, n$

since in this case

$$\mathbf{z}^T\mathbf{A}\mathbf{z} = \sum_{i=1}^{n} \sum_{j=1}^{n} a_{ij} z_i z_j = \sum_{i=1}^{n} a_{ii} z_i^2.$$

So for diagonal matrices, we may simply check the signs of the leading diagonal elements and conclude in accord with (a)–(d).

The reader who has not met this material before will probably want more detailed knowledge and is referred to the bibliographical notes.

Exercise 4

1. (a) On a sketch in R^2 indicate $C_f(-18)$, $UC_f(-18)$, $LC_f(-18)$ for the C^2 function $f: R^2 \to R$ defined by $f(\mathbf{x}) = -2x_1^2 - 2x_2^2$.
   (b) Evaluate $\mathbf{f}'(\mathbf{x})$ and the Hessian $\mathbf{f}''(\mathbf{x})$ for the function in (a).

2. By applying definition 4.1 and the analogous convex function definition, show that $f: R^n \to R$ is both concave and convex if

$$f(\mathbf{x}) = \sum_{i=1}^{n} a_i x_i + b.$$

3. By demonstrating the first derivative characterizations of both concave and convex functions, show that the linear function in question 2 is both concave and convex.

4. Using the second derivative characterizations of concave and convex functions evaluate whether the following C^2 functions $f:R^n \to R$ are (i) concave, (ii) convex, (iii) both, (iv) neither.

   (a) $n = 2$ and $f(\mathbf{x}) = -2x_1^2 - 2x_2^2$
   (b) n general and $f(\mathbf{x}) = -2\Sigma x_i^2$
   (c) $n = 2$ and $f(\mathbf{x}) = x_1 + 3x_1x_2 + 6x_1^2 + x_2^2$
   (d) $n = 2$ and $f(\mathbf{x}) = e^{x_1} + e^{x_2} - x_1 - x_2$
   (e) $n = 2$ and $f(\mathbf{x}) = -x_1^2 - x_2^2 - 2x_1x_2$.

5. Find the stationary points of the functions in question 4 and hence evaluate their global maxima, global minima and corresponding optimal values.
6. Can a concave function possess a global minimum?
7. (a) Prove that if $f:R^n \to R$ is concave then the set of global maxima of f is a convex set.
   (b) Prove that $f:R^n \to R$ is concave if and only if its hypograph is a convex set.
8. Prove that if $f:R^n \to R$ is a convex function then its lower contour sets are all convex sets.
9. Find whether the functions in question 4 are strictly concave or strictly convex (or neither).

5 Introduction to concave programming: Lagrange and Kuhn-Tucker

5.1 Introduction

We have already looked in some detail at maximization problems which required us to find the largest value of $f: R^n \to R$. To find such a value we were allowed to search through *all* $\mathbf{x} \in R^n$ to find an $\mathbf{x}^*$ at which f attains its largest value. The typical maximization problem thrown up by microeconomic theory is not of this form. Usually we are only allowed to search through those $\mathbf{x} \in R^n$ which satisfy certain *constraints* and we want to find the largest value of f *subject to* those constraints. The general concave programming problem is exactly such a constrained maximization problem. If $f: R^n \to R$ and $g_i: R^n \to R$, $i = 1, \ldots, m$ are $m + 1$ concave functions this general concave programming problem is

$$\text{(GCPP)} \quad \max f(\mathbf{x}) \quad \text{subject to} \quad g_1(\mathbf{x}) \geqslant 0, \ldots, g_m(\mathbf{x}) \geqslant 0$$

Notice that the constraints are all in *weak* inequality form. The g_i functions, $i = 1, \ldots, m$ are known as *constraint functions* and f is the *objective function*. The *feasible set* is

$$K = \{\mathbf{x} \in R^n | g_i(\mathbf{x}) \geqslant 0 \quad i = 1, \ldots, m\}$$

Alternatively (GCCP) can be written

$$\max f(\mathbf{x}) \quad \text{subject to} \quad \mathbf{x} \in K$$

A *solution* to this problem is $\mathbf{x}^* \in K$ such that $f(\mathbf{x}^*) \geqslant f(\mathbf{x})$, $\forall \mathbf{x} \in K$; $\mathbf{x}^*$ is then said to be a *global* maximum of f on K and $f(\mathbf{x}^*)$ is the *optimal value* of f on K.

The task of this chapter is to introduce an important *characterization* of solutions to (GCCP). For the earlier (unconstrained) maximization problems we found that (assuming f is C^1 and concave) stationarity characterized the solutions. However, stationarity of f is in general neither necessary nor sufficient for solutions to the new concave programming problem. For instance consider

$$\max -x^2 \quad \text{subject to} \quad x \geqslant 1 \text{ and } x \leqslant 2$$

The second constraint is $-x \geqslant -2$ and this is a special case of (GCCP) with feasible set $[1, 2]$. Inspection of the behaviour of $-x^2$ on this interval reveals that $x^* = 1$ is the (unique) solution. However, it is not a stationary point of f; $f'(1) = -2 \neq 0$. So stationarity of f is not *necessary* for solutions to (GCCP) in general. Moreover f has a stationary point at 0 but this is not in the feasible set and so is not a solution. So mere stationarity of f is not *sufficient* to ensure solutions to (GCCP) in general either.

On the other hand if in (GCCP) f has a stationary point at $\mathbf{x}^*$ *in* K, it follows that $\mathbf{x}^* \in K$ and since f is concave, $f(\mathbf{x}^*) \geqslant f(\mathbf{x})$, $\forall \mathbf{x}$; in particular then $f(\mathbf{x}^*) \geqslant f(\mathbf{x})$, $\forall \mathbf{x} \in K$ and $\mathbf{x}^*$ is a solution of (GCCP). So stationarity of f *in* K is sufficient to ensure a solution to (GCCP). But this condition is still not necessary, as the above one-variable example still demonstrates. In other words there is not an obvious *characterization* of solutions to (GCCP) in terms of the stationarity of f.

The characterization we want to introduce in this chapter in fact evolves from an attempt to produce *a new function* whose stationary points do characterize solutions to (GCCP). This new function is called the *Lagrangean function* for (GCCP) and the characterizing conditions are *Kuhn–Tucker conditions*, involving in fact a little more than mere stationarity of the Lagrangean. We introduce these concepts shortly by looking at a simple special case of (GCCP) where $m = n = 1$; i.e. there is one variable and one constraint. The generalization to n variables is studied in the next chapter, and the case of many constraints is not needed until much later.

Before proceeding two remarks are in order. The *linear programming problem* is

$$\text{(LP)} \quad \max f(\mathbf{x}) \quad \text{subject to} \quad g_i(\mathbf{x}) \geqslant 0, i = 1, \ldots, m$$
$$\text{and} \quad x_i \geqslant 0, i = 1, \ldots, n$$

where f and all g_i are *linear functions*. This is a *special case* of (GCCP) with $m + n$ linear (and so concave) constraints and a linear (hence concave) objective. Once we have mastered (GCCP) we can apply our knowledge to this (LP) special case. Because of the linearity, however, we will be able to find new results and procedures for (LP) not available in general for (GCCP). The discussions of these points come much later.

Secondly we will also want to generalize (GCCP) to the case where all functions are merely *quasi-concave*. This will lead us into *quasi-concave programming* and naturally we defer study of this until we have covered concave programming and quasi-concave functions more fully.

5.2 Concave programming on *R* with one constraint

The problem is:

$$\max f(x) \quad \text{subject to} \quad g(x) \geqslant 0 \tag{5.1}$$

Since there is only one constraint we do not bother subscripting g. $f:R \to R$ and $g:R \to R$ are assumed concave and C^1, although C^1 is not needed for all our statements. The feasible set is $K = \{x \in R \mid g(x) \geqslant 0\}$. Assuming 0 is in the range of f, K is non-empty and $K = \mathrm{UC}_g(0)$. However, the characterization of solutions to (5.1) which we want needs somewhat more than the non-emptiness of K. We assume that the following so-called constraint qualification (CQ) is satisfied:

$$\text{(CQ)} \quad \exists\, x \in R \quad \text{where } g(x) > 0$$

Since $K = \mathrm{UC}_g(0)$ we know from chapter 2 that K is a convex subset of R; i.e. K is an interval of R. In fact we can be more specific about the nature of this interval. For suppose $\mathrm{UC}_g(0)$ is of the form (a, b). Then for $\epsilon > 0$ and 'small', $g(a+\epsilon) \geqslant 0$. But g is continuous; so $\lim_{\epsilon \to 0} g(a+\epsilon) = g(a)$. Since $g(a+\epsilon) \geqslant 0$, $\forall \epsilon > 0$ and sufficiently small, the weak inequality must also remain true in the limit $\epsilon = 0$; hence $g(a) \geqslant 0$ and $a \in \mathrm{UC}_g(0)$ as well, and $\mathrm{UC}_g(0)$ cannot be of the form (a, b) as it must include a. Similarly it must include b. In fact this reasoning shows that $\mathrm{UC}_g(0)$ must be an interval of one of the following forms:

$$\text{(i) } [a, b], \quad \text{(ii) } [a, +\infty), \quad \text{(iii) } (-\infty, b], \quad \text{(iv) } (-\infty, +\infty)$$

In case (iv), (5.1) reduces to: $\max f(x)$, and stationarity of f does still characterize the solutions to (5.1). To find a more general characterization which in fact covers all four possibilities we consider case (i) in detail. Assuming (CQ), fig. 5.1 illustrates the typical K in this case. Notice that $x = a$ is the unique x where $g(x) = 0$ and $g'(x) > 0$ while $x = b$ is defined by $g(x) = 0$ and $g'(x) < 0$.

Now if f has a stationary point at $x^* \in [a, b]$ this will be solution to (5.1). If f does not have a stationary point in $[a, b]$ then $f'(x) \neq 0$, $\forall x \in [a, b]$ and so either $f'(x) > 0$, $\forall x \in [a, b]$ or $f'(x) < 0$, $\forall x \in [a, b]$ since f is C^1. In the first case G_f is increasing throughout $[a, b]$ and

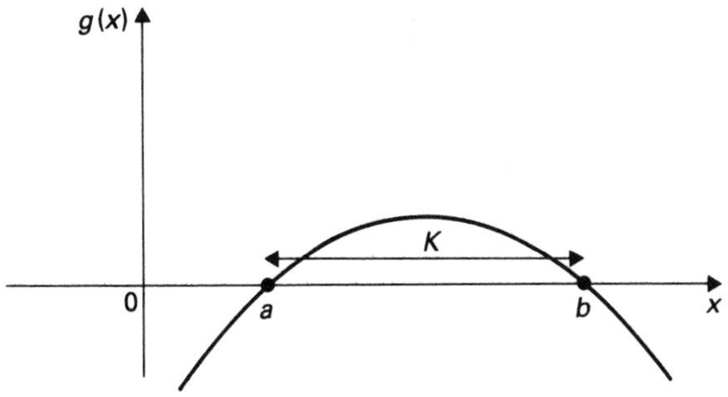

Figure 5.1

$x^* = b$ will be the solution: conversely $x^* = a$ is the solution in the second case. These are the only three possibilities: x^* solves (5.1) if and only if

either (1) $x^* \in [a, b]$ and $f'(x^*) = 0$
or (2) $x^* = b$ and $f'(x^*) > 0$
or (3) $x^* = a$ and $f'(x^*) < 0$.

Equivalently, x^* solves (7.3) if and only if

either (1) $g(x^*) \geqslant 0$ and $f'(x^*) = 0$
or (2) $g(x^*) = 0, g'(x^*) < 0$ and $f'(x^*) > 0$
or (3) $g(x^*) = 0, g'(x^*) > 0$ and $f'(x^*) < 0$.

This is a characterization of solutions to (5.1) but it does not have a useful generalization in higher dimensions. We try an alternative tack: can we find some new function whose stationary points do characterize solutions to (5.1) in case (i)?

Consider the *Lagrangean function* for (5.1) which is a function of the variables in the problem (x) and a new set of variables, one for each constraint, called *Lagrange multipliers*. Here there is only one constraint, so the one new variable is denoted λ and the Lagrangean function is

$$L: R^2 \to R \quad \text{where } L(x, \lambda) = f(x) + \lambda g(x)$$

We will give an intuitive justification for this choice of functional form later.

The introduction of λ has given us a new 'degree of freedom' in our search. Pose the question: can we find, for every possible solution to (5.1), a value of λ, λ^* say, which makes the solution a stationary point of L with respect to x? YES.

(1) If x^* is a 'type (1)' solution set $\lambda^* = 0$. Then $L(x, \lambda^*) = L(x, 0) = f(x)$ and $f'(x^*) = 0$ implies

$$\frac{\partial L}{\partial x}(x^*, 0) = 0$$

(2) If x^* is a 'type (2)' solution set

$$\lambda^* = -\frac{f'(x^*)}{g'(x^*)} > 0$$

Then

$$L(x, \lambda^*) = f(x) - \frac{f'(x^*)}{g'(x^*)} g(x)$$

$$\frac{\partial L}{\partial x}(x, \lambda^*) = f'(x) - \frac{f'(x^*)}{g'(x^*)} g'(x)$$

and so

$$\frac{\partial L}{\partial x}(x^*, \lambda^*) = 0 \text{ with } \lambda^* = -\frac{f'(x^*)}{g'(x^*)}$$

(3) If x^* is a 'type (3)' solution,

$$\lambda^* = -\frac{f'(x^*)}{g'(x^*)} > 0 \text{ ensures } \frac{\partial L}{\partial x}(x^*, \lambda^*) = 0 \text{ as in (2).}$$

Notice that $\lambda^* \geqslant 0$ in all cases.

So if x^* solves (5.1) in case (i) there is always a value of $\lambda^* \geqslant 0$ such that $(\partial L/\partial x)(x^*, \lambda^*) = 0$. In addition of course we must have $g(x^*) \geqslant 0$. But also either $\lambda^* = 0$ (case (1)) or $g(x^*) = 0$ (cases (2) and (3)): in all cases $\lambda^* g(x^*) = 0$.

The reader can check that our reasoning applies to feasible sets (ii), (iii) and (iv) as well. In case (iv), type (1) is the only possibility; in case (iii), (1) or (2) are the only possibilities; and (1) or (3) are the only possibilities for case (ii). In all cases, however, we can say: if x^* solves (5.1), there exists a real number λ^* such that

(a) $\dfrac{\partial L}{\partial x}(x^*, \lambda^*) = 0$

(b) $\lambda^* \geqslant 0$

(c) $\lambda^* g(x^*) = 0$

(d) $g(x^*) \geqslant 0$.

Condition (a) can be written alternatively. For $\lambda \geqslant 0$ and since f and g are concave it follows that $f(x) + \lambda g(x)$ is a concave function of x, for $x \in R$. For such functions stationarity characterizes the global maxima. Hence (a) is equivalent to, $L(x^*, \lambda^*) \geqslant L(x, \lambda^*)$, $\forall x \in R$. We have shown therefore that

If x^* solves (5.1), then there exists a real number λ^* such that

$$\left.\begin{array}{ll} \text{(A)} & L(x^*, \lambda^*) \geqslant L(x, \lambda^*) \quad \forall x \in R \\ \text{(B)} & \lambda^* \geqslant 0 \\ \text{(C)} & \lambda^* g(x^*) = 0 \\ \text{(D)} & g(x^*) \geqslant 0 \end{array}\right\} \quad \text{(K–T)}$$

The conditions indicated by (K–T) are the *Kuhn–Tucker* conditions for (5.1) and we have shown that they are *necessary conditions* at a solution to (5.1). Remarkably they are also sufficient, as follows.

From (A) $f(x^*) + \lambda^* g(x^*) \geqslant f(x) + \lambda^* g(x) \quad \forall x$

Using (C) $f(x^*) \geqslant f(x) + \lambda^* g(x) \quad \forall x$

From (B) $\lambda^* \geqslant 0$; hence, $\forall x$ such that $g(x) \geqslant 0$, $\lambda^* g(x) \geqslant 0$ and $f(x^*) \geqslant f(x)$, $\forall x$ such that $g(x) \geqslant 0$, i.e. $\forall x \in K$

From (D) $g(x^*) \geqslant 0$. So $x^* \in K$ and $f(x^*) \geqslant f(x)$, $\forall x \in K$. x^* is indeed a solution to (5.1).

(K–T) are therefore *necessary and sufficient* for, i.e. they characterize, solutions to (5.1) under our assumptions. We have proved:

Theorem 5.1 Suppose that f and g in (5.1) are concave and C^1 and suppose that (CQ) is satisfied. Then x^* solves (5.1) if and only if the Kuhn–Tucker conditions are satisfied.

A few remarks are in order. First our proof of theorem (5.1) has made use of the C^1 nature of f and g. The general proof of the next chapter does not need this: theorem 5.1 is true even if f and g are only concave. However, when f and g are C^1, (A) can be replaced by the previous Lagrangean stationarity condition (a). Secondly (CQ) is needed for the first part of our argument, the necessity of K–T. For instance suppose the graph of g is shown in fig. 5.2 (see example 3.3 for a specific such function): g is concave, K is convex but (CQ) is not satisfied. In fact $K = [0, 1]$. Suppose $f(x) = x$. Clearly $x^* = 1$ is the unique solution. But $g'(1) = 0$, $f'(1) = 1$ and there is no real number λ^* such that $1 + \lambda^*.\ 0 = 0$; so (CQ) is needed for necessity.

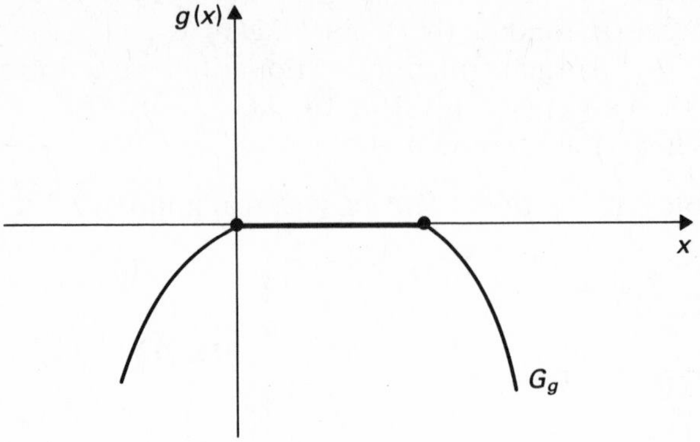

Figure 5.2

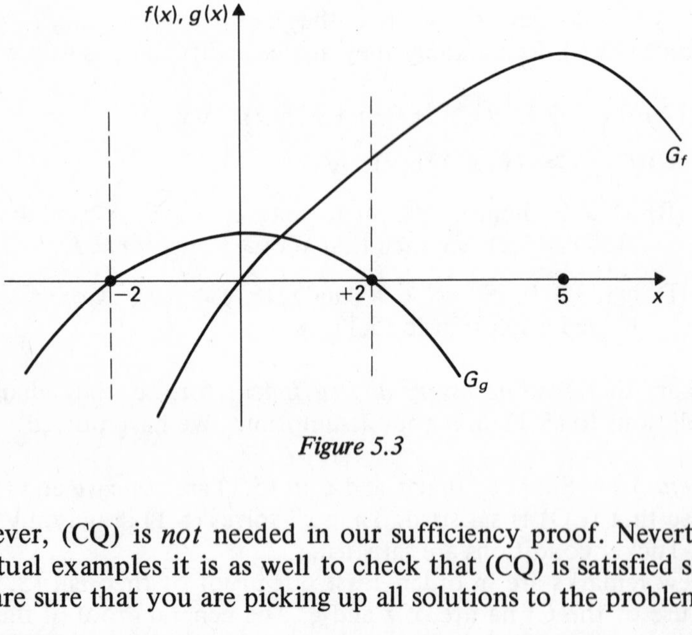

Figure 5.3

However, (CQ) is *not* needed in our sufficiency proof. Nevertheless in actual examples it is as well to check that (CQ) is satisfied so that you are sure that you are picking up all solutions to the problem.

Example 5.1 max $10x - x^2$ subject to $4 - x^2 \geqslant 0$. $f''(x) = -2 \leqslant 0$, $\forall x$, $g''(x) = -2 \leqslant 0$, $\forall x$ and f, g are concave; for instance, $4 - 0 > 0$ and (CQ) is satisfied. However, it is not necessary to use K–T to solve this. Figure 5.3 sketches G_g and G_f; the feasible set is $[-2, +2]$ and the solution is obviously $x^* = 2$. Nevertheless we work through the K–T derivation of this result to familiarize the reader with the mechanics. The Lagrangean is

$$L(x, \lambda) = 10x - x^2 + \lambda(4 - x^2)$$

(K–T) are:

(A) $\dfrac{\partial L}{\partial x} = 10 - 2x - 2\lambda x = 0$

(B) $\lambda \geqslant 0$

(C) $\lambda = 0$ or $4 - x^2 = 0$

(D) $4 - x^2 \geqslant 0$.

We have to find x^*, λ^* satisfying this system of equations and inequalities. There are three possibilities in (C): (a) $\lambda = 0$, (b) $x = -2$ or (c) $x = +2$. We try these in turn (even though we know it is the last one we want) to see if (A), (B) and (D) can also be satisfied.

(a) $\lambda = 0$. (A) $\Rightarrow x = 5$. (B) is satisfied, but $4 - 25 < 0$ and (D) is not.

(b) $x = -2$. (A) $\Rightarrow \lambda = -\frac{14}{4} < 0$ and (B) is not satisfied.

(c) $x = 2$. (A) $\Rightarrow \lambda = \frac{6}{4} = \frac{3}{2} > 0$ and (B) is satisfied. $4 - 4 = 0$ and (D) is satisfied.

So $x^* = +2$, $\lambda^* = \frac{3}{2}$ are the unique solutions to (K–T) and $x^* = +2$ *is the unique solution* to the original problem with *optimal value 16*.

Manipulation of K–T can be rather tedious even for very simple problems. Sometimes the objective function satisfies a condition which makes things easier. Suppose f has no *global unconstrained maximum*. In the C^1 case this is where f has no stationary point on R: we say f is *non-stationary*. Condition (A) can then never be satisfied with $\lambda^* = 0$. In this case (B) becomes '$\lambda^* > 0$', (C) therefore becomes '$g(x^*) = 0$' and (D) is redundant:

Corollary to theorem 5.1 Suppose in addition to the suppositions of theorem 5.1 that f is non-stationary. Then x^* solves (5.1) if and only if there exists a number λ^* such that,

(I) $L(x^*, \lambda^*) \geqslant L(x, \lambda^*) \quad \forall x \in R$

(II) $\lambda^* > 0$ and

(III) $g(x^*) = 0$.

(I)–(III) are the Kuhn–Tucker conditions for non-stationary objective functions. Of course non-stationarity of the objective is a strong assumption (not satisfied in example 5.1 for instance). Often in economics it will be satisfied, however, and the mechanics become easier.

Example 5.2 max $7x-4$ subject to $4-x^2 \geqslant 0$
f is linear and so concave and non-stationary; g is concave and (CQ) is satisfied as in example 5.1. The Lagrangean is

$$L(x, \lambda) = 7x - 4 + \lambda(4 - x^2)$$

$$\text{(I)} \quad \frac{\partial L}{\partial x} = 7 - 2\lambda x = 0$$

$$\text{(II)} \quad \lambda > 0$$

$$\text{(III)} \quad 4 - x^2 = 0$$

(III) $\Rightarrow x = -2$ or $x = +2$. If $x = -2$, (I) $\Rightarrow \lambda = -\frac{7}{4}$ and (II) is not satisfied. If $x = +2$, (I) $\Rightarrow \lambda = \frac{7}{4} > 0$ and (II) is satisfied. So $x^* = +2$, $\lambda^* = \frac{7}{4}$ are the unique solutions to (K–T) and $x^* = +2$ *is the unique solution* with *optimal value 10.*

5.3 Unique solutions

Concave programming problems like (5.1) may have no solution (e.g. max x subject to $x \geqslant 0$), one solution (e.g. examples 5.1 and 5.2) or more than one solution (see fig. 5.4); in fig. 5.4 any $x^* \in K$ is in fact a solution (the reader can supply functional forms for this: e.g. use example 3.3). As in the earlier unconstrained maximization discussion if there is more than one solution to a concave programming

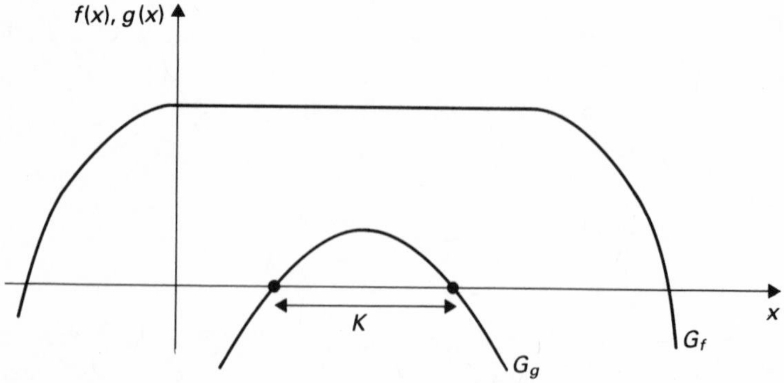

Figure 5.4

problem there are an infinite number of such solutions, and the set of solutions is convex (as is the case in fig. 5.4). To see why suppose x^1 and x^2 are two solutions to (5.1). Then $f(x^1) = f(x^2)$ and

$$g(x^1) \geqslant 0 \quad \text{and} \quad f(x^1) \geqslant f(x) \quad \forall x \in K$$

and

$$g(x^2) \geqslant 0 \quad \text{and} \quad f(x^2) \geqslant f(x) \quad \forall x \in K$$

Since g is concave,

$$g[\lambda x^1 + (1-\lambda)\, x^2] \geqslant \lambda g(x^1) + (1-\lambda)\, g(x^2) \geqslant 0 \qquad \forall \lambda \in [0, 1]$$

Since f is concave,

$$\begin{aligned} f[\lambda x^1 + (1-\lambda)\, x^2] &\geqslant \lambda f(x^1) + (1-\lambda)\, f(x^2) = f(x^1) = f(x^2) \qquad \forall \lambda \in [0, 1] \\ &\geqslant f(x) \quad \forall x \in K, \forall \lambda \in [0, 1] \end{aligned}$$

So, $g[\lambda x^1 + (1-\lambda)\, x^2] \geqslant 0$ and $f[\lambda x^1 + (1-\lambda)\, x^2] \geqslant f(x)$, $\forall x \in K$ and any convex combination of x^1 and x^2 is also a solution to (5.1).

As in chapter 3, strict concavity assumptions help rule out multiple solutions. There is now another case to note, however.

Theorem 5.2 Suppose that f and g in (5.1) are concave and C^1. If either (a) f is non-stationary or (b) f is strictly concave, then there is at most one solution to (5.1).

Proof (a) If f is non-stationary and C^1 either $f'(x) > 0$, $\forall x \in R$ or $f'(x) < 0$, $\forall x \in R$. In the former case the right-hand boundary of K (if there is one) must be the unique solution, while in the latter the left-hand boundary of K (if it exists) is the solution.

(b) Suppose f is strictly concave and let $x^1 \neq x^2$ be two solutions. Then

$$\begin{aligned} f[\lambda x^1 + (1-\lambda)\, x^2] &> \lambda f(x^1) + (1-\lambda)\, f(x^2) \qquad \forall \lambda \in (0, 1) \\ &= f(x^1) = f(x^2) \end{aligned}$$

since x^1, x^2 are solutions. Since g is concave, $g[\lambda x^1 + (1-\lambda)\, x^2] \geqslant \lambda g(x^1) + (1-\lambda)\, g(x^2) \geqslant 0$, $\forall \lambda \in [0, 1]$ since $x^1, x^2 \in K$. Hence, $\forall \lambda \in (0, 1)$

$$g[\lambda x^1 + (1-\lambda)\, x^2] \geqslant 0 \quad \text{and} \quad f[\lambda x^1 + (1-\lambda)\, x^2] > f(x^1)$$

and x^1 cannot be a solution. So there can be at most one solution.

Q.E.D.

Now suppose that (CQ) is satisfied in the concave programming problem (5.1) and suppose that (5.1) has a unique solution x^*. Then (K–T) will have a unique solution in x, namely x^*. Does it follow that there will be a unique value of λ^* satisfying (K–T) also? YES.

Theorem 5.3 Suppose that f and g in (5.1) are concave and C^1, and suppose that (CQ) is satisfied. If x^* is the unique solution to (5.1) there is a unique value of λ^* such that x^*, λ^* satisfies (K–T).

Proof If x^* solves (5.1) either (i) $g(x^*) > 0$ or (ii) $g(x^*) = 0$. In case (i), $\lambda^* = 0$ from (C) of (K–T) is the unique value of λ^* such that x^*, λ^* satisfy (K–T). In case (ii) suppose $\lambda_1^* \neq \lambda_2^*$ both satisfy (K–T) with x^*. From (C) of (K–T), $\lambda_1^*, \lambda_2^* > 0$. From (A)

$$f'(x^*) + \lambda_1^* g'(x^*) = f'(x^*) + \lambda_2^* g'(x^*) = 0$$

Therefore $(\lambda_1^* - \lambda_2^*) g'(x^*) = 0$ and $g'(x^*) = 0$ since $\lambda_1^* \neq \lambda_2^*$. But g is concave and so $g'(x^*) = 0$ implies x^* is a global maximum of g. Remembering $g(x^*) = 0$ in this case it follows that $g(x) \leqslant 0$, $\forall x \in R$, contradicting (CQ). So $\lambda_1^* = \lambda_2^*$ and there is a unique value of λ^* which satisfies (K–T) with x^*. *Q.E.D.*

So if either (a) or (b) of theorem 5.2 is satisfied, and if there is a solution to (5.1), there will be exactly one solution, x^* say, to (5.1) and exactly one solution x^*, λ^* to (K–T).

Both examples (5.1) and (5.2) exhibited such unique solutions, as do almost all the cases in this book. The uniqueness theorems 5.2 and 5.3 become very important in chapter 7.

5.4 Minimization problems

Consider:

$$\min f(x) \quad \text{subject to} \quad g(x) \geqslant 0 \tag{5.2}$$

For a solution, we require $x^* \in R$ with $g(x^*) \geqslant 0$ such that

$$f(x^*) \leqslant f(x), \forall x \quad \text{such that} \quad g(x) \geqslant 0$$

or

$$-f(x) \leqslant -f(x^*), \forall x \quad \text{such that} \quad g(x) \geqslant 0$$

But this last statement means exactly that x^* is a solution to the problem of type (5.1)

$$\max -f(x) \quad \text{subject to} \quad g(x) \geqslant 0 \tag{5.3}$$

So (5.3) is an equivalent maximization problem to the original minimization problem (5.2), in the sense that both have the same solution. But we can solve (5.3) now provided that $-f$ is concave and g is concave and satisfies (CQ). Hence, when presented with (5.2) we transform to the equivalent (5.3) and solve as before. Notice that $-f$ must be concave which means the original f is *convex*. To apply (K–T) to minimization problems the objective must be convex, with everything else as before.

Examples 5.3

$$\min x^2 - 4x + 1 \quad \text{subject to} \quad 1 - x^4 \geqslant 0$$

The equivalent maximization problem is

$$\max -x^2 + 4x - 1 \quad \text{subject to} \quad 1 - x^4 \geqslant 0$$

Now f is concave (quadratic with negative x^2 coefficient). $g''(x) = -12x^2 \leqslant 0$, $\forall x$ and g is concave. $g(0) = 1 > 0$, for instance and (CQ) is satisfied. f is not non-stationary so we need Kuhn–Tucker conditions (A)–(D). The Lagrangean is:

$$L(x, \lambda) = x^2 - 4x + 1 + \lambda(1 - x^4)$$

We need:

(A) $\dfrac{\partial L}{\partial x} = 2x - 4 - 4x^3\lambda = 0$

(B) $\lambda \geqslant 0$

(C) $\lambda = 0 \quad \text{or} \quad 1 - x^4 = 0$

(D) $1 - x^4 \geqslant 0$

Try $\lambda = 0$ first. Then, from (A) $x = 2$ and $1 - x^4 = 1 - 16 = -15 \ngeqslant 0$ and (D) is not satisfied. So there is no solution with $\lambda = 0$. Therefore try $1 - x^2 = 0$ or $x = \pm 1$. With $x = +1$, $\lambda = (-2/-4) = 1 > 0$ and $x = 1 = \lambda^*$ solves (A)–(D). Hence $x^* = 1$ solves our minimization problem since it solves the equivalent maximization problem. With $x = -1$, $\lambda = (-6/4) < 0$ and there is no solution. The optimal value in the min problem is -2.

Example 5.4

$$\min 3x + 1 \quad \text{subject to} \quad x^2 + x - 1 \leqslant 0$$

The constraint here is not in the form '$g(x) \geqslant 0$' which it must have for our results to apply. So we first rewrite the constraint as

$$1 - x - x^2 \geqslant 0$$

and our problem is

$$\min 3x + 1 \quad \text{subject to} \quad 1 - x - x^2 \geqslant 0$$

The equivalent maximization problem is:

$$\max -3x - 1 \quad \text{subject to} \quad 1 - x - x^2 \geqslant 0$$

f is linear and hence concave and non-stationary. g is concave and $g(0) = 1 > 0$ (for instance) so (CQ) is satisfied. The Lagrangean is:

$$L(x, \lambda) = -3x - 1 + \lambda(1 - x - x^2)$$

and Kuhn–Tucker conditions (I)–(III) require:

(I) $\dfrac{\partial L}{\partial x} = -3 - \lambda(1 + 2x) = 0$

(II) $\lambda > 0$

(III) $1 - x - x^2 = 0$

From (III)

$$x = \frac{-1 \pm \sqrt{1+4}}{2} = -\frac{1}{2} + \frac{1}{2}\sqrt{5} \quad \text{or} \quad -\frac{1}{2} - \frac{1}{2}\sqrt{5}$$

With

$$x = -\frac{1}{2} + \frac{1}{2}\sqrt{5}, \text{ from (I)}, \lambda = \frac{-3}{\sqrt{5}} < 0$$

and there is no solution.

With

$$x = -\frac{1}{2} - \frac{1}{2}\sqrt{5}, = \frac{-3}{-\sqrt{5}} > 0$$

and we have a solution,

$$x^* = -\frac{1}{2} - \frac{1}{2}\sqrt{5}, \lambda^* = \frac{3}{5}$$

Hence

$$x^* = -\frac{1}{2} - \frac{1}{2}\sqrt{5}$$

solves our minimization problem with optimal value

$$-\frac{1}{2}-\frac{3}{2}\sqrt{5}.$$

5.5 Interpreting Lagrangeans

The introduction of the Lagrangean function earlier evolved from the desire to find a function whose stationary points or global maxima on R characterized solutions to the concave programming problem. However, we chose the Lagrangean functional form without any justification. To allay any worries the reader may have about this magical Lagrangean appearance we now tell the reader a story which provides some motivation for the choice of the Lagrangean functional form.

Think of a person and call him (or her) 'the maximizer'. We are going to present the maximizer with a (concave) function on R with values $M(x)$, say, and the maximizer is going to choose an $x \in R$. We will then give to the maximizer an amount of money equal to $M(x)$. The maximizer, being greedy and being able to find global maxima of concave functions on R, will choose the global maximum of M. Now our problem is: if x^* solves the concave programming problem (5.1) can we find a function M such that the maximizer's choice is x^*? $M = f$ suffices if x^* is a 'type 1' solution to (5.1) but not otherwise.

The problem with $M = f$ when we have a type (2) or (3) solution is, of course, that the maximizer's choice (a global max of M on R) will then violate the constraint. How can we stop the maximizer violating the constraint? We cannot keep $M = f$ and forbid choices outside the constraint, as all we are then doing is presenting the maximizer with the concave programming problem and our whole objective is that the maximizer's problem be unconstrained. So we cannot *ban* choices outside the feasible set; but maybe we could make such choices less attractive? From the basis of the original suggestion of $M = f$, a natural possibility for us to try is that we offer the maximizer $f(x)$ if the choice is x but we reduce this by an amount which is proportional to the extent of his constraint violation at x. So if the choice is x outside the feasible set, i.e. where $g(x) < 0$, the maximizer would get $f(x)$ less a 'forfeit' which would be proportional to the size of $g(x)$. With a non-negative constant of proportionality $k \geqslant 0$, this would lead us to present the maximizer with $M(x) = f(x) + kg(x)$. So if the choice is x with $g(x) < 0$, the maximizer would get $f(x)$ plus the negative amount $kg(x)$. Incidentally, of course, we are then not only presenting the maximizer with a disincentive to choosing outside the feasible set (a forfeit of $kg(x) \leqslant 0$) but we are also simultaneously providing a positive incentive to choose inside this set (a 'bonus' of $kg(x) \geqslant 0$). Writing k as λ the Lagrangean functional form $f(x) + \lambda g(x)$ has emerged as a natural candidate to answer our original question. Section 5.2 now contains a demonstration that the Lagrangean does answer this question provided that λ is chosen as the λ^* which with x^* satisfies the Kuhn–Tucker conditions.

Hopefully this story helps to justify the appearance of the Lagrangean functional form. More importantly, and additionally, it suggests that the number λ^* may convey some useful information about solutions to concave programming problems: λ^* has emerged as a 'price' or 'cost' associated with constraint violations. In chapter 7 we give a precise description of this interpretation of Lagrange multipliers.

First we generalize to the case of n variables.

Exercise 5

1. Solve the following one variable maximization problems using (if possible) K–T:

   (a) max $1 - x^2$ subject to $(x-1)(x-2) \leqslant 0$
   (b) max $-e^x$ subject to $1 - x^2 \geqslant 0$

2. (a) Solve the following one-variable minimization problem using (if possible) K–T:

   $$\min\ (x-1)(x-2) \quad \text{subject to} \quad 1-x^2 \geqslant 0$$

   (b) Compare the answer with that to question 1(a).
   (c) Show that if x^* solves max $f(x)$ subject to $g(x) \geqslant 0$, then x^* also solves max $g(x)$ subject to $f(x) \geqslant f(x^*)$.

3. Prove that the following problem has at most one solution if f is strictly convex and g is concave:

   $$\min f(x) \text{ subject to } g(x) \geqslant 0.$$

6 Concave programming with one constraint

6.1 Introduction

We now generalize the Lagrangean/Kuhn–Tucker story of chapter 5 to the context of the following n-variable maximization problem:

$$\max f(\mathbf{x}) \quad \text{subject to } g(\mathbf{x}) \geqslant 0 \tag{6.1}$$

There is still only one constraint. Much later we will look at 'many-constraint' problems.

Throughout we assume that $f:R^n \to R$ and $g:R^n \to R$ are concave functions, of course, so that we do have a concave programming problem in (6.1). The discussion of chapter 5 generalizes for the most part in the obvious fashion.

6.2 The Kuhn–Tucker characterization

The feasible set for (6.1) is $K = UC_g(0) = \{\mathbf{x} \in R^n \mid g(\mathbf{x}) \geqslant 0\}$.

The constraint qualification for (6.1) is (CQ) $\exists\, \mathbf{x} \in R^n$ where $g(\mathbf{x}) > 0$.

The *Lagrangean function* for (6.1) is $L : R^{n+1} \to R$ where

$$L(\mathbf{x}, \lambda) = f(\mathbf{x}) + \lambda g(\mathbf{x})$$

The *Kuhn–Tucker conditions* for (6.1) are:

there exists a real number λ^* such that

(A) $L(\mathbf{x}^*, \lambda^*) \geqslant L(\mathbf{x}, \lambda^*) \quad \forall \mathbf{x}$

(B) $\lambda^* \geqslant 0$

(C) $\lambda^* g(\mathbf{x}^*) = 0$

(D) $g(\mathbf{x}^*) \geqslant 0$

Without more ado we state:

Theorem 6.1
Suppose f and g in (6.1) are concave and suppose (CQ) is satisfied. Then $\mathbf{x}^*$ solves (6.1) if and only if the Kuhn–Tucker conditions are satisfied.

Proof of 'if' Suppose $\mathbf{x}^*$, λ^* satisfy (A)–(D).

From (D) $\mathbf{x}^* \in K$

From (A) $f(\mathbf{x}^*) + \lambda^* g(\mathbf{x}^*) \geqslant f(\mathbf{x}) + \lambda^* g(\mathbf{x}) \quad \forall \mathbf{x}$

From (C) $f(\mathbf{x}^*) \geqslant f(\mathbf{x}) + \lambda^* g(\mathbf{x}) \quad \forall \mathbf{x}$

From (B) $\lambda^* g(\mathbf{x}) \geqslant 0$ whenever $g(\mathbf{x}) \geqslant 0$

Hence

$$f(\mathbf{x}^*) \geqslant f(\mathbf{x}) \ \forall \mathbf{x} \quad \text{where } g(\mathbf{x}) \geqslant 0.$$

That is, $f(\mathbf{x}^*) \geqslant f(\mathbf{x})$, $\forall \mathbf{x} \in K$. Since $\mathbf{x}^* \in K$ it follows that $\mathbf{x}^*$ solves (6.1).
Q.E.D.

Notice that (CQ) is not needed in this proof; it is, however, needed in the proof of 'only if'. The latter is a bit complicated and we relegate it to the end of the chapter.

Condition (A) is that $\mathbf{x}^*$ be a global maximum of $L(\mathbf{x}, \lambda^*)$ with respect to $\mathbf{x}$. Since f and g are concave and since $\lambda^* \geqslant 0$, L is a concave function of $\mathbf{x}$. So if f and g are in addition C^1 (then L is a C^1 function of $\mathbf{x}$), condition (A) is equivalent to the stationarity of L with respect to $\mathbf{x}$ at $\mathbf{x}^*$:

Corollary 1 to theorem 6.1 If f and g are in addition C^1 then (A) in theorem 6.1 can be replaced with:

$$(1) \quad \frac{\partial L}{\partial x_i}(\mathbf{x}^*, \lambda^*) = 0 \quad i = 1, \ldots, n$$

or

$$(2) \quad f_i'(\mathbf{x}^*) + \lambda^* g_i'(\mathbf{x}^*) = 0 \quad i = 1, \ldots, n$$

We give some examples to illustrate the mechanics of (K–T) application to higher dimensions.

Example 6.1

$$\max -x_1^2 - x_2^2 \quad \text{subject to } x_1 + x_2 \leqslant -1$$

We rewrite this as: max $-x_1^2-x_2^2$ subject to $-x_1-x_2-1\geqslant 0$. f and g are concave and C^1, (CQ) is satisfied; e.g. when $x_1=x_2=-2$, $-x_1-x_2-1=3>0$. The Lagrangean is:

$$L(\mathbf{x}, \lambda) = -x_1^2 - x_2^2 + \lambda(-x_1 - x_2 - 1)$$

(K–T) are:

(A) $-2x_1-\lambda=0, -2x_2-\lambda=0$

(B) $\lambda\geqslant 0$

(C) $\lambda=0$ or $-x_1-x_2-1=0$

(D) $-x_1-x_2-1\geqslant 0$

From (C) either $\lambda=0$ or $-x_1-x_2-1=0$. Try $\lambda=0$ first. From (A), $\mathbf{x}=(0, 0)$ but then (D) is not satisfied. So try $-x_1-x_2-1=0$. From (A), $x_1=x_2$ and so $x_1=x_2=-\frac{1}{2}$. From (A), $\lambda=1\geqslant 0$ and (B) is satisfied. So $\mathbf{x}^*=(-\frac{1}{2}, -\frac{1}{2})$ is the unique solution and the optimal value is $-\frac{1}{2}$.

We can usefully depict the solution visually by sketching the feasible set and contours of the objective function (see fig. 6.1). $C_g(0)$ is the line $x_1+x_2=-1$ and $UC_g(0)$, i.e. the feasible set, is the set of points on or below the line, which is the shaded half-space in the diagram. The range of the objective function is $(-\infty, 0]$ and for $y\in(-\infty, 0]$, $C_f(y)$ has equation $x_1^2+x_2^2=-y$. Of course these contours are circles, centre the origin and radius $\sqrt{-y}$; when $y=0$ the circle degenerates to a point, namely the origin. The global (unconstrained) maximum of f occurs at the origin where the value of f is zero and value of f increases as we move to circles closer to the origin. Our constrained maximization problem is visually to find the point in the feasible set which lies on the nearest contour to the origin. Clearly at such a point the contour through it will be tangential to the feasible set boundary, $C_g(0)$. Our calculations have found that $\mathbf{x}^*=(-\frac{1}{2}, -\frac{1}{2})$ is the unique point with this property, as indicated in fig. 6.1.

Example 6.2

$$\max -x_1^2 - x_2^2 \quad \text{subject to } x_1 + x_2 \geqslant -1$$

This is the same as example 6.1 except that the sense of the constraint inequality is reversed. The new feasible set is the set of points on or *above* the line $x_1+x_2=-1$ in fig. 6.1, and now the global unconstrained maximum of f (viz. $\mathbf{x}^*=(0, 0)$ is feasible, and must

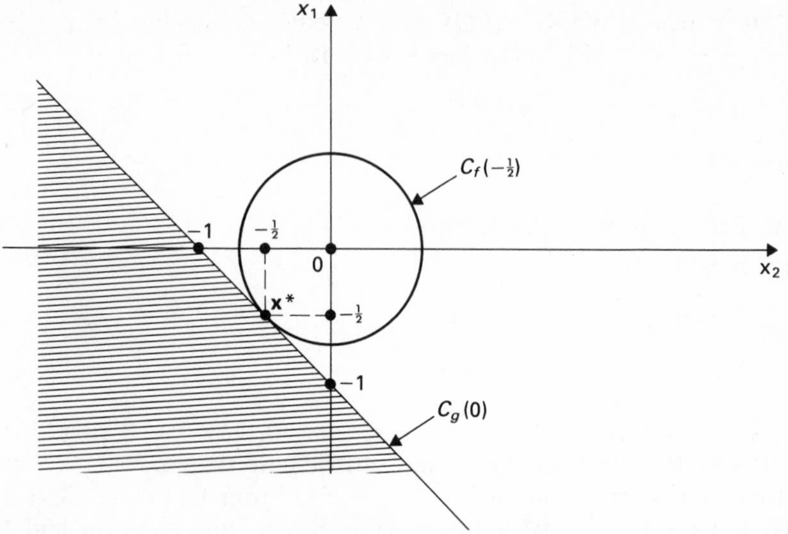

Figure 6.1

be the solution to the new problem. To confirm this, the new Lagrangean and (K–T) are:

$$L(\mathbf{x}, \lambda) = -x_1^2 - x_2^2 + \lambda(x_1 + x_2 + 1)$$

(A) $-2x_1 + \lambda = 0, -2x_2 + \lambda = 0$

(B) $\lambda \geqslant 0$

(C) $\lambda = 0$ or $x_1 + x_2 + 1 = 0$

(D) $x_1 + x_2 + 1 \geqslant 0$

With $\lambda = 0$ in (C), (B) is satisfied, $\mathbf{x} = (0, 0)$ satisfies (A) and $0 + 0 + 1 \geqslant 0$ satisfies (D). The reader can check that there is no solution with $x_1 + x_2 + 1 = 0$. So as expected $\mathbf{x}^* = (0, 0)$ is the unique solution with optimal value 0.

Analogously to chapter 5 if we assume f has no global unconstrained maximum (or in the C^1 case, f has no stationary point or is non-stationary), (A) cannot be satisfied with $\lambda^* = 0$. So (B) becomes $\lambda^* > 0$, (C) is $g(\mathbf{x}^*) = 0$ and (D) is redundant. Hence:

Corollary 2 to theorem 6.1

(a) Assuming f has no global unconstrained maximum and making the assumptions of theorem (6.1): $\mathbf{x}^*$ solves (6.1) if and only if there exists a real number λ^* such that

(I) $L(\mathbf{x}^*, \lambda^*) \geqslant L(\mathbf{x}, \lambda^*) \quad \forall \mathbf{x}$

(II) $\lambda^* > 0$

(III) $g(\mathbf{x}^*) = 0$

(b) If in addition the assumptions of corollary 1 are satisfied then (I) can be replaced with (1) or (2) of corollary 1 to theorem 6.1.

Example 6.3

$$\max x_1 + x_2 \quad \text{subject to } x_1^2 + x_2^2 \leqslant 1$$

We rewrite as

$$\max x_1 + x_2 \quad \text{subject to } 1 - x_1^2 - x_2^2 \geqslant 0$$

f and g are concave and C^1; (CQ) is satisfied, e.g. by $\mathbf{x} = (0, 0)$. Moreover f is now non-stationary. The Lagrangean is

$$L(\mathbf{x}, \lambda) = x_1 + x_2 + \lambda(1 - x_1^2 - x_2^2)$$

We can use (K–T) in the (I)–(III) version:

(I) $1 - 2\lambda x_1 = 0,\ 1 - 2\lambda x_2 = 0$

(II) $\lambda > 0$

(III) $1 - x_1^2 - x_2^2 = 0$

From (I) $x_1 = x_2$. From (III) $x_1 = x_2 = \pm(1/\sqrt{2})$. From (I) $\lambda = 1/2x_1$ and (II) is satisfied only when $x_1 > 0$. Hence $\mathbf{x}^* = (1/\sqrt{2}, 1/\sqrt{2})$ is the unique solution with optimal value $= 2/\sqrt{2} = \sqrt{2}$.

Figure 6.2 sketches the feasible set (shaded) and the solution, similarly to fig. 6.1. Notice again that at the solution the contour of f through the solution is tangential to $C_g(0)$.

The tangency of the solution between $C_g(0)$ and the contour of f through the solution in examples 6.1 and 6.3 is no fluke. It will characterize all solutions to (6.1) with two variables *provided* $\lambda^* > 0$. For if $\lambda^* > 0$ then $g(\mathbf{x}^*) = 0$ and

$$\frac{\partial L}{\partial x_1} = f_1'(\mathbf{x}^*) + \lambda^* g_1'(\mathbf{x}^*) = 0$$

$$\frac{\partial L}{\partial x_2} = f_2'(\mathbf{x}^*) + \lambda^* g_2'(\mathbf{x}^*) = 0$$

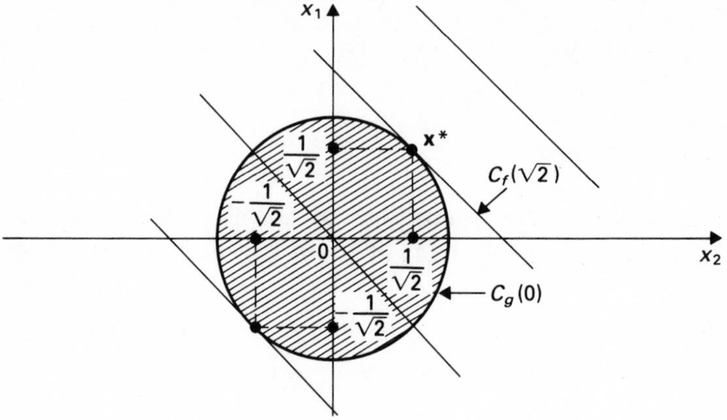

Figure 6.2

Eliminating λ^* from these two equations gives

$$-\frac{f_2'(\mathbf{x}^*)}{f_1'(\mathbf{x}^*)} = -\frac{g_2'(\mathbf{x}^*)}{g_1'(\mathbf{x}^*)}$$

which says that the contours of f and g through $\mathbf{x}^*$ have the same slope at $\mathbf{x}^*$. Since $g(\mathbf{x}^*) = 0$ the solution is indeed therefore characterized by tangency between the contour of f through the solution and $C_g(0)$.

In general the concave programming problem (6.1) may have 0, 1 or many solutions. However, if there is more than one solution then the set of solutions will be an (infinite) convex set; the reasoning in chapter 5 is straightforwardly adapted to show this. Conditions which rule out multiple solutions to (6.1) involve strict concavity and are rather different from those of theorem 5.2.

Theorem 6.2 Suppose that f and g in (6.1) are concave and C^1. If either (a) f is non-stationary *and* g is strictly concave or (b) f is strictly concave, then there is at most one solution to (6.1).

The proof of (b) follows exactly that of theorem 5.2(b)–details omitted.

The proof of (a) is given at the end of this chapter. If in addition (CQ) is satisfied then (K–T) characterize solutions to (6.1). If there is a unique solution $\mathbf{x}^*$ say to (6.1) (e.g. because of theorem 6.2) then there will be a unique solution $\mathbf{x}^*$, λ^* say to (K–T). The proof is very similar to that of theorem (5.3)–details are left to the reader.

Theorem 6.3 Suppose that f and g in (6.1) are concave and C^1 and suppose (CQ) is satisfied. If $\mathbf{x}^*$ is the unique solution to (6.1) then there is a unique value of λ^* such that $\mathbf{x}^*, \lambda^*$ satisfies (K–T).

All three earlier examples exhibited unique solutions and unique Lagrange multipliers. Non-unique solutions are exhibited by the following trivial problems:

(a) $\max x_1 + x_2 \quad \text{subject to } x_1 + x_2 \leqslant 0$

(b) $\max x_1 + x_2 \quad \text{subject to } x_1 + x_2 \geqslant 0$

Using a sketch or by applying K–T the reader should find that (b) has no solution while (a) has an infinite (convex) set of solutions, namely $\{\mathbf{x} \in R^2 | x_1 + x_2 = 0\}$. Most cases studied in this book will enjoy uniqueness. Theorems 6.2 and 6.3 give us conditions which ensure such uniqueness of solutions and multipliers, and these are useful later.

6.3 Minimization problems

If our problem is

$$\min f(\mathbf{x}) \quad \text{subject to } g(\mathbf{x}) \geqslant 0$$

then exactly as in chapter 5 a maximizing problem with the same solution is

$$\max -f(\mathbf{x}) \quad \text{subject to } g(\mathbf{x}) \geqslant 0$$

If g is concave and satisfies (CQ) and if $-f$ is concave (i.e. f is *convex*) we can solve the maximizing problem and hence the minimizing problem.

Example 6.4

$$\min x_1 + x_2 \quad \text{subject to } x_1^2 + x_2^2 \leqslant 1$$

The equivalent maximizing problem is

$$\max -x_1 - x_2 \quad \text{subject to } 1 - x_1^2 - x_2^2 \geqslant 0$$

As in example 6.3 g is concave and C^1 and (CQ) is satisfied. f is linear and so concave C^1 and non-stationary. The Lagrangean and (K–T) are

$$L(\mathbf{x}, \lambda) = -x_1 - x_2 + \lambda(1 - x_1^2 - x_2^2)$$

(I) $-1-2\lambda x_1 = 0, -1-2\lambda x_2 = 0$

(II) $\lambda > 0$

(III) $1-x_1^2-x_2^2 = 0$

From (I) and (III) $x_1 = x_2 = \pm(1/\sqrt{2})$. From (I), $\lambda = -(1/2x_1) > 0$ only when $x_1 < 0$. Hence $\mathbf{x}^* = (-(1/\sqrt{2}), -(1/\sqrt{2}))$ is the unique solution (to the minimization problem) with optimal value $-(2/\sqrt{2}) = -\sqrt{2}$.

Visually the feasible set for this minimization problem is the same as in example 6.3, the shaded area of fig. 6.2. f is also the same as in example 6.3 but now we want to *minimize* f. We have to find the *lowest* valued contour of f attainable in the feasible set and clearly this is the 'lowest' contour of f shown in fig. 6.2, the solution occurring at $(-(1/\sqrt{2}), -(1/\sqrt{2}))$.

6.4 Proof of 'only if' in theorem 6.1

Suppose $\mathbf{x}^*$ solves (6.1). We have to show that (K–T) are then satisfied. (D) follows immediately. Let

$$A = \{\mathbf{x} \in R^n | f(\mathbf{x}) > f(\mathbf{x}^*)\}$$

and

$$B = \{\mathbf{x} \in R^n | g(\mathbf{x}) > 0\}$$

B is non-empty from (CQ). Since $\mathbf{x}^*$ solves (6.1) it must be that $A \cap B = \emptyset$. Let

$$C = \{(\gamma, \delta) \in R^2 | \exists \mathbf{x} \in R^n \text{ with } f(\mathbf{x}) - f(\mathbf{x}^*) > \gamma \text{ and } g(\mathbf{x}) > \delta\}$$

Now if $\gamma, \delta \geqslant 0$ there *cannot* exist $\mathbf{x} \in R^n$ with $f(\mathbf{x}) - f(\mathbf{x}^*) > \gamma$ and $g(\mathbf{x}) > \delta$ since otherwise there would be $\mathbf{x} \in R^n$ with $f(\mathbf{x}) - f(\mathbf{x}^*) > 0$ and $g(\mathbf{x}) > 0$ contradicting the disjointness of A and B. So $(\gamma, \delta) \in R^2_+$ cannot belong to C, or

$$C \cap R^2_+ = \emptyset$$

R^2_+ is non-empty and convex. C is non-empty since $R^2_{--} \subset C$ for if $\gamma < 0$ and $\delta < 0$, $f(\mathbf{x}^*) - f(\mathbf{x}^*) = 0 > \gamma$ and $g(\mathbf{x}^*) \geqslant 0 > \delta$ and $x^* \in R^n$ satisfies the requirements for γ, δ to be in C. C is also convex, as follows.

Suppose (γ_1, δ_1) and $(\gamma_2, \delta_2) \in C$. Then $\exists\, \mathbf{x}^1, \mathbf{x}^2 \in R^n$ with

(1) $f(\mathbf{x}^1) - f(\mathbf{x}^*) > \gamma_1$

(2) $g(\mathbf{x}^1) > \delta_1$

(3) $f(\mathbf{x}^2) - f(\mathbf{x}^*) > \gamma_2$

(4) $g(\mathbf{x}^2) > \delta_2$

We have to show that $(\lambda\gamma_1 + (1-\lambda)\gamma_2, \lambda\delta_1 + (1-\lambda)\delta^2) \in C$, for all $\lambda \in (0, 1)$; $\lambda = 0$ or 1 is covered by the supposition. So we have to show that $\forall \lambda \in (0, 1)$, $\exists\, \mathbf{x} \in R^n$ such that

(5) $f(\mathbf{x}) - f(\mathbf{x}^*) > \lambda\gamma_1 + (1-\lambda)\gamma_2$

and

(6) $g(\mathbf{x}) > \lambda\delta_1 + (1-\lambda)\delta_2$

Let $\lambda \in (0, 1)$ and let $\mathbf{x} = \lambda\mathbf{x}^1 + (1-\lambda)\mathbf{x}^2$. Since f and g are concave

(7) $f(\mathbf{x}) \geqslant \lambda f(\mathbf{x}^1) + (1-\lambda) f(\mathbf{x}^2)$

and

(8) $g(\mathbf{x}) \geqslant \lambda g(\mathbf{x}^1) + (1-\lambda) g(\mathbf{x}^2)$

Using (1) and (3) in (7) we get, since $\lambda \in (0, 1)$,

$$f(\mathbf{x}) > \lambda\gamma_1 + \lambda f(\mathbf{x}^*) + (1-\lambda)\gamma_2 + (1-\lambda) f(\mathbf{x}^*)$$

and so

$$f(\mathbf{x}) - f(\mathbf{x}^*) > \gamma_1 + (1-\lambda)\gamma_2$$

which establishes (5). Similarly (2), (4) and (8) lead to (6). So C is convex.

Hence C and R^2_+ are two disjoint, non-empty convex sets in R^2. By the separating hyperplane theorem there is a hyperplane in R^2 which separates them; i.e. $\exists\, \alpha_1, \alpha_2$ and β where α_1 or α_2 is non-zero such that

(9) $\alpha_1\gamma + \alpha_2\delta \leqslant \beta \quad \forall(\gamma, \delta) \in C$

and

(10) $\alpha_1\gamma + \alpha_2\delta \geqslant \beta \quad \forall(\gamma, \delta) \in R^2_+$

Now (10) implies $\beta \leqslant 0$ (since $(0, 0) \in R^2_+$). In addition we must have $\alpha_1 \geqslant 0$ and $\alpha_2 \geqslant 0$, since $\delta = 0$ and γ very large would violate (10) if $\alpha_1 < 0$; similarly for α_2. From (9) then

(11) $\alpha_1\gamma + \alpha_2\delta \leqslant 0 \quad \forall(\gamma, \delta) \in C$

Now for any $\mathbf{x} \in R^n$ and $\epsilon > 0$, let

$$y_1 = f(\mathbf{x}) - f(\mathbf{x}^*) - \epsilon$$

and

$$y_2 = g(\mathbf{x}) - \epsilon$$

Then $f(\mathbf{x}) - f(\mathbf{x}^*) = y_1 + \epsilon > y_1$ and $g(\mathbf{x}) = y_2 + \epsilon > y_2$. So $(y_1, y_2) \in C$. From (11)

$$\alpha_1 y_1 + \alpha_2 y_2 \leqslant 0$$

Therefore, for any $\mathbf{x} \in R^n$ and $\epsilon > 0$

$$\alpha_1[f(\mathbf{x}) - f(\mathbf{x}^*) - \epsilon] + \alpha_2[g(\mathbf{x}) - \epsilon] \leqslant 0$$

or

$$\alpha_1[f(\mathbf{x}) - f(\mathbf{x}^*)] + \alpha_2 g(\mathbf{x}) \leqslant \epsilon(\alpha_1 + \alpha_2)$$

Since this is true for *any* $\epsilon > 0$ we must in fact have

$$\alpha_1[f(\mathbf{x}) - f(\mathbf{x}^*)] + \alpha_2 g(\mathbf{x}) \leqslant 0$$

or

$$\alpha_1 f(\mathbf{x}) + \alpha_2 g(\mathbf{x}) \leqslant \alpha_1 f(x^*) \quad \forall \mathbf{x} \in R^n$$

Suppose $\alpha_1 = 0$: then $\alpha_2 > 0$ and $g(\mathbf{x}) \leqslant 0$, $\forall \mathbf{x} \in R^n$ contradicting (CQ). So $\alpha_1 > 0$ and writing $\lambda^* = (\alpha_2/\alpha_1) \geqslant 0$, we have

$$f(\mathbf{x}^*) \geqslant f(\mathbf{x}) + \lambda^* g(\mathbf{x}) \quad \forall \mathbf{x} \in R^n$$

When $\mathbf{x} = \mathbf{x}^*$ we get $\lambda^* g(\mathbf{x}^*) \leqslant 0$. On the other hand we know $\lambda^* \geqslant 0$ and $g(\mathbf{x}^*) \geqslant 0$. So $\lambda^* g(x^*) \geqslant 0$. It must be that $\lambda^* g(x^*) = 0$ completing the proof.

6.5 Proof of theorem 6.2(a)

Suppose $\mathbf{x}^1 \neq \mathbf{x}^2$ are two solutions to (6.1) where f is non-stationary and g is strictly concave. We derive a contradiction. From the supposition $f(\mathbf{x}^1) = f(\mathbf{x}^2)$; also

$$g(\mathbf{x}^1) \geqslant 0 \text{ and } f(\mathbf{x}^1) \geqslant f(\mathbf{x}) \quad \forall \mathbf{x} \in K$$

and

$$g(\mathbf{x}^2) \geqslant 0 \text{ and } f(\mathbf{x}^2) \geqslant f(\mathbf{x}) \quad \forall \mathbf{x} \in K$$

Let $\mathbf{x} = \lambda \mathbf{x}^1 + (1-\lambda)\,\mathbf{x}^2$ for some $\lambda \in (0, 1)$. Then since g is strictly concave:

$$g(\mathbf{x}) > \lambda g(\mathbf{x}^1) + (1-\lambda)\, g(\mathbf{x}^2)$$

and so

$$g(\mathbf{x}) > 0$$

Since f is non-stationary, $f_i'(\mathbf{x}) \neq 0$, some i. Without loss of generality suppose $f_1'(\mathbf{x}) > 0$. Let $\mathbf{y} = (x_1 + \epsilon, x_2, x_3, \ldots, x_n)$; for $\epsilon > 0$ and sufficiently small we have $g(\mathbf{y}) > 0$ since $g(\mathbf{x}) > 0$ and g is continuous.

Since $f_1'(\mathbf{x}) > 0$, for $\epsilon > 0$ and sufficiently small it also follows that $f(\mathbf{y}) > f(\mathbf{x})$. But from the concavity of f

$$f(\mathbf{x}) \geqslant \lambda f(\mathbf{x}^1) + (1-\lambda) f(\mathbf{x}^2) = f(\mathbf{x}^1) = f(\mathbf{x}^2)$$

Hence $f(\mathbf{y}) > f(\mathbf{x}^1)$ in particular. Therefore

$$g(\mathbf{y}) > 0$$

and

$$f(\mathbf{y}) > f(\mathbf{x}^1)$$

and $\mathbf{x}^1$ cannot be a solution to (6.1), a contradiction. So there is at most one solution to (6.1).

Exercise 6

1. Convex programming. Consider the problem:

   $$\min f(\mathbf{x}) \quad \text{subject to } g(\mathbf{x}) \leqslant 0$$

   where $\exists\, \mathbf{x}$ with $g(\mathbf{x}) < 0$ and $f: R^n \to R$ and $g: R^n \to R$ are convex functions. Show that if $\mathbf{x}^*$, λ^* satisfy the following four conditions then x^* solves this minimization problem:

   (a) $L(\mathbf{x}^*, \lambda^*) \leqslant L(\mathbf{x}, \lambda^*) \quad \forall \mathbf{x}$

   (b) $\lambda^* \geqslant 0$

   (c) $\lambda^* g(\mathbf{x}^*) = 0$

   (d) $g(\mathbf{x}^*) \leqslant 0$

   where $L(\mathbf{x}, \lambda) = f(\mathbf{x}) + \lambda g(\mathbf{x})$.

2. Solve the following two variable problems:

   (a) $\max x_2 - x_1 \quad$ subject to $x_1 \geqslant e^{x_2}$

   (b) $\min x_1^2 + (x_2 - 1)^2 \quad$ subject to $x_1 \geqslant e^{x_2}$

3. For the problems in question 2 sketch in R^2 the feasible set and selected contours of the objective function indicating the solution.

4. Prove theorem 6.3.

7 Concave functions on convex domains

7.1 Introduction

So far we have studied concave functions, their unconstrained maxima and concave programming problems. However, throughout we have assumed that the domain of all functions under investigation is the whole of R^n (for some n). Unfortunately most of the problems thrown up by microeconomics involve functions whose domains are only a part of R^n. In fact these domains will always be *convex* subsets of R^n and usually they will be either R^n_+ or R^n_{++}. The objective of this chapter is to explain how the earlier story can be extended to apply to the case where functions have convex domains, not necessarily equal to R^n.

To start we define:

Definition 7.1 If $D \subset R^n$ is convex then $f:D \to R$ is a concave function if and only if

$$f[\lambda x^1 + (1-\lambda)\mathbf{x}^2] \geqslant \lambda f(\mathbf{x}^1) + (1-\lambda) f(\mathbf{x}^2)$$

$$\forall \lambda \in [0, 1], \forall \mathbf{x}^1, \mathbf{x}^2 \in D$$

Similarly for $f:D \to R$ to be a convex function requires the reverse inequality, while strict concavity (convexity) of $f:D \to R$ requires strict inequality in the concave (convex) definition for $\lambda \in (0, 1)$ and $\forall \mathbf{x}^1, \mathbf{x}^2 \in D$ where $\mathbf{x}^1 \neq \mathbf{x}^2$. The domains of all these classes of functions have to be convex since the definitions require that f be defined at every convex combination $(\lambda \mathbf{x}^1 + (1-\lambda)\,\mathbf{x}^2)$ of two points ($\mathbf{x}^1$ and $\mathbf{x}^2$) in the domain; thus D must contain every convex combination of two points in D and so D must be convex.

We wish to study derivative characterizations, maxima and concave programming (etc.) in this more general setting of functions with convex domains. However, we must distinguish two cases in order to do this. This is because there is a significant 'structural' difference between sets 'like' R^n_{++} and sets 'like' R^n_+. To see this, notice that from *any* point in R^n_{++} you can move a short distance in *any* direction and remain in the set. This is also true of R^n itself and sets with this property are called *open sets*. However, R^n_+ does *not* possess this property. For instance from any point $\mathbf{x}$ on the axes of R^n_+ (i.e. where $\mathbf{x} \in R^n_+$ and $x_i = 0$, some i) any decrease in some components of $\mathbf{x}$ (i.e. those where $x_i = 0$) will take you outside the set; R^n_+ is *not open*. As further illustration of this distinction we remark that an interval of R of the form (a, b) is open while $[a, b]$ is not open. A full and precise treatment of open sets comes later in the book. For the time being we shall be able to get by with only these brief remarks remembering that R^n and R^n_{++} are open while R^n_+ is not open. The importance of the open/not open distinction for our immediate purposes is that *everything* we said earlier about concave functions (etc.) on domain R^n has an *exact* analogue for functions whose domain is *convex and open*, whereas some significant differences emerge when the domain is convex and not open.

To explain all this we first concentrate on the convex open domain case running through the previous story and illustrate it with examples. Then we deal with the non-open problems.

First a few preliminaries. The range of $f: D \to R$, $D \subset R^n$ is $\{y \in R \mid y = f(\mathbf{x}), \text{ some } \mathbf{x} \in D\}$ and the graph of f is then $G_f = \{(y, \mathbf{x}) \in R^{n+1} \mid y = f(\mathbf{x}),\ \mathbf{x} \in D\}$. These are the same as in chapter 4 except $\mathbf{x} \in D$ replaces $\mathbf{x} \in R^n$. $C_f(y)$, $UC_f(y)$, $LC_f(y)$ (and HG_f, EG_f) are defined by making the same change. $f: D \to R$ is continuous if $\forall \mathbf{x}^* \in D$, $\lim f(\mathbf{x}) = f(\mathbf{x}^*)$ (where $\mathbf{x} \in D$ and $\mathbf{x} \to \mathbf{x}^*$) and again requires G_f to be an 'unbroken surface'.

7.2 Open, convex domains

Throughout this section we consider functions $f: D \to R$ where D is open and convex (e.g. R^n_{++} or R^n itself). Some examples are:

Examples 7.1

(a) $f: R_{++} \to R$ where $f(x) = \ln x$

(b) $f: R_{++} \to R$ where $f(x) = +x^{1/2}$

(c) $f: R^2_{++} \to R$ where $f(\mathbf{x}) = +x_1^{1/2} x_2^{1/2}$

(d) $f: R^n_{++} \to R$ where $f(\mathbf{x}) = \sum_{i=1}^{n} \alpha_i \ln x_i$, $\alpha_i > 0$, $\forall i$

(e) $f: R^n_{++} \to R$ where $f(x) = x^3$.

'Restricted domains' can arise either because we want to restrict a rule which can actually be applied more widely (e), or because the rule cannot be applied more widely (a).

Concavity of functions $f: D \to R$ has already been defined and corresponds (as ever) to the notion of the chord joining any two points on the graph lying entirely on or below the graph. Such a function is $C^1(C^2)$ if and only if, for all $\mathbf{x} \in D$ the first partial derivatives $f_i'(\mathbf{x})$ (second partial derivatives $f_{ij}''(\mathbf{x})$) are uniquely defined and continuous. Visually, as before C^1 corresponds to a graph with a unique non-vertical tangent hyperplane every point of the graph. In the current convex open-domain case all aspects of the previous story generalize in the obvious way. Consequently we merely list the important results, and stop only to give illustrative examples. Remember that throughout this list D is a convex and open subset of R^n.

1. If $f: D \to R$ is concave or convex then f is continuous.
2. Suppose $f: D \to R$ is C^1:

   (a) f is concave if and only if

   $$f(\mathbf{x}^*) + (\mathbf{x} - \mathbf{x}^*)\,\mathbf{f}'(\mathbf{x}^*) \geqslant f(\mathbf{x}) \quad \forall \mathbf{x}, \mathbf{x}^* \in D$$

   (b) f is strictly concave if and only if

   $$f(\mathbf{x}^*) + (\mathbf{x} - \mathbf{x}^*)\,\mathbf{f}'(\mathbf{x}^*) > f(\mathbf{x}^*) \quad \forall \mathbf{x}, \mathbf{x}^* \in D, \mathbf{x} \neq \mathbf{x}^*$$

3. Suppose $f: D \to R$ is C^2:

   (a) f is concave if and only if $\mathbf{f}''(\mathbf{x})$ is n.s.d., $\forall \mathbf{x} \in D$;

   (b) f is strictly concave if $\mathbf{f}''(\mathbf{x})$ is n.d., $\forall \mathbf{x} \in D$.

4. Reversing inequalities in (2) and (3) gives corresponding results for convex and strictly convex functions.

Examples 7.2 (a)–(e) are as in examples 7.1, and all have convex open domains. Hence

(a) $f'(x) = \dfrac{1}{x}$, $f''(x) = -\dfrac{1}{x^2} < 0$, $\forall x \in R_{++} \Rightarrow f$ is *strictly concave*;

(b) $f'(x) = +\dfrac{1}{2x^{1/2}}$, $f''(x) = -\dfrac{1}{4x^{3/2}} < 0$, $\forall x \in R_{++} \Rightarrow f$

is *strictly concave*,

(c) $f_1'(\mathbf{x}) = +\frac{1}{2}x_1^{-1/2}x_2^{1/2}$, $f_2'(\mathbf{x}) = +\frac{1}{2}x_1^{1/2}x_2^{-1/2}$. The Hessian is

$$\mathbf{f}''(\mathbf{x}) = \begin{bmatrix} -\frac{1}{4}x_1^{-3/2}x_2^{1/2} & +\frac{1}{4}x_1^{-1/2}x_2^{-1/2} \\ +\frac{1}{4}x_1^{-1/2}x_2^{-1/2} & -\frac{1}{4}x_1^{1/2}x_2^{-3/2} \end{bmatrix}$$

Now $\forall \mathbf{x} \in R^2_{++}$, (i) $f''_{11}(\mathbf{x}) < 0, f''_{22}(\mathbf{x}) < 0$ and (ii) $\det \mathbf{f}''(\mathbf{x}) = \frac{1}{16}x_1^{-1}x_2^{-1} - \frac{1}{16}x_1^{-1}x_2^{-1} = 0$.
So $\mathbf{f}''(\mathbf{x})$ is n.s.d. $\forall \mathbf{x} \in R^2_{++}$ (but not n.d.). Hence *f is concave*

(d) $f_i'(\mathbf{x}) = \dfrac{\alpha_i}{x_i}$; $f''_{ii}(\mathbf{x}) = -\dfrac{\alpha_i}{x_i^2}$; $f''_{ij}(\mathbf{x}) = 0, i \neq j$.

So the Hessian is a diagonal matrix as follows:

$$\mathbf{f}''(\mathbf{x}) = \begin{bmatrix} -\dfrac{\alpha_1}{x_1^2} & & 0 \\ & -\dfrac{\alpha_2}{x_2^2} & \\ 0 & & -\dfrac{\alpha_n}{x_n^2} \end{bmatrix}$$

(1) all 1st-order principal minors are of the form

$$-\frac{\alpha_i}{x_i^2} < 0, \forall \mathbf{x} \in R^n_{++} \text{ since } \alpha_i > 0$$

(2) all 2nd-order principal minors are of the form

$$\frac{\alpha_i\alpha_j}{x_i^2x_j^2} > 0, \forall \mathbf{x} \in R^n_{++}$$

(3) all 3rd-order principal minors are of the form

$$-\frac{\alpha_i\alpha_j\alpha_k}{x_i^2x_j^2x_k^2} < 0, \forall \mathbf{x} \in R^n_{++}$$

(n) $\det \mathbf{f}''(\mathbf{x}) = \prod_{i=1}^{n}\left[-\dfrac{\alpha_i}{x_i^2}\right] \begin{matrix} > 0 \text{ if } n \text{ is even} \\ < 0 \text{ if } n \text{ is odd} \end{matrix}$

$\mathbf{f}''(\mathbf{x})$ is indeed n.d. $\forall \mathbf{x} \in R^n_{++}$ and f is *strictly concave*.

(e) $f'(x) = 3x^2, f''(x) = 6x > 0, \forall x \in R_{++} \Rightarrow f$ is *strictly convex*.

(f) $f: R_{++} \to R$ where $f(x) = x^3 - x^2, f'(x) = 3x^2 - 2x$, and

$$f''(x) = 6x - 2\begin{bmatrix} \geqslant 0 \text{ if } x \geqslant 3 \\ \leqslant 0 \text{ if } x \leqslant 3 \end{bmatrix}$$

So f is *neither concave nor convex*.

For $f:D \to R$ we write the maximization problem of finding the largest value of f on its domain as,

$$\max_{\mathbf{x} \in D} f(\mathbf{x})$$

A solution to this problem (*a global maximum* of f on D) is $\mathbf{x}^* \in D$ such that $f(\mathbf{x}^*) \geqslant f(\mathbf{x})$, $\forall \mathbf{x} \in D$; $f(\mathbf{x}^*)$ is then the *optimal value* of f on D. For the corresponding minimization problem, solutions (or global minima) and optimal values are defined in the obvious fashion.

5. Suppose $f:D \to R$ is concave and C^1. $\mathbf{x}^*$ is a global maximum of f on D if and only if $\mathbf{x}^* \in D$ and $\mathbf{f}'(\mathbf{x}^*) = 0$.

6. Replacing maximum with minimum, and concave with convex, in 5 gives the convex function result.

Examples 7.3 (a)–(f) are as in examples 7.2
(a)–(d) are all concave and have no stationary points on their domains. Hence (a)–(d) have no global maximum. (e) is convex and has no stationary point on its domain and so has no global minimum. (f) has one stationary point on its domain ($x^* = \frac{2}{3}$) but as it is neither concave nor convex we can make no inference about this stationary point. (g) suppose $f:R_{++} \to R$ is defined by $f(x) = x^3 - 3x$ and we want to solve $\min_{x \in R_{++}} f(x)$. $f'(x) = 3x^2 - 3 = 0$ if $x^* = \pm 1$, $x^* = +1$ is the only stationary point in the domain. $f''(x) = 6x > 0$, $\forall x \in R_{++}$. Hence f is convex (in fact strictly convex) and $x^* = +1$ is its *global minimum* with optimal value -2. (h) Suppose $f:R^2_{++} \to R$ is given by $f(\mathbf{x}) = 2x_1^{1/2}x_2^{1/2} - x_1 - x_2$ and we want to solve $\max_{\mathbf{x} \in R^2_{++}} f(\mathbf{x})$. f has similar Hessian to example 7.2(c) and f is concave (but not strictly concave). $f_1'(\mathbf{x}) = x_1^{-1/2}x_2^{1/2} - 1$, $f_2'(\mathbf{x}) = x_1^{1/2}x_2^{-1/2} - 1$, $f_1'(\mathbf{x}) = f_2'(\mathbf{x}) = 0$ if and only if $x_1 = x_2$ and there are an infinite number of stationary points in the domain, namely any $\mathbf{x} = (a, a)$, $a > 0$. All these points are solutions to our problem with optimal value of 0.

7. (a) If $f:D \to R$ is concave there are either 0, 1 or an infinite convex set of solutions to $\max_{\mathbf{x} \in D} f(\mathbf{x})$.

   (b) If $f:D \to R$ is strictly concave there are either 0 or 1 solutions to $\max_{\mathbf{x} \in D} f(\mathbf{x})$.

8. Replacing maximum with minimum, and concave with convex in 7, gives the convex function results.

   Turning to concave programming, suppose $f:D \to R$ and $g:D \to R$ are concave functions and consider

$$\max_{\mathbf{x} \in D} f(\mathbf{x}) \quad \text{subject to } g(\mathbf{x}) \geqslant 0 \tag{7.1}$$

A solution is $\mathbf{x}^* \in D$ such that $f(\mathbf{x}^*) \geqslant f(\mathbf{x}), \forall \mathbf{x} \in D$; $f(\mathbf{x}^*)$ is then the optimal value. The constraint qualification is

$$\text{(CQ)}\ \exists\, \mathbf{x} \in D \quad \text{where } g(\mathbf{x}) > 0$$

The Lagrangean function is $L: D \times R \to R$ defined by

$$L(\mathbf{x}, \lambda) = f(\mathbf{x}) + \lambda g(\mathbf{x})$$

The Kuhn–Tucker conditions are: $\exists\, \lambda^*$ such that

(A) $L(\mathbf{x}^*, \lambda^*) \geqslant L(\mathbf{x}, \lambda^*) \quad \forall \mathbf{x} \in D$

(B) $\lambda^* \geqslant 0$

(C) $\lambda^* g(\mathbf{x}^*) = 0$

(D) $\mathbf{x}^* \in D$ and $g(\mathbf{x}^*) \geqslant 0$

9. Suppose f and g are concave and (CQ) is satisfied. Then $\mathbf{x}^*$ solves (7.1) if and only if the Kuhn–Tucker conditions (A)–(D) are satisfied.

10. In 9, if f has no global maximum on D the Kuhn–Tucker conditions become

    (I) $L(\mathbf{x}^*, \lambda^*) \geqslant L(\mathbf{x}, \lambda^*) \quad \forall \mathbf{x} \in D$

    (II) $\lambda^* > 0$

    (III) $\mathbf{x}^* \in D$ and $g(\mathbf{x}^*) = 0$

11. If in 9 and 10, f and g are C^1 then (A) and (I) can be replaced with either

    (a) $\dfrac{\partial L}{\partial x_i}(\mathbf{x}^*, \lambda^*) = 0 \quad i = 1, \ldots, n,$ or

    (b) $f_i'(\mathbf{x}^*) + \lambda^* g_i'(\mathbf{x}^*) = 0 \quad i = 1, \ldots, n.$

12. If f and g are concave and C^1 and (CQ) is satisfied, and if there is a unique solution $\mathbf{x}^*$ to (7.1) then there is a unique λ^* such that $\mathbf{x}^*, \lambda^*$ satisfies K–T.

13. There is at most one solution to (7.1) if either

    (a) f is strictly concave, or

    (b) g is strictly concave and f has no global maximum on D.

Examples 7.4

(a) $\max_{x \in R_{++}} \ln x$ subject to $x \leqslant 1$.

$f = \ln x$ and $g = 1 - x$ are concave and C^1 on R_{++}; f is non-stationary. (CQ) is satisfied by (e.g.) $x = \frac{1}{2}$. The Lagrangean is

$$L(x, \lambda) = \ln x + \lambda(1-x)$$

(K–T) are

(I) $\dfrac{1}{x} - \lambda = 0$

(II) $\lambda > 0$

(III) $x > 0$ and $x = 1$

Trivially $x^* = 1$ (with $\lambda^* = 1 > 0$) is the solution with optimal value 0.

(b) $\max_{\mathbf{x} \in R^2_{++}} x_1^{1/4} x_2^{1/4}$ subject to $x_1 + x_2 \leqslant 1$

$f = x_1^{1/4} x_2^{1/4}$ and computation of derivatives (details omitted) shows f is concave and non-stationary on R^2_{++}. $g = 1 - x_1 - x_2$ is concave on R^2_{++}. (CQ) is satisfied by, e.g. $\mathbf{x} = (\frac{1}{4}, \frac{1}{4})$. The Lagrangean and (K–T) are

$$L(\mathbf{x}, \lambda) = x_1^{1/4} x_2^{1/4} + \lambda(1 - x_1 - x_2)$$

(I) $\frac{1}{4} x_1^{-3/4} x_2^{1/4} - \lambda = 0$

$\frac{1}{4} x_1^{1/4} x_2^{-3/4} - \lambda = 0$

(II) $\lambda > 0$

(III) $x_1, x_2 > 0$ and $1 - x_1 - x_2 = 0$

From (I) $x_1 = x_2$. From (III) $x^* = (\frac{1}{2}, \frac{1}{2})$. From (I) $\lambda = \frac{1}{4}(\frac{1}{2})^{-1/2} = (\sqrt{2}/4) > 0$. Hence $x^* = (\frac{1}{2}, \frac{1}{2})$ is the solution with optimal value $(\frac{1}{4})^{1/4} = 1/\sqrt{2}$.

Figure 7.1 illustrates this solution to example 7.4(b).

Finally we mention:

14. The problem. $\min_{\mathbf{x} \in D} f(\mathbf{x})$ subject to $g(\mathbf{x}) \geqslant 0$, has the same solution as: $\max_{\mathbf{x} \in D} -f(x)$ subject to $g(\mathbf{x}) \geqslant 0$.

So 'minimization' problems can be solved by solving the equivalent maximization problem using 9, 10, or 11.

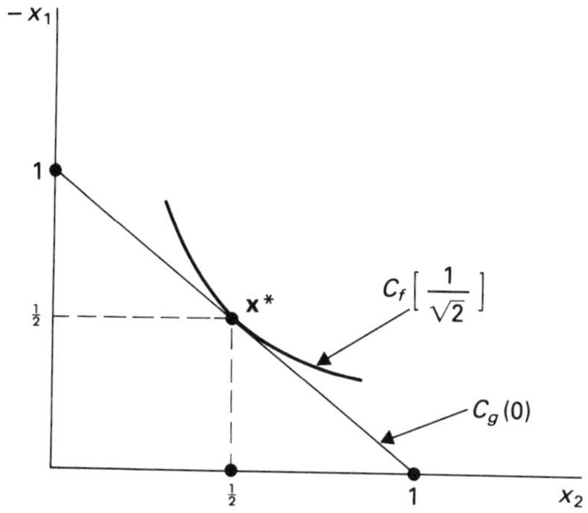

Figure 7.1

7.3 Convex, non-open domains

If D is convex but not open and $f:D\to R$ is concave it does not necessarily follow that f is continuous. For instance,

$$f:R_+\to R \quad \text{where } f(x)=\begin{cases}1 \text{ if } x>0\\ 0 \text{ if } x=0\end{cases}$$

is concave but not continuous (at 0). Consequently if the domain is merely convex we cannot infer continuity from concavity, and we have to assume it separately when needed.

A more substantive problem in our economic models will be that many of the functions of interest will have domain R^n_+ (convex but not open) and although they are continuous on R^n_+ they will be C^1 or C^2 only on R^n_{++}. A typical example is

$$f:R_+\to R \text{ where } f(x)=kx^\alpha \quad \text{where } \alpha\in(0,1)$$

Figure 7.2 illustrates the typical graph when $k>0$. As $x\to 0, f'(x)\to+\infty$, the tangent line becomes vertical at the origin and f is not C^1 on R_+ although it is C^1 (and C^2) on R_{++}. There is a simple and useful result which allows us to establish concavity of such functions even though they do not have derivatives everywhere on their domain. This result has no analogue earlier.

Theorem 7.1 If $f:R^n_+\to R$ is continuous on R^n_+ and concave on R^n_{++} then f is concave on R^n_+ as well.

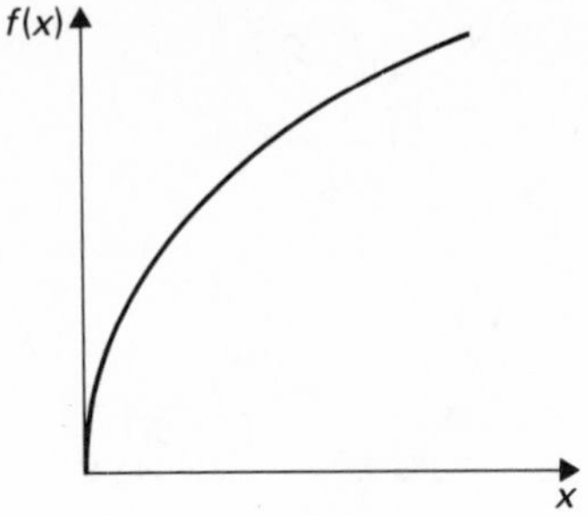

Figure 7.2

Proof Suppose $\mathbf{x}^1, \mathbf{x}^2 \in R^n_+$ and choose $\xi > 0$ and let $\boldsymbol{\xi} \in R^n_{++}$ with $\xi_i = \xi$, $i = 1, \ldots, n$. Then $\mathbf{x}^1 + \boldsymbol{\xi}$, $\mathbf{x}^2 + \boldsymbol{\xi} \in R^n_{++}$ and since f is concave on R^n_{++} we have, $\forall \lambda \in [0, 1]$,

$$f[\lambda(\mathbf{x}^1 + \boldsymbol{\xi}) + (1-\lambda)(\mathbf{x}^2 + \boldsymbol{\xi})] \geqslant \lambda f(\mathbf{x}^1 + \boldsymbol{\xi}) + (1-\lambda) f(\mathbf{x}^2 + \boldsymbol{\xi})$$

or

$$f[\lambda\mathbf{x}^1 + (1-\lambda)\mathbf{x}^2 + \boldsymbol{\xi}] \geqslant \lambda f(\mathbf{x}^1 + \boldsymbol{\xi}) + (1-\lambda) f(\mathbf{x}^2 + \boldsymbol{\xi})$$

However, since f is continuous on R^n_+, $f(\mathbf{x} + \boldsymbol{\xi}) \to f(\mathbf{x})$ as $\boldsymbol{\xi} \to 0$ for any $\mathbf{x} \in R^n_+$. Hence in the limit as $\boldsymbol{\xi} \to 0$, the last inequality becomes

$$f[\lambda\mathbf{x}^1 + (1-\lambda)\mathbf{x}^2] \geqslant \lambda f(\mathbf{x}^1) + (1-\lambda) f(\mathbf{x}^2)$$

and since this is true $\forall \mathbf{x}^1, \mathbf{x}^2 \in R^n_+$ and $\forall \lambda \in [0, 1]$, f is concave on R^n_+. *Q.E.D.*

For instance with the kx^α example where $k > 0$ and $\alpha \in (0, 1)$ we find that

$$f''(x) = k\alpha(\alpha-1)x^{\alpha-2} < 0 \quad \forall x \in R_{++}$$

and f is concave on R_{++}. Since it is continuous on R_+ we may infer from theorem 7.1 that f is also concave on R_+.

The main problem with convex non-open domains emerges in the maximization story. The stationary point characterization of solutions to

$$\max_{\mathbf{x} \in D} f(\mathbf{x})$$

and the Kuhn–Tucker characterization of solutions to

$$\max_{\mathbf{x} \in D} f(\mathbf{x}) \quad \text{subject to } g(\mathbf{x}) \geqslant 0$$

are simply not true if D is convex and not open. For instance suppose we have $f: R_+ \to R$ where $f(x) = -x$ and consider,

$$\max_{x \in R_+} -x$$

f is concave and C^1 and clearly $x^* = 0$ is the unique solution. But $f'(x^*) = -1 \neq 0$.

Rather than try to develop separate results to cover maximization problems on non-open domains we resort in what follows to a variety of procedures to reduce (or expand) any such problem that we meet to an open-domain problem for which the earlier results apply.

7.4 Local maxima and minima

Thus far the focus has been on characterizations of global maxima and minima of functions with and without weak inequality constraints. Indeed the development of this theory via concavity and convexity, and its applications to microeconomics, is the main theme of this book. However, the reader will no doubt have met elsewhere some discussion of *local* maxima and minima and we devote this section to a consideration of some of these local results. We start with unconstrained optimization and consider again:

$$\max_{\mathbf{x} \in D} f(\mathbf{x}) \quad \text{where } D \text{ is open and } f \text{ is } C^2$$

Now, however, we are interested in local solutions to this problem and we say that $\mathbf{x}^* \in D$ is a *local maximum* of f on D if and only if

$$f(\mathbf{x}^*) \geqslant f(\mathbf{x}) \quad \forall \mathbf{x} \text{ sufficiently close to } \mathbf{x}^*$$

Clearly if $\mathbf{x}^*$ is a global maximum of f then it is also local. However, local maxima need not be global. For instance $f: R \to R$ where $f(x) = x^3 - 3x$ has a local maximum at $x^* = -1$; but this is not a global maximum as its graph in fig. 7.3 shows.

It is hopefully known by the reader or fairly obvious that if $\mathbf{x}^*$ is a local maximum then it must be a stationary point of f. But stationary points need not be local maxima (e.g. $x = 1$ in fig. 7.3); stationarity is necessary for a local maximum but not sufficient, similar to the earlier global story. In the global development we restricted attention to functions f which are concave on D, and with this restriction stationarity is both necessary and sufficient for a global maximum. Not surprisingly if we now restrict attention to functions which are merely concave near $\mathbf{x}^*$ (i.e. $\mathbf{f}''(\mathbf{x})$ is n.s.d. for

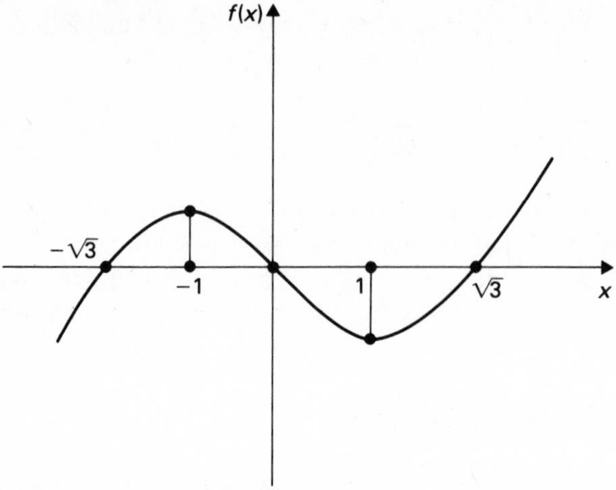

Figure 7.3

all $\mathbf{x}$ sufficiently close to $\mathbf{x}^*$) then stationarity becomes necessary and sufficient for a local maximum. However, although the global result is the most commonly used result for global maxima this is not true of its local analogue since there are alternatives which require only evaluation of the Hessian at $\mathbf{x}^*$. For instance if $\mathbf{f}''(\mathbf{x}^*)$ is n.d. then by continuity $\mathbf{f}''(\mathbf{x})$ will remain n.s.d. (in fact n.d.) sufficiently close to $\mathbf{x}^*$ and so a set of sufficient conditions for $\mathbf{x}^* \in D$ to be a local maximum of f on D are

(1) $\mathbf{f}'(\mathbf{x}^*) = 0$: '1st-order conditions';

(2) $\mathbf{f}''(\mathbf{x}^*)$ is n.d.: '2nd-order conditions'.

It is worth noting that (1) and (2) imply the stronger result that $\mathbf{x}^*$ is a *strict* local maximum of f on D; that is,

$$f(\mathbf{x}^*) > f(\mathbf{x}) \quad \forall \mathbf{x} \text{ sufficiently close to } \mathbf{x}^* \text{ where } \mathbf{x} \neq \mathbf{x}^*$$

So (1) and (2) are sufficient for a (strict) local maximum. (1) is also necessary but (2) is not quite necessary; however, it can be shown that (3) is a necessary 2nd-order condition

(3) $\mathbf{f}''(\mathbf{x}^*)$ is n.s.d.

Proofs of these assertions hinge on Taylor series expansions of C^2 functions, and the reader is referred to the bibliographical notes for references. Here we state:

Theorem 7.2 Suppose D is open and $f:D \to R$ is C^2. If (1) and (2) are satisfied at $\mathbf{x}^* \in D$ then $\mathbf{x}^*$ is a local maximum of f on D. Conversely if $\mathbf{x}^*$ is a local maximum of f on D then (1) and (3) are satisfied.

Local and strict local minima are defined in the obvious way changing '$\geqslant$' and '$>$' to '$\leqslant$' and '$<$' in the maxima definitions. The maxima results hold for minima upon changing 'n.s.d.' to 'p.s.d.' and 'n.d.' to 'p.d.'. The sufficient conditions of theorem 7.2 allow us to find (strict) local maxima (and minima) of functions in a probably familiar manner.

Examples 7.5

(a) $f:R \to D$ where $f(x) = x^3 - 3x$; stationary points are $x^* = \pm 1$, $f''(x) = 6x$ and $f''(1) = 6 > 0$, $f''(-1) = -6 < 0$. So $x^* = +1$ is a local minimum (strict) and $x^* = -1$ is a local maximum (strict).

(b) $f:R^2 \to R$ where $f(\mathbf{x}) = x_1^3 + x_1^2 - x_2^2$;

$$f_1'(\mathbf{x}) = 3x_1^2 + 2x_1 = 0 \text{ iff } x_1 = 0 \text{ or } -\tfrac{2}{3}$$

$$f_2'(\mathbf{x}) = -2x_2 = 0 \text{ iff } x_2 = 0$$

So there are two stationary points: $\mathbf{x}^* = (0, 0)$, $\mathbf{x}^* = (-\frac{2}{3}, 0)$.

The Hessian of f is

$$\mathbf{f}''(\mathbf{x}) = \begin{bmatrix} 6x_1 + 2 & 0 \\ 0 & -2 \end{bmatrix}$$

and

$$\mathbf{f}''(0, 0) = \begin{bmatrix} 2 & 0 \\ 0 & -2 \end{bmatrix} \quad \text{which is neither n.d. nor p.d.}$$

$$\mathbf{f}''(-\tfrac{2}{3}, 0) = \begin{bmatrix} -2 & 0 \\ 0 & -2 \end{bmatrix} \quad \text{which is n.d.}$$

Hence $\mathbf{x}^* = (-\frac{2}{3}, 0)$ is a local maximum (strict) and we have no inference about $(0, 0)$.

Turning to constrained maximization consider:

$$\max_{\mathbf{x} \in D} f(\mathbf{x}) \quad \text{subject to } g(\mathbf{x}) \geqslant 0$$

where D is open and f and g are C^2. A local solution to this problem (a local maximum of f on D subject to $g(\mathbf{x}) \geqslant 0$) is:

$$\mathbf{x}^* \in D \text{ where } g(\mathbf{x}^*) \geqslant 0 \text{ and } f(\mathbf{x}^*) \geqslant f(\mathbf{x})$$
$$\forall \mathbf{x} \text{ sufficiently close to } \mathbf{x}^*, \text{ where } g(\mathbf{x}) \geqslant 0$$

If we restrict attention to functions f and g which are concave near $\mathbf{x}^*$, then the K–T conditions become necessary and sufficient for a local solution to this problem, analogous to the local unconstrained maximization theory. Also analogously, alternative '2nd-order conditions' holding only at $\mathbf{x}^*$ can be found using the Taylor series expansion (see bibliographical notes for references). These are more usually stated for the equality constraint problem:

$$\max f(\mathbf{x}) \quad \text{subject to } g(\mathbf{x}) = 0$$

A local solution of this problem is a local maximum of f on D subject to $g(\mathbf{x}) = 0$ and is defined by:

$$\mathbf{x}^* \in D \text{ where } g(\mathbf{x}^*) = 0 \text{ and } f(\mathbf{x}^*) \geqslant f(\mathbf{x})$$
$$\forall \mathbf{x} \text{ sufficiently close to } \mathbf{x}^*, \text{ where } g(\mathbf{x}) = 0$$

The relevant conditions are:

$$\text{(4) (i)} \quad \frac{\partial L}{\partial x_i}(\mathbf{x}^*, \lambda^*) = 0 \quad i = 1, \ldots, n$$

$$\text{(ii)} \quad g(\mathbf{x}^*) = 0\left(= \frac{\partial L}{\partial \lambda}(\mathbf{x}^*, \lambda^*)\right)$$

where $L(\mathbf{x}, \lambda) = f(\mathbf{x}) + \lambda g(\mathbf{x})$ as usual.

$$\text{(5) (i)} \quad \begin{vmatrix} L''_{11} & L''_{12} & g'_1 \\ L''_{21} & L''_{22} & g'_2 \\ g'_1 & g'_2 & 0 \end{vmatrix} > 0$$

$$\text{(ii)} \quad \begin{vmatrix} L''_{11} & L''_{12} & L''_{13} & g'_1 \\ L''_{21} & L''_{22} & L''_{22} & g'_2 \\ L''_{31} & L''_{32} & L''_{33} & g'_3 \\ g'_1 & g'_2 & g'_3 & 0 \end{vmatrix} < 0$$

$$(n-1) \quad \begin{vmatrix} L''_{11} \ldots L''_{1n} & g'_1 \\ L''_{21} \ldots L''_{2n} & g'_2 \\ \ldots & \\ L''_{n1} \ldots L''_{nn} & g'_n \\ g'_1 \ldots g'_n & 0 \end{vmatrix} \quad \text{has sign } (-1)^n$$

where

$$L''_{ij} = \frac{\partial^2 L}{\partial x_i \, \partial x_j}(\mathbf{x}^*, \lambda^*) \text{ and } g'_i = g'_i(\mathbf{x}^*)$$

(6) The sequence of determinants in (5) have signs:

$$\geqslant 0, \quad \leqslant 0, \ldots, \quad (-1)^n \text{ or } 0.$$

And the theorem is:

Theorem 7.3 Suppose D is open and $f:D \to R$ and $g:D \to R$ are C^2. If (4) and (5) are satisfied at $\mathbf{x}^* \in D$ then $\mathbf{x}^*$ is a local maximum of f on D subject to $g(\mathbf{x}) = 0$. Conversely if $\mathbf{x}^*$ is a local maximum of f on D subject to $g(\mathbf{x}) = 0$ then (4) and (6) are satisfied.

As in theorem 7.2 the sufficient conditions here actually ensure a strict local constrained maximum. Local constrained minima are defined in the obvious way and theorem 7.3 prevails for such minima with *all* signs in (5) strictly negative and all signs in (6) non-positive.

Examples 7.6

$$\max_{\mathbf{x} \in R^2} x_1^3 + x_2^3 - \tfrac{1}{2}x_1^2 - \tfrac{1}{2}x_2^2 \quad \text{subject to } x_1 + x_2 + 1 = 0$$

$$L(\mathbf{x}, \lambda) = x_1^3 + x_2^3 - \tfrac{1}{2}x_1^2 - \tfrac{1}{2}x_2^2 + \lambda(x_1 + x_2 + 1)$$

$$\frac{\partial L}{\partial x_1} = 3x_1^2 - x_1 + \lambda = 0$$

$$\frac{\partial L}{\partial x_2} = 3x_2^2 - x_2 + \lambda = 0$$

$$\frac{\partial L}{\partial \lambda} = x_1 + x_2 + 1 = 0$$

Solving, $3x_1^2 - x_1 = 3x_2^2 - x_2$ and $x_1 + x_2 + 1 = 0$ implies $x_1 = x_2 = -\tfrac{1}{2}$ and $\lambda = -\tfrac{5}{4}$ (notice $\lambda > 0$ is not required).

For the '2nd-order condition'

$$L''_{11} = 6x_1 - 1 = -4, \quad L''_{21} = L''_{12} = 0 \quad \text{and} \quad L''_{22} = 6x_2 - 1 = -4$$

$$g'_1 = 1 \text{ and } g'_2 = 1$$

so the required determinant is

$$\begin{vmatrix} L''_{11} & L''_{12} & g'_1 \\ L''_{21} & L''_{22} & g'_2 \\ g'_1 & g'_2 & 0 \end{vmatrix} = \begin{vmatrix} -4 & 0 & 1 \\ 0 & -4 & 1 \\ 1 & 1 & 0 \end{vmatrix} = 8 > 0$$

and the sufficient conditions for a local maximum are satisfied. Hence $\mathbf{x}^* = (-\tfrac{1}{2}, -\tfrac{1}{2})$ is a local maximum of $x_1^3 + x_2^3 - x_1 - x_2$ subject to $x_1 + x_2 + 1 = 0$.

Exercise 7

1. Find whether the following C^2 functions are (i) concave, (ii) convex, (iii) both, or (iv) neither:

   (a) $f: R_{++} \to R$ where $f(x) = x^{\alpha}$ and $\alpha \in (0, 1)$

   (b) $f: R^2_{++} \to R$ where $f(x) = x_1^{\alpha} x_2^{1-\alpha}$ and $\alpha \in (0, 1)$

   (c) $f: R^n_{++} \to R$ where $f(\mathbf{x}) = \sum_{i=1}^{n} x_i^3$

   (d) $f: R^n_{++} \to R$ where $f(\mathbf{x}) = \sum_{i=1}^{n} x_i^{\alpha}$ and $\alpha \in (0, 1)$

2. Are any of the functions in question 1 strictly concave or strictly convex?

3. Solve the following problems:

   (a) $\max_{\mathbf{x} \in R^2_{++}} x_1^{1/4} x_2^{3/4} - x_1 - x_2$

   (b) $\max_{x \in R_{++}} x^5 - 5x$

   (c) $\max_{\mathbf{x} \in R^2_{++}} \ln x_1 + \ln x_2$ subject to $x_1 + 2x_2 \leqslant 1$

   (d) $\max_{\mathbf{x} \in R^2_{++}} x_1^{1/4} x_2^{3/4}$ subject to $x_1 + x_2 \leqslant 4$

   (e) $\max_{\mathbf{x} \in R^2_{++}} x_1 + x_2$ subject to $x_1^{1/2} + x_2^{1/2} \geqslant 3$

4. (a) Using the fact that the function $f: R_{++} \to R$ defined by $f(x) = \ln x$ is concave, and using the argument of exercise 2, question 8, prove that if $x^1, \ldots, x^m$ are m positive numbers and if $\lambda_1, \ldots, \lambda_m$ are all non-negative with $\Sigma_{i=1}^m \lambda_i = 1$ then

   $$\sum_{i=1}^{m} \lambda_i x^i \geqslant (x^1)^{\lambda_1} (x^2)^{\lambda_2} \ldots (x^m)^{\lambda_m} = \prod_{i=1}^{m} (x^i)^{\lambda_i}$$

   (b) Putting $\lambda_1 = \lambda_2 = \ldots = \lambda_m = 1/m$ show that the arithmetic mean of m positive numbers, $1/m \; \Sigma_{i=1}^m x^i$ is at least as large as the geometric mean, $\Pi_{i=1}^m (x^i)^{1/m}$.

5. Suppose that $D \subset R^n$ is a convex set and that $h: D \to R$ and $g: D \to R$ are both concave functions. Prove that $f: D \to R$ is also concave where

   $$f(\mathbf{x}) = \min[h(\mathbf{x}), g(\mathbf{x})]$$

8 Parameterized concave programming and the envelope theorem

8.1 Introduction

Before we start on the economics, we need to expand on the concave programming story of chapters 5, 6 and 7 in a particular direction. This is because in the economics discussion we will want to consider whole *families* of concave programming problems instead of just one problem in isolation as we did in chapters 5 and 6. To illustrate what we have in mind suppose that we have a constraint function which depends not only on the variables for which we want to solve, i.e. **x** (now known as *choice variables*), but also on some other 'variables' known as *parameters.* For instance, a very easy one-choice variable and one-parameter example is:

$$\max x \text{ subject to } \alpha - x^2 \geqslant 0 \quad \text{where } \alpha \in R_{++} \tag{8.1}$$

For any specification of the parameter $\alpha \in R_{++}$ this is a standard (chapter 5) one-variable concave programming problem. We can apply K–T to find the solution of any such problem; we do not need any new theory to do this. However, the solution we find will not be a specific numerical value for x^* but an expression for the solution x^* *in terms of* α. For the parameterized families of problems we encounter in economics (like, but more complicated than, (8.1)) a question of outstanding economic interest is: how does the solution vary with the parameters? At the moment we have no general theory to answer this question. The main objective of this chapter is to introduce the *envelope theorem*, which will allow us eventually to answer such questions. As a by-product this will also allow us to give precise expression to the interpretation of Lagrange multipliers as 'prices associated with constraint violations', hinted at towards the end of chapter 5.

8.2 Parameterized families of concave programming problems

Example 8.1 Consider again (8.1). For any $\alpha \in R_{++}$, (CQ) is satisfied, and f and g are concave and C^1. The Lagrangean is $x + \lambda[\alpha - x^2]$. Since f is non-stationary (K–T) are,

$$\text{(I) } 1 - 2\lambda x = 0 \quad \text{(II) } \lambda > 0 \quad \text{and} \quad \text{(III) } \alpha - x^2 = 0$$

From (III), $x = \pm\sqrt{\alpha}$ and from (I) $\lambda = (1/2x) > 0$ only when $x = +\sqrt{\alpha}$. Hence the solution of (K–T) is

$$x^* = +\sqrt{\alpha}, \quad \lambda^* = \frac{1}{2\sqrt{\alpha}}$$

So for any specification of $\alpha \in R_{++}$ the solution of (8.1) is $x^* = +\sqrt{\alpha}$ and the optimal value is $+\sqrt{\alpha}$.

In this example the solution, the Lagrange multiplier and the optimal value are all *functions* of α (i.e. uniquely defined given $\alpha \in R_{++}$): the above has therefore defined three functions associated with the family (8.1):

the solution function, $x^*: R_{++} \to R$ with values $x^*(\alpha) = +\sqrt{\alpha}$;
the multiplier function, $\lambda^*: R_{++} \to R$ with values $\lambda^*(\alpha) = 1/(2\sqrt{\alpha})$;
and the optimal value function, $V: R_{++} \to R$ with values $V(\alpha) = +\sqrt{\alpha}$.

For general parameterized families we are most interested in how the solution varies with the parameters. For (8.1) the above solution function tells us all we could want to know about this: for instance $dx^*/d\alpha = \frac{1}{2}\alpha^{-1/2} > 0$ and as α goes up, x^* goes up. This is the kind of statement economists would like to make about their parameterized families of problems; for instance in the theory of the firm choice variables might be quantities of inputs and outputs used by the firm, and parameters might be prices of inputs and outputs. The economist would like to know whether the quantity of an input used by the firm goes up or down as its (parametric) price goes up, for instance. To address this sort of question in the ensuing chapters we now provide some theory of general parameterized families of concave programming problems.

Let $\mathbf{x} = (x_1, \ldots, x_n)$ be the choice variables and $\boldsymbol{\alpha} = (\alpha_1, \ldots, \alpha_m)$ be a vector of all parameters appearing in our problem. To be general we allow that both *objective* and *constraint* functions may depend on $\boldsymbol{\alpha}$ and we write the values of these functions as $f(\mathbf{x}; \boldsymbol{\alpha})$ and $g(\mathbf{x}; \boldsymbol{\alpha})$; notice the semi-colon which separates choice variables from parameters. The parameters must belong to some set (R_{++} in (8.1) for example) which we name the *admissible parameter set* and denote by A. Then consider the general family of problems:

$$\max_{\mathbf{x} \in D} f(\mathbf{x}; \alpha) \text{ subject to } g(\mathbf{x}; \alpha) \geqslant 0 \quad \text{where } \alpha \in A \tag{8.2}$$

We also assume:

(A8.1) A is convex and open (usually R^m_{++}, as in (8.1), or R^m itself)

In addition for *every* $\alpha \in A$ we want the solutions to (8.2) to be characterized by the Kuhn–Tucker conditions. Hence we also assume:

(A8.2) D is convex and open (usually R^n_{++}, or, as in (8.1), R^n itself)
(A8.3) *For each* $\alpha \in A$, $f(\mathbf{x}; \alpha)$ and $g(\mathbf{x}; \alpha)$ are concave and C^2 functions of $\mathbf{x}$ for $\mathbf{x} \in D$.
(A8.4) *For each* $\alpha \in A$, $\exists\ \mathbf{x} \in D$ where $g(\mathbf{x}; \alpha) > 0$

Finally it would be very nice if for each $\alpha \in A$ there were exactly one solution to (8.2). For now we simply assume this,

(A8.5) *For each* $\alpha \in A$ there is exactly one solution to (8.2).

Conditions which ensure this are discussed much later. For the time being we carry (A8.5) as an (unsatisfactory) assumption. In examples we will be able to demonstrate (A8.5) by actually computing solutions.

For $\alpha \in A$ the Lagrangean is written

$$L(\mathbf{x}, \lambda; \alpha) = f(\mathbf{x}; \alpha) + \lambda g(\mathbf{x}; \alpha) \tag{8.3}$$

And (K–T) become

$$\mathbf{x}^* = \mathbf{x}^*(\alpha) \quad (\text{i.e. } x_i^* = x_i^*(\alpha), \forall i)$$

if and only if there exists a real number $\lambda^* = \lambda^*(\alpha)$ such that

(A) $L(\mathbf{x}^*, \lambda^*; \alpha) \geqslant L(\mathbf{x}, \lambda^*, \alpha) \quad \forall \mathbf{x} \in D$
(B) $\lambda^* \geqslant 0$
(C) $\lambda^* g(\mathbf{x}^*; \alpha) = 0$
(D) $\mathbf{x}^* \in D$ and $g(\mathbf{x}^*; \alpha) \geqslant 0$

Under our assumptions (A) can be replaced with the Lagrangean stationarity condition

$$\frac{\partial f}{\partial x_i}(\mathbf{x}^*; \alpha) + \lambda^* \frac{\partial g}{\partial x_i}(\mathbf{x}^*; \alpha) = 0 \quad i = 1, \ldots, n$$

And if $\partial f/\partial x_i\,(\mathbf{x}; \alpha) \neq 0$, $\forall \mathbf{x} \in D$, $\forall i$ (f is non-stationary with respect to $\mathbf{x}$) then (B) can be replaced by $\lambda^* > 0$ and (C) and (D) can be replaced by $\mathbf{x}^* \in D$ and $g(\mathbf{x}^*; \alpha) = 0$.

So to find solution and multiplier functions for problems like (8.2) under our assumption, we solve these K–T conditions for $\mathbf{x}^*, \lambda^*$; then $\mathbf{x}^*(\alpha) = \mathbf{x}^*$, $\lambda^*(\alpha) = \lambda^*$ and $V(\alpha) = f(\mathbf{x}^*; \alpha)$. We have already done this for example 8.1. Here are some more examples.

Example 8.2

(a) $\max_{x \in R_{++}} \ln x$ subject to $\alpha - x^2 \geqslant 0$ where $\alpha \in R_{++}$

The reader can easily check that (A8.1)–(A8.4) are satisfied. The Lagrangean is

$$L(x, \lambda; \alpha) = \ln x + \lambda(\alpha - x^2)$$

The objective is non-stationary and so K–T become:

$$\text{(I)} \frac{1}{x} - 2\lambda x = 0 \quad \text{(II)}\ \lambda > 0 \quad \text{(III)}\ x > 0 \quad \text{and} \quad \alpha - x^2 = 0$$

From (III), $x = +\sqrt{\alpha}$ and from (I) $\lambda = (1/2\alpha) > 0$ satisfying (II). So for all $\alpha > 0$ there is a unique solution and

$$x^*(\alpha) = +\sqrt{\alpha}, \quad \lambda^*(\alpha) = \frac{1}{2\alpha}, \quad V(\alpha) = \ln\sqrt{\alpha} = \tfrac{1}{2} \ln \alpha$$

(b) $\max_{x \in R_{++}} \alpha_1 x_1 - \alpha_2 x_2$ subject to $x_2^{1/2} - x_1 \geqslant 0$

where $(\alpha_1, \alpha_2) \in R^2_{++}$

Again the reader can easily check (A8.1)–(A8.4). The Lagrangean is,

$$L(\mathbf{x}, \lambda; \alpha) = \alpha_1 x_1 - \alpha_2 x_2 + \lambda(x_2^{1/2} - x_1)$$

Again the objective is non-stationary and (K–T) are

$$\text{(I)}\ \alpha_1 - \lambda = 0, -\alpha_2 + \tfrac{1}{2}\lambda x_2^{-1/2} = 0 \quad \text{(II)}\ \lambda > 0$$

$$\text{(III)}\ x_1, x_2 > 0 \quad \text{and} \quad x_2^{1/2} - x_1 = 0$$

From (I), $\lambda = \alpha_1 > 0$ satisfying (II). Also from (I) we get $x_2^{1/2} = \alpha_1/2\alpha_2$ and $x_2 = \alpha_1^2/4\alpha_2^2$, $x_1 = \alpha_1/2\alpha_2$. So (I)–(III) are satisfied, and there is a unique solution, with

$$x_1^*(\alpha) = \frac{\alpha_1}{2\alpha_2}, x_2^*(\alpha) = \frac{\alpha_1^2}{4\alpha_2^2}, \lambda^*(\alpha) = \alpha_1, V(\alpha) = \frac{\alpha_1^2}{4\alpha_2}$$

(c) $\max\ 10x - x^2$ subject to $\alpha - x \geqslant 0$, $\alpha \in R$. (A8.1)–(A8.4) are satisfied. The Lagrangean and (K–T) are $L(x, \lambda; \alpha) = 10x - x^2 + \lambda(\alpha - x)$

$$\text{(A) } 10 - 2x - \lambda = 0 \quad \text{(B) } \lambda \geqslant 0 \quad \text{(C) } \lambda = 0 \text{ or } \alpha = x$$

$$\text{(D) } \alpha - x \geqslant 0$$

Try $\lambda = 0$ in (C) so (B) is satisfied: then $x = 5$ for (A) and (D) is satisfied if and only if $\alpha \geqslant 5$. So if $\alpha \geqslant 5$ there is a solution with $x = 5$, $\lambda^* = 0$. Try $x = \alpha$ in (C) so (D) is satisfied. For (A) $\lambda = 10 - 2\alpha$ and (B) is satisfied if and only if $\alpha \leqslant 5$. So if $\alpha \leqslant 5$ there is a solution with $x^* = \alpha$, $\lambda^* = 10 - 2\alpha$. Summarizing, there is a unique solution for all α and

$$x^*(\alpha) = \begin{cases} 5 \text{ if } \alpha \geqslant 5 \\ \alpha \text{ if } \alpha \leqslant 5 \end{cases} \qquad \lambda^*(\alpha) = \begin{cases} 0 & \text{if } \alpha \geqslant 5 \\ 10 - 2\alpha & \text{if } \alpha \leqslant 5 \end{cases}$$

$$V(\alpha) = \begin{cases} 25 & \text{if } \alpha \geqslant 5 \\ 10\alpha - \alpha^2 & \text{if } \alpha \leqslant 5 \end{cases}$$

As we suggested earlier, the primary objective of this chapter is to evolve techniques which will allow us to sign derivatives of the solution functions in our later economic models. Example 8.2(c) throws up a significant problem for this plan; namely the solution, multiplier and optimal value functions are not even differentiable. When $\alpha = 5$ there are multiple tangent lines to the graphs of these functions. This was not a problem in example 8.1 or 8.2(a) and (b). In fact if it is the case that $\lambda^*(\alpha) > 0$ for all $\alpha \in A$ *or* if $\lambda^*(\alpha) = 0$, for all $\alpha \in A$ (not so in (c)) then 'usually' the solution, multiplier and optimal value functions will be differentiable. We do not engage in a detailed discussion of this matter and simply assume what we need (see chapter 17).

(A8.6) The solution and multiplier functions are C^1; the optimal value function is C^2.

For any given example we can check that (A8.6) is satisfied; for instance in example 8.1 and examples 8.2(a) and (b).

8.3 The envelope theorem

If we partially differentiate the Lagrangean (8.3) with respect to the parameter α_i we get,

$$\frac{\partial f}{\partial \alpha_i}(\mathbf{x}; \alpha) + \lambda \frac{\partial g}{\partial \alpha_i}(\mathbf{x}; \alpha)$$

Evaluating this at $\mathbf{x} = \mathbf{x}^*(\alpha)$ and $\lambda = \lambda^*(\alpha)$ gives

$$\frac{\partial f}{\partial \alpha_i}(\mathbf{x}^*(\alpha); \alpha) + \lambda^*(\alpha)\frac{\partial g}{\partial \alpha_i}(\mathbf{x}^*(\alpha); \alpha)$$

The envelope theorem says that this expression is equal to the partial derivative of the optimal value function with respect to α_i at α:

Theorem 8.1: The envelope theorem Under assumptions (A8.1)–(A8.6) the Lagrangean and optimal value functions for (8.2) possess the following property:

$$V_i'(\alpha) = \frac{\partial}{\partial \alpha_i} L(x, \lambda; \alpha) \quad i = 1, \ldots, n$$

after the right-hand side is evaluated at $\mathbf{x} = \mathbf{x}^*(\alpha)$ and $\lambda = \lambda^*(\alpha)$.

Proof From (C) of (K–T)

$$V(\alpha) = f[x^*(\alpha); \alpha] + \lambda^*(\alpha) g[\mathbf{x}^*(\alpha); \alpha]$$

Differentiating partially with respect to α_i

$$V_i'(\alpha) = \sum_{j=1}^{n} \frac{\partial f}{\partial x_j}\frac{\partial x_j^*}{\partial \alpha_i} + \frac{\partial f}{\partial \alpha_i} + g\frac{\partial \lambda^*}{\partial \alpha_i} + \lambda^*\left[\sum_{j=1}^{n} \frac{\partial g}{\partial x_j}\frac{\partial x_j^*}{\partial \alpha_i} + \frac{\partial g}{\partial \alpha_i}\right]$$

omitting the arguments $[\mathbf{x}^*(\alpha); \alpha]$ and (α) for convenience. Hence, rearranging

$$V_i'(\alpha) = \frac{\partial f}{\partial \alpha_i} + \lambda^*\frac{\partial g}{\partial \alpha_i} + g\frac{\partial \lambda^*}{\partial \alpha_i} + \sum_{j=1}^{n} \frac{\partial x_j^*}{\partial \alpha_i}\left[\frac{\partial f}{\partial x_j} + \lambda^*\frac{\partial g}{\partial x_j}\right]$$

But from (A) of (K–T) the last term is zero. We also know from (C) that $\lambda^*(\alpha) g[\mathbf{x}^*(\alpha); \alpha] = 0, \ \forall \alpha \in A$. Partially differentiating with respect to α_i and omitting brackets again

$$g\frac{\partial \lambda^*}{\partial \alpha_i} + \lambda^*\left[\Sigma \frac{\partial g}{\partial x_j}\frac{\partial x_j^*}{\partial \alpha_i} + \frac{\partial g}{\partial \alpha_i}\right] = 0$$

But either $g = 0$ or $\lambda^* = 0$. So in the last equation either the first term or the second term on the left-hand side is zero and the sum is zero: so both must be zero. In particular $g(\partial\lambda^*/\partial\alpha_i) = 0$. Hence

$$V_i'(\alpha) = \frac{\partial f}{\partial \alpha_i} + \lambda^* \frac{\partial g}{\partial \alpha_i}$$

$$= \frac{\partial f}{\partial \alpha_i}[\mathbf{x}^*(\alpha); \alpha] + \lambda^*(\alpha)\frac{\partial g}{\partial \alpha_i}[\mathbf{x}^*(\alpha); \alpha]$$

re-inserting brackets. This is the same as the statement in the theorem. *Q.E.D.*

The reader who would like to know the source of the name of this theorem can now read section 8.5. More importantly we proceed to an illustration of its usefulness in the next section.

8.4 Perturbation functions and Lagrange multipliers

Consider the typical concave programming problem of chapter 7:

$$\max_{\mathbf{x} \in D} f(\mathbf{x}) \quad \text{subject to } g(\mathbf{x}) \geqslant 0 \tag{8.4}$$

Now suppose that we *perturb* the constraint in (8.4) by an amount $\alpha \in R$ as follows:

$$\max_{\mathbf{x} \in D} f(\mathbf{x}) \quad \text{subject to } g(\mathbf{x}) + \alpha \geqslant 0 \tag{8.5}$$

Notice that (8.5) reduces to (8.4) when $\alpha = 0$.

Let us assume that for some set $A \subset R$ (with $0 \in A$), (8.5) is a parameterized family of problems satisfying the earlier assumptions (A8.1)–(A8.6). Then (8.5) gives rise to solution functions $\mathbf{x}^*(\alpha)$, a multiplier function $\lambda^*(\alpha)$ and an optimal value function $V(\alpha)$, all with domain A, as before. $V(\alpha)$ is known as the *perturbation function* for (8.4), whose importance stems from the application of the envelope theorem to (8.5), as follows. The Lagrangean for (8.5) is

$$L(\mathbf{x}, \lambda; \alpha) = f(\mathbf{x}) + \lambda(g(\mathbf{x}) + \alpha)$$

The partial derivative of this with respect to α is

$$\frac{\partial}{\partial \alpha} L(\mathbf{x}, \lambda; \alpha) = \lambda$$

Evaluated at $\lambda^*(\alpha)$ we get

$$\frac{\partial}{\partial \alpha} L(\mathbf{x}, \lambda; \alpha) = \lambda^*(\alpha)$$

Hence from the envelope theorem

$$\lambda^*(\alpha) = V'(\alpha)$$

In particular

$$\lambda^*(0) = V'(0) \tag{8.6}$$

Now $\lambda^*(0)$ is the value of the Lagrange multiplier associated with (8.4). Equation (8.6) gives us an interpretation of Lagrange multipliers; it tells us that the Lagrange multiplier for (8.4) is equal to the rate of change of the optimal value for (8.4) with respect to perturbations of the constraint.

Going back to our story of the maximizer (chapter 5) this is seen as a natural result. Remember we initially allowed the maximizer to violate the constraint at a charge of λ^* per unit of constraint violation. In order that the maximizer chooses not to violate the constraint, we should set the charge at a level where the marginal benefit from constraint violation is exactly offset by the marginal cost. But this means exactly that we should set $\lambda^* = V'(0)$, the result we arrived at formally above. Because of this, Lagrange multipliers are often referred to as *shadow values* or *shadow prices* of their associated constraints.

We have in fact already seen examples of perturbation problems like (8.5) and satisfying (A8.1)–(A8.6) in examples (8.1) and (8.2)(a). The multiplier and optimal value functions for these problems were for (8.1)

$$\lambda^*(\alpha) = \frac{1}{2\sqrt{\alpha}}, \quad V(\alpha) = \sqrt{\alpha}$$

and for (8.2)(a),

$$\lambda^*(\alpha) = \frac{1}{2\alpha}, \quad V(\alpha) = \tfrac{1}{2} \ln \alpha.$$

The examples confirm, of course, that $\lambda^*(\alpha) = V'(\alpha)$. More interestingly in both cases the optimal value function is *concave.* This is always the case for perturbation functions, and we need only a few of our assumptions to establish this:

Theorem 8.2 Suppose f and g are concave in the problem (8.5) where D is convex, and suppose a solution to (8.5) exists for $\alpha \in A$ where A is convex. Then the perturbation function, $V: A \to R$ [where $V(\alpha)$ is the optimal value of (8.5)], is a concave function.

Proof Let $\alpha^1, \alpha^2 \in A$ and let $\lambda \in [0, 1]$; we need to show that

$$V(\lambda\alpha^1 + (1-\lambda)\alpha^2) \geqslant \lambda V(\alpha^1) + (1-\lambda)V(\alpha^2)$$

For $i = 1, 2$ let $\mathbf{x}^i$ be a solution to (8.5) when $\alpha = \alpha^i$. Since A is convex a solution to (8.5) also exists when $\alpha = \lambda\alpha^1 + (1 - \lambda)\alpha^2$; let $\mathbf{x}$ denote such a solution. Notice that $V(\alpha^1) = f(\mathbf{x}^1)$, $V(\alpha^2) = f(\mathbf{x}^2)$ and $V(\lambda\alpha^1 + (1 - \lambda)\alpha^2) = f(\mathbf{x})$ in this notation; also

$$g(\mathbf{x}^1) + \alpha^1 \geqslant 0 \quad \text{and} \quad g(\mathbf{x}^2) + \alpha^2 \geqslant 0$$

Hence

$$\lambda g(\mathbf{x}^1) + (1 - \lambda)g(\mathbf{x}^2) + [\lambda\alpha^1 + (1 - \lambda)\alpha^2] \geqslant 0$$

Since g is concave and D convex, $\lambda\mathbf{x}^1 + (1 - \lambda)\mathbf{x}^2 \in D$ and

$$g[\lambda\mathbf{x}^1 + (1 - \lambda)\mathbf{x}^2] \geqslant \lambda g(\mathbf{x}^1) + (1 - \lambda)g(\mathbf{x}^2)$$

Therefore, $\lambda\mathbf{x}^1 + (1 - \lambda)\mathbf{x}^2 \in D$ and

$$g[\lambda\mathbf{x}^1 + (1 - \lambda)\mathbf{x}^2] + [\lambda\alpha^1 + (1 - \lambda)\alpha^2] \geqslant 0$$

which means that $\lambda\mathbf{x}^1 + (1 - \lambda)\mathbf{x}^2$ is in the feasible set for (8.5) when the parameter value is $\lambda\alpha^1 + (1 - \lambda)\alpha^2$. So $V(\lambda\alpha^1 + (1 - \lambda)\alpha^2)$ must be at least as large as the value of f at this feasible point; i.e.

$$V(\lambda\alpha^1 + (1 - \lambda)\alpha^2) \geqslant f(\lambda\mathbf{x}^1 + (1 - \lambda)\mathbf{x}^2)$$

Then, since f is concave we get

$$\begin{aligned} V(\lambda\alpha^1 + (1 - \lambda)\alpha^2) &\geqslant \lambda f(\mathbf{x}^1) + (1 - \lambda)f(\mathbf{x}^2) \\ &= \lambda V(\alpha^1) + (1 - \lambda)V(\alpha^2) \text{ as required} \end{aligned}$$

Q.E.D.

It is possible to start the concave programming story from this result and to develop (K–T) from it. For the reader interested in this alternative route, references are provided in the bibliographical notes.

There is a further consequence of theorem 8.2. Suppose we have a family of problems (8.5) which satisfy all our assumptions (A8.1)–(A8.6). Then we know

(i) $\lambda^*(\alpha) = V'(\alpha)$
(ii) V is concave

Since the multiplier function is C^1 by assumption we get from (i)

$$\frac{d\lambda^*}{d\alpha}(\alpha) = V''(\alpha)$$

But from (ii), $V''(\alpha) \leqslant 0$. Hence $(d\lambda^*/d\alpha)(\alpha) \leqslant 0$.

As the parameter increases (so that the feasible set in (8.5) 'expands') the multiplier decreases (or does not increase). Combining envelope theorem with the concavity of V has allowed us to ascertain the sign of $d\lambda^*/d\alpha$. This type of combination will be very fruitful in the later economics discussion.

To illustrate further, consider example 8.2(b): with a change of notation this is a typical problem in the theory of the firm which we shall meet in chapter 10. The envelope theorem tells us, for all $\alpha \in A$.

$$x_1^*(\alpha) = V_1'(\alpha) \quad \text{and} \quad -x_2^*(\alpha) = V_2'(\alpha) \tag{8.7}$$

since the derivative of the Lagrangean with respect to α_1 is x_1 and with respect to α_2 we get $-x_2$. The reader can check that, in this case,

$$V \text{ is a convex function.} \tag{8.8}$$

Now suppose that all we know about this example is (8.7) and (8.8). From (8.8) the Hessian of V is positive semidefinite, $\forall \alpha \in A$. From (8.7) we get

$$\begin{bmatrix} V_{11}''(\alpha) & V_{12}''(\alpha) \\ V_{21}''(\alpha) & V_{22}''(\alpha) \end{bmatrix} = \begin{bmatrix} \dfrac{\partial x_1^*}{\partial \alpha_1}(\alpha) & \dfrac{\partial x_1^*}{\partial \alpha_2}(\alpha) \\ -\dfrac{\partial x_2^*}{\partial \alpha_1}(\alpha) & -\dfrac{\partial x_2^*}{\partial \alpha_2}(\alpha) \end{bmatrix}$$

The left-hand matrix is the Hessian of V. The right-hand matrix is therefore p.s.d., $\forall \alpha \in A$. Hence in particular we can conclude

$$\frac{\partial x_1^*}{\partial \alpha_1}(\alpha) \geqslant 0 \quad \text{and} \quad \frac{\partial x_2^*}{\partial \alpha_2}(\alpha) \leqslant 0$$

We got this by coupling the envelope theorem with the curvature of the optimal value function as suggested.

8.5 The source of the envelope

From (A) of the Kuhn–Tucker conditions we get the following property of the Lagrangean of (8.2)

$$L[\mathbf{x}^*(\alpha), \lambda^*(\alpha); \alpha] \geqslant L[\mathbf{x}, \lambda^*(\alpha); \alpha] \quad \forall \mathbf{x} \in D, \forall \alpha \in A$$

In particular if $\mathbf{x} = \mathbf{x}^*(\hat{\alpha})$ where $\hat{\alpha} \in A$ we get

$$L[\mathbf{x}^*(\alpha), \lambda^*(\alpha); \alpha] \geqslant L[\mathbf{x}^*(\hat{\alpha}), \lambda^*(\alpha); \alpha] \quad \forall \alpha, \hat{\alpha} \in A \tag{8.9}$$

The left-hand side is just $V(\alpha)=f[\mathbf{x}^*(\alpha);\alpha]$ since from (C), $\lambda^*(\alpha)\,g[\mathbf{x}^*(\alpha);\alpha]=0$. The right-hand side depends on $\hat{\alpha}$ and α and we write it $l(\hat{\alpha},\alpha)$ for short; it is defined by

$$l(\hat{\alpha},\alpha)=f[\mathbf{x}^*(\hat{\alpha});\alpha]+\lambda^*(\alpha)\,g[\mathbf{x}^*(\hat{\alpha});\alpha]$$

Notice that when $\alpha=\hat{\alpha}$ the left- and right-hand sides of (8.9) are the same (namely $V(\alpha)$). This gives us what is known as an *envelope relation*: namely

$$V(\alpha)=l(\alpha,\alpha)\geqslant l(\hat{\alpha},\alpha)\quad \forall\alpha,\hat{\alpha}\in A \tag{8.10}$$

We may translate this general proposition into the easier terms of example 8.1. There, $V(\alpha)=+\sqrt{\alpha}$ and

$$l(\hat{\alpha},\alpha)=\sqrt{\hat{\alpha}}+\frac{1}{2\sqrt{\alpha}}(\alpha-\hat{\alpha})$$

since $f[x^*(\hat{\alpha})]=\sqrt{\hat{\alpha}}$ (f does not depend directly on α) and $g[x^*(\hat{\alpha});\alpha]=\alpha-[x^*(\hat{\alpha})]^2=\alpha-\hat{\alpha}$. Figure 8.1 shows the graph of $V(\alpha)$.

Now fix $\hat{\alpha}$, say at the value indicated in fig. 8.1, and consider the graph of $l(\hat{\alpha},\alpha)$ as a function of α alone. From the envelope relation this graph should touch the graph of $V(\alpha)$ when $\alpha=\hat{\alpha}$ (since $l(\hat{\alpha},\hat{\alpha})=V(\hat{\alpha})$) and everywhere else it should lie on or below the graph of $V(\alpha)$ (since $V(\alpha)\geqslant l(\hat{\alpha},\alpha)$), as shown. You can confirm this by sketching (for instance) $l(1,\alpha)=1+(\alpha-1)/(2\sqrt{\alpha})$ on top of $\alpha^{1/2}$; you will get something like fig. 8.1.

But suppose now we choose a different value of $\hat{\alpha}$, $\hat{\alpha}_1$ say. The same arguments apply to the graph of $l(\hat{\alpha}_1,\alpha)$ as a function of α as did above: it will touch the graph of V when $\alpha=\hat{\alpha}_1$, and lie on or below it everywhere else. Repeating for a few more values of $\hat{\alpha}$ you end up with fig. 8.2. If this exercise is repeated indefinitely

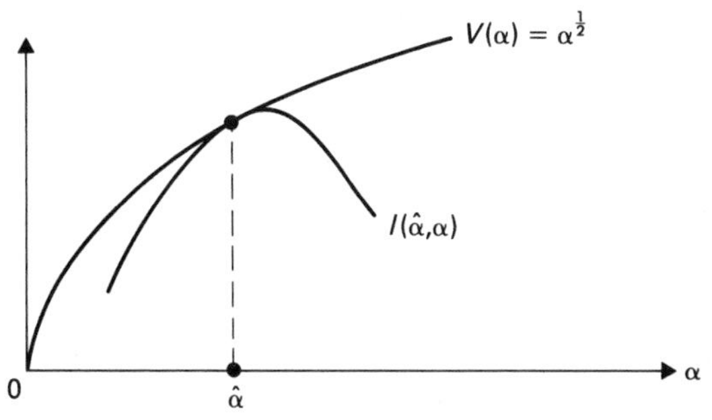

Figure 8.1

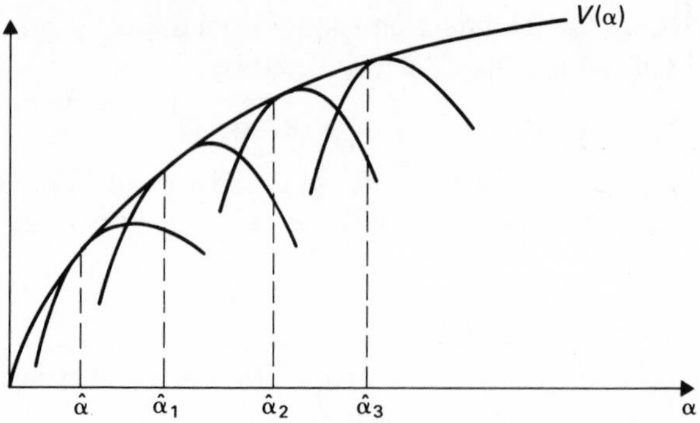

Figure 8.2

the graph of V emerges as the *outer envelope* of all the individual $l(\hat{\alpha}, \alpha)$ curves, as $\hat{\alpha}$ varies over A. This is where the term 'envelope relation' comes from.

The importance of the relation, however, is that it allows us to infer (using the differentiability assumption, of course) that the slope of V at $\hat{\alpha}$ equals the slope of the l curve for $\hat{\alpha}$ at $\alpha = \hat{\alpha}$; or

$$V'(\hat{\alpha}) = \frac{\partial}{\partial \alpha} l(\hat{\alpha}, \alpha) \text{ evaluated at } \alpha = \hat{\alpha}.$$

By (tedious) differentiation, the right-hand side is the same as

$$\frac{\partial}{\partial \alpha} L(x, \lambda; \alpha) \text{ evaluated at } \alpha = \hat{\alpha},\ x = x^*(\hat{\alpha}),\ \lambda = \lambda^*(\hat{\alpha})$$

Thus emerges the statement of the envelope theorem, so-called because of the envelope relation between V and l illustrated above.

Exercise 8

1. Find the solution functions, multiplier functions and optimal value functions for the following problems:

(a) $\max_{x \in R^2_{++}} x_1^{1/2} x_2^{1/2}$ subject to $\alpha_1 x_1 + \alpha_2 x_2 \leqslant \alpha_3$

where $\alpha \in R^3_{++}$

(b) $\min_{x \in R^2_{++}} \alpha_1 x_1 + \alpha_2 x_2$ subject to $x_1^{1/2} + x_2^{1/2} \geqslant \alpha_3$

where $\alpha \in R^3_{++}$.

2. State the envelope theorem and check its validity in question 1. In part (a) comment on $\partial V/\partial \alpha_3$ with respect to 'perturbations'.
3. Roy's identity (chapter 12). Suppose the following problem gives rise to solution functions, a multiplier function and an optimal value function so that the envelope theorem applies:

$$\max_{x \in R^n_{++}} U(\mathbf{x}) \text{ subject to } \sum_{i=1}^{n} p_i x_i \leqslant m$$

$$\text{where } (\mathbf{p}, m) \in R^{n+1}_{++}$$

Applying the envelope theorem prove that for $i = 1, \ldots, n$ the ith solution function equals $-(\partial V/\partial p_i)/(\partial V/\partial m)$.

9 Homogeneous functions

9.1 Introduction

This chapter is something of a digression from our main theme, albeit a necessary digression. It will emerge in chapters 10–12 that many of the functions appearing from solutions of the parameterized families of problems occurring in economics are *homogeneous functions*. Consequently we devote this chapter to a discussion of this class of functions.

A function, $f: D \to R$, $D \subset R^n$, is said to be *homogeneous of degree r*, where $r \in R$, if the rule defining the function satisfies

$$f(t\mathbf{x}) = t^r f(\mathbf{x}) \quad \forall t > 0, \forall \mathbf{x} \in D$$

For instance homogeneity of degree zero requires $f(t\mathbf{x}) = f(\mathbf{x})$, $\forall t > 0$, $\forall \mathbf{x} \in D$ so that multiplying all variables by $t > 0$ leaves the value of f unchanged; $f: R^2_{++} \to R$ where $f(\mathbf{x}) = x_1/x_2$ has this property since $f(t\mathbf{x}) = tx_1/tx_2 = x_1/x_2 = f(\mathbf{x})$. On the other hand homogeneity of degree one requires $f(t\mathbf{x}) = tf(\mathbf{x})$, $\forall t > 0$, $\forall \mathbf{x} \in D$ so that multiplying all variables by $t > 0$ multiplies the value of the function by t; any linear function on R^n has this property as do some non-linear functions (e.g. $f: R^2_{++} \to R$ where $f(\mathbf{x}) = x_1^2/x_2$). Nevertheless, functions which are homogeneous of degree one are sometimes referred to as *linearly homogeneous*. However, in this chapter, we consider the general case of homogeneity of degree r.

The domain of a homogeneous function must satisfy the following requirement:

$$\text{if } \mathbf{x} \in D \text{ then } t\mathbf{x} \in D \quad \forall t > 0$$

A set $D \subset R^n$ which satisfies this restriction is known as a *cone*. A cone need not be a convex set: for instance $D = \{\mathbf{x} \in R^2 | x_1 = 0$ or $x_2 = 0\}$ is a non-convex cone consisting of the 'axes' of R^2. Moreover, convex sets need not be cones: any bounded convex set will not be a cone. However, there are many sets which are both cones and convex. For instance R^n, R^n_+, R^n_{++}, $R^n_{++} \cup \{0\}$ are all convex cones. Since most of the economics discussion of homogeneity is in the context of functions whose domain is R^n_{++} we restrict attention to homogeneous functions on R^n_{++} for the most part in this chapter; the reader should note, however, that many of the ideas of this chapter can be extended to homogeneous functions whose domains are merely cones.

We now look in detail at the properties of homogeneous functions on R^n_{++}, starting with the one variable case.

9.2 Homogeneous functions of one variable

This is easy. $f: R_{++} \to R$ is homogeneous of degree r if and only if $f(x) = x^r f(1)$; $f(1)$ is merely some real number and so f is homogeneous of degree r if and only if

$$f(x) = kx^r \quad \text{some } k \in R \tag{9.1}$$

For instance the only homogeneous of degree 1 functions of one variable are linear functions, $f(x) = kx$, and so on.

It now follows that homogeneous functions of one variable $f: R_{++} \to R$ are C^2 functions with derivatives

$$f'(x) = krx^{r-1} = r\frac{f(x)}{x}$$

and

$$f''(x) = kr(r-1)\,x^{r-2}$$

A number of important properties of one variable homogeneous of degree r functions follow from this:

1. Euler's theorem. $xf'(x) = rf(x)$, $\forall x \in R_{++}$; the product of variable and derivative is the value of the function multiplied by the degree of homogeneity.
2. The first derivative function, $f': R_{++} \to R$ with values $f'(x)$ is homogeneous of degree $r-1$ since $f'(tx) = t^{r-1}krx^{r-1} = t^{r-1}f'(x)$, $\forall x \in R_{++}$, $\forall t > 0$. [Note when $r = 0$, $f(x) = k$, $f'(x) = 0$, and this derivative property is rather trivial.]

From the second derivative formula we see that f is concave (convex) if and only if $kr(r-1) \leqslant (\geqslant)\ 0$; since we must have one or other of these inequalities it follows that:

3. Any one variable homogeneous function is either concave or convex.

Specific concavity or convexity can easily be checked from the sign of $kr(r-1)$. Since many of our homogeneous functions have the property that they are *positively valued*, i.e. the value of f is strictly positive everywhere on the domain, the following is worth special mention:

4. A one-variable, homogeneous of degree r, positively valued function $f: R_{++} \to R$ is concave if and only if $0 \leqslant r \leqslant 1$ and convex if and only if $r \geqslant 1$ or $r \leqslant 0$; this is because positive valuedness means $k > 0$ and f is concave (convex) if and only if $r(r-1) \leqslant (\geqslant)\, 0$, which implies the stated result.

9.3 Homogeneous functions of many variables

Things are not so straightforward here. There is no simple formula like (9.1) governing all n-variable homogeneous functions, and indeed such functions need not be continuous let alone differentiable. So we will typically assume continuity and differentiability as required. Properties 1 and 2 of the last section do then generalize:

Theorem 9.1. Euler's theorem Suppose $f: R^n_{++} \to R$ is C^1 and homogeneous of degree r. Then

$$\sum_{i=1}^{n} x_i f_i'(\mathbf{x}) = rf(\mathbf{x}) \quad \forall \mathbf{x} \in R^n_{++}$$

Proof Since f is homogeneous of degree r

$$f(t\mathbf{x}) = t^r f(\mathbf{x}) \quad \forall \mathbf{x} \in R^n_{++} \quad \forall t > 0$$

For fixed $\mathbf{x} \in R^n_{++}$, differentiate with respect to t

$$\sum_{i=1}^{n} x_i f_i'(t\mathbf{x}) = rt^{r-1} f(\mathbf{x})$$

Putting $t = 1$ gives

$$\sum_{i=1}^{n} x_i f_i'(\mathbf{x}) = rf(\mathbf{x}). \qquad \textit{Q.E.D.}$$

So for homogeneous functions the sum of variables times partial derivatives equals r times the value of the function. We remark (without proof) that this Euler relation is sufficient (as well as necessary) for homogeneity of C^1 functions.

Theorem 9.2 Suppose $f: R^n_{++} \to R$ is C^1 and homogeneous of degree r. Then $f'_i: R^n_{++} \to R$ is homogeneous of degree $r-1$, $i = 1, \ldots, n$.

Proof Since f is homogeneous of degree r

$$f(t\mathbf{x}) = t^r f(\mathbf{x}) \quad \forall \mathbf{x} \in R^n_{++}, \forall t > 0$$

Now fix $t > 0$ and differentiate with respect to x_i:

$$t f'_i(t\mathbf{x}) = t^r f'_i(\mathbf{x})$$

Hence $f'_i(t\mathbf{x}) = t^{r-1} f'_i(\mathbf{x})$ and f'_i is homogeneous of degree $r-1$.
Q.E.D.

This result has a useful geometric consequence most easily seen when $n = 2$. The slope of the contour through $\mathbf{x}$ of a function of two variables at $\mathbf{x}$, assuming $f'_1(\mathbf{x}) \neq 0$, is

$$-\frac{f'_2(\mathbf{x})}{f'_1(\mathbf{x})}$$

So the slope at $t\mathbf{x}$ is

$$-\frac{f'_2(t\mathbf{x})}{f'_1(t\mathbf{x})} = -\frac{t^{r-1} f'_2(\mathbf{x})}{t^{r-1} f'_1(\mathbf{x})} = -\frac{f'_2(\mathbf{x})}{f'_1(\mathbf{x})}$$

The slope of the contour is the same at $\mathbf{x}$ as at $t\mathbf{x}$. Figure 9.1 illustrates this property, which says that for homogeneous functions of two variables, the contours are 'parallel displacements of each other'.

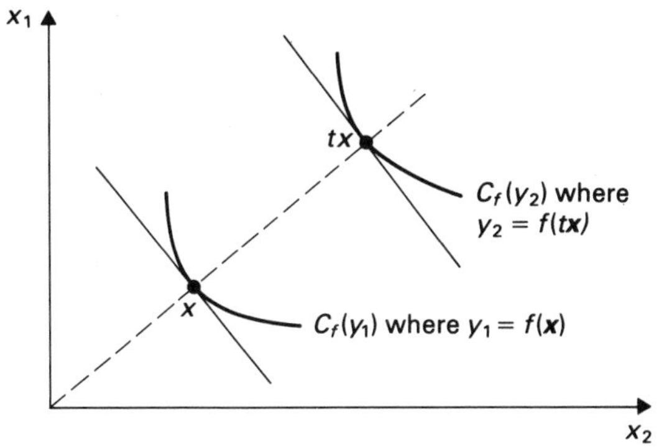

Figure 9.1

Unlike the one-variable case we cannot write down a single simple formula to capture all homogeneous functions of n variables. Shortly we will look at two very well-known classes of functional forms for n-variable homogeneous functions, *the Cobb–Douglas functions* and the *C.E.S. (constant elasticity of substitution) functions*. At the moment, however, we merely note that all such homogeneous functional forms on n variables $(x_1, \ldots, x_n)$, will collapse to the expression kx^r for some k where r is degree of homogeneity and when $x = x_1 = x_2 = \ldots = x_n$. To see why, suppose that $f: R^n_{++} \to R$ is homogeneous of degree r: then,

$$f(tx_1, tx_2, \ldots, tx_n) = t^r f(x_1, \ldots, x_n) \quad \forall \mathbf{x} \in R^n_{++}, \forall t > 0$$

Hence

$$f(tx, tx, \ldots, tx) = t^r f(x, \ldots, x) \quad \forall x \in R_{++}, \forall t > 0$$

Now define $g: R_{++} \to R$ by $g(x) = f(x, \ldots, x)$. This is a one-variable function and from the last equality

$$g(tx) = t^r g(x) \quad \forall x \in R_{++}, \forall t > 0$$

Hence g is a one-variable, homogeneous of degree r function and from (9.1), $g(x) = kx^r$ some $k \in R$. So we do indeed have

$$f(x, x, \ldots, x) = kx^r \quad \text{some } k \in R$$

In particular, the Cobb–Douglas and C.E.S. forms will collapse to such an expression whenever $x_1 = x_2 = \ldots = x_n = x$.

Another of the nice features of the one-variable case fails to generalize: in the many-variable setting homogeneous functions may be neither concave nor convex. For instance, $f: R^2_{++} \to R$ defined by $f(\mathbf{x}) = x_1 x_2$ is homogeneous of degree 2 since $f(t\mathbf{x}) = t^2 x_1 x_2 = t^2 f(\mathbf{x})$. However, the Hessian of f is

$$\begin{bmatrix} 0 & 1 \\ 1 & 0 \end{bmatrix}$$

which is neither p.s.d. nor n.s.d.; recalling the second derivative characterizations, f is neither concave nor convex although it is homogeneous.

Despite this there is a *partial* generalization of property 4 earlier.

Theorem 9.3 Suppose $f: R^n_{++} \to R$ is homogeneous of degree r and positively valued. Then

(a) if f is concave then $0 \leqslant r \leqslant 1$

(b) if f is convex then either $r \leqslant 0$ or $r \geqslant 1$.

Proof Suppose $f: R^n_{++} \to R$ is homogeneous of degree r and positively valued. Define (as earlier), $g: R_{++} \to R$ by

$$g(x) = f(x, x, \ldots, x)$$

From the earlier discussion we know that g is also homogeneous of degree r. For (a) suppose in addition that f is concave. Then, for any $x^1, x^2 \in R$ and for any $\lambda \in [0, 1]$,

$$\begin{aligned} &f[\lambda x^1 + (1-\lambda)x^2, \lambda x^1 + (1-\lambda)x^2, \ldots, \lambda x^1 + (1-\lambda)x^2] \\ &\quad \geqslant \lambda f[x^1, x^1, \ldots, x^1] + (1-\lambda) f[x^2, x^2, \ldots, x^2] \end{aligned}$$

which means

$$g[\lambda x^1 + (1-\lambda)x^2] \geqslant \lambda g(x^1) + (1-\lambda) g(x^2)$$

Hence g is a concave as well as homogeneous of degree r function of one variable. From 4. of section 9.2 it follows that $0 \leqslant r \leqslant 1$. The proof of (b) is similar. *Q.E.D.*

So far we have allowed the degree of homogeneity to be negative, zero or positive. If $r < 0$, homogeneity of degree r requires

$$f(t\mathbf{x}) = \frac{1}{t^{-r}} f(\mathbf{x})$$

If $f(\mathbf{x}) > 0$ (for instance) you see that $f(t\mathbf{x}) \to +\infty$ as $t \to 0$ and $f(0)$ is not defined. This is why so far we have considered only homogeneous functions on the domain R^n_{++}; functions which are homogeneous of negative degree cannot be defined at 0. However, most of the following homogeneous functions will be of degree $r \geqslant 0$ and for such functions there is no problem in extending the domain to R^n_+, for instance, an extension which is sometimes useful later. Hence,

$f: R^n_+ \to R$ is homogeneous of degree $r \geqslant 0$ if and only if

$$f(t\mathbf{x}) = t^r f(\mathbf{x}) \quad \forall t > 0 \text{ and } \forall \mathbf{x} \in R^n_+$$

In the one-variable setting such functions on R_+ must have $f(x) = kx^r$ and must be continuous on R_+ and C^2 on R_{++} (but not necessarily C^2 on R_+ since when $r < 1$ the tangent line to G_f becomes vertical at the origin). In the n-variable case we can assume f is continuous on R^n_+ and C^2 on R^n_{++} and theorems 9.1–9.3 will continue to apply to the restrictions of f to R^n_{++}.

9.4 The Cobb–Douglas functions

This family of functions is defined by $f: R^n_+ \to R$ where $n > 1$ and

$$f(\mathbf{x}) = k \prod_{i=1}^{n} x_i^{\alpha_i} \quad \text{where } k > 0 \text{ and } \alpha_i > 0, i = 1, \ldots, n$$

($\Pi_{i=1}^n$ means 'the continued product of . . .' from $i = 1, \ldots, n$; so when $n = 2$, $f(\mathbf{x}) = kx_1^{\alpha_1}x_2^{\alpha_2}$ while with $n = 3$, $f(\mathbf{x}) = kx_1^{\alpha_1}x_2^{\alpha_2}x_3^{\alpha_3}$, and so on.)

Since $x_i^{\alpha_i}$ where $\alpha_i > 0$ is continuous on R_+ and C^2 on R_{++} it follows that Cobb–Douglas functions are continuous on R^n_+ and C^2 on R^n_{++}. Notice also that $f(\mathbf{x}) = 0$ if some $x_i = 0$, $f(\mathbf{x}) \geqslant 0$, $\forall \mathbf{x} \in R^n_+$ and $f(\mathbf{x}) > 0$, $\forall \mathbf{x} \in R^n_{++}$. The following formula for the first partial derivatives of f is useful later: for $\mathbf{x} \in R^n_{++}$ and $j = 1, \ldots, n$.

$$f'_j(\mathbf{x}) = k\alpha_j x_j^{\alpha_j - 1} \prod_{i \neq j} x_i^{\alpha_i}$$

$$= \frac{k\alpha_j}{x_j} \prod_{i=1}^{n} x_i^{\alpha_i} = \frac{\alpha_j}{x_j} f(\mathbf{x})$$

In particular, $f'_j(\mathbf{x}) > 0$, $\forall \mathbf{x} \in R^n_{++}$, $\forall j = 1, \ldots, n$.

For homogeneity we examine $f(t\mathbf{x})$:

$$f(t\mathbf{x}) = k \prod_{i=1}^{n} (tx_i)^{\alpha_i} = k \prod_{i=1}^{n} t^{\alpha_i} x_i^{\alpha_i}$$

$$= kt^{\Sigma\alpha_i} \prod_{i=1}^{n} x_i^{\alpha_i} = t^{\Sigma\alpha_i} f(\mathbf{x})$$

Hence *f is homogeneous of degree $\Sigma_{i=1}^n \alpha_i$*, notice in particular that a Cobb–Douglas function is linearly homogeneous if and only if the 'sum of the exponents', $\Sigma\alpha_i$ equals one.

From theorem 9.3, and since the Cobb–Douglas function on R^n_{++} is positive valued, we know that when $\Sigma\alpha_i < 1$, f cannot be convex and when $\Sigma\alpha_i > 1$, f cannot be concave. To establish positive results on the concavity (etc.) of the Cobb–Douglas we would need to look at its $n \times n$ Hessian matrix which is a totally frightening prospect. Fortunately there are easier methods, but these will not become available until chapter 13. So for the time being we state, without proof:

Theorem 9.4 A Cobb–Douglas function is concave if and only if $\Sigma_{i=1}^n \alpha_i \leqslant 1$ (i.e. homogeneous of degree $r \leqslant 1$).

When $\Sigma_{i=1}^{n} \alpha_i > 1$ a Cobb–Douglas function is neither concave nor convex. In fact it is then (and so always) *quasi-concave*, and again we fill out this picture in chapter 13. For the time being let us remind the reader that quasi-concave functions always have convex upper contour sets; so the upper contour sets of *any* Cobb–Douglas function are always convex sets.

As a result of all this we know quite a lot about contours of a Cobb–Douglas function. When $n = 2$ and for $y > 0$ we have:

(i) $C_f(y)$ is downward-sloping since $f'_1(\mathbf{x}), f'_2(\mathbf{x}) > 0$, $\forall \mathbf{x} \in R^2_{++}$;

(ii) the set of points on or above $C_f(y)$ is $UC_f(y)$ and is a convex set;

(iii) the equation defining a contour is $kx_1^{\alpha_1}x_2^{\alpha_2} = y$, or

$$x_1 = \frac{y^{1/\alpha_1}}{k^{1/\alpha_1}x_2^{\alpha_2/\alpha_1}}$$

which is a hyperbola in R^2_{++}. As $x_2 \to 0$, $x_1 \to +\infty$ and as $x_1 \to 0$, $x_2 \to +\infty$; the contours are asymptotic to (i.e. tend to) the axes of R^2_{++}.

(iv) The absolute value of the slope of the contour through $\mathbf{x}$ is

$$\frac{f'_2(\mathbf{x})}{f'_1(\mathbf{x})} = \frac{\alpha_2 \, x_1}{\alpha_1 \, x_2}$$

Since f is homogeneous this ratio is the same at $\mathbf{x}$ as at $t\mathbf{x}$ and contours will be 'parallel displacements of each other'.

There is a fifth property worth introducing now, relating to how quickly the contour slope changes as we move along the contour or how 'curved' the contour is. A measure of such curvature is the 'elasticity of substitution', $\sigma(\mathbf{x})$. In fig. 9.2 we have drawn a downward-sloping, convex $UC_f(y)$ contour of an (unspecified) function of two variables. The absolute value of the slope of this contour is larger at the point where it intersects $x_1/x_2 = C_2$ than at its intersection with $x_1/x_2 = C_1$ where $C_2 > C_1$. In other words

$$\frac{\mathrm{d}}{\mathrm{d}(x_1/x_2)}\left[\frac{f'_2(\mathbf{x})}{f'_1(\mathbf{x})}\right] > 0$$

or the absolute value of the slope increases as x_1/x_2 increases. If the contour is 'very flat' we would expect this derivative to be small, and it would be large for 'sharply curved' contours. However, for the same reasons that elasticity of demand is a better measure of the

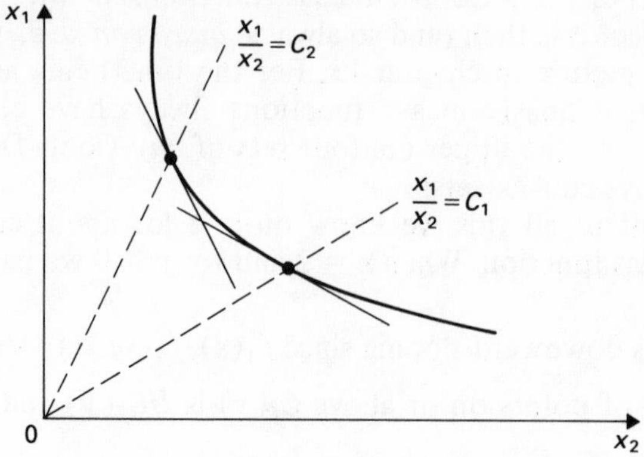

Figure 9.2

price responsiveness of quantity demanded than the slope of the demand curve, consider instead the following 'elasticity' derived from the above derivative:

$$\frac{x_1/x_2}{f_2'(\mathbf{x})/f_1'(\mathbf{x})}\,\frac{\mathrm{d}}{\mathrm{d}(x_1/x_2)}\left[\frac{f_2'(\mathbf{x})}{f_1'(\mathbf{x})}\right]$$

Just to be awkward the *elasticity of substitution* is the *reciprocal* of this measure:

$$\sigma(\mathbf{x}) = \frac{\dfrac{f_2'(\mathbf{x})}{f_1'(\mathbf{x})}\Big/\dfrac{x_1}{x_2}}{\dfrac{\mathrm{d}}{\mathrm{d}(x_1/x_2)}\left[\dfrac{f_2'(\mathbf{x})}{f_1'(\mathbf{x})}\right]}$$

So when $\sigma(\mathbf{x})$ is *low* the contour through $\mathbf{x}$ is 'sharply curved' while when $\sigma(\mathbf{x})$ is *high* the contour is relatively flat. In fact $\sigma(\mathbf{x}) \to 0$ as the contour through $\mathbf{x}$ becomes flat (i.e. a line) while $\sigma(\mathbf{x}) \to +\infty$ as the contour through $\mathbf{x}$ becomes 'L-shaped' (see fig. 9.3).

For two-variable Cobb–Douglas functions $\sigma(\mathbf{x}) = 1,\ \forall x \in R^2_{++}$. This is very, very special: $\sigma(\mathbf{x})$ always and everywhere equals one, no matter what k, α_1, α_2 are. It is easy to see why using the previous slope formula:

$$\sigma(\mathbf{x}) = \frac{\dfrac{f_2'}{f_1'}\Big/\dfrac{x_1}{x_2}}{\dfrac{\mathrm{d}}{\mathrm{d}(x_1/x_2)}\left(\dfrac{f_2'}{f_1'}\right)} = \frac{\dfrac{\alpha_2}{\alpha_1}\dfrac{x_1}{x_2}\Big/\dfrac{x_1}{x_2}}{\dfrac{\mathrm{d}}{\mathrm{d}(x_1/x_2)}\left(\dfrac{\alpha_2 x_1}{\alpha_1 x_2}\right)} = \frac{\alpha_2/\alpha_1}{\alpha_2/\alpha_1} = 1$$

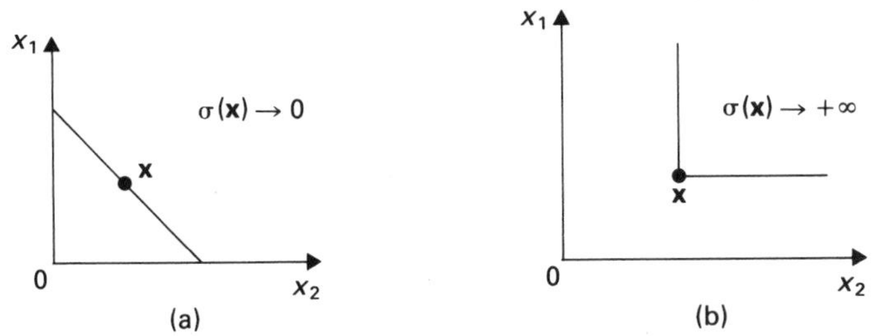

Figure 9.3

Roughly speaking this means that as we move along a contour of a Cobb–Douglas function, to induce a 10% change in x_1/x_2 will require exactly a 10% change in the slope of the contour. This is a very restrictive feature of Cobb–Douglas functions.

9.5 The C.E.S. function

The family of constant elasticity of substitution (C.E.S.) functions is $f: R^n_+ \to R$, $(n > 1)$ defined by $f(0) = 0$ and

$$f(\mathbf{x}) = k\left[\sum_{i=1}^{n} \delta_i x_i^{-\rho}\right]^{-v/\rho} \quad \text{otherwise, where}$$

(a) $k > 0, v > 0$

(b) $\rho > -1$ and $\rho \neq 0$

(c) $\delta_i > 0, \forall i$ and $\sum_{i=1}^{n} \delta_i = 1$

It can be shown that f is continuous on R^n_+ and C^2 on R^n_{++}. In addition $f(0) = 0$, $f(\mathbf{x}) \geqslant 0$, $\forall \mathbf{x} \in R^n_+$ and $f(\mathbf{x}) > 0$, $\forall \mathbf{x} \in R^n_{++}$. Partially differentiating at $\mathbf{x} \in R^n_{++}$, for any $i = 1, \ldots, n$ we get

$$\begin{aligned} f_i'(\mathbf{x}) &= k\left(-\frac{v}{\rho}\right)[\Sigma \delta_i x_i^{-\rho}]^{-(v/\rho)-1}(-\rho \delta_i x_i^{-\rho-1}) \\ &= \frac{kv\delta_i}{x_i^{1+\rho}}[\Sigma \delta_i x_i^{-\rho}]^{-(v/\rho)-1} = \frac{v\delta_i}{x_i^{1+\rho}} \frac{f(\mathbf{x})}{\Sigma \delta_i x_i^{-\rho}} \\ &= \frac{v\delta_i}{x_i^{1+\rho}} \frac{f(\mathbf{x})}{[f(\mathbf{x})/k]^{-\rho/v}} = k^{-\rho/v} v \delta_i \frac{[f(\mathbf{x})]^{1+\rho/v}}{x_i^{1+\rho}} \end{aligned}$$

In the (common) special case $k=v=1$ this becomes

$$f_i'(\mathbf{x}) = \delta_i\left[\frac{f(\mathbf{x})}{x_i}\right]^{1+\rho}$$

We need these formulae later but not too often! Notice that $f_i'(\mathbf{x}) > 0$, $\forall i$ and $\forall \mathbf{x} \in R^n_{++}$.

For homogeneity we evaluate $f(t\mathbf{x})$:

$$f(t\mathbf{x}) = k[\Sigma\delta_i(tx_i)^{-\rho}]^{-v/\rho} = k[t^{-\rho}\Sigma\delta_i x_i^{-\rho}]^{-v/\rho}$$
$$= t^v k[\Sigma\delta_i x_i^{-\rho}]^{-v/\rho} = t^v f(\mathbf{x})$$

Hence *a C.E.S. function is homogeneous of degree v.*

As in the Cobb–Douglas case a C.E.S. function is always quasi-concave, never convex and *concave if and only if it is homogeneous of degree less than or equal to one (i.e. $v \leqslant 1$).* Proofs and further discussion of this are left to the quasi-concavity chapter, later.

The reader will have noticed that $\rho = 0$ is excluded from this discussion obviously because $-v/\rho$ is not then defined. However, it is interesting to ask what happens to a C.E.S. function in *the limit as $\rho \to 0$.* The answer is even more interesting.

Theorem 9.5 In the limit as $\rho \to 0$ a C.E.S. function becomes a Cobb–Douglas function of the same degree of homogeneity. A proof is given at the end of this chapter.

In addition when $\rho = -1$ (the lower bound on its possible values) the C.E.S. function becomes

$$f(\mathbf{x}) = k[\Sigma\delta_i x_i]^v$$

In this case the equation of a contour is

$$k[\Sigma\delta_i x_i]^v = y \quad \text{or} \quad \Sigma\delta_i x_i = \left(\frac{y}{k}\right)^{1/v}$$

which is a hyperplane in R^n. So when $n = 2$ and $\rho = -1$ contours of C.E.S. functions become straight lines; the elasticity of substitution $\sigma(x) \to +\infty$. On the other hand when $\rho \to 0$, contours of C.E.S. functions approach the hyperbolic contours of a Cobb–Douglas function with $\sigma(\mathbf{x}) = 1$. In fact as ρ increases from -1 the contours of a C.E.S. function become more and more 'curved'; i.e. $\sigma(\mathbf{x})$ decreases as ρ increases. The formula linking $\sigma(\mathbf{x})$ and ρ is easily found, using the earlier derivative formula:

$$\sigma(\mathbf{x}) = \frac{\dfrac{f_2'}{f_1'}\bigg/\dfrac{x_1}{x_2}}{\dfrac{\mathrm{d}}{\mathrm{d}(x_1/x_2)}\left(\dfrac{f_2'}{f_1'}\right)} = \frac{\dfrac{\delta_2}{\delta_1}\left(\dfrac{x_1}{x_2}\right)^{1+\rho}\bigg/\dfrac{x_1}{x_2}}{\dfrac{\mathrm{d}}{\mathrm{d}(x_1/x_2)}\left[\dfrac{\delta_2}{\delta_1}\left(\dfrac{x_1}{x_2}\right)^{1+\rho}\right]}$$

$$= \frac{(\delta_2/\delta_1)(x_1/x_2)^{\rho}}{(1+\rho)(\delta_2/\delta_1)(x_1/x_2)^{\rho}} = \frac{1}{1+\rho}$$

The elasticity of substitution for a two-variable C.E.S. function is $\sigma(\mathbf{x}) = (1/(1+\rho)$, $\forall \mathbf{x} \in R^2_{++}$. Here the elasticity is the same everywhere (i.e. $\forall \mathbf{x} \in R^2_{++}$) and so there is a *constant* elasticity of substitution. Note, however, that this varies with the parameter ρ, according to $\sigma(\mathbf{x}) = 1/(1+\rho)$. Notice too that

(i) as $\rho \to -1$, $\sigma(\mathbf{x}) \to +\infty$: this is the linear contour case;

(ii) when $\rho = 0$, $\sigma(\mathbf{x}) = 1$: this is the case where C.E.S. collapses to Cobb–Douglas;

(iii) when $\rho \to +\infty$, $\sigma(\mathbf{x}) \to 0$: we would expect the contours to become L-shaped (like fig. 9.3(b)). A functional form which gives rise to such contours (when $n = 2$) is that of the *Leontief or fixed coefficients function*

$$f : R^n_+ \to R \text{ where } f(\mathbf{x}) = \left\{\min\left[\frac{x_1}{\gamma_1}, \frac{x_2}{\gamma_2}, \ldots, \frac{x_n}{\gamma_n}\right]\right\}^{\alpha}$$

where $\gamma_i > 0$, $\forall i$ and $\alpha > 0$. This is continuous on R^n_+, homogeneous of degree α, always quasi-concave, never convex, and concave if and only if $\alpha \leqslant 1$. However, it is not differentiable even on R^n_{++} which is why it is not given the same attention as earlier cases. When $n = 2$ the typical contour is

$$y = \left\{\min\left[\frac{x_1}{\gamma_1}, \frac{x_2}{\gamma_2}\right]\right\}^{\alpha} \quad \text{or} \quad y^{1/\alpha} = \begin{cases} \dfrac{x_1}{\gamma_1} \text{ if } x_1 \leqslant \dfrac{\gamma_1}{\gamma_2} x_2 \\ \dfrac{x_2}{\gamma_2} \text{ if } x_1 \geqslant \dfrac{\gamma_1}{\gamma_2} x_2 \end{cases}$$

or

$$x_1 = \gamma_1 y^{1/\alpha} \quad \text{when } x_1 \leqslant \frac{\gamma_1}{\gamma_2} x_2$$

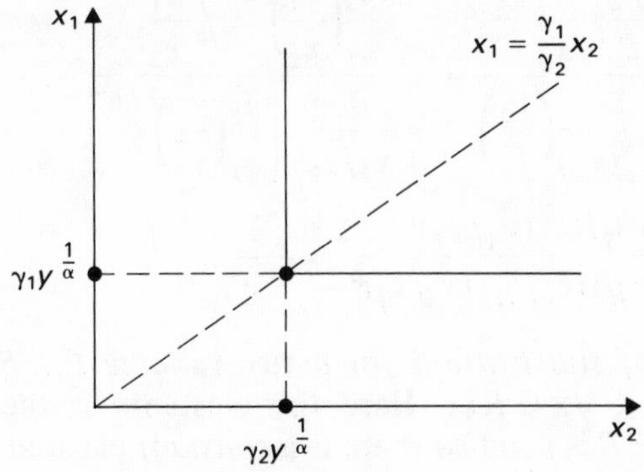

Figure 9.4

and

$$x_2 = \gamma_2 y^{1/\alpha} \quad \text{when } x_1 \geqslant \frac{1}{\gamma_2} x_2$$

Figure 9.4 provides a sketch, confirming the L-shape.

It can be shown (details omitted) that a C.E.S. function becomes a Leontief function with the same degree of homogeneity in the limit as $\rho \to +\infty$, as the behaviour of $\sigma(\mathbf{x})$ had led us to expect.

So C.E.S. functions (like Cobb–Douglas) have the same value of $\sigma(\mathbf{x})$ throughout R^2_{++}. Unlike Cobb–Douglas, however, this value varies as the parameter ρ varies, allowing a full range of C.E.S. contour shapes from straight lines at one extreme to L-shapes at the other.

9.6 Proof of theorem 9.5

The proof uses the following well-known result:

L'Hopital's rule: Suppose g and h are two C^1 functions of one variable, t say, where

$$\text{(i) } g(t^*) = h(t^*) = 0 \quad \text{and} \quad \text{(ii) } h'(t^*) \neq 0$$

Then

$$\lim_{t \to t^*} \frac{g(t)}{h(t)} = \lim_{t \to t^*} \frac{g'(t)}{h'(t)}$$

That is, the limit of the ratio of two functions is the limit of the ratio of their derivatives. We now apply this to prove theorem 9.5, as follows

Suppose f is C.E.S. Then for $\mathbf{x} \in R^n_{++}$,

$$\ln f = \ln k - v \frac{\ln[\Sigma \delta_i x_i^{-\rho}]}{\rho}$$

We can use l'Hopital's rule to evaluate

$$\lim_{\rho \to 0} \frac{\ln[\Sigma \delta_i x_i^{-\rho}]}{\rho}$$

The derivative of the bottom line is 1. Using the fact that $(\mathrm{d}/\mathrm{d}\rho) x_i^{-\rho} = -x_i^{-\rho} \ln x_i$ [exercise: prove that] the derivative of the top line with respect to ρ is

$$\frac{-\Sigma \delta_i x_i^{-\rho} \ln x_i}{\Sigma \delta_i x_i^{-\rho}}$$

and from l'Hopital's rule the desired limit is,

$$\lim_{\rho \to 0} \frac{-\Sigma \delta_i x_i^{-\rho} \ln x_i}{\Sigma \delta_i x_i^{-\rho}} = -\frac{\Sigma \delta_i \ln x_i}{\Sigma \delta_i} \quad \text{since } x_i^0 = 1$$

$$= -\Sigma \delta_i \ln x_i \text{ since } \Sigma \delta_i = 1$$

Hence as $\rho \to 0$, $\ln f$ converges to

$$\ln k + v \sum_{i=1}^{n} \delta_i \ln x_i = \ln \left\{ k \prod_{i=1}^{n} x_i^{v\delta_i} \right\}$$

and so f converges to $k \Pi_{i=1}^n x_i^{v\delta_i}$, which is Cobb–Douglas, homogeneous of degree $\Sigma v \delta_i = v \Sigma \delta_i = v$. *Q.E.D.*

Exercise 9

1. Find whether the following functions $f: R^n_{++} \to R$ are homogeneous or not, and if so state the degree

   (a) $f(\mathbf{x}) = \sum_{i=1}^{n} \alpha_i \ln x_i \quad$ where $\alpha_i > 0$, $i = 1, \ldots, n$

   (b) $f(\mathbf{x}) = \left(\sum_{i=1}^{n} x_i^4 \right)^{1/2}$

(c) $f(\mathbf{x}) = g(\mathbf{x})/h(\mathbf{x})$ where g is homogeneous of degree r_1 and h is homogeneous of degree r_2.

2. $f: R^2_{++} \to R$ is C^1 and linearly homogeneous. Show using Euler's theorem that the Hessian of f is singular (i.e. the determinant of the Hessian is zero).

3. Compute the elasticity of substitution for $f: R^2_{++} \to R$ where $f(\mathbf{x}) = x_1^2 + x_2^2$.

4. (a) Using Euler's theorem and the first derivative characterization of concave functions, prove that the linearly homogeneous, C^1 function $f: R^n_{++} \to R$ is concave if and only if $\mathbf{x}f'(\mathbf{x}^*) \geqslant f(\mathbf{x}), \forall \mathbf{x}, \mathbf{x}^* \in R^n_{++}$.
   (b) Hence show that the linearly homogeneous, Cobb–Douglas function ($f(x) = k \prod_{i=1}^n x_i^{\alpha_i}$ where $k > 0$, $\alpha_i > 0$ for all i and $\Sigma\alpha_i = 1$) is concave using also exercise 7, question 4(a).

10 Theory of the firm

10.1 Introduction

A firm is an economic entity which transforms inputs of goods into outputs of goods by some production process. For simplicity, although most aspects can be generalized, we assume that the firm can produce quantities, denoted x_0, of a single output from quantities of n inputs, denoted $\mathbf{x} = (x_1, \ldots, x_n)$. All such quantities correspond to the physical magnitude of output produced or inputs used; hence throughout $x_0 \in R_+$ and $\mathbf{x} \in R_+^n$, so $(x_0, \mathbf{x}) \in R_+^{n+1}$. $(x_0, \mathbf{x})$ is then an $n+1$-dimensional vector indicating output produced and inputs used, and is referred to as a *production plan*. Not all production plans in R_+^{n+1} are feasible for the firm, and our assumption is that the only such plans which are feasible are those which satisfy the additional constraint

$$x_0 \leqslant f(\mathbf{x})$$

Here $f: R_+^n \to R$ is known as the firm's *production function*; $f(\mathbf{x})$ measures the maximum attainable output from the input vector, $\mathbf{x}$. A production plan is feasible for the firm if and only if it belongs to the firm's *production set*, Y, where

$$Y = \{(x_0, \mathbf{x}) \in R_+^{n+1} | x_0 \leqslant f(\mathbf{x})\}$$

The production set (and the production function) are intended to reflect the firm's 'technological' knowledge regarding transformations of inputs into output, and indeed Y is sometimes referred to as the firm's technology. It is purely an 'engineering' type of concept and we take it to be a datum of our model of the firm; i.e. a firm's technology is given and is not 'explained'.

We assume that the firm buys inputs and sells output on markets where the prices are respectively $(p_1, \ldots, p_n) = \mathbf{p}$ and p_0: throughout we assume all these prices are strictly positive so $(p_0, \mathbf{p}) R_{++}^{n+1}$.

We also assume that the firm can (in principle, but subject to its technology constraint) buy and sell any quantities on these $n+1$ markets at the prices $(p_0, \mathbf{p})$. However, it cannot control the prices at which it trades on these markets; that is all prices are parameters for, or parametric to, the firm. These two assumptions of parametric prices and no market restrictions on quantities are intended to reflect the economist's notion of perfect competition; consequently firms will be perfect competitors in this sense throughout our discussion.

The production plan $(x_0, \mathbf{x})$ requires the firm to incur costs $\Sigma_{i=1}^n p_i x_i$ to buy the inputs so as to acquire revenue $p_0 x_0$ from the sale of output. *Profits* are therefore $p_0 x_0 - \Sigma_{i=1}^n p_i x_i$. The crucial assumption which generates our model of firm behaviour is that the firm chooses its production plan so as to maximize profits subject to the technology constraint given the parametric prices. Expressing this concisely, we get

$$\text{(FP)} \qquad \max_{(x_0, \mathbf{x}) \in R_+^{n+1}} p_0 x_0 - \sum_{i=1}^{n} p_i x_i \quad \text{subject to } x_0 \leqslant f(\mathbf{x})$$
$$\text{where } (p_0, \mathbf{p}) R_{++}^{n+1}$$

This is a parameterized family of maximization problems and naturally we will be using the techniques of chapter 8 to analyse behaviour of the firm.

10.2 The production function

We make a number of assumptions about the production function (and hence the production set or technology).

(A10.1) $f: R_+^n \to R$ is continuous on R_+^n, C^2 on R_{++}^n and $f(0) = 0$

The assumption that $f(0) = 0$ is natural: the firm can get no output if it uses no inputs. The other parts of (A10.1) are for technical convenience.

(A10.2) For all $\mathbf{x} \in R_{++}^n$, $f_i'(\mathbf{x}) > 0$, $i = 1, \ldots, n$

$f_i'(\mathbf{x})$ is referred to as the *marginal product* of input i at $\mathbf{x}$ and measures the rate of change of output as the quantity of input i is increased from x_i, quantities of other inputs remaining fixed. (A10.2) tells us that such an increase in x_i leads to an *increase* in output and is therefore the assumption that inputs are *productive* in the sense that more input gives more output. (A10.1) and (A10.2) imply that $f(\mathbf{x}) > 0$, $\forall \mathbf{x} \in R^n_{++}$.

(A10.3) f is a strictly concave function on R^n_{++}.

From theorem 7.1 it follows from (A10.1) and (A10.3) that f is concave on R^n_+.

(A10.3) is probably the least defensible of these three assumptions with the real world in mind. Coupled with the other assumptions it implies that the production set is typically as shown in fig. 10.1, when $n = 1$ (i.e. when the firm uses only one input). When $n = 2$ the contours of the production function are typically as shown in fig. 10.2.

Contours of production functions are referred to in economics as *isoquants*; fig. 10.2 is then a typical isoquant map under our assumptions when $n = 2$.

(A10.3) has consequences for the economist's concept of returns to scale. A production function $f: R^n_+ \to R$ is said to exhibit decreasing returns to scale if

$$f(t\mathbf{x}) < tf(\mathbf{x}) \quad \forall t > 1, \forall \mathbf{x} \in R^n_+ \text{ except } \mathbf{x} = 0$$

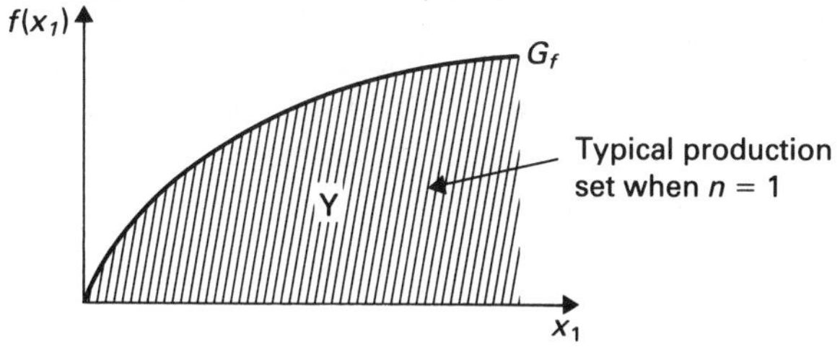

Figure 10.1

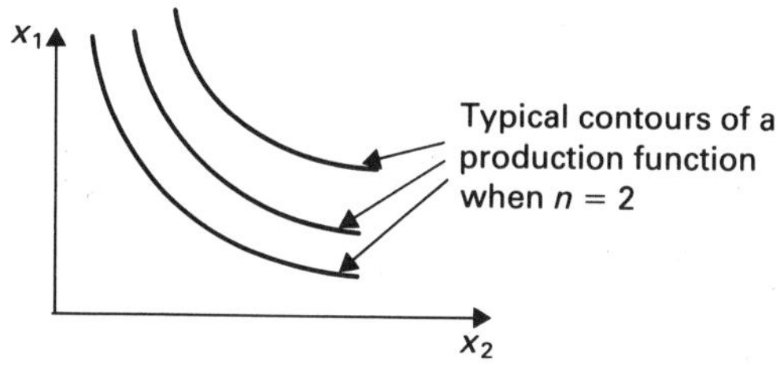

Figure 10.2

For instance with $t = 2$ this requires that doubling all input levels leads to less than double the output level. Increasing returns to scale requires $f(t\mathbf{x}) > tf(\mathbf{x})\ \forall t > 1$ and $\forall \mathbf{x} \in R^n$ except $\mathbf{x} = 0$ while constant returns is equivalent to linear homogeneity.

Theorem 10.1 If a production function satisfies (A10.1) and (A10.3) then the production function exhibits either constant or decreasing returns to scale.

Proof Choose any $t > 1$ and any $\mathbf{x} \in R^n_+$ where $\mathbf{x} \neq 0$. Then $1/t \in (0, 1)$ and $\mathbf{x} = (1/t)(t\mathbf{x}) + [1 - (1/t)]\,0$, trivially. Since f is concave on R^n_+,

$$f(\mathbf{x}) = f\left[\frac{1}{t}(t\mathbf{x}) + \left(1 - \frac{1}{t}\right)0\right] \geqslant \frac{1}{t}f(t\mathbf{x}) + \left(1 - \frac{1}{t}\right)f(0) = \frac{1}{t}f(t\mathbf{x})$$

Hence $f(t\mathbf{x}) \leqslant tf(\mathbf{x})$ and since this is true $\forall t > 1$ and $\forall \mathbf{x} \in R^n_+$ except $\mathbf{x} = 0$, the theorem follows. *Q.E.D.*

So, amongst other things, our assumptions rule out increasing returns. Often it is argued by economists that, at least in some real world situations and at least for low levels of output, doubling inputs will lead to more than double the output; i.e. there are increasing returns at least over some part of the domain of the production function. The reader should note therefore that results derived from (A10.1)–(A10.3) will not (necessarily) apply to such situations. Despite this we assume (A10.1)–(A10.3) in most of our firm discussions. In fact since f is strictly concave on R^n_{++} it also follows from (A10.1)–(A10.3) that

$$f(t\mathbf{x}) < tf(\mathbf{x}) \quad \forall t > 1 \text{ and } \forall \mathbf{x} \in R^n_{++}$$

and f exhibits (strictly) decreasing returns at least on R^n_{++}. So constant returns are also excluded by our assumptions. However, this is mainly a technical convenience to help generate unique solutions to (FP) shortly.

Two examples of functional forms which satisfy (A10.1)–(A10.3) are:

(a) The Cobb–Douglas production function, $f: R^n_+ \to R$ where

$$f(\mathbf{x}) = k \prod_{i=1}^{n} x_i^{\alpha_i}$$

where $\alpha_i > 0$, $\forall i$ and $\Sigma\alpha_i < 1$ and $k > 0$

(b) The C.E.S. production function, $f: R^n_+ \to R$ where

$$f(\mathbf{x}) = k\left[\sum_{i=1}^{n} \delta_i x_i^{-\rho}\right]^{-v/\rho}$$

where $\delta_i \in (0, 1)$, $\forall i$, $\sum_{i=1}^{n} \delta_i = 1$, $k > 0$, $v \in (0, 1)$ and $\rho > -1$, $\rho \neq 0$.

See chapter 9 for a detailed discussion of these functional forms. Of course both of these are also homogeneous. Notice generally that if the degree of homogeneity of a production function is 1 we have constant returns, while non-increasing returns follow from homogeneity of degree less than 1 (and homogeneity of degree greater than 1 would imply non-decreasing returns).

10.3 The profit maximization problem

As stated in the introduction, the basic assumption of our theory of the firm is that the firm chooses the input levels it buys and uses and the output level it produces and sells so as to solve the optimization problem (FP) given the prices of output and inputs

$$\text{(FP)} \qquad \max_{(x_0, \mathbf{x}) \in R^{n+1}_+} p_0 x_0 - \Sigma p_i x_i \quad \text{subject to } x_0 \leqslant f(\mathbf{x})$$
$$\text{where } (p_0, \mathbf{p}) \in R^{n+1}_{++}$$

Technically speaking we have an immediate difficulty in that the domain of this problem, namely R^{n+1}_+, is not open. One way out of this would be to find extra assumptions which ensured that any solution to (FP) must in fact belong to R^{n+1}_{++}. Such assumptions will be studied eventually (see section 11.5); for the time being we merely assume

(A10.4) For all $(p_0, \mathbf{p}) \in R^{n+1}_{++}$, any solution to (FP) must belong to R^{n+1}_{++}

We remark (see section 11.5) that if in addition to (A10.1)–(A10.3) f is Cobb–Douglas or C.E.S. then (A10.4) will be satisfied. (A10.4) ensures that FP is now equivalent to the following open domain problem:

$$\max_{(x_0, \mathbf{x}) \in R^{n+1}_{++}} p_0 x_0 - \Sigma p_i x_i \quad \text{subject to } x_0 \leqslant f(\mathbf{x})$$
$$\text{where } (p_0, \mathbf{p}) \in R^{n+1}_{++} \qquad (10.1)$$

For this problem the objective function is concave and non-stationary (linear); the constraint function is concave (since f is concave); and (CQ) is satisfied (by e.g. $(\mathbf{x}, 0)$, $\mathbf{x} \in R^n_{++}$ since then $f(\mathbf{x}) > 0$). Hence solutions are characterized by the usual (K–T) conditions for such problems. The Lagrangean is

$$L(x_0, \mathbf{x}, \lambda; p_0, \mathbf{p}) = p_0 x_0 - \Sigma p_i x_i + \lambda[f(\mathbf{x}) - x_0]$$

And (K–T) are: $\exists\, \lambda^*$ such that

(I) $p_0 - \lambda^* = 0; \quad -p_i + \lambda^* f_i'(\mathbf{x}^*) = 0,\ i = 1, \ldots, n$

(II) $\lambda^* > 0$ and

(III) $(x_0^*, \mathbf{x}^*) \in R^{n+1}_{++}$ and $f(\mathbf{x}^*) - x_0^* = 0$

From (I), $\lambda^* = p_0 > 0$ and (II) is redundant. Substituting $\lambda^* = p_0$ elsewhere in (I) gives:

Theorem 10.2 Assuming (A10.1)–(A10.4), $(x_0^*, \mathbf{x}^*)$ solves (FP) at $(p_0, \mathbf{p})$ if and only if

(a) $p_0 f_i'(\mathbf{x}^*) = p_i,\ i = 1, \ldots, n$ and $x^* \in R^n_{++}$

(b) $x_0^* = f(\mathbf{x}^*)$

(with $\lambda^* = p_0$).

This theorem characterizes the profit-maximizing production plan for a firm at prices $(p_0, \mathbf{p})$ under our assumptions. As we now see the characterization makes good intuitive sense. For instance condition (b) tells us that the firm produces 'on the production function' rather than 'inside the production set'; the latter would effectively involve the firm throwing away output and is obviously inconsistent with profit maximization since $p_0 > 0$. In condition (a), $p_0 f_i'(\mathbf{x}^*)$ is the value of the marginal product of input i, $VMP_i(\mathbf{x}^*)$. To maximize profits (a) tells us that this should equal the price of input i for all $i = 1, \ldots, n$ at the chosen production plan. If this were not so and $VMP_i(\mathbf{x}^*) > p_i$ some $i = 1, \ldots, n$, a small increase in the use of input i (and hence in output to satisfy (b)) would lead to a rate of increase of additional revenue of $VMP_i(\mathbf{x}^*)$ and a rate of increase of costs of p_i; since $VMP_i(\mathbf{x}^*) > p_i$, profits would be increased. Similarly a small reduction in x_i^* when $VMP_i(\mathbf{x}^*) < p_i$ leads to increased profits and indeed we should have $VMP_i(\mathbf{x}^*) = p_i$, for all $i = 1, \ldots, n$ for a profit maximum.

Alternatively we can depict the solution to (FP) visually when $n=1$, as in fig. 10.3. The feasible set for (FP) is the production set Y. Contours of the objective function are linear ($p_0x_0-p_1x_1=y$) with positive slope (p_1/p_0) and the value of the objective function increases as we move 'north-west' in fig. 10.3. Clearly x_0^*, x_1^* is then the solution to (FP) as shown in fig. 10.3. This is 'on the production function', i.e. $x_0^*=f(x_1^*)$, and at this point the slope of the contour, p_1/p_0, equals the slope of the production function $f'(x_1^*)$ and so conditions (a) and (b) are satisfied.

10.4 Output supply, input demand and profit functions

The firm's profit maximization problem (FP) gives rise to a family of maximization problems, for $(p_0, \mathbf{p}) \in R_{++}^{n+1}$, each one of which has solution characterized by the Kuhn–Tucker conditions which led to the simple and intuitive characterization of such solutions in the last section. In this section we apply the methods of chapter 8 to analyse the functions thrown up by the solutions to this family of problems. To proceed in this direction we need the additional property that for every $(p_0, \mathbf{p}) \in R_{++}^{n+1}$ there is exactly one solution to (FP). The following gives us part of this property:

Lemma 10.1 If (A10.1)–(A10.3) are satisfied then there is at most one solution to (FP) for any $(p_0, \mathbf{p}) \in R_{++}^{n+1}$.

Proof Suppose not, and let $(x_0^1, \mathbf{x}^1) \neq (x_0^2, \mathbf{x}^2)$ be two solutions to (FP) at $(p_0, \mathbf{p})$. Then

(a) $p_0x_0^1 - \Sigma p_i x_i^1 = p_0 x_0^2 - \Sigma p_i x_i^2$

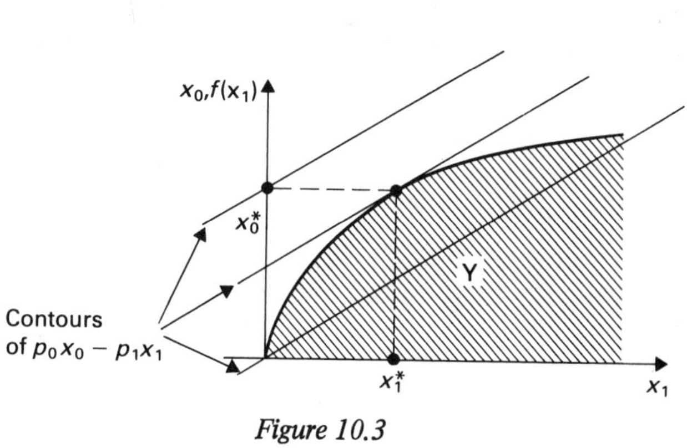

Figure 10.3

(b) $(x_0^1, \mathbf{x}^1), (x_0^2, \mathbf{x}^2) \in R_+^{n+1}$

(c) $f(\mathbf{x}^1) - x_0^1 = 0$ and $f(\mathbf{x}^2) - x_0^2 = 0$

From (c) we must have $\mathbf{x}^1 \neq \mathbf{x}^2$ and since f is strictly concave

$$f[\lambda \mathbf{x}^1 + (1-\lambda)\mathbf{x}^2] > \lambda f(\mathbf{x}^1) + (1-\lambda) f(\mathbf{x}^2) \quad \forall \lambda \in (0,1)$$
$$= \lambda x_0^1 + (1-\lambda) x_0^2$$

Hence for $\lambda \in (0,1)$ and for some $\epsilon > 0$, $f[\lambda \mathbf{x}^1 + (1-\lambda)\mathbf{x}^2] \geqslant \lambda x_0^1 + (1-\lambda)x_0^2 + \epsilon$ and $(x_0, \mathbf{x}) = (\lambda x_0^1 + (1-\lambda) x_0^2 + \epsilon,\ \lambda \mathbf{x}^1 + (1-\lambda)\mathbf{x}^2) \in R_+^{n+1}$; so $(x_0, \mathbf{x})$ is a feasible production plan. It would give profits

$$p_0 x_0 - \Sigma p_i x_i = \lambda[p_0 x_0^1 - \Sigma p_i x_i^1] + (1-\lambda)[p_0 x_0^2 - \Sigma p_i x_i^2] + p_0 \epsilon$$
$$= \text{(from (a))}\ p_0 x_0^1 - \Sigma p_i x_i^1 + p_0 \epsilon > p_0 x_0^1 - \Sigma p_i x_i^1$$

Hence $(x_0^1, \mathbf{x}^1)$ cannot be a profit-maximizing plan, a contradiction. Therefore there is at most one solution to (FP). *Q.E.D.*

However, we need there to be exactly one solution: for now we merely assume,

(A10.5) For all $(p_0, \mathbf{p}) \in R_{++}^{n+1}$ there is at least one solution to (FP)

In actual examples we can check this by verifying that K–T can be satisfied for any $(p_0, \mathbf{p}) \in R_{++}^{n+1}$; much later we will look at results which will give sufficient conditions to ensure (A10.5)–see chapter 17. For the time being in our general discussion we merely assume it. Coupled with lemma 10.1 it ensures that there is exactly one solution to (FP) for all $(p_0, \mathbf{p}) \in R_{++}^{n+1}$. Hence it now follows that the solutions to (FP) define the following set of functions.

1. The solution functions $x_i^*: R_{++}^{n+1} \to R$ with values $x_i^*(p_0, \mathbf{p})$, $i = 0, \ldots, n$. The function x_0^* here is the firm's *output supply function* while x_i^*, $i = 1, \ldots, n$ are the firm's *input demand functions*.
2. The optimal value function, traditionally denoted (instead of V) $\Pi: R_{++}^{n+1} \to R$ with values $\Pi(p_0, \mathbf{p}) = p_0 x_0^*(p_0, \mathbf{p}) - \Sigma_{i=1}^n p_i x_i^*(p_0, \mathbf{p})$. Π is the firm's *profit function*.
3. The multiplier function, $\lambda^*: R_{++}^{n+1} \to R$ with values $\lambda^*(p_0, \mathbf{p})$. This has no particular new name; indeed most interest will focus on 1 and 2 above.

Examples 10.1 These are the same as examples 8.2(a) and (b) except for notation.

(a) The production function is $f: R_+ \to R$ where $f(x_1) = x_1^{1/2}$ and satisfies (A10.1)–(A10.3); f is Cobb-Douglas so (A10.4) is satisfied too. Hence (x_0, x_1) solves (FP) at (p_0, p_1) if and only if

(1) $p_0 \frac{1}{2} x_1^{-1/2} = p_1$; $x_1 > 0$

(2) $x_0 = x_1^{1/2}$

From (1) $x_1^* = p_0^2/4p_1^2$ and from (2) $x_0^* = p_0/2p_1$. Hence $x_0^*(p_0, p_1) = p_0/2p_1$, $x_1^*(p_0, p_1) = p_0^2/4p_1^2$, $\Pi(p_0, p_1) = p_0^2/4p_1$, $\lambda^*(p_0, p_1) = p_0$.

(b) The production function is $f: R_+^2 \to R$ where $f(\mathbf{x}) = x_1^{1/4} x_2^{1/4}$ and satisfies (A10.1)–(A10.4). $(x_0, \mathbf{x})$ solves FP at $(p_0, \mathbf{p})$ if and only if

(1) $p_0 \frac{1}{4} x_1^{-3/4} x_2^{1/4} = p_1$

$p_0 \frac{1}{4} x_1^{1/4} x_2^{-3/4} = p_2$; $x_1 > 0$, $x_2 > 0$

(2) $x_0 = x_1^{1/4} x_2^{1/4}$

Solving (as earlier) gives

$$x_0^*(p_0, \mathbf{p}) = \frac{p_0}{4 p_1^{1/2} p_2^{1/2}}, \quad x_1^*(p_0, \mathbf{p}) = \frac{p_0^2}{16 p_1^{1/2} p_2^{3/2}},$$

$$x_2^*(p_0, \mathbf{p}) = \frac{p_0^2}{16 p_1^{3/2} p_2^{1/2}}, \quad \Pi(p_0, \mathbf{p}) = \frac{p_0^2}{8 p_1^{1/2} p_2^{1/2}}$$

and $\lambda^*(p_0, \mathbf{p}) = p_0$

In these examples and generally under assumptions (A10.1)–(A10.5), $x_0^*(p_0, \mathbf{p})$ tells us the profit-maximizing output level at prices $(p_0, \mathbf{p})$ and $x_i^*(p_0, \mathbf{p})$, $i = 1, \ldots, n$ tell us the profit-maximizing input levels at these prices. The issue of most interest to economists is: how do these output supplies and input demands vary as prices change? In economics this is known as the *comparative statics* question. We provide an answer by uncovering various properties of output supply and input demand functions using the methods suggested in chapter 8. To do this we have to assume suitable differentiability of the functions thrown up by (FP).

(A10.6) (i) For $i = 0, \ldots, n$, $x_i^*: R_{++}^{n+1} \to R$ is C^1.

(ii) $\Pi: R_{++}^{n+1} \to R$ is C^2.

(iii) $\lambda^*: R_{++}^{n+1} \to R$ is C^1

Once again we can check this in examples: it is certainly true in example 10.1 for instance. Later (chapter 17) we shall look at general results which give sufficient conditions for (A10.6); in fact 'almost always' when (A10.1)–(A10.5) are satisfied, (A10.6) will follow.

At last we are in a position to carry through the strategy suggested in chapter 8. First we apply the envelope theorem to (FP) giving directly:

Theorem 10.3: Hotelling's lemma Assume (A10.1)–(A10.6). Then

(i) $\Pi_0'(p_0, \mathbf{p}) = x_0^*(p_0, \mathbf{p}), \forall (p_0, \mathbf{p}) \in R_{++}^{n+1}$

(ii) for $i = 1, \ldots, n$, $\Pi_i'(p_0, \mathbf{p}) = -x_i^*(p_0, \mathbf{p}), \forall (p_0, \mathbf{p}) \in R_{++}^{n+1}$

Proof The Lagrangean for (FP) is

$$p_0 x_0 - \sum_{i=1}^{n} p_i x_i + \lambda[f(\mathbf{x}) - x_0]$$

Differentiating with respect to p_0 gives x_0 and hence (i) from the envelope theorem; similarly differentiating with respect to p_i gives $-x_i$ and (ii) follows. *Q.E.D.*

Next notice (or believe) that the profit functions in example 10.1 are both *convex* functions. This is no fluke:

Theorem 10.4 Assume (A10.1)–(A10.5). Then the profit function $\Pi : R_{++}^{n+1} \to R$ is a convex function.

Proof For shorthand we write $(p_0, \mathbf{p})$ merely as $\mathbf{p}$ in this proof. We have to show,

$$\Pi[\lambda \mathbf{p}^1 + (1-\lambda)\mathbf{p}^2] \leqslant \lambda \Pi(\mathbf{p}^1) + (1-\lambda)\Pi(\mathbf{p}^2)$$
$$\forall \lambda \in [0, 1], \forall \mathbf{p}^1, \mathbf{p}^2 \in R_{++}^{n+1}$$

Let $(x_0, \mathbf{x})$ be a solution to (FP) at prices $\lambda \mathbf{p}^1 + (1-\lambda)\mathbf{p}^2$ where $\lambda \in [0, 1]$ and $\mathbf{p}^1, \mathbf{p}^2 \in R_{++}^{n+1}$. Then $(x_0, \mathbf{x})$ must be feasible for (FP) and

$$\begin{aligned}\Pi[\lambda \mathbf{p}^1 + (1-\lambda)\mathbf{p}^2] &= x_0(\lambda p_0^1 + (1-\lambda)p_0^2) \\ &\quad - \sum_{i=1}^{n} x_i(\lambda p_i^1 + (1-\lambda)p_i^2) \\ &= \lambda[p_0^1 x_0 - \Sigma p_i^1 x_i] + (1-\lambda)[p_0^2 x_0 - \Sigma p_i^2 x_i]\end{aligned}$$

But $p_0^1 x_0 - \Sigma p_i^1 x_i$ is the profits accruing from the (feasible) production plan $(x_0, \mathbf{x})$ at prices $\mathbf{p}^1$ and this cannot exceed the maximum profits attainable at $\mathbf{p}^1$. Hence

$$\Pi(\mathbf{p}^1) \geqslant p_0^1 x_0 - \sum_{i=1}^{n} p_i^1 x_i$$

and similarly

$$\Pi(\mathbf{p}^2) \geqslant p_0^2 x_0 - \sum_{i=1}^{n} p_i^2 x_i$$

Therefore $\Pi[\lambda \mathbf{p}^1 + (1-\lambda)\mathbf{p}^2] \leqslant \lambda \Pi(\mathbf{p}^1) + (1-\lambda)\Pi(\mathbf{p}^2)$; since this is true for any $\lambda \in [0, 1]$ and for all $\mathbf{p}^1, \mathbf{p}^2 \in R_{++}^{n+1}$, it follows that Π is convex. *Q.E.D.*

Assuming (A10.1)–(A10.6) we can now proceed as follows:

(a) From theorem 10.4 the Hessian of Π, $\mathbf{\Pi}''(p_0, \mathbf{p})$ is p.s.d., $\forall (p_0, \mathbf{p}) \in R_{++}^{n+1}$; this matrix is also symmetric since it is the Hessian of a C^2 function.

(b) From theorem 10.3 we get

$$\mathbf{\Pi}''(p_0, \mathbf{p}) = \begin{bmatrix} \Pi''_{00} \dots \Pi''_{0n} \\ \Pi''_{10} \dots \Pi''_{1n} \\ \dots \\ \Pi''_{n0} \dots \Pi''_{nn} \end{bmatrix} = \begin{bmatrix} \dfrac{\partial x_0^*}{\partial p_n} & \dots & \dfrac{\partial x_0^*}{\partial p_n} \\ -\dfrac{\partial x_1^*}{\partial p_0} & \dots & -\dfrac{\partial x_1^*}{\partial p_n} \\ & \dots & \\ -\dfrac{\partial x_n^*}{\partial p_0} & \dots & -\dfrac{\partial x_n^*}{\partial p_n} \end{bmatrix}$$

where all derivatives are evaluated at $(p_0, \mathbf{p})$.

(c) We can conclude that the following matrix is symmetric and p.s.d., $\forall (p_0, \mathbf{p}) \in R_{++}^{n+1}$

$$\mathbf{T}(p_0, \mathbf{p}) = \begin{bmatrix} \dfrac{\partial x_0^*}{\partial p_0} & \dots & \dfrac{\partial x_0^*}{\partial p_n} \\ -\dfrac{\partial x_1^*}{\partial p_0} & \dots & \dfrac{\partial x_1^*}{\partial p_n} \\ & \dots & \\ -\dfrac{\partial x_n^*}{\partial p_0} & \dots & -\dfrac{\partial x_n^*}{\partial p_n} \end{bmatrix} \tag{10.2}$$

where derivatives in the matrix are evaluated at $(p_0, \mathbf{p})$.

Hence we have shown:

Theorem 10.5 Assuming (A10.1)–(A10.6) the matrix $\mathbf{T}(p_0, \mathbf{p})$ defined in (10.2) is symmetric and p.s.d. for all $(p_0, \mathbf{p}) R^{n+1}_{++}$.

This is the central result in the comparative statics of the theory of the firm. Shortly we shall spell out some of its consequences. First we note that the solution functions and optimal value function of (FP) possess homogeneity properties:

Theorem 10.6 Assuming (A10.1)–(A10.5)

(a) for $i = 0, \ldots, n$, $x_i^*: R^{n+1}_{++} \to R$ is homogeneous of degree 0

(b) $\Pi: R^{n+1}_{++} \to R$ is homogeneous of degree 1.

Proof (a) From theorem 10.2 $(x_0^*, \mathbf{x}^*)$ solves (FP) at $(p_0, \mathbf{p})$ if and only if

$$p_0 f_i'(\mathbf{x}^*) = p_i,\ i = 1, \ldots, n;\ \mathbf{x}^* \in R^n_{++}$$

and

$$x_0^* = f(\mathbf{x}^*)$$

For $(tp_0, t\mathbf{p})$ where $t > 0$, $(x_0, \mathbf{x})$ solves (FP) if and only if

$$tp_0 f_i'(\mathbf{x}) = tp_i,\ i = 1, \ldots, n;\ \mathbf{x} \in R^n_{++}$$

$$x_0 = f(\mathbf{x})$$

t cancels in the first equation and so $(x_0^*, \mathbf{x}^*)$ solves (FP) at $(tp_0, t\mathbf{p})$ as well as at $(p_0, \mathbf{p})$. Hence for any $t > 0$,

$$x_0^*(tp_0, t\mathbf{p}) = x_0^*(p_0, \mathbf{p})$$

and

$$x_i^*(tp_0, t\mathbf{p}) = x_i^*(p_0, \mathbf{p})$$

which means $x_i^*: R^{n+1}_{++} \to R$ is homogeneous of degree 0, $i = 0, \ldots, n$.

(b) By definition

$$\Pi(p_0, \mathbf{p}) = p_0 x_0^*(p_0, \mathbf{p}) - \sum_{i=1}^{n} p_i x_i^*(p_0, \mathbf{p})$$

Hence, for any $t > 0$

$$\begin{aligned}\Pi(tp_0, t\mathbf{p}) &= tp_0 x_0^*(tp_0, t\mathbf{p}) - \Sigma t p_i x_i^*(tp_0, t\mathbf{p}) \\ &= \text{(using (a))}\ t[p_0 x_0^*(p_0, \mathbf{p}) - \Sigma p_i x_i^*(p_0, \mathbf{p})] = t\Pi(p_0, \mathbf{p})\end{aligned}$$

So $\Pi: R^{n+1}_{++} \to R$ is homogeneous of degree 1. *Q.E.D.*

As a result of theorem 10.6 we can apply Euler's theorem (assuming (A10.6) as well) to get, for $i = 0, \ldots, n$ and for all $(p_0, \mathbf{p}) \in R^{n+1}_{++}$

$$\sum_{j=0}^{n} p_j \frac{\partial x_i^*}{\partial p_j}(p_0, \mathbf{p}) = 0$$

We can now set out some consequences of all this for the comparative statics issue. We start with the simplest case of a single input ($n = 1$) and assume throughout that (A10.1)–(A10.6) are satisfied.

(i) *The single-input case*

From theorem 10.5 the following matrix is symmetric and positive semidefinite, $\forall (p_0, p_1) \in R^2_{++}$,

$$\mathbf{T}(p_0, p_1) = \begin{bmatrix} \dfrac{\partial x_0^*}{\partial p_0} & \dfrac{\partial x_0^*}{\partial p_1} \\[2ex] -\dfrac{\partial x_1^*}{\partial p_0} & -\dfrac{\partial x_1^*}{\partial p_1^*} \end{bmatrix} \quad \text{derivatives evaluated at } (p_0, p_1)$$

Hence, in particular

$$\frac{\partial x_0^*}{\partial p_0} \geqslant 0 \tag{10.3}$$

$$\frac{\partial x_1^*}{\partial p_1} \leqslant 0 \tag{10.4}$$

The first result says that as the price of output goes up (other prices constant or 'ceteris paribus', as economists say) the quantity of output goes up. Conversely from (10.4) as the input price increases (cet. par.) quantity of input used goes down.

From Euler's theorem

$$p_0 \frac{\partial x_0^*}{\partial p_0} + p_1 \frac{\partial x_0^*}{\partial p_1} = 0 \quad \text{and} \quad p_0 \frac{\partial x_1^*}{\partial p_0} + p_1 \frac{\partial x_1^*}{\partial p_0} = 0$$

Hence

$$\frac{\partial x_0^*}{\partial p_1} = -\frac{p_0}{p_1}\frac{\partial x_0^*}{\partial p_0} \quad \text{and} \quad \frac{\partial x_1^*}{\partial p_0} = -\frac{p_1}{p_0}\frac{\partial x_1^*}{\partial p_1}$$

From (10.3) and (10.4) we get,

$$\frac{\partial x_0^*}{\partial p_1} \leqslant 0 \tag{10.5}$$

$$\frac{\partial x_1^*}{\partial p_0} \geqslant 0 \tag{10.6}$$

So as the input price increases (cet. par.) output produced goes down, and as the output price goes up (cet. par.) input used goes up.

We can conclude that in this case the sign pattern of the $\mathbf{T}(p_0, p_1)$ matrix is always

$$\begin{bmatrix} + & - \\ - & + \end{bmatrix}$$

All this is fairly obvious in the context of fig. 10.3. As p_1/p_0 increases the contours of $p_0 x_0 - p_1 x_1$ in fig. 10.3 become steeper. The tangency point with G_f (i.e. the solution to (FP)) shifts downwards along G_f towards the origin so that x_0^* and x_1^* decline. (10.3)–(10.6) are merely manifestations of this.

(ii) *The general case*

Generally we know from theorem 10.5 that $\mathbf{T}(p_0, \mathbf{p})$ is positive semi-definite. Hence its leading diagonal elements are non-negative:

$$\frac{\partial x_0^*}{\partial p_0} \geqslant 0 \tag{10.7}$$

$$\text{For } i = 1, \ldots, n, \ \frac{\partial x_i^*}{\partial p_i} \leqslant 0 \tag{10.8}$$

These are the obvious generalization of (10.3) and (10.4) with similar interpretation. From Euler's theorem

$$p_i \frac{\partial x_i^*}{\partial p_i} = -\sum_{j \neq i} p_j \frac{\partial x_i^*}{\partial p_j} \quad \text{for } i = 0, \ldots, n$$

In particular,

$$\sum_{j \neq 0} p_j \frac{\partial x_0^*}{\partial p_j} = -p_0 \frac{\partial x_0^*}{\partial p_0} \leqslant 0$$

and for $i = 1, \ldots, n$,

$$\sum_{j \neq i} p_j \frac{\partial x_i}{\partial p_j} = -p_i \frac{\partial x_i^*}{\partial p_i} \geqslant 0$$

Hence we can only conclude:

$$\text{For some } j = 1, \ldots, n, \ \frac{\partial x_0^*}{\partial p_j} \leqslant 0 \tag{10.9}$$

$$\text{For each } i = 1, \ldots, n, \text{ either } \frac{\partial x_i^*}{\partial p_0} \geqslant 0 \text{ or } \frac{\partial x_i^*}{\partial p_j} \geqslant 0$$

$$\text{some } j = 1, \ldots, n, j \neq i \quad (10.10)$$

In the general case we cannot be sure of the signs of *all* elements of the $\mathbf{T}(p_0, \mathbf{p})$ matrix. We do know the signs of the leading diagonal elements ($\geqslant 0$ giving 10.7 and 10.8) but all we can say about the off-diagonal elements is that in every row there is at least one off-diagonal element which is non-positive (giving 10.9 and 10.10). By symmetry it follows that at least one off-diagonal element in every column is non-positive. For instance a ceteris paribus increase in output price leads to an increase in output and an increase in the use of *some* input but not necessarily all inputs when $n > 1$. On the other hand an increase in the price input i leads to a reduction in the use of this input and either a reduction in output or an increase in the use of some input (but not necessarily both and not necessarily all inputs).

These rather complicated statements should not detract from the definite results we have achieved. If output price goes up (cet. par.) output goes up; if an input price goes up (cet. par.) use of that input goes down. These simple definitive statements are most useful in economics.

10.5 The classical approach to comparative statics

The derivation of the comparative static properties of output supply and input demand functions of the last section has been rooted in the properties of the profit function. This route to comparative statics is relatively modern, becoming increasingly fashionable over the past 20 years or so. Prior to that an alternative tack was taken emanating from Samuelson's *Foundations of Economic Analysis*. We call this the classical approach and roughly speaking it is based on the Lagrangean for (FP). The reader should be aware of this alternative. However, there are many texts which provide comprehensive treatment of its application to microeconomics (see bibliographical notes for references) and consequently we devote little space to it. We now run through its application to the one-input firm and refer the reader to later exercises and to the alternative texts for more widespread discussion.

Under the assumptions (A10.1) and (A10.2) on production functions of this chapter we know that the profit-maximizing firm will produce 'on' the production function. With $n = 1$ the firm's problem thus can be effectively written as an equality constraint problem:

$$\max_{(x_0, x_1) \in R^2_{++}} \; p_0 x_0 - p_1 x_1 \quad \text{subject to } x_0 = f(x_1),\ (p_0, p_1) \in R^2_{++}$$

assuming interior solutions as earlier. The Lagrangean is:

$$L(x_0, x_1, \lambda) = p_0 x_0 - p_1 x_1 + \lambda[f(x_1) - x_0]$$

From chapter 7 the sufficient conditions for a local solution to this problem are:

(a) $$\frac{\partial L}{\partial x_0} = p_0 - \lambda = 0$$

$$\frac{\partial L}{\partial x_1} = -p_1 + \lambda f_1'(x_1) = 0$$

$$\frac{\partial L}{\partial \lambda} = f(x_1) - x_0 = 0$$

(b) $L''_{00} = 0$, $L''_{01} = 0 = L''_{10}$ and $L''_{11} = \lambda f''_{11}(x_1)$;

$g_0' = -1$, $g_1' = f_1'(x_1)$ so that the 2nd-order condition for a local profit maximum is:

$$\begin{vmatrix} 0 & 0 & -1 \\ 0 & f''_{11}(x_1) & f_1'(x_1) \\ -1 & f_1'(x_1) & 0 \end{vmatrix} = -\lambda f''_{11}(x_1) > 0$$

The classical approach assumes that the 2nd-order condition in (b) is satisfied; thus (A10.1), (A10.2), interior solutions and (b) are its four assumptions. Here $\lambda = p_0 > 0$ and the (b) condition is merely $f''_{11}(x_1) > 0$–more or less the same as strict concavity of f. Rewriting the 1st-order conditions, they become

$$-\lambda = -p_0 \tag{1}$$

$$\lambda f_1'(x_1) = p_1 \tag{2}$$

$$-x_0 + f(x_1) = 0 \tag{3}$$

The matrix of derivatives of the left-hand side with respect to x_0, x_1 and λ respectively is:

$$\begin{bmatrix} 0 & 0 & -1 \\ 0 & \lambda f''_{11}(x_1) & f_1'(x_1) \\ -1 & f_1'(x_1) & 0 \end{bmatrix}$$

which is the matrix in the 2nd-order conditions (b). Assuming this matrix is non-singular (ensured by the 2nd-order conditions) the implicit function theorem tells us we can solve (1)–(3) locally for x_0, x_1, and λ as C^1 functions of p_0, p_1 giving us $x_0^*(p_0, p_1)$, $x_1^*(p_0, p_1)$ and $\lambda^*(p_0, p_1)$. Hence

$$-\lambda^*(p_0, p_1) = -p_0$$
$$\lambda^*(p_0, p_1) f_1'[x_1^*(p_0, p_1)] = p_1$$
$$-x_0^*(p_0, p_1) + f[x_1^*(p_0 p_1)] = 0$$

Differentiating this system partially with respect to p_0 gives (omitting arguments of the functions):

$$-\frac{\partial \lambda^*}{\partial p_0} = -1$$
$$\lambda^* f_{11}'' \frac{\partial x_1^*}{\partial p_0} + f_1' \frac{\partial \lambda^*}{\partial p_0} = 0$$
$$-\frac{\partial x_0^*}{\partial p_0} + f_1' \frac{\partial x_1^*}{\partial p_0} = 0$$

or

$$\begin{bmatrix} 0 & 0 & -1 \\ 0 & \lambda^* f_{11}'' & f_1' \\ -1 & f_1' & 0 \end{bmatrix} \begin{bmatrix} \partial x_0^*/\partial p_0 \\ \partial x_1^*/\partial p_0 \\ \partial \lambda^*/\partial p_0 \end{bmatrix} = \begin{bmatrix} -1 \\ 0 \\ 0 \end{bmatrix}$$

Similar differentiation with respect to p_1 leads to:

$$\begin{bmatrix} 0 & 0 & -1 \\ 0 & \lambda^* f_{11}'' & f_1' \\ -1 & f_1' & 0 \end{bmatrix} \begin{bmatrix} \partial x_0^*/\partial p_1 \\ \partial x_1^*/\partial p_1 \\ \partial \lambda^*/\partial p_1 \end{bmatrix} = \begin{bmatrix} 0 \\ 1 \\ 0 \end{bmatrix}$$

Hence

$$\begin{bmatrix} 0 & 0 & -1 \\ 0 & \lambda^* f_{11}'' & f_1' \\ -1 & f_1' & 0 \end{bmatrix} \begin{bmatrix} \partial x_0^*/\partial p_0 & \partial x_0^*/\partial p_1 \\ \partial x_1^*/\partial p_0 & \partial x_1^*/\partial p_1 \\ \partial \lambda^*/\partial p_0 & \partial \lambda^*/\partial p_1 \end{bmatrix} = \begin{bmatrix} -1 & 0 \\ 0 & 1 \\ 0 & 0 \end{bmatrix}$$

Since the 3×3 matrix on the left is non-singular by (b) we have

$$\begin{bmatrix} \partial x_0^*/\partial p_0 & \partial x_0^*/\partial p_1 \\ \partial x_1^*/\partial p_0 & \partial x_1^*/\partial p_1 \\ \partial \lambda^*/\partial p_0 & \partial \lambda^*/\partial p_1 \end{bmatrix} = \begin{bmatrix} 0 & 0 & -1 \\ 0 & \lambda^* f_{11}'' & f_1' \\ -1 & f_1' & 0 \end{bmatrix}^{-1} \begin{bmatrix} -1 & 0 \\ 0 & 1 \\ 0 & 0 \end{bmatrix}$$

The required inverse here is easy to compute as:

$$-\frac{1}{\lambda^* f''_{11}}\begin{bmatrix} -(f'_1)^2 & -f'_1 & -\lambda^* f''_{11} \\ -f'_1 & -1 & 0 \\ -\lambda^* f''_{11} & 0 & 0 \end{bmatrix}$$

Hence we find:

$$\frac{\partial x_0^*}{\partial p_0} = -\frac{(f'_1)^2}{\lambda^* f''_{11}} > 0$$

$$\frac{\partial x_0^*}{\partial p_1} = \frac{f'_1}{\lambda^* f''_{11}} < 0$$

$$\frac{\partial x_1^*}{\partial p_0} = -\frac{f'_1}{\lambda^* f''_{11}} > 0$$

$$\frac{\partial x_1^*}{\partial p_1} = \frac{1}{\lambda^* f''_{11}} < 0$$

Of course these comparative statics findings are in accord with those of section 10.4 when $n = 1$. One drawback with this classical approach, as we have presented it, is that it is based on only 'local' 2nd-order conditions; however, this is superficial and can be easily remedied. A more substantial drawback is that the classical approach requires a matrix inversion. With $n = 1$ the required matrix algebra is simple; for an investigation of the case of unspecified n the matrix algebra is not so simple. Generally the classical approach involves the following steps:

(a) Formulate the Lagrangean for the problem.

(b) Write down 1st-order (Kuhn–Tucker) conditions for its solution.

(c) Substitute solution functions in the 1st-order conditions and differentiate with respect to the parameters.

(d) Solve the resulting system for the derivatives of the solution functions with respect to the parameters, using 2nd-order conditions to sign these derivatives.

Since the 1st-order conditions are only implicit equations for the solutions, the transition from (c) to (d) will require matrix inversion. The alternative approach of sections 10.1 to 10.4 focuses on the profit function rather than the Lagrangean. Instead of implicit equations for solutions in the 1st-order Kuhn–Tucker conditions we had the explicit equations of Hotelling's

Lemma. Mere differentiation gave direct information on the derivatives of interest and the '2nd-order conditions' of the concavity of the profit function provided the desired comparative statics conclusions.

In essence the new approach has evolved from application of some of the many constructs of convex and concave analysis to micro-economic problems. The reader should be aware that the analysis offered in the first few sections of this chapter provides insight into only some of these applications. A complete catalogue of such applicable constructs is beyond the scope of this book. However, mention should be made of two points.

(i) The optimal value function for a problem which maximizes a linear function on a convex set (expressing maximum value as a function of the parameters of the linear function) is known as the *support function* of the convex set, for reasons which emerge in chapters 16 and 18. Consequently, the profit function of a firm is the support function of the firm's technology.

(ii) The property of the profit function which we have named Hotelling's Lemma is a general property of support functions and can be derived without recourse to the envelope property of the Lagrangean. For instance, and in the context of the firm discussion, let $(x_0^*, \mathbf{x}^*)$ denote a profit-maximizing plan for a firm at prices $(p_0^*, \mathbf{p}^*)$. Then, by definition

$$\Pi(p_0^*, \mathbf{p}^*) = p_0^* x_0^* - \Sigma p_i^* x_i^*$$

Also we know that $(x_0^*, \mathbf{x}^*)$ is technologically feasible so that maximum profits at some other prices, $(p_0, \mathbf{p})$ say, cannot be less than those accruing from use of the plan $(x_0^*, \mathbf{x}^*)$ at the new prices: that is,

$$\Pi(p_0, \mathbf{p}) \geqslant p_0 x_0^* - \Sigma p_i x_i^*$$

Hence

$$G(p_0, \mathbf{p}) = \Pi(p_0, \mathbf{p}) - p_0 x_0^* + \Sigma p_i x_i^* \geqslant 0 \quad \forall (p_0, \mathbf{p}) \in R_{++}^{n+1}$$

and

$$G(p_0^*, \mathbf{p}^*) = 0$$

Hence G has a global minimum at $(p_0^*, \mathbf{p}^*)$. G is also a convex function since Π is convex; hence G is stationary at $(p_0^*, \mathbf{p}^*)$. Therefore,

$$\frac{\partial \Pi}{\partial p_0}(p_0^*, \mathbf{p}^*) = x_0^* = x_0^*(p_0^*, \mathbf{p}^*)$$

and for $i = 1, \ldots, n$, $\dfrac{\partial \Pi}{\partial p_i}(p_0^*, \mathbf{p}^*) = -x_i^* = -x_i^*(p_0^*, \mathbf{p}^*)$

which is Hotelling's Lemma derived without the Lagrangean envelope property.

The reader who would like to pursue properties of support functions (and many other constructs of convex/concave analysis such as conjugate functions, distance functions etc. which are not treated in this book) is referred to the bibliographical notes.

Exercise 10

1. Work through question 2 for the special case $n = 2$, $\alpha_1 = \alpha_2 = \frac{1}{4}$ (see example 10.1).
2. Consider the Cobb–Douglas production function, $f: R_+^n \to R$ where

$$f(\mathbf{x}) = \prod_{i=1}^{n} x_i^{\alpha_i} \text{ and } \alpha_i > 0 \quad \forall i, \Sigma\alpha_i < 1$$

(a) Show that the demand function for input i is:

$$x_i^*(p_0, \mathbf{p}) = \frac{\alpha_i}{p_i} p_0^{1/(1-\Sigma\alpha_j)} \theta(\mathbf{p})$$

where

$$\theta(\mathbf{p}) = \prod_{j=1}^{n} \left[\frac{\alpha_j}{p_j}\right]^{\alpha_j/(1-\Sigma\alpha_k)}$$

(b) Show that the output supply function is:

$$x_0^*(p_0, \mathbf{p}) = p_0^{\Sigma\alpha_j/(1-\Sigma\alpha_j)}\, \theta(\mathbf{p})$$

(c) Hence show that the profit function is:

$$\Pi(p_0, \mathbf{p}) = (1-\Sigma\alpha_j)\, p_0^{1/(1-\Sigma\alpha_j)}\, \theta(\mathbf{p})$$

(d) Check that Hotelling's Lemma is satisfied here.

(e) Taking natural logs in (a) and (b), show that for $i = 0, \ldots, n$ we can write output supply and input demands in the log-linear form:

$$\ln x_i^*(p_0, \mathbf{p}) = \beta_i + \sum_{k=0}^{n} \gamma_{ik} \ln p_k$$

specifying the values of β_i and γ_{ik}.

(f) In (e), $\gamma_{ik} = \dfrac{\partial \ln x_i^*}{\partial \ln p_k} = \dfrac{\partial x_i^*}{\partial p_k} \dfrac{p_k}{x_i^*}$

which is the response elasticity of x_i^* to changes in p_k. Comment on the nature of these elasticities from the information found in (e).

(g) Show that all off-diagonal elements in $\mathbf{T}(p_0, \mathbf{p})$ are negative in this case.

3. Work through question 4 for the special case $v = \frac{1}{2}$, $\rho = -\frac{1}{2}$.

4. Consider the C.E.S. production function $f: R_+^n \to R$ where $f(\mathbf{x}) = [\Sigma x_i^{-\rho}]^{-v/\rho}$ where $\rho > -1$ (and $\neq 0$) and $v \in (0, 1)$.

(a) Show that the demand function for input i is:

$$x_i^*(p_0, \mathbf{p}) = \frac{(p_0 v)^{1/(1-v)}}{p_i^{1/(1+\rho)}} \{\Gamma(\mathbf{p})\}^{v+p}$$

where $\Gamma(\mathbf{p}) = \left[\sum_{j=1}^{n} p_j^{\rho/(1+\rho)}\right]^{-[1/\rho(1-v)]}$

(b) Show that the output supply function is:

$$x_0^*(p_0, \mathbf{p}) = (p_0 v)^{v/(1-v)} \{\Gamma(\mathbf{p})\}^{v(1+\rho)}$$

(c) Show that the profit function is:

$$\Pi(p_0, \mathbf{p}) = (1 - v)\, p_0^{1/(1-v)} v^{v/(1-v)} \{\Gamma(\mathbf{p})\}^{-v(1+\rho)}$$

(d) Show that all off-diagonal elements in $\mathbf{T}(p_0, \mathbf{p})$ are negative in this case also.

11 Cost minimization

11.1 Introduction

Chapter 10 has analysed the behaviour of competitive profit maximizing firms and has provided us with most of the results that economists could want (or at any rate, can get) about such behaviour. However, there is another issue in the theory of the firm which is of economic interest but which is separate from (although related to) the behaviour of profit maximizing firms. This is the analysis of the so-called *cost minimization* problem for a firm. In this problem the parameters facing the firm are the input prices **p** and a *preassigned output level* $\bar{x}_0$. Given values for these parameters, the choice variables are the input levels and the typical cost minimization problem is

$$\min_{\mathbf{x} \in R^n_+} \sum_{i=1}^{n} p_i x_i \quad \text{subject to } f(\mathbf{x}) \geqslant \bar{x}_0 \tag{11.1}$$

In other words, we ask the firm: what choice of inputs leads to the minimum cost production of (at least) the given output level $\bar{x}_0$, given the input prices **p**? In a sense the cost minimization is 'part' of the profit maximization problem; if a profit maximizing firm produces x_0^* from inputs $\mathbf{x}^*$ at prices p_0, **p** then it must be that the chosen input levels $\mathbf{x}^*$ constitute the minimum cost method for producing x_0^* given input prices **p**. Otherwise the firm would not be maximizing profits! However, the cost minimization problem is of independent interest to economists since it will give information on how the firm's costs of production behave, and the structure of the firm's costs is of interest to economists over and above the behaviour of profit maximizing firms. Consequently this chapter is devoted to a detailed study of (11.1).

11.2 The cost minimization problem

We continue to make the same three basic assumptions about the production function as in chapter 10:

(A11.1) $f: R^n_+ \to R$ is continuous on R^n_+, C^2 on R^n_{++} and $f(0) = 0$.

(A11.2) For all $\mathbf{x} \in R^n_{++}$, $f'_i(\mathbf{x}) > 0$, $i = 1, \ldots, n$.

(A11.3) f is strictly concave on R^n_{++}.

The cost minimization problem (11.1) involves $n + 1$ parameters, $\mathbf{p}$ and $\bar{x}_0$. The admissible set of prices is R^n_{++}. With respect to the output level we naturally assume that $\bar{x}_0$ belongs to the range of f and under the above assumptions this range will be a subset of R of the form $[0, a)$ where a may be $+\infty$. However, when $\bar{x}_0 = 0$, (11.1) trivially has the unique solution $\mathbf{x}^* = 0$ irrespective of $\mathbf{p}$. So we exclude this and assume that the admissible range for $\bar{x}_0$ is $(0, a)$ which for shorthand are described merely as A. So the family of cost minimization problems is now:

$$\text{(CM)} \quad \min_{\mathbf{x} \in R^n_+} \sum_{i=1}^{n} p_i x_i \quad \text{subject to } f(\mathbf{x}) \geqslant \bar{x}_0 \text{ where } (\mathbf{p}, \bar{x}_0) \in R^n_{++} \times A$$

We analyse (CM) following the pattern of chapters 8 and 10.

(A11.4) For all $(\mathbf{p}, \bar{x}_0) \in R^n_{++} \times A$ any solution to (CM) must belong to R^n_{++}

Again we will look at sufficient conditions for (A11.4) later (see section 11.9), and again we remark without proof that if (as well as (A11.1)–(A11.3)) f is Cobb–Douglas or C.E.S. then (A11.4) does indeed follow. Now (CM) becomes equivalent to the open domain problem:

$$\min_{\mathbf{x} \in R^n_{++}} \sum_{i=1}^{n} p_i x_i \quad \text{subject to } f(\mathbf{x}) \geqslant \bar{x}_0 \text{ where } (\mathbf{p}, \bar{x}_0) \in R^n_{++} \times A \tag{11.2}$$

The equivalent 'max' problem to (11.2) is

$$\max_{\mathbf{x} \in R^n_{++}} - \sum_{i=1}^{n} p_i x_i \quad \text{subject to } f(x) \geqslant \bar{x}_0 \text{ where } (\mathbf{p}, \bar{x}_0) \in R^n_{++} \times A \tag{11.3}$$

The objective in (11.3) is concave and non-stationary, the constraint function is concave and (CQ) is satisfied, for any $(\mathbf{p}, \bar{x}_0) \in R^n_{++} \times A$. The Lagrangean for (11.3) is

$$L(\mathbf{x}, \lambda; \mathbf{p}, \bar{x}_0) = -\sum_{i=1}^{n} p_i x_i + \lambda[f(\mathbf{x}) - \bar{x}_0]$$

And K–T are: $\exists \lambda^*$ such that

(I) $-p_i + \lambda^* f_i'(\mathbf{x}^*) = 0, i = 1, \ldots, n$

(II) $\lambda^* > 0$ and

(III) $\mathbf{x}^* \in R^n_{++}$ and $f(\mathbf{x}^*) = \bar{x}_0$

From (I), $\lambda^* = p_i / f_i'(\mathbf{x}^*) > 0$ and (II) is redundant. Eliminating λ^* from (I) we get, equivalently to (I)–(III):

(a) $\dfrac{f_i'(\mathbf{x}^*)}{f_j'(\mathbf{x}^*)} = \dfrac{p_i}{p_j}$ for all $i, j = 1, \ldots, n$

(b) $f(\mathbf{x}^*) = \bar{x}_0$

The solutions to (11.3) coincide with those of (11.2), which in turn are the same as those of (CM). Hence:

Theorem 11.1 Assuming (A11.1)–(A11.4), $\mathbf{x}^*$ solves (CM) at $\mathbf{p}, \bar{x}_0$ if and only if:

(a) $\dfrac{f_i'(\mathbf{x}^*)}{f_j'(\mathbf{x}^*)} = \dfrac{p_i}{p_j}$ $\forall i, j = 1, \ldots, n$

(b) $f(\mathbf{x}^*) = \bar{x}_0$

(with $\lambda^* = p_i / f_i'(\mathbf{x}^*), i = 1, \ldots, n$).

When $n = 1$ (a) gives no information ($1 = 1$) and so the solution is always defined by $f(x_1^*) = \bar{x}_0$ in this case. This makes sense. In fig. 11.1 to produce at least $\bar{x}_0$ you need at least x_1^* input. Clearly the minimum cost way of producing $\bar{x}_0$ is then to use exactly (no more than) x_1^*: but x_1^* is defined by $f(x_1^*) = \bar{x}_0$ which thus always (no matter the value of p_1) defines the solution to (CM) when $n = 1$.

When $n = 2$ the feasible set for (CM) is the set of input combinations on or above the isoquant for the output level $\bar{x}_0$ (i.e. $UC_f(\bar{x}_0)$), typically as shown by the shaded region in fig. 11.2. The contours of the objective are straight lines of slope $-p_2/p_1$ with objective value

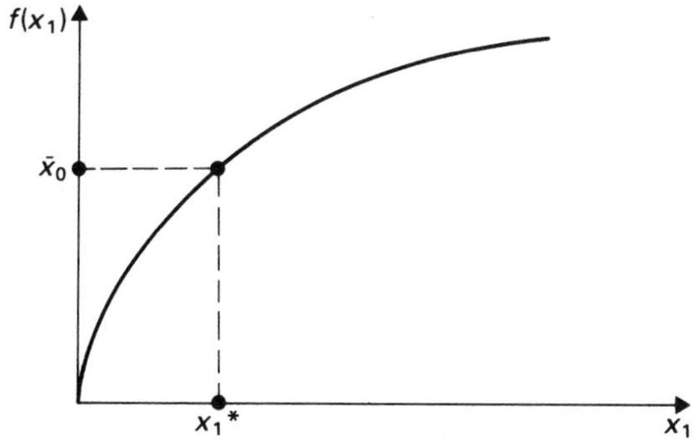

Figure 11.1

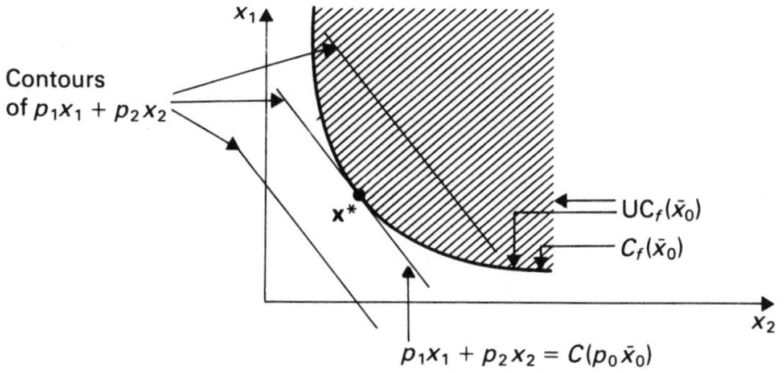

Figure 11.2

decreasing as we move towards the origin (south-west). The lowest valued such contour is clearly attained at $\mathbf{x}^*$ in fig. 11.2, which is therefore the solution to (CM). $\mathbf{x}^*$ lies on $C_f(\bar{x}_0)$, so that $f(\mathbf{x}^*) = \bar{x}_0$, and the tangency of the objective contour and $C_f(\bar{x}_0)$ at $\bar{x}_0$ means

$$\frac{f_2'(\mathbf{x}^*)}{f_1'(\mathbf{x}^*)} = \frac{p_2}{p_1}$$

Thus (a) and (b) of theorem 11.1 indeed emerge in fig. 11.2 as characterizations of solutions to (CM) when $n = 2$.

We can invoke the 'uniqueness' results of chapter 7 directly for (CM) to ensure that for each $(\mathbf{p}, \bar{x}_0) \in R^n_{++} \times A$ there is at most one solution to (CM). In fact (as we see in chapter 17) the assumptions made so far are enough to ensure also that there is *at least* one solution. So (A11.1)–(A11.5) guarantee exactly one solution to (CM) for all $(\mathbf{p}, \bar{x}_0) \in R^n_{++} \times A$ and we need not list this as a separate assumption. As a consequence of it, the family (CM) defines solution, optimal value and multiplier functions. To distinguish from chapter 10 we use the following notation for these:

1. The solution functions, $x_i^c: R_{++}^n \times A \to R$ with values $x_i^c(\mathbf{p}, \bar{x}_0)$, $i = 1, \ldots, n$; these are known as the firm's *conditional input demand functions.*
2. The optimal value function, $C: R_{++}^n \times A \to R$ with values
$$C(\mathbf{p}, \bar{x}_0) = \sum_{i=1}^{n} p_i x_i^c(\mathbf{p})$$
is known as the firm's *cost function.*
3. The multiplier function, $\lambda^c: R_{++}^n \times A \to R$ with values $\lambda^c(\mathbf{p}, \bar{x}_0)$.

The conditional demand functions $\mathbf{x}^c(\mathbf{p})$ tell us the minimum cost method of producing (at least) output $\bar{x}_0$ at input prices $\mathbf{p}$, and the cost function tells us the minimum cost of producing $\bar{x}_0$ at $\mathbf{p}$.

Examples 11.1 These are the same as in examples 10.1.

(a) $f: R_+ \to R$ where $f(x_1) = x_1^{1/2}$ is the production function and $A = R_{++}$. Then (A11.1)–(A11.5) are satisfied, as the reader can check. With $n = 1$ the conditional input demand is defined by

$$\bar{x}_0 = f(x_1) \quad \text{or} \quad \bar{x}_0 = x_1^{1/2}$$

Hence $x_1^c(p_1, \bar{x}_0) = \bar{x}_0^2$ and so $C(p_1, \bar{x}_0) = p_1 \bar{x}_0^2$ (with $\lambda^c(p_1, \bar{x}_c) = p_1/\frac{1}{2}x_1^{-1/2} = 2p_1\bar{x}_0$).

(b) The production function is $f: R_+^2 \to R$ where $f(\mathbf{x}) = x_1^{1/4}x_2^{1/4}$; again (A11.1)–(A11.5) are satisfied and $A = R_{++}$. $\mathbf{x}$ solves (CM) if and only if

$$\frac{f_1'(\mathbf{x})}{f_2'(\mathbf{x})} = \frac{p_1}{p_2} \quad \text{or} \quad \frac{\frac{1}{4}x_1^{-3/4}x_2^{1/4}}{\frac{1}{4}x_1^{1/4}x_2^{-3/4}} = \frac{p_1}{p_2} \quad \text{or} \quad \frac{x_2}{x_1} = \frac{p_1}{p_2}$$

and $f(\mathbf{x}) = \bar{x}_0$ or $x_1^{1/4}x_2^{1/4} = \bar{x}_0$.

Solving these two equations gives

$$x_1^2 \frac{p_1}{p_2} = \bar{x}_0^4$$

and so

$$x_1^c(\mathbf{p}, \bar{x}_0) = \bar{x}_0^2 \frac{p_2^{1/2}}{p_1^{1/2}}, \quad x_2^c(\mathbf{p}, \bar{x}_0) = \bar{x}_0^2 \frac{p_1^{1/2}}{p_2^{1/2}}$$

and $C(\mathbf{p}, \bar{x}_0) = 2\bar{x}_0^2 p_1^{1/2} p_2^{1/2}$

(with $\lambda^c(\mathbf{p}, \bar{x}_0) = p_1/f_1'(\mathbf{x}) = 4\bar{x}_0 p_1^{1/2} p_2^{1/2}$).

To proceed to a general comparative static analysis of conditional input demands as prices change we assume:

(A11.5) (i) For $i = 1, \ldots, n$, $x_i^c : R_{++}^n \times A \to R$ is C^1

(ii) $C : R_{++}^n \times A \to R$ is C^2

(iii) $\lambda^c : R_{++}^n \times A \to R$ is C^1

Now applying the envelope theorem with respect to prices to the Lagrangean for (11.3) we get:

Theorem 11.2: Shephard's Lemma Assuming (A11.1)–(A11.5)

$$\frac{\partial C}{\partial p_i}(\mathbf{p}, \bar{x}_0) = x_i^c(\mathbf{p}, \bar{x}_0), \; i = 1, \ldots, n$$

Proof Differentiating the Lagrangean for (11.3) with respect to p_i gives $-x_i$. The optimal value function for (11.3) is $-C(\mathbf{p}, \bar{x}_0)$. Hence from the envelope theorem,

$$-\frac{\partial C}{\partial p_i}(\mathbf{p}, \bar{x}_0) = -x_i^c(\mathbf{p}, \bar{x}_0) \qquad \textit{Q.E.D.}$$

For fixed $\bar{x}_0 \in A$, the cost function (as a function of $\mathbf{p}$) has a nice 'curvature' property:

Theorem 11.3 Assuming (A11.1)–(A11.4) the cost function $C : R_{++}^n \times A \to R$ is a concave function of $\mathbf{p}$ for fixed $\bar{x}_0$.

Proof Fix $\bar{x}_0 \in A$ and for convenience delete it as an argument of the cost function. We have to show that,

$$C[\lambda \mathbf{p}^1 + (1-\lambda)\mathbf{p}^2] \geqslant \lambda C(\mathbf{p}^1) + (1-\lambda) C(\mathbf{p}^2)$$
$$\forall \lambda \in [0, 1], \forall \mathbf{p}^1, \mathbf{p}^2 \in R_{++}^n$$

Let $\mathbf{x}$ be a solution to (CM) at output $\bar{x}_0$ and prices $\lambda \mathbf{p}^1 + (1-\lambda)\mathbf{p}^2$ where $\lambda \in [0, 1]$ and $\mathbf{p}^1, \mathbf{p}^2 \in R_{++}^n$. $\mathbf{x}$ must then be feasible at these parameter values (i.e. $f(\mathbf{x}) \geqslant \bar{x}_0$) and

$$C[\lambda \mathbf{p}^1 + (1-\lambda)\mathbf{p}^2] = \sum_{i=1}^n x_i(\lambda p_i^1 + (1-\lambda) p_i^2)$$

$$= \lambda \sum_{i=1}^n p_i^1 x_i + (1-\lambda) \sum_{i=1}^n p_i^2 x_i$$

But $\Sigma_{i=1}^{n} p_i^1 x_i$ is the cost of producing $\bar{x}_0$ at prices $\mathbf{p}^1$ using the input combination of $\mathbf{x}$ and cannot be less than the minimum cost of producing $\bar{x}_0$ at prices $\mathbf{p}^1$. Hence

$$C(\mathbf{p}^1) \leqslant \sum_{i=1}^{n} p_i^1 x_i$$

and similarly

$$C(\mathbf{p}^2) \leqslant \sum_{i=1}^{n} p_i^2 x_i$$

Therefore $C[\lambda \mathbf{p}^1 + (1-\lambda)\mathbf{p}^2] \geqslant \lambda C(\mathbf{p}^1) + (1-\lambda) C(\mathbf{p}^2)$. Since this is true for any $\lambda \in [0, 1]$ and any $\mathbf{p}^1, \mathbf{p}^2 \in R_{++}^n$ the result follows. *Q.E.D.*

As in chapter 10 we also get homogeneity properties of x_i^c and C, with respect to $\mathbf{p}$ for fixed $\bar{x}_0$.

Theorem 11.4 Assuming (A11.1)–(A11.4)

(a) For $i = 1, \ldots, n$, $x_i^c : R_{++}^n \times A \to R$ is a homogeneous of degree zero function of $\mathbf{p}$, for fixed $\bar{x}_0 \in A$.

(b) $C : R_{++}^n \times A \to R$ is a homogeneous of degree one function of $\mathbf{p}$, for fixed $\bar{x}_0 \in A$.

Proof (a) Given the fixed $\bar{x}_0$ and given $\mathbf{p} \in R_{++}^n$, $\mathbf{x}$ solves (CM) if and only if

$$\frac{f_i'(\mathbf{x})}{f_j'(\mathbf{x})} = \frac{p_i}{p_j} \quad \forall i, j = 1, \ldots, n$$

and

$$f(\mathbf{x}) = \bar{x}_0$$

But with $\bar{x}_0$ unchanged and with $\mathbf{p}$ changed to $t\mathbf{p}$, where $t > 0$ the conditions are exactly the same. Hence $x_i^c(\mathbf{p}, \bar{x}_0) = x_i^c(t\mathbf{p}, \bar{x}_0)$, $i = 1, \ldots, n$ and $\forall t > 0$ which is the desired result.

(b) $$C(t\mathbf{p}, \bar{x}_0) = \sum_{i=1}^{n} t p_i x_i^c(t\mathbf{p}, \bar{x}_0)$$

$$= \text{(using (a))}\ t \Sigma p_i x_i^c(\mathbf{p}, \bar{x}_0) = tC(\mathbf{p}, \bar{x}_0) \text{ as required.}$$

Q.E.D.

Bringing all this together we now get the desired comparative static results, at least with respect to price changes. First a definition:

$$\mathbf{S}(\mathbf{p}, \bar{x}_0) = \begin{bmatrix} \dfrac{\partial x_1^c}{\partial p_1} \cdots \dfrac{\partial x_1^c}{\partial p_n} \\ \cdots\cdots\cdots \\ \dfrac{\partial x_n^c}{\partial p_1} \cdots \dfrac{\partial x_n^c}{\partial p_n} \end{bmatrix}$$

where derivatives are evaluated at $(\mathbf{p}, \bar{x}_0)$ is the firm's *Slutsky matrix*; it is the matrix of first partials of conditional demands with respect to prices. From Shephard's lemma

$$\mathbf{S}(\mathbf{p}, \bar{x}_0) = \begin{bmatrix} \dfrac{\partial^2 C}{\partial p_1^2} & \cdots & \dfrac{\partial^2 C}{\partial p_1 \partial p_n} \\ \cdots & \cdots & \cdots \\ \dfrac{\partial^2 C}{\partial p_n \partial p_1} & \cdots & \dfrac{\partial^2 C}{\partial p_n^2} \end{bmatrix}$$

And from theorem 11.3 the right-hand matrix is the Hessian of C with respect to $\mathbf{p}$ and so is symmetric and n.s.d. We have shown:

Theorem 11.5 Assuming (A11.1)–(A11.5), the firm's Slutsky matrix, $\mathbf{S}(\mathbf{p}, \bar{x}_0)$ is symmetric and n.s.d. for all $(\mathbf{p}, \bar{x}_0) \in R^n_{++} \times A$.

We now spell out in detail some of the consequences of theorems 11.4 and 11.5. From theorem 11.5 we have

$$\frac{\partial x_i^c}{\partial p_i} \leqslant 0, i = 1, \ldots, n \tag{11.4}$$

So a 'cet. par.' increase in the price of input i leads to a reduction of the conditional demand for input i. Applying Euler's theorem in the light of theorem 11.4 we get

$$\sum_{j=1}^{n} p_j \frac{\partial x_i^c}{\partial p_j} = 0, i = 1, \ldots, n$$

so

$$\sum_{j \neq i} p_j \frac{\partial x_i^c}{\partial p_j} = -p_i \frac{\partial x_i^c}{\partial p_i} \geqslant 0 \text{ from (11.4)}$$

It follows that at least one off-diagonal element in the ith row of the Slutsky matrix must be non-negative. For each i

$$\frac{\partial x_i^c}{\partial p_j} \geqslant 0 \text{ some } j \neq i \tag{11.5}$$

In the case where $n = 2$ it follows that the sign pattern of the Slutsky matrix is

$$\begin{bmatrix} - & + \\ + & - \end{bmatrix}$$

In this case as the price of input 2 goes up (cet. par.) the conditional demand for input 1 goes up, while the conditional demand for input 2 goes down. This is obvious from fig. 11.2: as p_2 goes up (cet. par.), p_2/p_1 goes up, contours of the (CM) objective become 'more vertical' and the contour/isoquant tangency for the solution must occur 'to the left' of $\mathbf{x}^*$ in fig. 11.2 leading to an increase in x_1 and a reduction in x_2.

In the general case ($n > 2$) all we can infer is that as p_j goes up (cet. par.) then the conditional demand for *some* input i ($\neq j$) goes up while the conditional demand for j goes down.

We have not addressed the dependence of solution to (CM) on the parameter $\bar{x}_0$ as yet. We come to this next as it is the issue which generates the various cost 'curves' discussed by economists in micro-economics. We already have a full picture of the dependence of costs and conditional demands on input prices. This will be very useful in the next chapter.

11.3 Cost curves

In the last section we analysed in detail the relation between costs and input prices; we now investigate the relation between costs and output. This (one-variable) relationship gives rise to the 'cost curves' used so freely in elementary microeconomics. First remember that if $\bar{x}_0 = 0$ then the firm will use no inputs and thus incur no costs, no matter what input prices are; in other words $C(\mathbf{p}, 0) = 0$, $\forall \mathbf{p} \in R^n_{++}$. The question of interest, however, is: if we fix $\mathbf{p}$, how does C vary with $\bar{x}_0$ for positive output levels? A first property in answer to this question comes from application of the envelope theorem for the parameter $\bar{x}_0$ to the (CM) problem (Shephard's lemma came from envelope application to (CM) for input prices). You find

$$\lambda^c(\mathbf{p}, \bar{x}_0) = \frac{\partial C}{\partial \bar{x}_0}(\mathbf{p}, \bar{x}_0)$$

In other words the Lagrange multiplier function for (CM) measures the rate of change of cost with respect to output, or what economists call *marginal cost*. An immediate implication is that marginal cost is always strictly positive, i.e. the cost curve is always upward-sloping.

This is pretty obvious anyway: if output goes up, with input prices constant, then clearly cost will rise. Less obvious is the following consequence of our assumptions in the last section:

Theorem 11.6 Assuming (A11.1)–(A11.5), the cost function $C: R^n_{++} \times A \to R$ is a convex function of $\bar{x}_0$ for fixed $\mathbf{p} \in R^n_{++}$.

Proof Fix $\mathbf{p} \in R^n_{++}$ and for shorthand write $C(\mathbf{p}, \bar{x}_0)$ as $C(\bar{x}_0)$. We need to show, $\forall \lambda \in [0, 1]$ and $\forall \bar{x}_0^1, \bar{x}_0^2 \in A$ that

$$C(\lambda \bar{x}_0^1 + (1-\lambda)\bar{x}_0^2) \leqslant \lambda C(\bar{x}_0^1) + (1-\lambda)C(\bar{x}_0^2)$$

Choose any $\bar{x}_0^1$, $\bar{x}_0^2 \in A$. Let $\mathbf{x}^1$ be the input vector which solves (CM) at $\mathbf{p}, \bar{x}_0^1$ and let $\mathbf{x}^2$ solve at $\mathbf{p}, \bar{x}_0^2$; then

$$C(\bar{x}_0^1) = \sum_{i=1}^{n} p_i x_i^1 \quad \text{and} \quad C(\bar{x}_0^2) = \sum_{i=1}^{n} p_i x_i^2$$

Since f is concave

$$f[\lambda \mathbf{x}^1 + (1-\lambda)\mathbf{x}^2] \geqslant \lambda f(\mathbf{x}^1) + (1-\lambda) f(\mathbf{x}^2) \quad \forall \lambda \in [0, 1]$$

i.e.

$$f[\lambda \mathbf{x}^1 + (1-\lambda)\mathbf{x}^2] \geqslant \lambda \bar{x}_0^1 + (1-\lambda)\bar{x}_0^2 \quad \forall \lambda \in [0, 1]$$

since $f(\mathbf{x}) = \bar{x}_0$ at solutions to (CM).

So when the parameters in (CM) are $(\mathbf{p}, \lambda \bar{x}_0^1 + (1-\lambda)\bar{x}_0^2)$, $\lambda \in [0, 1]$, the input vector $\lambda \mathbf{x}^1 + (1-\lambda)\mathbf{x}^2$ is feasible for (CM) and would give rise to costs of $\lambda \Sigma p_i x_i^1 + (1-\lambda)\Sigma p_i x_i^2 = \lambda C(\bar{x}_0^1) + (1-\lambda) C(\bar{x}_0^2)$. But $C(\lambda \bar{x}_0^1 + (1-\lambda)\bar{x}_0^2)$ is the minimum cost of producing $\lambda \bar{x}_0^1 + (1-\lambda)\bar{x}_0^2$ at $\mathbf{p}$. Hence

$$C(\lambda \bar{x}_0^1 + (1-\lambda)\bar{x}_0^2) \leqslant \lambda C(\bar{x}_0^1) + (1-\lambda) C(\bar{x}_0^2)$$

This is true for any $\bar{x}_0^1, \bar{x}_0^2 \in R_{++}$ and any $\lambda \in [0, 1]$. *Q.E.D.*

If we continue the practice of writing $C(\mathbf{p}, \bar{x}_0)$ as $C(\bar{x}_0)$ (i.e. fixing $\mathbf{p}$) we see that the first derivative characterization of convex functions tells us

$$C(\bar{x}_0^*) + (\bar{x}_0 - \bar{x}_0^*) C'(\bar{x}_0^*) \leqslant C(\bar{x}_0) \quad \forall \bar{x}_0, \bar{x}_0^* \in A$$

But as $C(0) = 0$ it follows that putting $\bar{x}_0 = 0$ in the above formula (strictly speaking a 'limit' argument is needed here, but it works),

$$C(\bar{x}_0^*) \leqslant \bar{x}_0^* C'(\bar{x}_0^*) \quad \forall \bar{x}_0^* \in A$$

Hence

$$C'(\bar{x}_0^*) \geqslant \frac{C(\bar{x}_0^*)}{\bar{x}_0^*} \quad \forall \bar{x}_0^*$$

The left-hand side is just marginal cost. The right-hand side is the ratio of total cost to output and is cost per unit or *average cost*. Under our assumptions the marginal cost curve lies everywhere above the average cost curve. Moreover, since C is convex, $C''(\bar{x}_0) \geqslant 0$ and so the marginal cost curve is upward-sloping. The first derivative of average cost is

$$\frac{C'(\bar{x}_0)\,\bar{x}_0 - C(\bar{x}_0)}{\bar{x}_0^2} = \frac{1}{\bar{x}_0^3}\left[C'(\bar{x}_0) - \frac{C(\bar{x}_0)}{\bar{x}_0}\right] \geqslant 0$$

since marginal exceeds average cost. So the average cost curve is upward-sloping too. Figure 11.3 sketches typical total, average and marginal cost curves under our assumptions.

The configuration in fig. 11.3(b) may surprise the reader who is accustomed to U-shaped marginal and average cost curves. Remember, however, that our assumptions on the production function differ from those of the typical elementary microeconomics treatment, and this difference causes the changed nature of the cost curves. The traditional configuration emerges in chapter 15 when we change our production function assumptions.

11.4 Relation between profit maximization and cost minimization

Suppose we know the cost function (or the conditional input demand functions) of a firm satisfying the assumptions of this chapter. Can we find from this information the firm's profit function and the (unconditional) output supply and input demand functions? If $C(\mathbf{p}, \bar{x}_0)$ represents the minimum cost of producing the given output

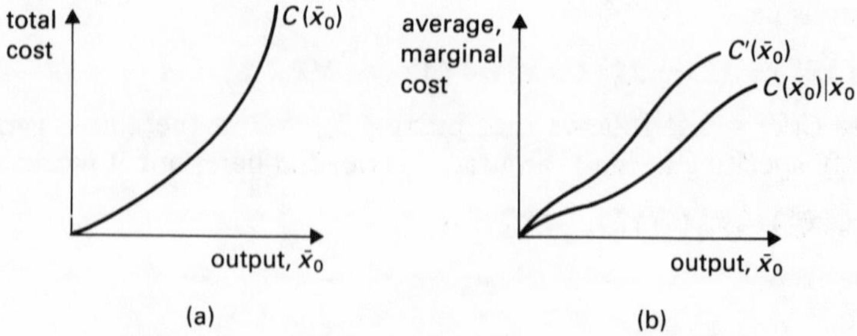

Figure 11.3

$\bar{x}_0$ at input prices $\mathbf{p}$ then profits from producing $\bar{x}_0$ at price p_0, given costs $C(\mathbf{p}, \bar{x}_0)$, are

$$p_0\bar{x}_0 - C(\mathbf{p}, \bar{x}_0)$$

It follows that if we now maximize this expression, treating $p_0, \mathbf{p}$ as parameters and $\bar{x}_0$ now as a variable, the solution expressing $\bar{x}_0$ as a function of $(p_0, \mathbf{p})$ should give us the firm's output supply function. Indeed this is the case. Moreover, to produce $\bar{x}_0$ at minimum cost given input prices $\mathbf{p}$ requires use of input i in the amount $(\partial C/\partial p_i)(\mathbf{p}, \bar{x}_0) = x_i^c(\mathbf{p}, \bar{x}_0)$ from Shephard's lemma. Hence if we substitute the formula for the output supply function found above for $\bar{x}_0$ in the conditional input demand functions we should get the input levels which lead to maximum profits at $(p_0, \mathbf{p})$; in other words we should get the *unconditional* input demand functions from this substitution. Of course once we know the unconditional output supply and input demand functions we can find the profit function since

$$\Pi(p_0, \mathbf{p}) = p_0 x_0^*(p_0, \mathbf{p}) - \sum_{i=1}^{n} p_i x_i^*(p_0, \mathbf{p})$$

Thus it seems that we have a method of going from information about cost functions (or conditional input demand functions) to profit functions and unconditional output supply and input demand functions. This is so and we assert:

Theorem 11.7 Under assumptions (A11.1)–(A11.4) and (A10.4):

(a) $x_0^*(p_0, \mathbf{p})$ is the solution function for $\bar{x}_0$ in

$$\max_{\bar{x}_0 \in R_{++}} \; p_0\bar{x}_0 - C(\mathbf{p}, \bar{x}_0) \quad \text{where } (p_0, \mathbf{p}) \in R_{++}^{n+1}$$

(b) for $i = 1, \ldots, n$, $x_i^*(p_0, \mathbf{p}) = x_i^c[\mathbf{p}, x_0^*(p_0, \mathbf{p})]$

Examples 11.2 From examples 11.1.

(a) $n = 1$ and suppose we know only that $x_1^c(p_1, \bar{x}_0) = \bar{x}_0^2$. Then profits are $p_0\bar{x}_0 - p_1\bar{x}_0^2$ and maximization of this concave function of $\bar{x}_0$ requires $p_0 - 2p_1\bar{x}_0 = 0$ so that $\bar{x}_0 = p_0/2p_1$. Hence

$$x_0^*(p_0, p_1) = \frac{p_0}{2p_1}$$

Substituting this for $\bar{x}_0$ in $x_1^c(p_1, \bar{x}_0)$ gives

$$x_1^*(p_0, p_1) = \frac{p_0^2}{4p_1^2}$$

Hence

$$\Pi(p_0, p_1) = \frac{p_0^2}{4p_1}$$

(b) $n = 2$ and suppose we know only that $C(\mathbf{p}, \bar{x}_0) = 2\bar{x}_0^2 p_1^{1/2} p_2^{1/2}$. Profits are $p_0\bar{x}_0 - 2\bar{x}_0^2 p_1^{1/2} p_2^{1/2}$ and the maximum with respect to $\bar{x}_0$ occurs when $p_0 = 4\bar{x}_0 p_1^{1/2} p_2^{1/2}$. Hence

$$x_0^*(p_0, \mathbf{p}) = \frac{p_0}{4p_1^{1/2} p_2^{1/2}}$$

From Shephard's lemma

$$x_1^c(\mathbf{p}, \bar{x}_0) = \frac{\partial C}{\partial p_1} = \bar{x}_0^2 \frac{p_2^{1/2}}{p_1^{1/2}}$$

and

$$x_2^c(\mathbf{p}, \bar{x}_0) = \frac{\partial C}{\partial p_2} = \bar{x}_0^2 \frac{p_1^{1/2}}{p_2^{1/2}}$$

Substituting $x_0^*(p_0, \mathbf{p})$ for $\bar{x}_0$ gives

$$x_1^*(p_0, \mathbf{p}) = \frac{p_0^2}{16p_1 p_2} \frac{p_2^{1/2}}{p_1^{1/2}} = \frac{p_0^2}{16p_1^{3/2} p_2^{1/2}}$$

$$x_2^*(p_0, \mathbf{p}) = \frac{p_0^2}{16p_1^{1/2} p_2^{3/2}}$$

Hence

$$\Pi(p_0, \mathbf{p}) = p_0 x_0^*(p_0, \mathbf{p}) - \sum_{i=1}^{2} p_i x_i^*(p_0, \mathbf{p})$$

$$= \frac{p_0^2}{4p_1^{1/2} p_2^{1/2}} - \frac{p_0^2}{8p_1^{1/2} p_2^{1/2}} = \frac{p_0^2}{8p_1^{1/2} p_2^{1/2}}$$

Figure 11.4 summarizes the links between (CM) and (FP) we have discovered, and also the links within each problem between solution functions and optimal value functions.

In chapter 18 we will add a production function box, $f(\mathbf{x})$ to this diagram and show that it is possible to infer the contents of all (five) boxes from knowledge of the contents of *any* one of them.

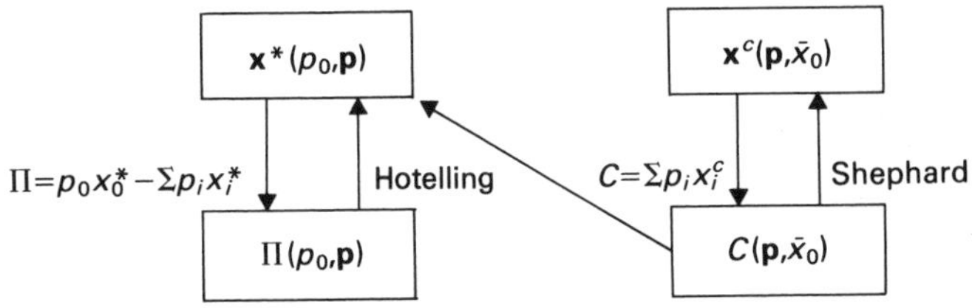

Figure 11.4

11.5 Interior solutions in the theory of the firm

We have employed interior solution assumptions in chapters 10 and 11 (A10.4 and A11.4). In this section we provide sufficient conditions on the production function to ensure satisfaction of those interior solution assumptions.

Consider first the cost minimization problem (CM), where $(\mathbf{p}, \bar{x}_0) \in R^n_{++} \times A$ so that $\bar{x}_0 > 0$. Suppose the following assumption is satisfied by the production function.

Interior isoquants $UC_f(\bar{x}_0) \subset R^n_{++} \quad \forall \bar{x}_0 > 0$

For positive output levels this requires that the isoquants of f never touch the axes of R^n_+. Since the feasible set for (CM) is then $UC_f(\bar{x}_0)$, any solution $\mathbf{x} \in UC_f(\bar{x}_0) \subset R^n_{++}$ and so $\mathbf{x} \in R^n_{++}$: interior solutions to (CM) are indeed guaranteed by interior isoquants.

Turning to (FP) and chapter 10 consider the following assumption:

Infinite derivatives at the origin

Let $\mathbf{x} = (x, x, \ldots, x)$, the n vector with all components equal to x where $x > 0$. The assumption is

$$\lim_{x \to 0} \sum_{i=1}^{n} f_i'(\mathbf{x}) = +\infty$$

We show that this rules out zero output solutions to (FP) at any $(p_0, \mathbf{p}) \in R^{n+1}_{++}$. Zero output gives zero profits so we have to show that some positive output will give strictly positive profits at any $(p_0, \mathbf{p}) \in R^n_{++}$. If the firm uses inputs $(x, x, \ldots, x)$, $x > 0$, output is $f(x, x, \ldots, x) = f(\mathbf{x})$, say, and profits are

$$p_0 f(\mathbf{x}) - x \sum_{i=1}^{n} p_i$$

Given $(p_0, \mathbf{p}) \in R^n_{++}$ the derivative of profits with respect to x is

$$p_0 \sum_{i=1}^{n} f_i'(\mathbf{x}) - \Sigma p_i$$

and for all x sufficiently small and strictly positive, profits are strictly increasing with x from the infinite derivative assumption. Since profits are continuous for $x \geqslant 0$ and zero at $x = 0$ it follows that $p_0 f(\mathbf{x}) - x\Sigma p_i > 0$ for some strictly positive x, sufficiently small. Hence at any $(p_0, \mathbf{p}) \in R^{n+1}_{++}$ output will be strictly positive. At any solution to (FP) whatever output is produced must be produced at minimum cost given the output prices; it follows that if interior isoquants prevail also then all input levels must be strictly positive. Hence interior solutions to (FP) are guaranteed by interior isoquants and infinite derivatives at the origin.

If the production function f satisfies (A10.1)–(A10.3) (= A11.1–A11.3) *and* if f is homogeneous then f will have infinite derivatives at the origin (see question 7 of exercise 11). In particular Cobb–Douglas and C.E.S. production functions satisfy the infinite derivatives at the origin assumption. Unfortunately the addition of homogeneity to (A10.1)–(A10.3) is not enough to ensure interior isoquants. However, Cobb–Douglas production functions or C.E.S. production function with $\rho > 0$ do satisfy interior isoquants (see question 8 of exercise 11). For C.E.S. with $\rho \in (-1, 0)$ isoquants touch the axes but an alternative argument guarantees interior solutions to (CM) in this case (see question 9 of exercise 11).

To sum up: suppose f satisfies (A10.1)–(A10.3) or (A11.1)–(A11.3). If, in addition:

(a) f has interior isoquants then (A10.4) follows;

(b) f has interior isoquants and infinite derivatives at the origin then (A11.4) follows;

(c) f is Cobb–Douglas or C.E.S. then (A10.4) and (A11.4) follow.

11.6 Inverse functions: an introduction

Earlier in this chapter (fig. 11.1) we alluded to the concept of an inverse of a function of one variable. We use this concept later in the book and so devote here a section to remedying the earlier evasion.

Suppose $f:D \to R$ is a function of one variable ($D \subset R$) with range E say and with values $f(x)$. The inverse *mapping* to f is a mapping $g:E \to R$ with values $g(y)$ such that

$$x \in g(y) \quad \text{if and only if } f(x) = y$$

The inverse mapping thus defined need not be a function even though f is a function. For instance suppose we define $f:R \to R$ by $f(x) = x^2$. Then the range of f is R_+ and the inverse mapping is $g:R_+ \to R$ where $g(y) = \{x \,|\, x^2 = y\} = \{x \,|\, x = +y^{1/2} \text{ or } x = -y^{1/2}\}$. So the inverse mapping maps $y \in R_+$ into *two* points in general and is not a function. On the other hand for $f:R \to R$ given by $f(x) = 1 + 2x$, the range is R and we find that the inverse $g:R \to R$ is given by $g(y) = \{x \,|\, 1 + 2x = y\} = \{x \,|\, x = (y-1)/2\}$ which does define a function. The crucial result here is:

If $f:D \to R$, where D is open, is a C^1 function with range E and with $f'(x) > 0$, $\forall x \in D$ or $f'(x) < 0$, $\forall x \in D$ then the inverse mapping to f is a function, usually written $f^{-1}:E \to R$ with values $f^{-1}(y)$ where:

$$f^{-1}(y) = x \text{ if and only if } f(x) = y$$

For instance when $f:R \to R$ has $f(x) = 1 + 2x$ then the inverse function is $f^{-1}:R \to R$ with values $f^{-1}(y) = (y-1)/2$. Notice that $f^{-1}(y)$ does not mean $1/f(y)$.

For functions of one variable which possess an inverse function there are close links between the derivatives of the function and those of its inverse. To see this notice that

$$f^{-1}[f(x)] = x$$

Differentiating with respect to x and omitting arguments

$$(f^{-1})'f' = 1 \quad \text{and hence} \quad (f^{-1})' = \frac{1}{f'}$$

or, fully

$$(f^{-1})'(f(x) = \frac{1}{f'(x)}$$

That is the derivative of the inverse $(f^{-1})'$ evaluated at $f(x)$ equals the reciprocal of the derivative of f evaluated at x. Differentiating again

$$(f^{-1})''f'f' + (f^{-1})'f'' = 0$$

so that

$$(f^{-1})'' = -\frac{(f^{-1})'f''}{(f')^2} \quad \text{assuming } f' \neq 0$$

$$= -\frac{f''}{(f')^3}$$

or fully

$$(f^{-1})''(f(x)) = -\frac{f''(x)}{[f'(x)]^3}$$

Notice in particular that if $f'(x) > 0$, $\forall x \in D$ and f is concave then f^{-1} is convex.

The earlier observation surrounding fig. 11.1 can now be stated more succinctly. For a production function with $n = 1$ there is an inverse function since we assume $f'(x_1) > 0$, $\forall x_1 \in R_{++}$. The conditional input demand, given p_1 and $\bar{x}_0$, is the solution of $\bar{x}_0 = f(x_1)$ for x_1 in terms of $\bar{x}_0$. We now know that this means

$$x_1^c(p_1, \bar{x}_0) = f^{-1}(\bar{x}_0)$$

Hence $C(p_1, \bar{x}_0) = p_1 f^{-1}(\bar{x}_0)$, and since f is concave, f^{-1} is convex; it follows immediately that C is convex in $\bar{x}_0$ for given p_1.

Exercise 11

1. Work through question 2 for the special case $n = 2$ and $\alpha_1 = \alpha_2 = \frac{1}{4}$.
2. For the Cobb–Douglas production function

$$f(\mathbf{x}) = \prod_{i=1}^{n} x_i^{\alpha_i}, \alpha_i > 0, \forall i \text{ and } \Sigma\alpha_i < 1:$$

(a) Show that the conditional input demand functions and the cost function are

$$x_i^c(\mathbf{p}, \bar{x}_0) = \frac{\alpha_i}{p_i} \bar{x}_0^{1/\Sigma\alpha_j} \prod_{j=1}^{n} \left[\frac{p_j}{\alpha_j}\right]^{\alpha_j/\Sigma\alpha_j} \qquad i = 1, \ldots, n$$

$$C(\mathbf{p}, \bar{x}_0) = \bar{x}_0^{1/\Sigma\alpha_j} \left[\sum_{j=1}^{n} \alpha_j\right] \prod_{j=1}^{n} \left[\frac{p_j}{\alpha_j}\right]^{\alpha_j/\Sigma\alpha_j}$$

(b) Show that the conditional input demands can be written in log-linear form

$$\ln x_i^c = \beta_i + \gamma_i \ln \bar{x}_0 + \sum_{j=1}^{n} \delta_{ij} \ln p_j \quad i = 1, \ldots, n$$

(c) Comment on the conditional input demand price elasticities, $\delta_{ij}, i, j = 1, \ldots, n$.
(d) Show that the off-diagonal elements of the Slutsky matrix are all positive.
(e) Check Shephard's lemma.

3. Work through question 4 for the special case $n = 2$, $v = \frac{1}{2}$, $\rho = -\frac{1}{2}$.

4. For the C.E.S. production function

$$f(\mathbf{x}) = \left[\sum_{i=1}^{n} x_i^{-\rho}\right]^{-v/\rho}$$

where $\rho > -1$ and $\rho \neq 0$, $v \in (0, 1)$:

(a) Show that the conditional input demand functions and the cost function are

$$x_i^c(\mathbf{p}, \bar{x}_0) = \frac{\bar{x}_0^{1/v}}{p_i^{1+\rho}}\left[\sum_{j=1}^{n} p_j^{\rho/1+\rho}\right]^{1/\rho} \quad i = 1, \ldots, n$$

$$C(\mathbf{p}, \bar{x}_0) = \bar{x}_0^{1/v}\left[\sum_{j=1}^{n} p_j^{-\rho}\right](\Sigma p_j^{\rho/1+\rho})^{1/\rho}$$

(b) Show that the off-diagonal elements of the Slutsky matrix are all positive.
(c) Check Shephard's lemma.
(d) Can the conditional demand equations be written in log-linear form?

5. For the cost function in question 2(a) show that the solution in $\bar{x}_0$ to: $\max_{\bar{x}_0 \in R_{++}} p_0 \bar{x}_0 - C(\mathbf{p}, \bar{x}_0)$, is the output supply function of exercise 10, question 2. Show that substitution of this output supply function in the conditional input demands in question 2(a) of exercise 11 produces the unconditional input demands of exercise 10, question 2.

6. With $n = 2$ the 1st- and 2nd-order conditions for a local solution to (CM) (written in 'max' form) are:

$$\begin{aligned} -p_1 + \lambda f_1'(\mathbf{x}) &= 0 \\ -p_2 + \lambda f_2'(\mathbf{x}) &= 0 \\ f(\mathbf{x}) - \bar{x}_0 &= 0 \end{aligned} \quad \text{and} \quad \begin{vmatrix} f_{11}'' & f_{12}'' & f_1' \\ f_{21}'' & f_{22}'' & f_2' \\ f_1' & f_2' & 0 \end{vmatrix} > 0$$

Use the classical comparative statics method to show that the sign pattern of the Slutsky matrix is

$$\begin{bmatrix} - & + \\ + & - \end{bmatrix}$$

7. Suppose $f:R^n_+ \to R$ is a production function satisfying (A10.1)–(A10.3) and suppose further that f is homogeneous of degree r ($0 < r < 1$, from strict concavity). From chapter 9 we know that if $\mathbf{x} = (x, x, \ldots, x)$ where $x > 0$, $f(\mathbf{x}) = kx^r$ some $k > 0$. Prove that

$$\lim_{x \to 0} \sum_{i=1}^{n} f_i'(\mathbf{x}) = +\infty$$

8. Prove that $UC_f(y) \subset R^n_{++}$ if $y > 0$ and

   (a) f is Cobb–Douglas, or
   (b) f is C.E.S. with $\rho > 0$.

9. For a C.E.S. production function with $\rho \in (-1, 0)$,

   (a) Show that if $n = 1$ there must be interior solutions to (CM) for all $(p_1, \bar{x}_0) \in R_{++} \times A$.
   (b) Show, by induction on n, that for any n there must be interior solutions to (CM) for all $(\mathbf{p}, \bar{x}_0) \in R^n_{++} \times A$.

12 Consumer theory

12.1 Introduction

A consumer is an economic entity, usually thought of as a person, who gains satisfaction from the consumption of commodities and who uses the resources available (income) to buy commodities in order to maximize the satisfaction gained from their consumption.

To make this precise we assume that there are n commodities or goods available; let $\mathbf{x} \in R^n_+$ denote a typical consumption vector. Not all consumption vectors are biologically feasible, however; denote by $X \in R^n_+$ the set of biologically feasible consumption vectors. X is known as the consumer's *consumption set*. Usually, for simplicity, we assume that $X = R^n_+$. The consumer is presumed to have *preferences* between alternative consumption vectors in the consumption set. That is, given, $\mathbf{x}^1, \mathbf{x}^2 \in X$, the consumer can tell us whether (a) $\mathbf{x}^1$ is preferred to $\mathbf{x}^2$, (b) $\mathbf{x}^2$ is preferred to $\mathbf{x}^1$ or (C) the consumer is indifferent between $\mathbf{x}^1$ and $\mathbf{x}^2$. We give a functional expression to these preferences by assuming that the consumer has a *utility function*, $U: X \to R$ which represents the consumer's preferences in the following sense:

(i) $\mathbf{x}^1, \mathbf{x}^2 \in X$ and $U(\mathbf{x}^1) > U(\mathbf{x}^2)$ if and only if (a) above is true;

(ii) $\mathbf{x}^1, \mathbf{x}^2 \in X$ and $U(\mathbf{x}^1) < U(\mathbf{x}^2)$ if and only if (b);

(iii) $\mathbf{x}^1, \mathbf{x}^2 \in X$ and $U(\mathbf{x}^1) = U(\mathbf{x}^2)$ if and only if (c).

Higher values of U thus indicate increased satisfaction and the consumer's objective of 'maximum satisfaction' translates into the mathematical requirement of 'maximizing U'. However, the consumer does not have a free choice of any consumption vector in X. We assume that the consumer has an exogenously given income $m > 0$ and that the consumer can purchase a unit of good i for the price $p_i > 0$, $i = 1, \ldots, n$; the vector $\mathbf{p} = (p_1, \ldots, p_n) \in R^n_{++}$. The purchase of the vector $\mathbf{x}$ at prices $\mathbf{p}$ incurs the consumer in an outlay of $\Sigma_{i=1}^{n} p_i x_i$ and this outlay cannot exceed the consumer's income. Thus the consumer's *budget constraint* is

budget constraint

$$\sum_{i=1}^{n} p_i x_i \leqslant m$$

and the consumer can acquire only consumption vectors which satisfy this constraint. We also assume that the consumer has no control over the prices on the goods market so that $\mathbf{p}$ is a parameter to the consumer, and that the consumer is free to buy any quantities (subject to the budget constraint) on these markets. Together these assumptions reflect the economist's assumption of a consumer who is a perfect competitor on all the markets on which the consumer trades.

Bringing all of this together, our model of consumer behaviour is that the consumer purchases goods $\mathbf{x}$ so as to solve the following *utility maximization problem*

utility max

$$\text{(UM)} \quad \max_{\mathbf{x} \in R_+^n} U(\mathbf{x}) \text{ subject to } \sum_{i=1}^{n} p_i x_i \leqslant m \text{ where } (\mathbf{p}, m) \in R_{++}^{n+1}$$

The ultimate objective of this chapter is a study of the solutions to (UM) and their properties. However, it is useful to start the consumer analysis by looking at another problem in which the consumer is asked to minimize the cost of reaching a pre-assigned utility level, $\bar{u}$:

cost min.

$$\min_{\mathbf{x} \in R_+^n} \Sigma p_i x_i \text{ subject to } U(\mathbf{x}) \geqslant \bar{u}$$

This is the consumer's *expenditure minimization problem* and is in a sense 'part of' of the utility maximization problem since if the consumer attains utility level $\bar{u}$ at the solution to (UM), the consumer must be choosing an $\mathbf{x}$ to solve (UM) which is the minimum cost way of reaching $\bar{u}$–otherwise utility is not being maximized! Analytically, it is easiest to look at the expenditure minimization problem first before addressing the full (UM) problem.

12.2 Assumptions on utility functions

Our analysis of utility maximization and expenditure minimization employs the following three assumptions on utility functions:

(A12.1) $U: R_+^n \rightarrow R$ is continuous on R_+^n and C^2 on R_{++}^n.

(A12.2) For $\mathbf{x} \in R^n_{++}$, $U_i'(\mathbf{x}) > 0$, $i = 1, \ldots, n$

The partial derivative $U_i'(\mathbf{x})$ measures the rate of change of utility as consumption of good i is increased from $\mathbf{x}$ and is referred to as the *marginal utility* of good i at $\mathbf{x}$. That marginal utility is positive merely reflects the assumption that the consumer prefers more goods to less, or that goods are always 'goods' and never become 'bads'. The third assumption is

(A12.3) U is strictly concave on R^n_{++}

When $n = 2$ (the case $n = 1$ has no economic interest) these assumptions imply that contours of U are typically as shown in fig. 12.1. Contours of utility functions are known as *indifference curves*: since U is constant along a contour the consumer is indifferent between any two consumption vectors on the same contour, and hence the name. Consequently, fig. 12.1 is the typical *indifference map* under our assumptions. In particular our assumptions imply that:

$$\text{if } U(\mathbf{x}^1) = U(\mathbf{x}^2),\ \mathbf{x}^1 \neq \mathbf{x}^2, \text{ then } U[\lambda \mathbf{x}^1 + (1-\lambda)\mathbf{x}^2] > U(\mathbf{x}^1)$$
$$= U(\mathbf{x}^2) \text{ for all } \lambda \in (0, 1)$$

This follows from (A12.3) and means that if the consumer is indifferent between $\mathbf{x}^1$ and $\mathbf{x}^2$ then the consumer will prefer any weighted average of $\mathbf{x}^1$ and $\mathbf{x}^2$ to either $\mathbf{x}^1$ or $\mathbf{x}^2$. Loosely the consumer prefers 'mixtures' of goods. However, our assumptions involve much more than this mixture preference which also follows from the weaker assumption of strict quasi-concavity. For a number of reasons it will, in fact, be desirable to replace (A12.3) by strict quasi-concavity, but we leave this replacement until we have studied quasi-concavity. For the moment we press on with (A12.3).

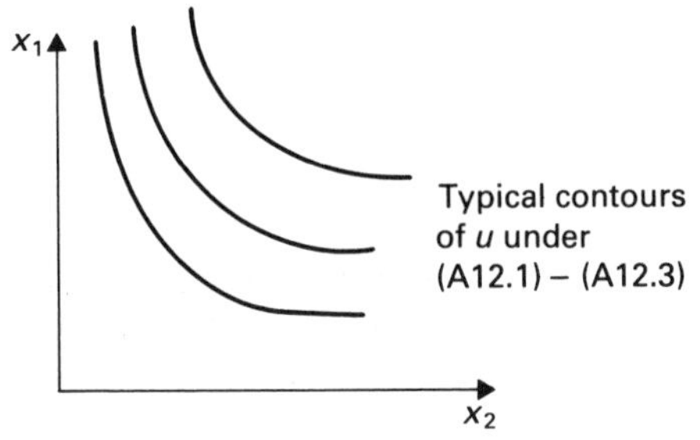

Figure 12.1

12.3 The expenditure minimization problem

In the expenditure minimization problem the parameters are the prices $\mathbf{p} \in R^n_{++}$ and the pre-assigned utility level, $\bar{u}$. Naturally we assume that $\bar{u}$ belongs to the range of U and this range will be some subset of R of the form $[a, b)$, where $U(0) = a$; b may be $+\infty$. However, if $\bar{u} = a$ the expenditure minimization problem has a trivial solution with $\mathbf{x} = 0$. We exclude this case from subsequent analysis and assume that $\bar{u} \in (a, b)$; for shorthand we denote (a, b) by A so that the complete specification of the expenditure minimization problem is:

$$\text{(EM)} \quad \min_{\mathbf{x} \in R^n_+} \sum_{i=1}^{n} p_i x_i \text{ subject to } U(\mathbf{x}) \geqslant \bar{u}, \text{ where } (\mathbf{p}, \bar{u}) \in R^n_{++} \times A$$

There is a complete formal equivalence, however, between this problem and the cost minimization problem of chapter 11; simply change U to f, $\bar{u}$ to $\bar{x}_0$ and (EM) becomes (CM). Consequently we can immediately transport the arguments of chapter 11 to the current context. We now do this.

(A12.4) For all $(\mathbf{p}, \bar{u}) \in R^n_{++} \times A$, any solution to (EM) must belong to R^n_{++}

This ensures interior solutions to (EM), and gives the following Kuhn–Tucker characterization of its solutions:

Theorem 12.1 Assuming (A12.1)–(A12.4), $\mathbf{x}^*$ solves (EM) at $\mathbf{p}, \bar{u}$ if and only if:

(a) $$\frac{U_i'(\mathbf{x}^*)}{U_j'(\mathbf{x}^*)} = \frac{p_i}{p_j} \quad \forall i, j = 1, \ldots, n$$

(b) $U(\mathbf{x}^*) = \bar{u}$

(with $\lambda^* = p_i / U_i'(\mathbf{x}^*)$, $i = 1, \ldots, n$)

Figure 12.2 illustrates the typical solution when $n = 2$. (b) requires the solution to lie on the contour of U for the value $\bar{u}$ while (a) requires the solution to be at the point on this contour where the contour slope, known as the consumer's *marginal rate of substitution*, equals the slope of the contour of $p_1x_1 + p_2x_2$ through this point.

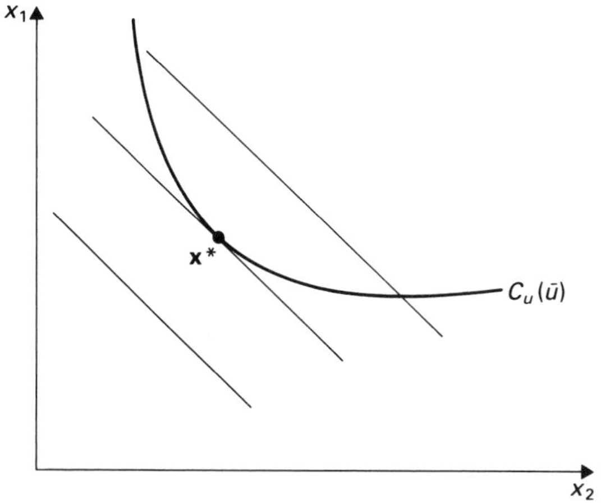

Figure 12.2

That is, $\mathbf{x}^*$ is visually characterized as the point on the indifference curve for utility level $\bar{u}$ where the marginal rate of substitution equals the relative price.

From chapter 7 there is at most one solution to (EM) at $(\mathbf{p}, \bar{u}) \in R^n_{++} \times A$. In chapter 17 we will see that (A12.1)–(A12.4) imply that, for all $(\mathbf{p}, \bar{u}) \in R^n_{++} \times A$, there is exactly one solution to (EM). Hence solutions to (EM) define the following three types of function.

1. The solution functions, now denoted $x_i^H : R^n_{++} \times A \to R$ with values $x_i^H(\mathbf{p}, \bar{u})$, $i = 1, \ldots, n$ and known as the consumer's *Hicksian demand functions.*
2. The optimal value function, denoted $e : R^n_{++} \times A \to R$ with values $e(\mathbf{p}, \bar{u}) = \Sigma p_i x_i^H(\mathbf{p}, \bar{u})$ and known as the consumer's *expenditure function.*
3. The multiplier function, $\lambda^H : R^n_{++} \times A \to R$ with values $\lambda^H(\mathbf{p}, \bar{u})$.

The expenditure function tells us the minimum expenditure required by the consumer to reach utility level $\bar{u}$ when the prices are $\mathbf{p}$; the Hicksian demand functions tell us the vector of goods the consumer will buy to reach this point. To proceed, we introduce differentiability assumptions about 1–3:

(A12.5) (i) for $i = 1, \ldots, n$, $x_i^H : R^n_{++} \times A \to R$ is C^1

(ii) $e : R^n_{++} \times A \to R$ is C^2

(iii) $\lambda^H : R^n_{++} \times A \to R$ is C^1

This allows us to apply the envelope theorem giving:

Theorem 12.2: Shephard's lemma for consumers Assuming (A12.1)–(A12.5)

$$\frac{\partial e}{\partial p_i}(\mathbf{p}, \bar{u}) = x_i^H(\mathbf{p}, \bar{u})$$

Of course this is the exact analogue of Shephard's lemma in chapter 11. In addition:

Theorem 12.3 Assuming (A12.1)–(A12.4), the expenditure function $e : R^n_{++} \times A \to R$ is a concave function of $\mathbf{p}$ for fixed $\bar{u}$.

Theorem 12.4 Assuming (A12.1)–(A12.4):

(a) for $i = 1, \ldots, n$, x_i^H is a homogeneous of degree zero function of $\mathbf{p}$ for fixed $\bar{u} \in A$.

(b) e is a homogeneous of degree one function of $\mathbf{p}$, for fixed $\bar{u} \in A$.

Combining these three theorems allows comparative static conclusions for (EM), at least with respect to price changes. The consumer's *Slutsky* matrix is defined as:

$$\mathbf{S}(\mathbf{p}, \bar{u}) = \begin{bmatrix} \frac{\partial x_1^H}{\partial p_1} & \cdots & \frac{\partial x_1^H}{\partial p_n} \\ \cdots & \cdots & \cdots \\ \frac{\partial x_n^H}{\partial p_1} & \cdots & \frac{\partial x_n^H}{\partial p_n} \end{bmatrix}$$

where derivatives are evaluated at $\mathbf{p}, \bar{u}$. The Slutsky matrix is the matrix of price derivatives of the Hicksian demand functions.

Using Shephard's lemma and the concavity property of theorem 12.3 gives:

Theorem 12.5 Assuming (A12.1)–(A12.5) the consumer's Slutsky matrix $\mathbf{S}(\mathbf{p}, \bar{u})$ is symmetric and n.s.d. for all $(\mathbf{p}, \bar{u}) \in R^n_{++} \times A$.

In particular we can conclude:

$$\frac{\partial x_i^H}{\partial p_i} \leqslant 0, \; i = 1, \ldots, n \tag{12.1}$$

so that a ceteris paribus increase in p_i leads to a reduction in the Hicksian demand for good i. In general, the only statement about the signs of off-diagonal elements of the Slutsky matrix is:

$$\text{for each } i, \frac{\partial x_i^H}{\partial p_j} \geqslant 0, \text{ some } j \neq i \tag{12.2}$$

which follows from theorems 12.5, 12.4 and Euler's theorem.

The signs of the off-diagonal elements of $\mathbf{S}(\mathbf{p}, \bar{u})$ give rise to a well-known definition. If the price of margarine goes up you would expect a rise in demand for butter as these goods are in some sense 'substitutes'. To be precise, i is said to be a *Hicksian net substitute* for j at $(\mathbf{p}, \bar{u})$ if $\partial x_i^H/\partial p_j\,(\mathbf{p}, \bar{u}) > 0$ while i is a *Hicksian net complement* for j at $(\mathbf{p}, \bar{u})$ if $\partial x_i^H/\partial p_j\,(\mathbf{p}, \bar{u}) < 0$. Some properties of this categorization of commodities which follow from our analysis are:

(a) From symmetry, i is a Hicksian net substitute (complement) for j at $(\mathbf{p}, \bar{u})$ if and only if j is a Hicksian net substitute (complement) for i at $(\mathbf{p}, \bar{u})$.

It is perhaps as well that (a) is true since without it the definition would be rather unappealing. Less attractive is:

(b) From (12.2), every good has at least one Hicksian net substitute (excluding zero values for Slutsky matrix elements).

In particular when there are just two goods, both goods must always be Hicksian net substitutes. Although this is intuitively unattractive, the Hicksian net substitute/complement classification is the most popular such classification used by economists, although it will not feature much in our later analysis.

Theorem 12.5 and (12.1), (12.2) are the substantial comparative static conclusions for (EM) which we carry forward now to our analysis of the full utility maximization problem.

12.4 The utility maximization problem

To refresh the reader this problem is:

$$\text{(UM)} \quad \max_{\mathbf{x} \in R_+^n} U(\mathbf{x}) \text{ subject to } \sum_{i=1}^{n} p_i x_i \leqslant m \text{ where } (\mathbf{p}, m) \in R_{++}^{n+1}$$

We embark on an analysis of this problem in the usual fashion:

(A12.6) For all $(\mathbf{p}, m) \in R^{n+1}_{++}$, any solution to (UM) must belong to R^n_{++}.

We assert that (A12.6) follows if U is Cobb–Douglas or C.E.S. (see section 12.9). (A12.6) ensures that we can write (UM) as:

$$\max_{\mathbf{x} \in R^n_{++}} U(\mathbf{x}) \text{ subject to } \sum_{i=1}^{n} p_i x_i \leqslant m \text{ where } (\mathbf{p}, m) \in R^{n+1}_{++}$$

Under our utility function assumptions this is now a standard parameterized concave programming problem (the reader can check this), with a non-stationary objective function. The Lagrangean and Kuhn–Tucker conditions are

$$L(\mathbf{x}, \lambda; \mathbf{p}, m) = U(\mathbf{x}) + \lambda\left[m - \sum_{i=1}^{n} p_i x_i\right]$$

(I) $U_i'(\mathbf{x}^*) - \lambda^* p_i = 0, i = 1, \ldots, n$

(II) $\lambda^* > 0$

(III) $m = \sum_{i=1}^{n} p_i x_i^*$ and $\mathbf{x}^* \in R^n_{++}$

(II) is implied by (I) since $p_i > 0$ and $U_i'(\mathbf{x}^*) > 0$; and (I) is equivalent to

$$\frac{U_i'(\mathbf{x}^*)}{U_j'(\mathbf{x}^*)} = \frac{p_i}{p_j} \quad \forall i, j = 1, \ldots, n$$

Hence the following characterization of solutions to (UM):

Theorem 12.6 Assuming (A12.1)–(A12.3) and (A12.6), $\mathbf{x}^*$ solves (UM) at $(\mathbf{p}, m)$ if and only if:

(a) $\dfrac{U_i'(\mathbf{x}^*)}{U_j'(\mathbf{x}^*)} = \dfrac{p_i}{p_j} \quad \forall i, j = 1, \ldots, n$

(b) $\mathbf{x}^* \in R^n_{++}$ and $m = \sum_{i=1}^{n} p_i x_i^*$

(with $\lambda^* = U_i'(\mathbf{x}^*)/p_i, i = 1, \ldots, n$).

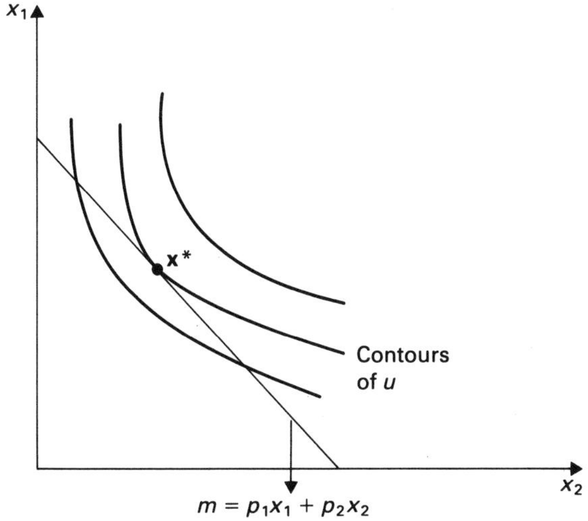

Figure 12.3

Figure 12.3 sketches a typical solution when $n = 2$. (b) tells us that the solution lies on the 'budget line', $m = p_1x_1 + p_2x_2$, and (a) tells us that the solution is at the point on this line where its slope equals the 'marginal rate of substitution' (i.e. the slope of the contour of U through the point). Figure 12.3 will no doubt be a familiar picture. Notice the similarity to fig. 12.2 but also notice the difference; in fig. 12.2 the *curve* $C_u(\bar{u})$ is the constraint, while in fig. 12.3 the constraint is the *line* $m = p_1x_1 + p_2x_2$.

Since U is strictly concave it follows from chapter 7 that there is at most one solution to (UM) at any $(\mathbf{p}, m) \in R^{n+1}_{++}$. Later we will show that in fact there is exactly one solution. This gives rise to the usual set of functions:

1. The solution functions denoted $x_i^M : R^{n+1}_{++} \to R$ with values $x_i^M(\mathbf{p}, m)$, $i = 1, \ldots, n$ and known as the consumer's *Marshallian demand functions*.
2. The optimal value function $\psi : R^{n+1}_{++} \to R$ with values $\psi(\mathbf{p}, m) = U[\mathbf{x}(\mathbf{p}, m)]$ and known as the consumer's *indirect utility function*.
3. The multiplier function, $\lambda^M : R^{n+1}_{++} \to R$ with values $\lambda^M(\mathbf{p}, m)$.

The Marshallian demand functions tell us what the consumer will purchase and consume at prices $\mathbf{p}$ with income m, and the indirect utility function indicates the level of utility thus attained.

Example 12.1 $n = 2$ and $U(\mathbf{x}) = x_1^{1/2} + x_2^{1/2}$. The reader can easily check that (A12.1)–(A12.3) are satisfied; U is C.E.S. so (A12.6) is satisfied. Hence $\mathbf{x}$ solves (UM) for this consumer if and only if:

(a) $$\frac{U_2'(\mathbf{x}^*)}{U_1'(\mathbf{x}^*)} = \frac{\frac{1}{2}x_2^{-1/2}}{\frac{1}{2}x_1^{-1/2}} = \frac{x_1^{1/2}}{x_2^{1/2}} = \frac{p_2}{p_1} \text{ and}$$

(b) $m = p_1 x_1 + p_2 x_2, \mathbf{x} \in R^2_{++}$.

From (a) $x_1 = \dfrac{p_2^2}{p_1^2} x_2$ and so from (b) $m = \dfrac{p_2^2}{p_1} x_2 + p_2 x_2$.

Hence $x_2 = \dfrac{p_1 m}{p_2(p_1 + p_2)}$ and $x_1 = \dfrac{p_2 m}{p_1(p_1 + p_2)}$ giving

$$x_1^M(\mathbf{p}, m) = \frac{p_2 m}{p_1(p_1 + p_2)}, \; x_2^M(\mathbf{p}, m) = \frac{p_1 m}{p_2(p_1 + p_2)},$$

$$\psi(\mathbf{p}, m) = \frac{m^{1/2}(p_1 + p_2)^{1/2}}{p_1^{1/2} p_2^{1/2}}$$

In order to apply the envelope theorem to (UM) we assume:

(A12.7) (i) For $i = 1, \ldots, n$, $x_i^M : R^{n+1}_{++} \to R$ is C^1

(ii) $\psi : R^{n+1}_{++} \to R$ is C^2

(iii) $\lambda^M : R^{n+1}_{++} \to R$ is C^1

These assumptions are satisfied in the above example; at a later stage we address the conditions on U which ensure (A12.7).

Applying the envelope theorem to (UM) with respect to p_i, $i = 1, \ldots, n$ gives

$$\frac{\partial L}{\partial p_i} = -\lambda x_i = -\lambda^M(\mathbf{p}, m)\, x_i^M(\mathbf{p}, m) = \frac{\partial \psi}{\partial p_i}, \; i = 1, \ldots, n$$

And for the parameter m we get

$$\frac{\partial L}{\partial m} = \lambda = \lambda^M(\mathbf{p}, m) = \frac{\partial \psi}{\partial m}$$

From these two relations we get

$$x_i^M(\mathbf{p}, m) = -\frac{\partial \psi / \partial p_i}{\partial \psi / \partial m}, \; i = 1, \ldots, n$$

This is a well-known result:

Theorem 12.7: Roy's identity Assuming (A12.1)–(A12.3) and (A12.6), (A12.7),

$$x_i^M(\mathbf{p}, m) = -\frac{\partial\psi/\partial p_i}{\partial\psi/\partial m}, \; i = 1, \ldots, n$$

where the right-hand side derivatives are evaluated at $(\mathbf{p}, m)$.

Roy's identity tells us that we can derive the consumer's Marshallian demand functions from knowledge of the indirect utility function simply by differentiation and use of Roy's formula. For instance, the reader can check that the indirect utility function found in example 12.1 does indeed give rise to the Marshallian demands of that example under application of Roy's identity. You can also see in example 12.1 that the Marshallian demand functions and the indirect utility function are homogeneous of degree zero in $(\mathbf{p}, m)$; this is generally true.

Theorem 12.8 Assuming (12.1)–(A12.3) and (A12.6):

(a) For $i = 1, \ldots, n$, $x_i^M(t\mathbf{p}, tm) = x_i^M(\mathbf{p}, m)$, $\forall t > 0$, $\forall(\mathbf{p}, m) \in R_{++}^{n+1}$; i.e. x_i^M is homogeneous of degree zero.

(b) $\psi(t\mathbf{p}, tm) = \psi(\mathbf{p}, m)$, $\forall t > 0$, $\forall(\mathbf{p}, m) \in R_{++}^{n+1}$; i.e. ψ is homogeneous of degree zero.

Proof

(a) From theorem 12.6, $\mathbf{x} = \mathbf{x}(\mathbf{p}, m)$ if and only if

$$\frac{U_i'(\mathbf{x})}{U_j'(\mathbf{x})} = \frac{p_i}{p_j} \quad \forall i, j = 1, \ldots, n$$

and

$$m = \sum_{i=1}^{n} p_i x_i, \; \mathbf{x} \in R_{++}^n$$

But the conditions characterizing the solution to (UM) at $(t\mathbf{p}, tm)$, $t > 0$ are exactly the same since

$$\frac{tp_i}{tp_j} = \frac{p_i}{p_j} \text{ and } m = \sum_{i=1}^{n} p_i x_i \text{ if and only if } tm = t\sum_{i=1}^{n} p_i x_i$$

Hence the solutions at $(\mathbf{p}, m)$ and $(t\mathbf{p}, tm)$, $t > 0$ are the same, which means

$$x_i^M(t\mathbf{p}, tm) = x_i^M(\mathbf{p}, m) \quad \forall t > 0, \forall i = 1, \ldots, n$$

as required.

(b) From (a), $U[\mathbf{x}(t\mathbf{p}, tm)] = U[\mathbf{x}(\mathbf{p}, m)]$, $\forall t > 0$ which means $\psi(t\mathbf{p}, tm) = \psi(\mathbf{p}, m)$, $\forall t > 0$. *Q.E.D.*

We now take a different direction from the one which the reader may be anticipating. Instead of trying to establish a 'curvature' property of ψ and using Roy's identity to uncover comparative statics results for (UM), it is much more fruitful and straightforward to attack this comparative static issue by first tracing links between the (UM) problem and the earlier (EM) problem–and then using the earlier results for (EM) with these 'links' to establish results for (UM). We start with the relation between (EM) and (UM).

12.5 Relations between utility maximization and expenditure minimization

We trace the desired links between (UM) and (EM) by looking at fig. 12.4 where the typical solution to a two good (EM) problem is sketched (again similar to fig. 12.2). Notice that the contour of the objective function for (EM) at the solution has equation $p_1x_1 + p_2x_2 = e(\mathbf{p}, \bar{u})$ since both equal $p_1x_1^H(\mathbf{p}, \bar{u}) + p_2x_2^H(\mathbf{p}, \bar{u})$. Now keep p_1, p_2 as they are and define $m = e(\mathbf{p}, \bar{u})$: the line in fig. 12.4 then becomes a budget line. Ask the consumer to solve (UM) given this budget constraint. Clearly (see fig. 12.3 if you need) the consumer will solve this constructed (UM) problem by choosing the tangency point in fig. 12.4. In other words:

$$\text{if } m = e(\mathbf{p}, \bar{u}) \text{ then } x_i^M(\mathbf{p}, m) = x_i^H(\mathbf{p}, \bar{u}), i = 1, 2$$

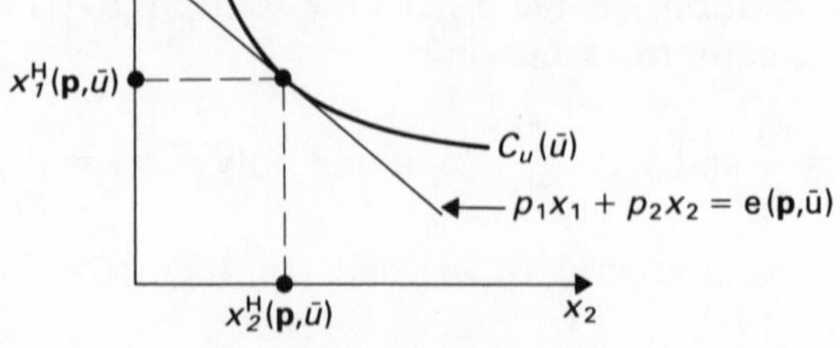

Figure 12.4

or

$$x_i^M(\mathbf{p}, e(\mathbf{p}, \bar{u})) = x_i^H(\mathbf{p}, \bar{u}), i = 1, 2$$

Furthermore, the indifference curve labelled $C_u(\bar{u})$ in fig. 12.4 now becomes the indifference curve through the solution of our constructed (UM) problem and hence is associated with utility level $\psi(\mathbf{p}, m)$, where, remember, $m = e(\mathbf{p}, \bar{u})$. Hence

$$\bar{u} = \psi(\mathbf{p}, e(\mathbf{p}, \bar{u}))$$

We have established the following two properties:

(D1) $x_i^M(\mathbf{p}, e(\mathbf{p}, \bar{u})) = x_i^H(\mathbf{p}, \bar{u}) \quad \forall i$

(D2) $\psi(\mathbf{p}, e(\mathbf{p}, \bar{u})) = \bar{u}$

These properties are often referred to as duality relations between (EM) and (UM), hence the labels (D1), (D2). (D1) tells us that we can find Hicksian demands simply by substituting the expenditure function formula, $e(\mathbf{p}, \bar{u})$, for m in the Marshallian demand function formula. (D2) tells us that if we solve the equation $\psi(\mathbf{p}, m) = \bar{u}$ for m in terms of $(\mathbf{p}, \bar{u})$, the resulting formula is the formula for the expenditure function. Examples illustrating these results follow soon.

First, however, reverse the argument to that so far. Start with fig. 12.5, a sketch of the typical solution to (UM) when $n = 2$. Now define $\bar{u} = \psi(\mathbf{p}, m)$ and present the consumer with the (EM) problem where p_1, p_2 are as they were and $\bar{u} = \psi(\mathbf{p}, m)$. Clearly:

(D3) $x_i^H(\mathbf{p}, \psi(\mathbf{p}, m)) = x_i^M(\mathbf{p}, m) \quad \forall i$

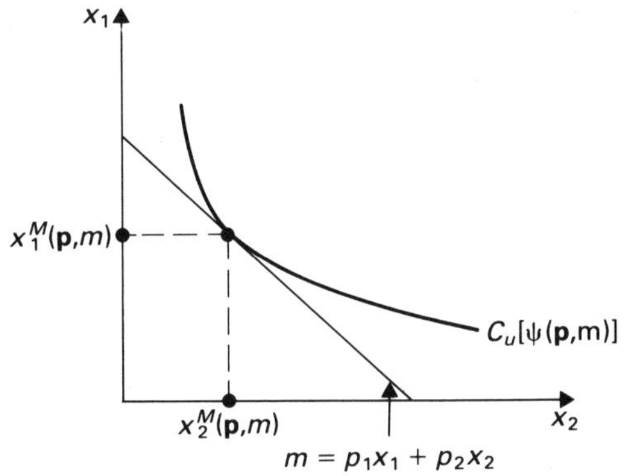

Figure 12.5

Moreover, the line in fig. 12.5 now has equation $p_1x_1+p_2x_2=e(\mathbf{p},\bar{u})$ where, remember, $\bar{u}=\psi(\mathbf{p},m)$. Hence:

(D4) $m = e(\mathbf{p}, \psi(\mathbf{p}, m))$

(D3) shows that substitution of the indirect utility function for $\bar{u}$ in Hicksian demand formulae produces the Marshallian demand functions while (D4) shows that if we solve $m = e(\mathbf{p}, \bar{u})$ for $\bar{u}$ in terms of $\mathbf{p}, m$ the result is the formula for the indirect utility function. Again illustrative examples follow soon.

We now assert that (D1)–(D4) are generally true and not just when $n = 2$:

Theorem 12.9 Under assumptions (A12.1)–(A12.3), the 'duality' relations (D1)–(D4) are satisfied.

Figure 12.6 is a visual representation of these links between (UM) and (EM), plus the links between solution functions and optimal values within each problem. Notice that knowledge of $\psi(\mathbf{p}, m)$ alone, $e(\mathbf{p}, \bar{u})$ alone or $\mathbf{x}^H$ alone is sufficient to allow derivation of the other three functions in fig. 12.6; knowledge of $\mathbf{x}^M(\mathbf{p}, m)$ requires knowledge of U or e to do this, however.

Example 12.2

(a) Suppose we know $\psi(\mathbf{p}, m) = \dfrac{m^{1/2}(p_1+p_2)^{1/2}}{p_1^{1/2}p_2^{1/2}}$

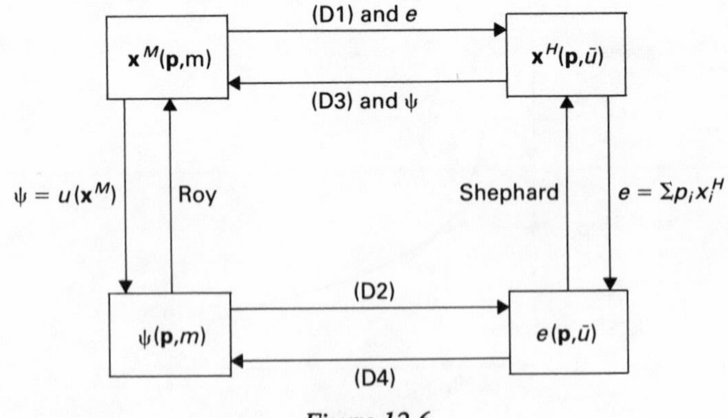

Figure 12.6

(i) To find e set $\bar{u} = \dfrac{m^{1/2}(p_1+p_2)^{1/2}}{p_1^{1/2}p_2^{1/2}}$ and solve for m giving

$$m = \frac{p_1p_2}{p_1+p_2}\,\bar{u}^2 = e(\mathbf{p}, \bar{u})$$

(ii) To find $\mathbf{x}^H$ apply Shephard's lemma to e giving

$$x_1^H(\mathbf{p}, \bar{u}) = \frac{\partial e}{\partial p_1} = \bar{u}^2\,\frac{p_2(p_1+p_2)-p_1p_2}{(p_1+p_2)^2} = \left[\frac{p_2\bar{u}}{p_1+p_2}\right]^2$$

$$x_2^H(\mathbf{p}, u) = \frac{\partial e}{\partial p_2} = \left[\frac{p_1\bar{u}}{p_1+p_2}\right]^2$$

(iii) To find $\mathbf{x}^M$ from (ii) substitute $\bar{u} = \psi(\mathbf{p}, m)$ giving

$$x_1^M(\mathbf{p}, m) = \frac{p_2^2}{(p_1+p_2)^2}\,\frac{m(p_1+p_2)}{p_1p_2} = \frac{p_2m}{p_1(p_1+p_2)} \text{ and}$$

$$x_2^M(\mathbf{p}, m) = \frac{p_1m}{p_2(p_1+p_2)}$$

Alternatively, apply Roy's identity directly to ψ giving, of course, the same answers.

(b) Suppose, on the other hand, that we start with the knowledge of

$$e(\mathbf{p}, \bar{u}) = \frac{p_1p_2}{p_1+p_2}\,\bar{u}^2$$

To find ψ equate $e(\mathbf{p}, \bar{u})$ to m, i.e.

$$\frac{p_1p_2}{p_1+p_2}\,\bar{u}^2 = m$$

and solve for $\bar{u}$ in terms of m giving

$$\bar{u} = \frac{m^{1/2}(p_1+p_2)^{1/2}}{p_1^{1/2}p_2^{1/2}}$$

which is ψ.

(c) Finally starting from

$$x_1^H(\mathbf{p}, \bar{u}) = \left[\frac{p_2\bar{u}}{p_1+p_2}\right]^2,\ x_2^H(\mathbf{p}, \bar{u}) = \left[\frac{p_1\bar{u}}{p_1+p_2}\right]^2$$

we can find e by $e(\mathbf{p}, \bar{u}) = p_1 x_1^H + p_2 x_2^H$ which gives

$$e(\mathbf{p}, \bar{u}) = \frac{p_1 p_2}{p_1 + p_2} \bar{u}^2$$

and (b) shows how to derive the rest.

The close links between Marshallian demands and Hicksian demands, in (D1) and (D3) in particular, suggest that there will be close links between the derivatives of these functions also. Indeed there are, and the *Slutsky equation* expresses this relation.

12.6 The Slutsky equation

We find this relation between the derivatives of Marshallian and Hicksian demands by differentiating the duality formula (D1) of the last section; this was

$$x_i^M(\mathbf{p}, e(\mathbf{p}, \bar{u})) = x_i^H(\mathbf{p}, \bar{u})$$

and differentiating partially with respect to p_j gives

$$\frac{\partial x_i^M}{\partial p_j}(\mathbf{p}, e(\mathbf{p}, \bar{u})) + \frac{\partial x_i^M}{\partial m}(\mathbf{p}, e(\mathbf{p}, \bar{u}))\frac{\partial e}{\partial p_j}(\mathbf{p}, \bar{u}) = \frac{\partial x_i^H}{\partial p_j}(\mathbf{p}, \bar{u})$$

Now by Shephard's lemma,

$$x_j^H(\mathbf{p}, \bar{u}) = \frac{\partial e}{\partial p_j}(\mathbf{p}, \bar{u})$$

thus giving

$$\frac{\partial x_i^M}{\partial p_j}(\mathbf{p}, e(\mathbf{p}, \bar{u})) + x_j^H(\mathbf{p}, \bar{u})\frac{\partial x_i^M}{\partial m}(\mathbf{p}, e(\mathbf{p}, \bar{u})) = \frac{\partial x_i^H}{\partial p_i}(\mathbf{p}, \bar{u})$$

Now let $e(\mathbf{p}, \bar{u}) = m$ so that $\bar{u} = \psi(\mathbf{p}, m)$ from (D4) earlier. This substitution gives, using (D3),

$$\frac{\partial x_i^M}{\partial p_j}(\mathbf{p}, m) + x_j^M(\mathbf{p}, m)\frac{\partial x_i^M}{\partial m}(\mathbf{p}, m) = \frac{\partial x_i^H}{\partial p_j}(\mathbf{p}, \psi(\mathbf{p}, m))$$

This is the Slutsky equation linking Marshallian derivatives on the left-hand side with Hicksian derivatives on the right. It is more usual to write it in the following form:

Theorem 12.10: The Slutsky equation Assuming (A12.1)–(A12.7), for any $i, j = 1, \ldots, n$ and for any $(\mathbf{p}, m) \in R_{++}^{n+1}$,

$$\frac{\partial x_i^M}{\partial p_j}(\mathbf{p}, m) = \frac{\partial x_i^H}{\partial p_j}(\mathbf{p}, \psi(\mathbf{p}, m)) - x_j^M(\mathbf{p}, m)\frac{\partial x_i^M}{\partial m}(\mathbf{p}, m)$$

Thus the total effect of a change in p_j on the Marshallian demand for good i can be split into the sum of two parts:

(i) $\partial x_i^H/\partial p_j\,(\mathbf{p}, \psi(\mathbf{p}, m))$, known as the *substitution effect* of a change in p_j on the Marshallian demand for i; and

(ii) $-x_j^M(\mathbf{p}, m)\,\partial x_i^M/\partial m\,(\mathbf{p}, m)$, known as the *income effect* of a change in p_j on the Marshallian demand for i.

A ceteris paribus change in p_j, say an increase, makes the consumer worse off (since income and all other prices are constant). If the consumer were compensated for this reduction in utility with extra income to bring back the original utility level (but at the new prices) the consumer's consumptions would differ from the original levels because of the price change. The difference between the original and these 'compensated' consumptions corresponds to the substitution effect (i), while the income effect (ii) corresponds to the difference between the compensated values and the final consumption point. In due course some pictures of this Slutsky decomposition of 'total' effects into 'income' and 'substitution' effects will aid the understanding of readers not already familiar with the notion. More importantly, we must address now the comparative static issue for Marshallian demands, and we do so by looking at the possibility of definitive signs for income and substitution effects. In fact there is hardly anything definite to be had; but the process of discovering this is instructive.

12.7 Income effects and inferior goods

Consider a utility maximizing consumer faced with a ceteris paribus increase in income. The consumer will certainly increase consumption of at least some goods, and first thoughts may suggest that the consumer will increase consumption of all goods. However, if originally the consumer is very poor and buying lots of bread as a cheap food, the increase in income could cause a switch out of bread into more luxurious foods and bread consumption may actually fall. In fact, the assumptions made so far for the (UM) problem do allow this sort of behaviour. The situations depicted in fig. 12.7 are both entirely consistent with utility functions satisfying (A12.1)–(A12.3) and our other assumptions.

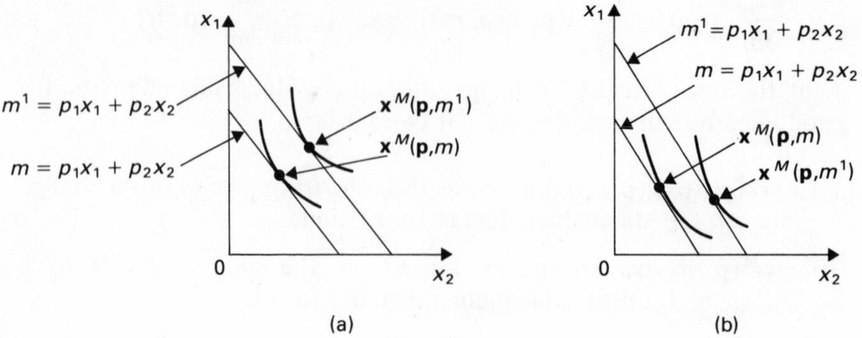

Figure 12.7

In both figs 12.7(a) and 12.7(b) the consumer undergoes a ceteris paribus rise in income from m to m^1; prices do not change so this increase shifts the budget line outwards, parallel to its original position. In fig. 12.7(a) the effect on Marshallian demands is to increase consumption of both goods, while in fig. 12.7(b), although consumption of good 2 increases, that of good 1 goes down; good 1 is like the bread in the earlier story.

Consider now $\partial x_i^M/\partial m\ (\mathbf{p}, m)$. Figure 12.7 shows that such income derivatives of Marshallian demands can be either positive or negative. We say:

(i) good i is *an inferior good* at $(\mathbf{p}, m)$ if $\partial x_i^M/\partial m\ (\mathbf{p}, m) < 0$;

(ii) good i is *a non-inferior good* at $(\mathbf{p}, m)$ if it is not inferior at $(\mathbf{p}, m)$.

So good 1 in fig. 12.7(b) would be inferior at least at some $(\mathbf{p}, m)$, corresponding to bread in the earlier example.

Now we know from the Slutsky equation that the effect of a ceteris paribus increase in p_j on the Marshallian demand for good i can be decomposed into income and substitution effects. The income effect is

$$-x_j^M(\mathbf{p}, m)\,\frac{\partial x_i^M}{\partial m}\,(\mathbf{p}, m)$$

Since $x_j^M(\mathbf{p}, m) > 0$ it follows that the income effect works for a reduction in consumption of good i if i is non-inferior, while the income effect works for an increase in consumption of good i if i is inferior. The problematic nature of the sign of the income effect should make you pessimistic about the possibility of putting a definite sign on the total effect $\partial x_i^M/\partial p_j$ $(\mathbf{p}, m)$. There is good reason for this pessimism.

12.8 Substitution effects, total effects and Giffen goods

The substitution effect in the Slutsky equation corresponds to an element of the consumer's Slutsky matrix. Hence we draw on our earlier analyses of this matrix for the following information about its sign:

(a) for $i = 1, \ldots, n$, $\partial x_i^H/\partial p_i$ $(\mathbf{p}, \psi(\mathbf{p}, m)) \leqslant 0$;

(b) for $i, j = 1, \ldots, n$ where $i \neq j$, the sign of $\partial x_i^H/\partial p_j$ $(\mathbf{p}, \psi(\mathbf{p}, m))$ can be either positive or negative if $n > 2$.

From (a) we say that the 'own-price' substitution effect is negative, while from (b) the 'cross-price' substitution effect has indeterminate sign, at least when $n > 2$.

Consider now the 'total' effect, $\partial x_i^M/\partial p_j$ $(\mathbf{p}, m)$. If $i \neq j$ this total effect is the sum of an indeterminate sign substitution effect and an indeterminate sign income effect. Indeed, the total 'cross' effect, $\partial x_i^M/\partial p_j$ $(\mathbf{p}, m)$, $i \neq j$ can be either positive or negative. On the other hand, if $i = j$ the total 'own-price' effect is the sum of a negative substitution effect and an indeterminate sign income effect. The sign of the income effect depends on whether good i is inferior or not. Logically there are three potential outcomes for the total own-price effect:

(i) Good i is non-inferior giving a negative income effect which reinforces the negative substitution effect producing a negative total effect.

This is the outcome suggested by first thoughts: as p_i goes up (ceteris paribus) demand for good i goes down. The same ultimate outcome would emerge in the following case:

(ii) Good i is inferior giving a positive income effect, but this income effect is 'small' in magnitude so that it is outweighed by the negative substitution effect producing a negative total effect again.

The last logical possibility is:

(iii) Good i is 'strongly' inferior giving a 'large' positive income effect which outweighs the negative substitution effect and produces a positive total effect.

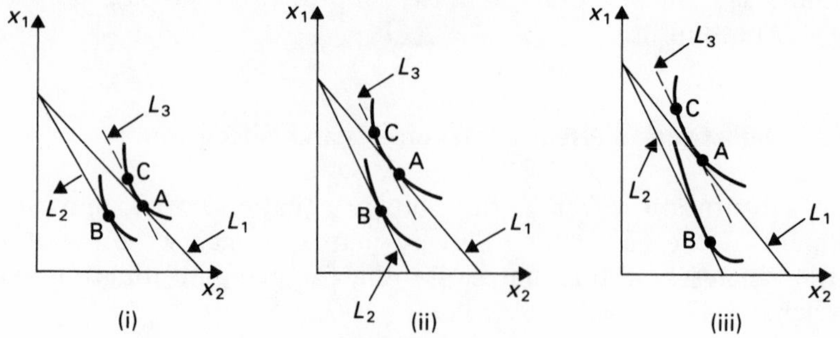

Figure 12.8

We now assert that all three of these cases can occur under our assumptions (A12.1)–(A12.3) and (A12.6), (A12.7). Figure 12.8 provides an illustration. In each case L_1 represents the initial budget line and A the initial solution to (UM) while L_2 is the budget line after a ceteris paribus increase in p_2 and B is the new solution to (UM). The dotted line L_3 compensates the consumer for the loss of utility by increasing income and keeping prices at their new levels so that the consumer can just reach the original utility level at point C. The move from A to C is then the substitution effect while C to B is the income effect; A to B is, of course, the total effect. Concentrating on the effects on good 2 (i.e. the own-price effects) you see that:

(a) in case (i) substitution and income effects both lead to a reduction in x_2 producing a negative total effect;

(b) in case (ii) the income effect is positive but is outweighed by the substitution effect producing a negative total effect again;

(c) in case (iii) the income effect is positive but now large enough to outweigh the substitution effect producing the perverse positive total effect.

We say that good i is a *Giffen good* at $(\mathbf{p}, m)$ if $\partial x_i^M(\mathbf{p}, m)/\partial p_i > 0$ while i is non-Giffen otherwise; case (iii) thus corresponds to the case of a Giffen good while the other two cases are non-Giffen. Notice that 'good i is Giffen at $(\mathbf{p}, m)$' implies 'good i is inferior at $(\mathbf{p}, m)$', but not vice-versa. Inferior goods are not necessarily Giffen (case (ii)); you need a 'strongly' inferior good (case (iii)).

12.9 Interior solutions in consumer theory

Let $a = U(0)$. An assumption which generates interior solutions is the following analogue of interior isoquants:

Interior indifference curves $UC_u(y) \subset R^n_{++}$ if $y > a$

In the firm discussion we imposed $f(0) = 0$; for consumers $U(0)$ need not be zero. This apart, the interior indifference curves assumption is the same as interior isoquants and implies interior solutions to (EM). However, now this assumption also implies interior solutions to (UM). For the consumer can achieve a utility level $y > a$ in (UM) since $(\mathbf{p}, m) \in R^{n+1}_{++}$. Hence solutions to (UM) must belong to $UC_u(y)$ some $y > a$ and so these solutions must belong to R^n_{++}. In particular if U satisfies (A12.1)–(A12.3) and is Cobb–Douglas or C.E.S. with $\rho > 0$ then (A12.4) and (A12.6) follow. For C.E.S. utility functions with $\rho \in (-1, 0)$ the argument of question 9 of exercise 11 ensures interior solutions to (EM), and a straightforward re-working of this exercise shows that interior solutions to (UM) are also ensured.

To sum up: suppose U satisfies (A12.1)–(A12.3); if in addition,

(a) U has interior indifference curves then (A12.4) and (A12.6) follow,

(b) U is Cobb–Douglas or C.E.S. then (A12.4) and (A12.6) follow.

Exercise 12

1. For the Cobb–Douglas utility function, $U(\mathbf{x}) = \Pi_{i=1}^n x_i^{\alpha_i}$, $\alpha_j > 0$, $\forall i$ and $\Sigma\alpha_i < 1$:

   (a) Write down the Hicksian demand functions and the expenditure function from question 2(a) of exercise 11.

   (b) Hence show that the indirect utility function is

$$\psi(\mathbf{p}, m) = \frac{m^{\Sigma\alpha_j}}{\left[\sum_{j=1}^{n} \alpha_j\right]^{\Sigma\alpha_j} \prod_{j=1}^{n} \left[\frac{p_j}{\alpha_j}\right]^{\alpha_j}}$$

   (c) By substituting the indirect utility function for $\bar{u}$ in the Hicksian demands (or by using Roy's identity), show that the Marshallian demand functions are

$$x_i^M(\mathbf{p}, m) = \frac{\alpha_i m}{p_i \sum_{j=1}^{n} \alpha_j}, i = 1, \ldots, n$$

(d) Show that all goods are non-inferior, non-Giffen and (using question 2(a) of exercise 11), that every pair of goods are Hicksian net substitutes.

2. Repeat questions 1(a)–1(d) for the C.E.S. utility function $U(\mathbf{x}) = [\Sigma x_i^{-\rho}]^{-v/\rho}$, $\rho > -1$, $\rho \neq 0$, $v \in (0, 1)$ referring to question 4 of exercise 11 and substituting

$$\psi(\mathbf{p}, m) = \frac{m^v}{\left[\sum_{j=1}^{n} p_j^{-\rho}\right]^v \left[\sum_{j=1}^{n} p_j^{\rho/1+\rho}\right]^{v/\rho}}$$

and

$$x_i^M(\mathbf{p}, m) = \frac{m}{p_i^{1+\rho} \sum_{j=1}^{n} p_j^{-\rho}}, i = 1, \ldots, n$$

3. The Marshallian budget share for good i is

$$w_i(\mathbf{p}, m) = \frac{p_i x_i^M(\mathbf{p}, m)}{m}$$

(a) Show that w_i is homogeneous of degree zero in $(\mathbf{p}, m)$ and $\Sigma_{i=1}^n w_i = 1$.

(b) For the Cobb–Douglas and C.E.S. cases write down the formulae for $w_i(\mathbf{p}, m)$ and show that both exhibit the following additional homogeneity properties:

(i) w_i is homogeneous of degree zero in $\mathbf{p}$ for fixed m;

(ii) w_i is homogeneous of degree zero in m for fixed $\mathbf{p}$.

4. The Marshallian income elasticity for good i is

$$\eta_i(\mathbf{p}, m) = \frac{m}{x_i^M(\mathbf{p}, m)} \frac{\partial x_i^M}{\partial m}(\mathbf{p}, m)$$

(a) By differentiation of the budget constraints show that

$$\sum_{i=1}^{n} w_i(\mathbf{p}, m)\, \eta_i(\mathbf{p}, m) = 1$$

Hence note that $\eta_i(\mathbf{p}, m) > 0$ for at least one i.

(b) Evaluate the formulae for $\eta_i(\mathbf{p}, m)$ in the Cobb–Douglas and C.E.S. cases.

5. The Marshallian price elasticity for good i with respect to j is

$$\epsilon_{ij}(\mathbf{p}, m) = \frac{p_j}{x_i^M(\mathbf{p}, m)} \frac{\partial x_i^M(\mathbf{p}, m)}{\partial p_j}$$

(a) By differentiation of the budget constraint show that

$$w_j(\mathbf{p}, m) + \sum_{i=1}^{n} w_i(\mathbf{p}, m)\, \epsilon_{ij}(\mathbf{p}, m) = 0, \; j = 1, \ldots, n$$

Hence note that for each j, there is at least one i (which may equal j) where $\epsilon_{ij}(\mathbf{p}, m) > 0$.

(b) Evaluate the formulae for $\epsilon_{ij}(\mathbf{p}, m)$ in the Cobb–Douglas and C.E.S. cases.

(c) Good i is a Hicksian gross substitute (complement) for j at $(\mathbf{p}, m)$ if $\partial x_i^M/\partial p_j\ (\mathbf{p}, m) > (<)\ 0$ or if $\epsilon_{ij}(\mathbf{p}, m) > (<)\ 0$. Investigate Hicksian gross substitutability/complementary in the Cobb–Douglas and C.E.S. cases.

6. When $n = 2$ consider

$$\begin{bmatrix} \dfrac{\partial x_1^M}{\partial p_1} & \dfrac{\partial x_1^M}{\partial p_2} \\ \dfrac{\partial x_2^M}{\partial p_1} & \dfrac{\partial x_2^M}{\partial p_2} \end{bmatrix}$$

Using the Slutsky equation:

(a) Find which of the elements of the matrix can be definitely signed if:

(i) both goods are non-inferior;

(ii) good 1 is inferior (so good 2 is non-inferior).

(b) Ascertain whether the matrix is necessarily symmetric and comment on the resulting intuitive appeal of the Hicksian gross substitute/complement classification of question 5 above.

7. Subsistence consumption. Suppose the consumption set is $X = \{\mathbf{x} \in R^n_+ | x_i \geqslant \gamma_i,\ i = 1, \ldots, n\}$ where $\gamma_i \geqslant 0$ is the subsistence consumption of good i. Let $z_i = x_i - \gamma_i$ and let $U: R^n_+ \to R$, with values $U(\mathbf{z})$, represent consumer preferences among vectors which at least meet subsistence requirements. The budget constraint is $\Sigma p_i x_i \leqslant m$ or $\Sigma p_i z_i \leqslant m - \Sigma p_i \gamma_i = \hat{m}$, say; $\hat{m}$ is income left over after meeting subsistence requirements and we assume $\hat{m} > 0$. In terms of $\mathbf{z}$ the (UM) problem is (assuming 'interior solutions')

$$\max_{\mathbf{z} \in R^n_{++}} U(\mathbf{z}) \text{ subject to } \Sigma p_i z_i \leqslant \hat{m} \text{ where } (\mathbf{p}, \hat{m}) \in R^{n+1}_{++}$$

which is exactly the standard (UM) problem with a different interpretation. With a Cobb–Douglas specification of

$$U(\mathbf{z}) = \prod_{i=1}^{n} z_i^{\alpha_i}, \quad \Sigma \alpha_i < 1$$

the utility in terms of $\mathbf{x}$ is $\Pi(x_i - \gamma_i)^{\alpha_i}$ which is known as the Stone–Geary utility function. Question 1(c) above provides the solution of (UM) for $\mathbf{z}$ in terms of $\mathbf{p}, \hat{m}$. Re-writing this as $\mathbf{x}$ in terms of $\mathbf{p}, m$ show that for a Stone–Geary utility function

(a) $$p_i x_i^M(\mathbf{p}, m) = p_i \gamma_i + \frac{\alpha_i}{\sum_{j=1}^{n} \alpha_j} \left[m - \sum_{j=1}^{n} p_j \gamma_j \right] \quad i = 1, \ldots, n$$

(known as the linear expenditure system since expenditure on good i is a linear function of $\mathbf{p}, m$)

(b) $$\psi(\mathbf{p}, m) = \frac{\left(m - \sum_{j=1}^{n} p_j \gamma_j \right)^{\Sigma \alpha_j}}{(\Sigma \alpha_j)^{\Sigma \alpha_j} \prod_{j=1}^{n} \left[\frac{p_j}{\alpha_j} \right]^{\alpha_j}}$$

(c) $$x_i^H(\mathbf{p}, \bar{u}) = \gamma_i + \frac{\alpha_i}{p_i} \bar{u}^{1/\Sigma \alpha_j} \prod_{j=1}^{n} \left[\frac{p_j}{\alpha_j} \right]^{\alpha_j / \Sigma \alpha_j}$$

(d) $$e(\mathbf{p}, \bar{u}) = \sum_{j=1}^{n} p_j \gamma_j + \bar{u}^{1/\Sigma \alpha_j} (\Sigma \alpha_j) \, \Pi \left[\frac{p_j}{\alpha_j} \right]^{\alpha_j / \Sigma \alpha_j}$$

13 Quasi-concavity

13.1 Introduction

The theory of concave functions and concave programming developed earlier has been most useful in allowing us to study the basic models of the theory of the firm and the theory of the consumer. However, as already remarked, the assumptions of concave production and utility functions are assumptions that we would prefer to relax. Attention is thus focused on generalizing the concept of a concave function and the subsequent theory of optimization involving generalized concave functions. This chapter and the next are devoted to the most well-known and most useful concept of generalized concavity, namely quasi-concavity. We start by defining quasi-concave functions; we look in detail at their properties and finally we turn to quasi-concave programming. Since there is rather too much material for one chapter various bits (including quasi-concave programming) are saved for chapter 14.

13.2 Quasi-concave functions

The definition has been mentioned earlier:

Definition 13.1 Suppose $D \subset R^n$ is convex. Then $f: D \to R$ is *quasi-concave* if and only if $UC_f(y)$ is a convex set for all y in the range of f.

Now any concave function will have the property that its upper contour sets are convex sets. However, there are functions whose upper contour sets are all convex which are not concave functions; for instance the earlier example of such a function was $f: R \to R$ where $f(x) = x^3$. It follows that the class of quasi-concave functions includes, but is larger than, the class of concave functions; quasi-concavity is indeed a generalization of concavity. To expand on this remark we now engage in some further discussion of the geometry of quasi-concave functions in the one- and two-variable cases.

Suppose then that $f:R \to R$ is a quasi-concave function of one variable. The only requirement that f must satisfy is that all its upper contour sets are convex sets. Any concave f will have this property: however, fig. 13.1 shows the graphs of various unspecified functions of one variable which also have this property but which are not concave (you can put the graph of x^3 alongside as another example). In each case a typical $UC_f(y)$ is shown and is convex: the reader can see by inspection that all upper contour sets will be convex in fig. 13.1. Hence all functions whose graphs are shown there are quasi-concave functions. Further inspection of (a) and (b) will also reveal the fact that any C^1, *non-stationary* function of one variable will be quasi-concave since then G_f is either upward-sloping throughout (like (a)) or downward sloping throughout (like (b)): in either case $UC_f(y)$ will always be a convex set. One lesson from fig. 13.1 is that the *graph* of a quasi-concave function need not have the 'nice' properties possessed by the graphs of concave functions; in particular there is no reason why the graph of a quasi-concave function should have a convex hypograph, unlike the concave case. A convex upper contour set is all that is needed for quasi-concavity.

In the two-variable setting we have typically used contour maps (in R^2) rather than graphs (in R^3) to acquire a visualization of such functions. However, both concave and quasi-concave functions have the same contour property that $UC_f(y)$ is convex. For instance fig. 13.2 sketches a few contours of an unspecified C^1 function $f:R^2 \to R$ with positive partial derivatives everywhere.

Since derivatives are positive $UC_f(y_i)$ is the set of points on or above $C_f(y_i)$, $i = 1, 2, 3$ and is drawn as a convex set. Consequently f could be concave or merely quasi-concave. Both possibilities are consistent with the picture. Like the one-variable case the visual difference between concave and merely quasi-concave two-variable functions lies in their graphs which are subsets of R^3. Concave functions must have convex hypographs while this is not necessarily true

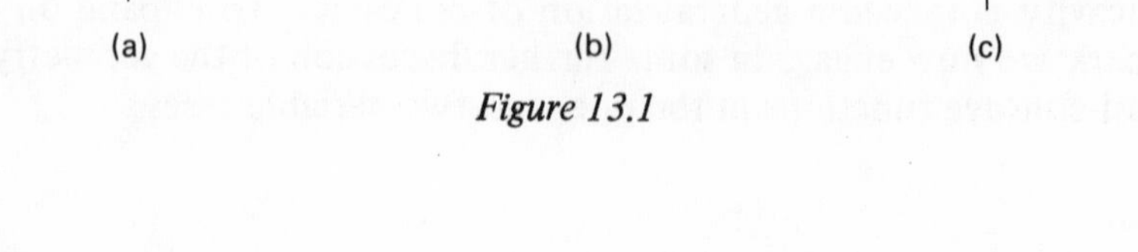

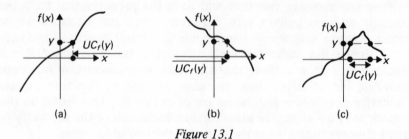

Figure 13.1

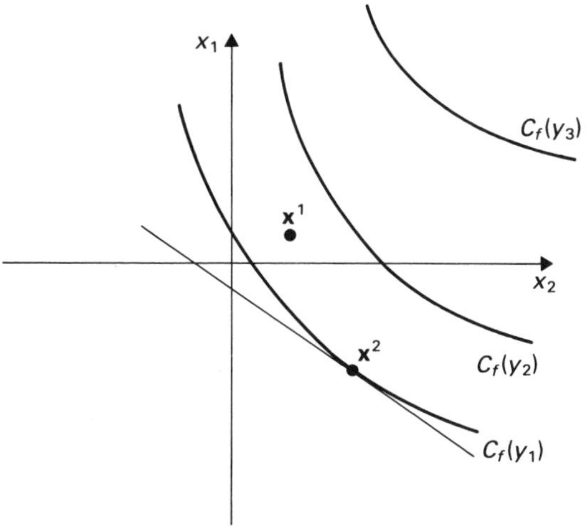

Figure 13.2

of quasi-concave functions. For instance consider $f: R^2_{++} \to R$ where $f(\mathbf{x}) = x_1 x_2$. The range is R_{++} and for any $y \in R_{++}$, $UC_f(y) = \{\mathbf{x} \in R^2_{++} \mid x_1 \geqslant y/x_2\}$ and is the set of points on or above a rectangular hyperbola in R^2_{++} which is certainly a convex set; this function is therefore certainly quasi-concave. However, the function is not concave; for instance the Hessian is $\begin{pmatrix} 0 & 1 \\ 1 & 0 \end{pmatrix}$ which is not n.s.d. Yet the shape of the contours gives no information to indicate this lack of concavity. The visual feature which does betray this lack of concavity is the hypograph of f but unfortunately this is a subset of R^3 and difficult to sketch. However, consider the subset of the hypograph corresponding to $x_1 = x_2 = x$ say. The hypograph itself is $\{(y, \mathbf{x}) \in R^3 \mid y \leqslant x_1 x_2\}$ and the subset of the hypograph where $x_1 = x_2 = x$ is $\{(y, x) \in R^2 \mid y \leqslant x^2\}$. Figure 13.3 shows this subset of HG_f which is clearly not a convex set and which means that HG_f itself cannot be a convex set; for instance $y = 1, x_1 = x_2 = 1$ and $y = 4, x_1 = x_2 = 2$ are two points in HG_f but convex combinations of these are not in HG_f. The visual lesson is complete. For a function to be quasi-concave its upper contour sets must be convex sets–and that is all. Concave functions have this property but must *also* have the property that their hypographs are convex sets; there are functions which are quasi-concave (convex $UC_f(y)$) but not concave (convex $UC_f(y)$ but non-convex HG_f).

So far the discussion of quasi-concavity has been very visual, emanating from the 'geometric' definition 13.1. For some purposes

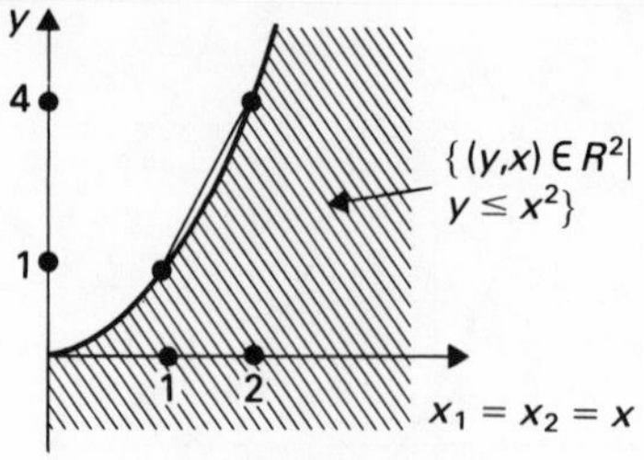

Figure 13.3

an algebraic expression of definition 13.1 is useful. There are a number of possibilities, the most popular of which is;

Theorem 13.1 Suppose $D \subset R^n$ is convex. $f: D \to R$ is quasi-concave if and only if

$$\mathbf{x}^1, \mathbf{x}^2 \in D \text{ and } f(\mathbf{x}^1) \geqslant f(\mathbf{x}^2) \text{ implies } f[\lambda \mathbf{x}^1 + (1-\lambda)\mathbf{x}^2] \geqslant f(\mathbf{x}^2), \quad \forall \lambda \in [0, 1]$$

Proof *'if'* Suppose the implication in the theorem is satisfied and let $\mathbf{x}^1, \mathbf{x}^2 \in UC_f(y)$. Then $f(\mathbf{x}^1) \geqslant y$, $f(\mathbf{x}^2) \geqslant y$ and $\mathbf{x}^1, \mathbf{x}^2 \in D$. Without loss of generality assume $f(\mathbf{x}^1) \geqslant f(\mathbf{x}^2)$: then

$$f[\lambda \mathbf{x}^1 + (1-\lambda)\mathbf{x}^2] \geqslant f(\mathbf{x}^2) \geqslant y, \ \forall \lambda \in [0, 1]$$

Hence $\forall \lambda \in [0, 1]$, $\lambda \mathbf{x}^1 + (1-\lambda)\mathbf{x}^2 \in UC_f(y)$ and $UC_f(y)$ is a convex set, as required.

'only if' Suppose $UC_f(y)$ is convex and suppose $f(\mathbf{x}^1) \geqslant f(\mathbf{x}^2)$. Let $y = f(\mathbf{x}^2)$. Then $\mathbf{x}^1, \mathbf{x}^2 \in UC_f(y)$ and $\forall \lambda \in [0, 1]$, $\lambda \mathbf{x}^1 + (1-\lambda)\mathbf{x}^2 \in UC_f(y)$ since this is convex. Hence

$$f[\lambda \mathbf{x}^1 + (1-\lambda)\mathbf{x}^2] \geqslant y = f(\mathbf{x}^2)$$

which is the desired implication. *Q.E.D.*

Theorem 13.1 says that if $\mathbf{x}^1$ is in $UC_f(y)$ where $y = f(\mathbf{x}^2)$ then any point on the line joining $\mathbf{x}^1$ to $\mathbf{x}^2$ (also in $UC_f(y)$) is in $UC_f(y)$, which makes the equivalence of theorem 13.1 to convex upper contours fairly transparent: the above proof merely confirms this.

Quasi-concave functions (even on open domains) need not be continuous unlike the concave case. For instance $f: R \to R$ where

$$f(x) = \begin{cases} x & \text{if } x > 0 \\ x - 1 & \text{if } x \leqslant 0 \end{cases}$$

is easily seen to be quasi-concave but is not continuous. Consequently we shall assume continuity where we need it (which is most of the time).

As in the concave case the theory of differentiable quasi-concave functions is very useful. There is indeed a first derivative characterization of quasi-concave functions. Consider again fig. 13.2 where we have imposed the tangent line at $\mathbf{x}^2$ to the contour through $\mathbf{x}^2$. The equation of this tangent line is

$$(\mathbf{x}-\mathbf{x}^2)\,\mathbf{f}'(\mathbf{x}^2)=0$$

You see from fig. 13.2 that *if* $f(\mathbf{x}^1)\geqslant f(\mathbf{x}^2)$, as drawn, then $\mathbf{x}^1$ must be above this tangent line. That is, $\mathbf{x}^1, \mathbf{x}^2\in D$ and $f(\mathbf{x}^1)\geqslant f(\mathbf{x}^2)$ implies $(\mathbf{x}^1-\mathbf{x}^2)\,\mathbf{f}'(\mathbf{x}^2)\geqslant 0$. In fact this implication is equivalent to the quasi-concavity of C^1 functions since it is equivalent to convexity of the upper contour sets. A formal statement is as follows:

Theorem 13.2 Suppose $D\subset R^n$ is convex and open and suppose $f:D\to R$ is C^1. Then f is quasi-concave if and only if:

$$\mathbf{x}^1, \mathbf{x}^2\in D \text{ and } f(\mathbf{x}^1)\geqslant f(\mathbf{x}^2) \text{ implies } (\mathbf{x}^1-\mathbf{x}^2)\,\mathbf{f}'(\mathbf{x}^2)\geqslant 0$$

A proof is given at the end of this chapter.

The restriction to open domains here is no problem. Indeed if a function $f:R^n_+\to R$ is continuous and if f is quasi-concave on R^n_{++} then f is quasi-concave on all of R^n_+; the proof is similar to that of theorem 7.1 (details left to the reader). Since many of the functions of major interest here are continuous on R^n_+ but C^1 only on R^n_{++}, this remark plus theorem 13.2 suffices to cover the cases of interest.

A concave function must be quasi-concave. So it should be the case that the first derivative characterization of a C^1 concave function should imply the first derivative characterization of a C^1 quasi-concave function. That this is so is easily checked. The C^1 concave characterization is

$$f(\mathbf{x}^2)+(\mathbf{x}^1-\mathbf{x}^2)\,\mathbf{f}'(\mathbf{x}^2)\geqslant f(\mathbf{x}^1),\ \forall \mathbf{x}^1, \mathbf{x}^2\in D \tag{13.1}$$

Hence $(\mathbf{x}^1-\mathbf{x}^2)\,\mathbf{f}'(\mathbf{x}^2)\geqslant f(\mathbf{x}^1)-f(\mathbf{x}^2)$, $\forall \mathbf{x}^1, \mathbf{x}^2\in D$. Now if $\mathbf{x}^1, \mathbf{x}^2\in D$ and $f(\mathbf{x}^1)\geqslant f(\mathbf{x}^2)$ then $f(\mathbf{x}^1)-f(\mathbf{x}^2)\geqslant 0$ and from the last inequality $(\mathbf{x}^1-\mathbf{x}^2)\,\mathbf{f}'(\mathbf{x}^2)\geqslant 0$. So indeed,

$$\mathbf{x}^1, \mathbf{x}^2\in D \text{ and } f(\mathbf{x}^1)\geqslant f(\mathbf{x}^2) \text{ implies } (\mathbf{x}^1-\mathbf{x}^2)\,\mathbf{f}'(\mathbf{x}^2)\geqslant 0 \tag{13.2}$$

as expected; (13.1) implies (13.2) although of course the reverse implication does not follow in general.

We have just emphasized the fact, laboured during the visual discussion, that although a concave function must be quasi-concave, in general a quasi-concave function need not be concave. However, there is an important class of functions for which quasi-concavity implies concavity and so quasi-concavity is equivalent to concavity for these functions. The class of functions for which this is always true is the class of C^1, *linearly homogeneous* and *positive-valued* functions $f:R^n_{++} \to R$. This is very useful. Here is a formal statement and proof; the proof shows that (13.2) implies (13.1) for such functions.

Theorem 13.3 Suppose $f:R^n_{++} \to R$ is C^1, linearly homogeneous and positive-valued. Then f is concave if and only if f is quasi-concave.

Proof *'only if'* is always true even without homogeneity, etc.

'if' Suppose $f:R^n_{++} \to R$ is C^1, linearly homogeneous, positive-valued and quasi-concave: (13.2) is then true and we have to show (13.1) with $D = R^n_{++}$. Choose any $\mathbf{x}^1, \mathbf{x}^2 \in R^n_{++}$ and since f is positive-valued we can define t by $t = f(\mathbf{x}^1)/f(\mathbf{x}^2)$ and $t > 0$. Since f is linearly homogeneous this implies $f(\mathbf{x}^1) = tf(\mathbf{x}^2) = f(t\mathbf{x}^2)$. Since f is quasi-concave and since $f(\mathbf{x}^1) = f(t\mathbf{x}^2)$, (13.2) tells us that

$$(\mathbf{x}^1 - t\mathbf{x}^2)\,\mathbf{f}'(t\mathbf{x}^2) \geqslant 0$$

But f_i' is homogeneous of degree zero, $i = 1, \ldots, n$ since f is homogeneous of degree one. Hence $\mathbf{f}'(t\mathbf{x}^2) = \mathbf{f}'(\mathbf{x}^2)$ and

$$\mathbf{x}^1\mathbf{f}'(\mathbf{x}^2) - t\mathbf{x}^2\mathbf{f}'(\mathbf{x}^2) \geqslant 0$$

By Euler's theorem $\mathbf{x}^2\mathbf{f}'(\mathbf{x}^2) = f(\mathbf{x}^2)$. Therefore

$$\begin{aligned}\mathbf{x}^1\mathbf{f}'(\mathbf{x}^2) &\geqslant tf(\mathbf{x}^2)\\ &= f(\mathbf{x}^1) \text{ from the definition of } t\end{aligned}$$

So $\mathbf{x}^1\mathbf{f}'(\mathbf{x}^2) \geqslant f(\mathbf{x}^1)$ and from Euler's theorem again

$$\mathbf{x}^2\mathbf{f}'(\mathbf{x}^2) = f(\mathbf{x}^2)$$

Subtracting this last equation from the previous inequality gives

$$\mathbf{x}^1\mathbf{f}'(\mathbf{x}^2) - \mathbf{x}^2\mathbf{f}'(\mathbf{x}^2) \geqslant f(\mathbf{x}^1) - f(\mathbf{x}^2)$$

Hence

$$(\mathbf{x}^1 - \mathbf{x}^2)\,\mathbf{f}'(\mathbf{x}^2) \geqslant f(\mathbf{x}^1) - f(\mathbf{x}^2)$$

which is (13.1). Since this is true for any $\mathbf{x}^1, \mathbf{x}^2 \in R^n_{++}$ it follows that f is concave. *Q.E.D.*

Effectively what happens here is that quasi-concavity ensures convex upper contours (as ever) while the addition of linear homogeneity and positive-valuedness produces a convex hypograph as well and hence a concave function. In particular if $f:R^n_{++} \to R$ is linear homogeneous and $x_1 = x_2 = x$ it follows from chapter 9 that $f(x, x) = kx$, some $k \in R$ and the type of non-convex hypograph of fig. 13.3 is ruled out, for instance.

Precise identification of quasi-concave functions is not an issue we have properly addressed so far. There are second derivative results for quasi-concavity. However, these are a bit more tricky than the corresponding concave result and like the latter involve 'large' determinants which can easily be unmanageable for large n; in the concave case we ran up against this unmanageability in chapter 9 for the Cobb–Douglas and C.E.S. functions for instance. Consequently instead we look at a set of results for both the quasi-concave and concave cases, which are at least as useful as the second derivative results for n-variable functions. These are the *composition* results since they pertain to cases where a function is composed of various simple functions.

Before moving on to the composition results we briefly invert the previous story and look at *quasi-convex* functions, $f:D \to R$, $D \subset R^n$ and convex, defined by the property that $LC_f(y)$ is a convex set for all y in the range of f; or algebraically by

$$\mathbf{x}^1, \mathbf{x}^2 \subset D \text{ and } f(\mathbf{x}^1) \leqslant f(\mathbf{x}^2) \text{ implies } f[\lambda\mathbf{x}^1 + (1-\lambda)\,\mathbf{x}^2] \leqslant f(\mathbf{x}^2), \quad \forall\lambda \in [0, 1]$$

The first derivative characterization of quasi-convex functions is

$$\mathbf{x}^1, \mathbf{x}^2 \in D \text{ and } f(\mathbf{x}^1) \leqslant f(\mathbf{x}^2) \text{ implies } (\mathbf{x}^1 - \mathbf{x}^2)\,\mathbf{f}'(\mathbf{x}^2) \leqslant 0$$

and if $f:R^n_{++} \to R$ is C^1, linear homogeneous and positive-valued, then f is convex if and only if f is quasi-convex.

A glance at fig. 13.1 will confirm that the lower contours are all convex in (a) and (b) but not in (c); (a) and (b) correspond to quasi-convex (as well as quasi-concave) function while (c) is merely quasi-concave. Functions which are both quasi-convex and quasi-concave are worth a final comment. If $f:D \to R$, $D \subset R^n$ has contours which are all *hyperplanes* in R^n then the *upper and lower* contour sets will be half-spaces and will be convex sets; hence such f will be quasi-convex and quasi-concave. Now if f itself is a linear function then of course it has hyperplane contours and will be both quasi-convex and quasi-concave; alternatively linear functions are both convex and concave and hence must be quasi-convex and quasi-concave. However, perhaps surprisingly, there are many non-linear functions whose contours are all hyperplanes. For instance suppose α, $\beta \in R^n_{++}$ and

$\gamma, \delta \in R_{++}$ and define $f: R^n_{++} \to R$ by

$$f(\mathbf{x}) = \frac{\sum_{i=1}^{n} \alpha_i x_i + \gamma}{\sum_{i=1}^{n} \beta_i x_i + \delta}$$

a ratio of linear functions but itself non-linear. The range of f will be R_{++} and for any $y \in R_{++}$,

$$\begin{aligned} C_f(y) &= \left\{ \mathbf{x} \in R^n_{++} \,\middle|\, \frac{\Sigma\, \alpha_i x_i + \gamma}{\Sigma\, \beta_i x_i + \delta} = y \right\} \\ &= \{\mathbf{x} \in R^n_{++} \mid \Sigma\, \alpha_i x_i + \gamma = y\, \Sigma\, \beta_i x_i + y\delta\} \\ &= \{\mathbf{x} \in R^n_{++} \mid \Sigma\, (\alpha_i - y\beta_i)\, x_i = y\delta - \gamma\} \end{aligned}$$

which is a hyperplane in R^n. Since this is so for any y in the range R_{++}, f is both quasi-convex and quasi-concave.

13.3 Composition results for concave functions

It is very easy to show the following two results:

Theorem 13.4 Suppose $D \subset R^n$ is convex and suppose $f: D \to \mathrm{R}$ and $g: D \to R$ are two functions such that $f(x) = kg(x)$ where $k \in R$. Then

(a) if g is concave, f is concave if $k > 0$ and f is convex if $k < 0$;

(b) if g is convex, f is convex if $k > 0$ and f is concave if $k < 0$.

Theorem 13.5 Suppose $D \subset R^n$ is convex and suppose $f: D \to R$, $g: D \to R$ and $h: D \to R$ are three functions such that $f(\mathbf{x}) = h(\mathbf{x}) + g(\mathbf{x})$. Then

(a) f is concave if h and g are concave;

(b) f is convex if h and g are convex.

The proofs are left as an exercise for the reader: simply apply the definitions of concave/convex functions. Together, for instance, these results show that $f(\mathbf{x}) = \Sigma_{i=1}^n k_i g_i(\mathbf{x})$ is concave if for all i, $k_i > 0$ and g_i is concave. The next result is much more substantive and concerns the case where f is a function (h, say) of a function (g, say); i.e. $f(x) = h[g(\mathbf{x})]$. To be more precise suppose $g: D \to R$ where $D \subset R^n$ is a function of n variables with range $E \subset R$, say, and suppose $h: E \to R$ is a function of one variable defined on the range of values of g. Then f is defined by

$$f: D \to R \text{ with values } f(\mathbf{x}) = h[g(\mathbf{x})]$$

A simple example is

$$g: R^2_{++} \to R \text{ where } g(\mathbf{x}) = x_1 + x_2$$

The range is R_{++} and let $h: R_{++} \to R$ be given by $h(\mathbf{x}) = \ln g$. Then $f: R^2_{++} \to R$ is defined by $f(\mathbf{x}) = \ln(x_1 + x_2)$ and is a 'function of a function' (ln of $x_1 + x_2$).

Suppose that both h and g are concave functions. Does it follow that the composite function of a function f is also concave? The answer is: no, not always. For instance, and very simply, suppose $g: R_{++} \to R$ has $g(x) = \ln x, h: R_{++} \to R$ has $h(g) = -g$. Then g is concave, h is linear and so concave but $f(x) = -\ln x$ and is *convex*.

Suppose, however, now, that h is a C^1 function with the property that $h'(g) > 0$, $\forall g \in E$; we say that h is a *monotone increasing function* and f (defined by $f(\mathbf{x}) = h[g(\mathbf{x})]$) is a *monotone increasing transformation of* g. It is true that if g is concave and h is concave and *monotone increasing* then f is concave. Similarly for the convex case:

Theorem 13.6 Suppose $D \subset R^n$ is convex, suppose $g: D \to R$ has range E and suppose $h: E \to R$ is defined on the range of g. Define $f: D \to R$ by $f(\mathbf{x}) = h[g(\mathbf{x})]$. Then

(a) if g is concave and h is concave, C^1 and monotone increasing then f is concave;

(b) if g is convex and h is convex, C^1 and monotone increasing then f is convex.

Proof (a) Suppose g is concave and h is concave and monotone increasing. Since g is concave

$$g[\lambda \mathbf{x}^1 + (1-\lambda)\mathbf{x}^2] \geqslant \lambda g(\mathbf{x}^1) + (1-\lambda) g(\mathbf{x}^2), \quad \forall \lambda \in [0, 1], \forall \mathbf{x}^1, \mathbf{x}^2 \in D$$

Since h is monotone increasing $g^1 \geqslant g^2$ implies $h(g^1) \geqslant h(g^2)$. Hence

$$h\{g[\lambda \mathbf{x}^1 + (1-\lambda)\mathbf{x}^2]\} \geqslant h\{\lambda g(\mathbf{x}^1) + (1-\lambda) g(\mathbf{x}^2)\}, \quad \forall \lambda \in [0, 1], \forall \mathbf{x}^1, \mathbf{x}^2 \in D$$

And since h is concave

$$h\{\lambda g(\mathbf{x}^1)+(1-\lambda)g(\mathbf{x}^2)\} \geqslant \lambda h[g(\mathbf{x}^1)]+(1-\lambda)h[g(\mathbf{x}^2)],$$
$$\forall\lambda\in[0,1],\ \forall\mathbf{x}^1,\mathbf{x}^2\in D$$

Hence

$$h\{g[\lambda\mathbf{x}^1+(1-\lambda)\mathbf{x}^2]\} \geqslant \lambda h[g(\mathbf{x}^1)]+(1-\lambda)h[g(\mathbf{x}^2)],$$
$$\forall\lambda\in[0,1],\ \forall\mathbf{x}^1,\mathbf{x}^2\in D$$

That is

$$f[\lambda\mathbf{x}^1+(1-\lambda)\mathbf{x}^2] \geqslant \lambda f(\mathbf{x}^1)+(1-\lambda)f(\mathbf{x}^2),$$
$$\forall\lambda\in[0,1],\ \forall\mathbf{x}^1,\mathbf{x}^2\in D$$

Hence f is concave.

The proof of (b) is similar. *Q.E.D.*

So, in particular, concave, monotone increasing transformations of concave functions are also concave. For instance the earlier example in which $f(x) = \ln(x_1 + x_2)$, had $h(g) = \ln g$ which is concave and monotone increasing and $g(\mathbf{x}) = x_1 + x_2$ which is linear and so concave. Hence we can conclude that f is concave, also. Further examples using theorems 13.4, 13.5 and 13.6 come shortly. We should stress that although *concave, monotone increasing* transformations of concave functions are concave it is *not* in general true that (i) concave transformations of concave functions are concave or (ii) monotone increasing transformations of concave functions are concave. Both the concave *and* monotone increasing properties of the transforming functions are needed to preserve the concavity. A counter-example to (i) has been provided already. A simple counter-example for (ii) is $D = R$, $g(x) = x$ and $h(g) = g^3 + g$ so that $f(x) = x^3 + x$. g is linear and so concave, $h'(g) = 3g^2 + 1 > 0$ and h is monotone increasing: but f is not concave since $f''(x) = 6x$ whose sign varies with x.

13.4 Composition results for quasi-concave functions

Immediately from the algebraic definition of quasi-concavity we get the analogue of theorem 13.4:

Theorem 13.7 Under the suppositions about f and g of theorem 13.4:

(a) if g is quasi-concave then f is quasi-concave if $k > 0$ and quasi-convex if $k < 0$;

(b) if g is quasi-convex then f is quasi-convex if $k > 0$ and quasi-concave if $k < 0$.

Most surprisingly however, it is not true, in general, that the sum of two quasi-concave functions is quasi-concave. For instance suppose $h(x) = x^3 + x$ and $g(x) = -2x$, both on domain R. Then h is non-stationary ($h'(x) = 3x^2 + 1 > 0$, $\forall x$–in fact h is monotone increasing) and so quasi-concave; g is linear and so concave and quasi-concave. But $f(x) = h(x) + g(x) = x^3 - x$ which is definitely not quasi-concave; e.g. $UC_f(0) = [-1, 0] \cup [+1, +\infty]$ which is not a convex set. So in general sums of quasi-concave functions need not be quasi-concave and similarly sums of quasi-convex functions need not be quasi-convex.

We now turn to functions of a function, and suppose that $f(x) = h[g(x)]$, domains as described in section 13.3. The situation turns out as the expected analogue of the concave result, theorem 13.6. In particular any quasi-concave, monotone increasing transformation of a quasi-concave function is quasi-concave. However, to describe h as quasi-concave *and* monotone increasing is superfluous since any monotone increasing function of one variable is necessarily quasi-concave (and quasi-convex). Hence:

Theorem 13.8 Under the suppositions about g, h and f of theorem 13.6:

(a) if h is monotone increasing and g is quasi-concave then f is quasi-concave;

(b) if h is monotone increasing and g is quasi-convex then f is quasi-convex.

In particular then any monotone increasing transformation of a quasi-concave (quasi-convex) function is also quasi-concave (quasi-convex). The operation of taking a monotone increasing transformation of any function (not just of quasi-concave or quasi-convex functions) has the important general property that it leaves the contours (and upper and lower contour sets) unchanged in a certain sense. We now describe this precisely; it will as a by-product provide us with a simple proof of theorem 13.8.

Theorem 13.9 If f is a monotone increasing transformation (h) of the function g (i.e. under the suppositions about g, h and f of theorem 13.6) then for all y in the range of g:

(a) $UC_g(y) = UC_f[h(y)]$

(b) $LC_g(y) = LC_f[h(y)]$

(c) $C_g(y) = C_f[h(y)]$

Proof

(a) $$UC_g(y) = \{\mathbf{x} \in D \mid g(\mathbf{x}) \geqslant y\}$$

and $$UC_f[h(y)] = \{\mathbf{x} \in D \mid f(\mathbf{x}) \geqslant h(y)\}$$
$$= \{\mathbf{x} \in D \mid h[g(\mathbf{x})] \geqslant h(y)\}$$

Since h is monotone increasing, $h(a) \geqslant h(b)$ if and only if $a \geqslant b$. Hence

$$UC_f[h(y)] = \{\mathbf{x} \in D \mid g(\mathbf{x}) \geqslant y\} = UC_g(y)$$

The proofs of (b) and (c) are similar. *Q.E.D.*

Hence, in particular, the subset of R^n which is $C_g(y)$ is precisely one of the contours of f, namely that for the value of f of $h(y)$. When a function undergoes a monotone increasing transformation its contour map remains the same except that the value labelling on a contour changes from y to $h(y)$. Similarly for upper and lower contours. Theorem 13.8 follows immediately now since if g is quasi-concave we know $UC_g(y)$ is a convex set and theorem 13.9 tells us that the upper contours of f are the same as those of g (except for the labelling) and so must also be convex sets; hence f is quasi-concave and similarly for (b) of theorem 13.8.

One consequence of theorem 13.8 is worth stressing: since any monotone increasing transformation of a quasi-concave function is quasi-concave it follows in particular that any monotone increasing transformation of a *concave* function will also be *quasi-concave*. But be reminded of the warning of the last section; it is *not* true in general that (merely) monotone increasing transformations of concave functions are *concave*.

Some examples illustrating these composition results are:

Example 13.1

(a) $f: R^n_{++} \to R$ where $f(\mathbf{x}) = \ln\left(\sum_{i=1}^{n} x_i\right)$

Define $g: R^n_{++} \to R$ by $g(\mathbf{x}) = \Sigma x_i$ and $h: R_{++} \to R$ by $h(g) = \ln g$. Then $f(\mathbf{x}) = h[g(\mathbf{x})]$, g is linear and so both concave and convex and h is monotone increasing and concave. It follows that f is concave as it is a monotone increasing, concave transformation of a concave function. It also follows, however, that f is a monotone increasing transformation of a convex function and so must be quasi-convex. Hence f is both concave and quasi-convex. Notice in particular that f is therefore both quasi-concave and quasi-convex and does indeed have hyperplane contours;

$$C_f(y) = \{\mathbf{x} \in R^n_{++} \mid \ln(\Sigma x_i) = y\} = \{\mathbf{x} \in R^n_{++} \mid \Sigma x_i = e^y\}$$

a hyperplane for any $y \in R_{++}$, the range of f.

(b) $f: R^n_{++} \to R$ where $f(\mathbf{x}) = \ln\left(\sum_{i=1}^{n} x_i^2\right)$

With domains as in (a) let $g(\mathbf{x}) = \Sigma x_i^2$ and $h(g) = \ln g$. Now g is a convex function since its Hessian is an $n \times n$ diagonal matrix with all diagonal elements equal to 2. As above h is monotone increasing (and concave). So now f is a monotone increasing transformation of a convex function and is therefore quasi-convex which is all the composition results give us here.

(c) $f: R^n_{++} \to R$ where $f(\mathbf{x}) = \left(\sum_{i=1}^{n} x_i^2\right)^{1/2}$

With domains as in (b) let $g(\mathbf{x}) = \Sigma x_i^2$ and $h(g) = g^{1/2}$. Then f is a monotone increasing (concave) transformation of a convex function and is quasi-convex, similar to (b). Now, however, f is linear homogeneous, [since $f(t\mathbf{x}) = [\Sigma(tx_i)^2]^{1/2} = t[\Sigma x_i^2]^{1/2} = tf(\mathbf{x})$], C^1 and positive-valued. Hence f is convex as well as quasi-convex from the convex analogue of theorem 13.3.

Theorems 13.3–13.8 together provide extremely useful results for identification of concavity or quasi-concavity of perhaps complicated n-variable functional forms. In particular we now devote the next section to an analysis of the Cobb–Douglas and C.E.S. functions from this base, tying up some loose ends left in chapter 9.

13.5 Concavity and quasi-concavity of Cobb–Douglas and C.E.S. functions

We start with the Cobb–Douglas case, $f: R^n_+ \to R$ defined by

$$f(\mathbf{x}) = k \prod_{i=1}^{n} x_i^{\alpha_i}$$

and $k > 0$, $\alpha_i > 0$, $\forall_i$. We asserted in chapter 9 that f is continuous. Hence, we look at $f: R^n_{++} \to R$ since concavity or quasi-concavity there can be extended to all of R^n_+ (theorem 7.1 and section 13.2). Since $k > 0$ we may set it equal to 1 without affecting the results, from theorems 13.4 and 13.7. There are three stages in our argument.

1. First we look at $\ln f(\mathbf{x})$ since this transforms the continued product into a sum whose concavity etc. is easy to handle:

$$\ln f(\mathbf{x}) = \sum_{i=1}^{n} \alpha_i \ln x_i$$

   The Hessian of $\ln f(\mathbf{x})$ is then a diagonal matrix with the ith leading diagonal element equal to $-(\alpha_i/x_i^2)$; this matrix is certainly n.s.d. $\forall \mathbf{x} \in R^n_{++}$. Hence $\ln f(\mathbf{x})$ is a concave function. Writing $g(\mathbf{x}) = \ln f(\mathbf{x})$ it follows that $f(\mathbf{x}) = e^{g(\mathbf{x})}$ and f is a (convex), monotone increasing transformation of the concave function g. It follows that *f is always quasi-concave*.

2. The degree of homogeneity of f is $\Sigma \alpha_i$. Hence *if* $\Sigma \alpha_i = 1$ *f is concave*, from theorem 13.3, since f is C^1 and positive-valued.

3. We can always write $f(\mathbf{x})$ as follows:

$$f(\mathbf{x}) = [\Pi x_i^{\alpha_i/\Sigma \alpha_i}]^{\Sigma \alpha_i}$$

   which decomposes f into a function $(h(g) = g^{\Sigma \alpha_i})$ of a function $g(\mathbf{x}) = \Pi x_i^{\alpha_i/\Sigma \alpha_i}$. Now g itself is a Cobb–Douglas function constructed, however, so that the sum of the exponents $\Sigma(\alpha_i/\Sigma \alpha_i)$ equals unity. Hence from (2), g is concave. h, on the other hand, is always monotone increasing and is concave if $\Sigma \alpha_i \leqslant 1$ and convex if $\Sigma \alpha_i \geqslant 1$. Consider the case $\Sigma \alpha_i \leqslant 1$. Here f is a concave, monotone increasing transformation (h) of the concave function g. Hence *if* $\Sigma \alpha_i \leqslant 1$, *$f$ is concave*. When $\Sigma \alpha_i > 1$, f is a convex monotone increasing transformation of a concave function and we cannot improve on the quasi-concavity of (1).

We have proved:

Theorem 13.10 A Cobb–Douglas function is always quasi-concave and is concave if and only if the degree of homogeneity $\Sigma_{i=1}^n \alpha_i \leqslant 1$.

The C.E.S. function is $f: R^n_+ \to R$ where $f(0) = 0$ and for $\mathbf{x} \neq 0$,

$$f(\mathbf{x}) = k\left[\sum_{i=1}^{n} \delta_i x_i^{-\rho}\right]^{-v/\rho}$$

with $k>0$, $\delta_i>0$, $\forall i$ and $\Sigma_{i=1}^n \delta_i = 1$, $v>0$ and $\rho>-1$, $\rho \neq 0$. As in the Cobb–Douglas case we can set $k = 1$ and we need only look at $f:R^n_{++}\to R$ to get results for all of R^n_+ since f is continuous. In fact the same steps used for Cobb-Douglas give the desired result here.

1. Let $g(\mathbf{x}) = \ln f(\mathbf{x}) = -v/\rho \ln[\Sigma\, \delta_i x_i^{-\rho}]$ and let $h(\mathbf{x}) = \Sigma\, \delta_i x_i^{-\rho}$. The Hessian of h is a diagonal matrix with ith leading diagonal element equal to $-\rho(-\rho-1)\, x_i^{-\rho-2} = \rho(1+\rho)\, x_i^{-\rho-2}$ which is $\leqslant 0$, $\forall \mathbf{x}\in R^n_{++}$ if $\rho\in(-1,0)$ and $\geqslant 0$, $\forall \mathbf{x}\in R^n_{++}$ if $\rho\in(0,+\infty)$. Hence h is concave if $\rho\in(-1,0)$ and h is convex if $\rho\in(0,+\infty)$. Consider these two cases in turn:

   (a) $\rho\in(-1,0)$. h is concave then, $\ln h$ is a concave increasing transformation of h and so is concave and $-(v/\rho)$ is a positive constant; hence g is concave. Now $f(\mathbf{x}) = e^{g(\mathbf{x})}$ and so f is quasi-concave, as it is a (convex) monotone increasing transformation of the concave g.

   (b) $\rho\in(0,+\infty)$. Here h is convex, $\ln h$ is quasi-convex as it is a (concave) monotone increasing transformation of h and $-(v/\rho)$ is a *negative* constant. Hence g is quasi-concave as it is a negative multiple of a quasi-convex function. $f(\mathbf{x}) = e^{g(\mathbf{x})}$ and f is quasi-concave as it is a monotone increasing transform of a quasi-concave function.

   In every case f is quasi-concave.

2. The degree of homogeneity is v, f is C^1 and positive-valued and so *if $v = 1$, f is concave.*

3. Write

$$f(\mathbf{x}) = \{[\Sigma\, \delta_i x_i^{-\rho}]^{-1/\rho}\}^v = h(g(\mathbf{x}))$$

   where $g(\mathbf{x}) = (\Sigma\, \delta_i x_i^{-\rho})^{-1/\rho}$ and $h(g) = g^v$. g is linear homogeneous, C.E.S. and so is concave from (2). When $v\leqslant 1$, h is concave and monotone increasing. So when $v\leqslant 1$, *f is concave*. Hence:

Theorem 13.11 A C.E.S. function is always quasi-concave and is concave if and only if the degree of homogeneity $v\leqslant 1$.

The arguments used in (2) and (3) in both these cases have produced a general principle worthy of separate note. Suppose $f:R^n_{++}\to R$ is quasi-concave, C^1, positive-valued and homogeneous of degree $r>0$. Write

$$f(\mathbf{x}) = \{[f(\mathbf{x})]^{1/r}\}^r = h(g(x))$$

where $g(\mathbf{x}) = [f(\mathbf{x})]^{1/r}$ and $h(g) = g^r$. g is quasi-concave as it is a monotone increasing transformation ($f^{1/r}$ where $r > 0$) of f. g is also linearly homogeneous since

$$
\begin{aligned}
g(t\mathbf{x}) &= [f(t\mathbf{x})]^{1/r} \\
&= [t^r f(\mathbf{x})]^{1/r} \text{ since } f \text{ is homogeneous of degree } r \\
&= t[f(\mathbf{x})]^{1/r} = tg(\mathbf{x})
\end{aligned}
$$

Hence g is concave. h is concave *and* monotone increasing if $r \leqslant 1$ and so f is concave since it is a concave, monotone increasing transformation of a concave function. We have proved the following generalization of theorem 13.3.

Theorem 13.12 Suppose $f: R^n_{++} \to R$ is C^1, homogeneous of degree r, $0 < r \leqslant 1$ and positive-valued. Then f is concave if and only if f is quasi-concave.

13.6 Strict quasi-concavity

Strictly concave functions were those concave functions whose graphs contained no linear segments. Similarly strictly quasi-concave functions are those quasi-concave functions whose *contours* contain no linear segments. A precise algebraic definition is:

Definition 13.2 Suppose $D \subset R^n$ is convex. The $f: D \to R$ is *strictly quasi-concave* if and only if

$$
\mathbf{x}^1, \mathbf{x}^2 \in D,\ \mathbf{x}^1 \neq \mathbf{x}^2 \text{ and } f(\mathbf{x}^1) \geqslant f(\mathbf{x}^2) \text{ implies}
$$
$$
f[\lambda \mathbf{x}^1 + (1-\lambda)\mathbf{x}^2] > f(\mathbf{x}^2),\ \forall \lambda \in (0, 1)
$$

Any strictly concave function will be strictly quasi-concave, but not of course, vice-versa. For instance in the one-variable setting, any non-stationary function will be strictly quasi-concave–see fig. 13.1(a) and (b) again. More interestingly, for a two-variable strictly quasi-concave function, definition 13.2 tells us that if $f(\mathbf{x}^1) = f(\mathbf{x}^2)$ and $\mathbf{x}^1 \neq \mathbf{x}^2$ so that $\mathbf{x}^1$ and $\mathbf{x}^2$ are on the same contour, then

$$
f[\lambda \mathbf{x}^1 + (1-\lambda)\mathbf{x}^2] > f(\mathbf{x}^2) = f(\mathbf{x}^1),\ \forall \lambda \in (0, 1)
$$

That is, the line joining $\mathbf{x}^1$ to $\mathbf{x}^2$ lies entirely 'above' the contour containing $\mathbf{x}^1$ and $\mathbf{x}^2$, apart from the end-points, of course. Visually speaking strictly quasi-concave functions are those quasi-concave functions whose *contours* contain no 'flat sections' (whereas strictly concave functions are those concave functions whose *graphs* contain no flat sections).

Strictly quasi-concave functions need not be continuous; but any strictly quasi-concave function which is continuous will also be quasi-concave (but not vice-versa). More surprisingly the expected first derivative characterization of strictly quasi-concave functions fails to materialize. In fact there seems to be no useful first derivative characterization of the entire class of strictly quasi-concave functions, although in the next chapter we provide such a characterization for the sub-class of strictly quasi-concave functions which are also non-stationary. Currently we shift attention to composition results for strict quasi-concavity, and, naturally for strict concavity too.

Finally we mention that f is strictly quasi-convex if and only if

$$\mathbf{x}^1, \mathbf{x}^2 \in D, \ \mathbf{x}^1 \neq \mathbf{x}^2 \text{ and } f(\mathbf{x}^1) \leqslant f(\mathbf{x}^2) \text{ implies}$$
$$f[\lambda \mathbf{x}^1 + (1-\lambda)\,\mathbf{x}^2] < f(\mathbf{x}^2), \quad \forall \lambda \in (0, 1)$$

There are obvious analogues to the strict quasi-concavity properties above for strict quasi-convexity—details are left to the reader.

13.7 Compositions of strictly concave and strictly quasi-concave functions

The composition results of sections 13.3 and 13.4 earlier have the expected analogues for the cases of strict concavity and strict quasi-concavity. We merely list these results.

1. A scalar multiple, k, of a strictly concave function is strictly concave if $k > 0$ and strictly convex if $k < 0$. This is also true interchanging 'concave' and 'convex'.
2. A scalar multiple, k, of a strictly quasi-concave function is strictly quasi-concave if $k > 0$ and strictly quasi-convex if $k < 0$. This is also true interchanging 'concave' and 'convex'.
3. The sum of two strictly concave (convex) functions is strictly concave (convex).

   Once again, however, note that the sum of two strictly quasi-concave functions need not be strictly quasi-concave, or even quasi-concave.
4. A strictly concave (convex), monotone increasing transformation of a strictly concave (convex) function is strictly concave (convex).

   Finally a strictly quasi-concave, monotone increasing transformation of a strictly quasi-concave function is strictly quasi-concave; but as any monotone increasing function of one variable is strictly quasi-concave we avoid superfluity by stating:

5. A monotone increasing transformation of a strictly quasi-concave (convex) function is strictly quasi-concave (convex).

It is useful to apply these results to the earlier Cobb–Douglas and C.E.S. analyses. In each case under step (1) these functions were shown to be monotone increasing transformations of concave functions: however, the Hessians of these concave functions were in fact negative definite so that these functions are actually strictly concave. Hence both Cobb–Douglas and C.E.S. functions are strictly quasi-concave on R^n_{++} since they are then monotone increasing transformations of strictly concave functions. However, we cannot 'improve' on step (2) since linearly homogeneous strictly quasi-concave functions are only concave. The following then helps with step (3); a proof is given at the end of the chapter.

Theorem 13.13 A strictly concave, monotone increasing transformation of a concave *and* strictly quasi-concave function is strictly concave.

Armed with this we see that at each step (3) when the *degree of homogeneity is strictly less than one*, f is a strictly concave, monotone increasing transformation of a concave, strictly quasi-concave function and so is strictly concave. The following table summarizes all these results about Cobb–Douglas and C.E.S.

	Strictly quasi-concave (s.q.c.) and strictly concave	*S.q.c. and concave*	*S.q.c. and not concave*
Cobb–Douglas	$\Sigma\alpha_i < 1$	$\Sigma\alpha_i = 1$	$\Sigma\alpha_i > 1$
C.E.S.	$v < 1$	$v = 1$	$v > 1$

13.8 Proof of theorem 13.2

For convenience we follow the general strategy used to prove the first derivative characterization of concave functions and stick with the one-variable case. The n-variable extension follows the concave analogue in chapter 5 and the details of this are omitted.

Suppose $f:D \to R$, $D \subset R$ and convex and open, is quasi-concave and C^1. Then

$$f(x^1) \geqslant f(x^2) \Rightarrow f[\lambda x^1 + (1-\lambda)x^2] \geqslant f(x^2), \forall \lambda \in [0, 1]$$

$$\therefore f(x^1) \geqslant f(x^2) \Rightarrow (x^1 - x^2) \frac{[f\{\lambda x^1 + (1-\lambda)x^2\} - f(x^2)]}{\lambda(x^1 - x^2)} \geqslant 0,$$
$$\forall \lambda \in (0, 1] \text{ if } x^1 \neq x^2$$

$$\therefore f(x^1) \geqslant f(x^2) \Rightarrow \lim_{\lambda \to 0} (x^1 - x^2) \frac{[f\{\lambda x^1 + (1-\lambda)x^2\} - f(x^2)]}{\lambda(x^1 - x^2)} \geqslant 0$$
$$\text{if } x^1 \neq x^2$$

$$\therefore f(x^1) \geqslant f(x^2) \Rightarrow (x^1 - x^2) f'(x^2) \geqslant 0, \text{ if } x^1 \neq x^2$$

If $x^1 = x^2$ the desired implication is trivial, completing 'only if' when $n = 1$.

Conversely suppose

$$f(x^1) \geqslant f(x^2) \Rightarrow (x^1 - x^2) f'(x^2) \geqslant 0, \forall x^1, x^2 \in D$$

We want to show f is then quasi-concave; i.e. that

$$f(x^1) \geqslant f(x^2) \Rightarrow f[\lambda x^1 + (1-\lambda)x^2] \geqslant f(x^2), \forall \lambda \in [0, 1]$$

Suppose not and that $f(x^1) \geqslant f(x^2)$ but $f(\hat{x}) < f(x^2)$ where $\hat{x} = \lambda x^1 + (1-\lambda)x^2$, $\lambda \in (0, 1)$. It must be that $x^1 \neq x^2$. Also since $f(x^1) \geqslant f(\hat{x})$ and $f(x^2) \geqslant f(\hat{x})$

$$(x^1 - \hat{x}) f'(\hat{x}) \geqslant 0$$

and

$$(x^2 - \hat{x}) f'(\hat{x}) \geqslant 0$$

Substituting the formula for $\hat{x}$ gives, since $\lambda \in (0, 1)$

$$(x^1 - x^2) f'(\hat{x}) \geqslant 0$$

and

$$(x^1 - x^2) f'(\hat{x}) \leqslant 0$$

Hence since $x^1 \neq x^2$, $f'(\hat{x}) = 0$. Without loss of generality suppose $x^2 > x^1$; a similar argument is constructed if $x^2 < x^1$. Then $\hat{x} \in (x^1, x^2)$. Now there must be a point in $(\hat{x}, x^2)$, $\tilde{x}$ say, where $f'(\tilde{x}) > 0$ and $f(\tilde{x}) < f(x^2)$; otherwise f is non-increasing on the interval $(\hat{x}, x^2)$ and $f(x^2) \leqslant f(\hat{x})$, a contradiction. Since $f(x^1) \geqslant f(x^2)$ we also have $f(x^1) > f(\tilde{x})$. Hence $(x^1 - \tilde{x}) f'(\tilde{x}) \geqslant 0$ and $x^1 \geqslant \tilde{x}$ since $f'(\tilde{x}) > 0$. But $\tilde{x} > \hat{x} > x^1$, a contradiction which establishes 'if' when $n = 1$.

Q.E.D.

13.9 Proof of theorem 13.13

Suppose g is concave and strictly quasi-concave and h is strictly concave and monotone increasing, domains as earlier: we want to show that f is strictly concave where

$$f(\mathbf{x}) = h[g(\mathbf{x})]$$

Choose any $\mathbf{x}^1, \mathbf{x}^2 \in D$ where $\mathbf{x}^1 \neq \mathbf{x}^2$ and let $\lambda \in (0, 1)$. Since g is concave

(1) $g[\lambda \mathbf{x}^1 + (1-\lambda)\mathbf{x}^2] \geqslant \lambda g(\mathbf{x}^1) + (1-\lambda) g(\mathbf{x}^2)$

Moreover since g is strictly quasi-concave

(2) $g[\lambda \mathbf{x}^1 + (1-\lambda)\mathbf{x}^2] > \lambda g(\mathbf{x}^1) + (1-\lambda) g(\mathbf{x}^2)$ *if* $g(\mathbf{x}^1) = g(\mathbf{x}^2)$

Since h is monotone increasing

(3) $h\{g[\lambda \mathbf{x}^1 + (1-\lambda)\mathbf{x}^2]\} \geqslant h\{\lambda g(\mathbf{x}^1) + (1-\lambda) g(\mathbf{x}^2)\}$ with strict inequality if $g(\mathbf{x}^1) = g(\mathbf{x}^2)$.

Since h is strictly concave

(4) $h\{\lambda g(\mathbf{x}^1) + (1-\lambda) g(\mathbf{x}^2)\} \geqslant \lambda h(g(\mathbf{x}^1)) + (1-\lambda) h(g(\mathbf{x}^2))$ with strict inequality if $g(\mathbf{x}^1) \neq g(\mathbf{x}^2)$.

Combining (3) and (4) whether $g(\mathbf{x}^1) = g(\mathbf{x}^2)$ or $g(\mathbf{x}^1) \neq g(\mathbf{x}^2)$ we get

$$h\{g[\lambda \mathbf{x}^1 + (1-\lambda)\mathbf{x}^2]\} > \lambda h(g(\mathbf{x}^1) + (1-\lambda) h(g(\mathbf{x}^2))$$

Since this is true $\forall \mathbf{x}^1, \mathbf{x}^2 \in D$, $\mathbf{x}^1 \neq \mathbf{x}^2$ and $\forall \lambda \in (0, 1)$ it follows that f is strictly concave. *Q.E.D.*

Exercise 13

1. Are the following functions $f: R^n_{++} \to R$ concave, quasi-concave, convex, quasi-convex?

   (a) $f(\mathbf{x}) = \ln(\Sigma \alpha_i x_i^2)$ where $\alpha_i > 0$, $\forall i$.

(b) $f(\mathbf{x}) = (\Sigma e^{x_i})^\beta$ where

(i) $\beta = \frac{1}{2}$

(ii) $\beta = 2$

(iii) $\beta = -1$

2. Show that the following functions $f: R^n_{++} \to R$ are quasi-concave:

(a) $f(\mathbf{x}) = \dfrac{\Sigma \alpha_i x_i + \beta}{(\Sigma \gamma_i x_i + \delta)^2}$ where $\beta, \delta > 0$ and $\alpha, \gamma \in R^n_{++}$
[Hint: consider $UC_f(y)$]

(b) $f(\mathbf{x}) = h(\mathbf{x})/g(\mathbf{x})$ where $h(\mathbf{x}) > 0$ and $g(\mathbf{x}) > 0$, $\forall \mathbf{x} \in R^n_{++}$ and h is concave, g is convex. [Hint: as in (a)].

(c) $f(\mathbf{x}) = [h(\mathbf{x})]^\alpha [g(\mathbf{x})]^{1-\alpha}$ where $\alpha \in (0, 1)$, $h(\mathbf{x}) > 0$ and $g(\mathbf{x}) > 0$, $\forall \mathbf{x} \in R^n_{++}$ and both h and g are concave and linearly homogeneous. [Hint: consider $\ln f(\mathbf{x})$].

(d) Show that the function in (c) above is concave by proving that it is linearly homogeneous.

3. Prove that the following functions $f: R^n_{++} \to R$ are quasi-convex:

(a) $f(\mathbf{x}) = k \Pi x_i^{\alpha_i}$ where $k > 0$ and $\alpha_i < 0, i = 1, \ldots, n$.

(b) $f(\mathbf{x}) = k[\Sigma x_i^{-\rho}]^{-v/\rho}$ where $v > 0$, $\rho < -1$ and $k > 0$.
Are these functions strictly quasi-convex? Convex?

4. Prove theorems 13.4 and 13.5

5. The Diewert cost function is

$$C(\mathbf{p}, \bar{x}_0) = \bar{x}_0^\alpha \sum_{i=1}^{n} \sum_{j=1}^{n} b_{ij} p_i^{1/2} p_j^{1/2}$$

where $b_{ij} = b_{ji}$ and $b_{ij} > 0$ for all i, j and $\alpha > 1$. Show that:

(a) for fixed $\bar{x}_0 > 0$, C is a concave linearly homogeneous function of $\mathbf{p}$;

(b) for fixed $\mathbf{p} \in R^n_{++}$, C is convex and homogeneous of degree α in $\bar{x}_0$.

14 More on quasi-concavity

14.1 Introduction

Quasi-concave programming and second derivative properties of quasi-concave functions are the major gaps left from chapter 13 and we now set about filling these gaps. As was suggested in chapter 13, the theory of quasi-concave programming is a messy business made especially awkward by the fact that a stationary point of a C^1, quasi-concave function need not be a global maximum or even a local maximum. In order to sidestep the difficulties thus thrown up, we concentrate exclusively on quasi-concave programming problems where the functions involved are C^1 and *non-stationary*. Before we do this, however, we need to look again at the first derivative characterization of C^1, quasi-concave functions now under the additional assumption of non-stationarity, since this addition allows us to improve upon the first derivative results of chapter 13 in a way which is most helpful for the theory of quasi-concave programming. Finally, we turn to second derivatives and here the literature is quite complicated. Consequently we do not discuss second derivatives of general quasi-concave functions but only of strictly quasi-concave functions and again under the earlier simplifying assumptions plus the assumption that the function is monotone increasing: this is all we shall need later.

14.2 First derivative characterization of non-stationary, quasi-concave functions

Suppose D is convex and open and suppose $f:D \to R$ is a C^1, non-stationary, quasi-concave function. From chapter 13 we know that, for C^1, quasi-concave functions

$$f(\mathbf{x}) \geqslant f(\mathbf{x}^*) \Rightarrow (\mathbf{x}-\mathbf{x}^*)\,\mathbf{f}'(\mathbf{x}^*) \geqslant 0 \qquad (14.1)$$

However, we can now see that the new, non-stationary feature of f allows us to reach the additional conclusion

$$f(\mathbf{x}) > f(\mathbf{x}^*) \Rightarrow (\mathbf{x}-\mathbf{x}^*)\,\mathbf{f}'(\mathbf{x}^*) > 0 \tag{14.2}$$

To see why, first note that since f is non-stationary we may suppose without loss of generality that $f_1'(\mathbf{x}^*) \neq 0$; suppose further that $f_1'(\mathbf{x}^*) > 0$ – a similar argument for the case $f_1'(\mathbf{x}^*) < 0$ is easily constructed. Now suppose that $f(\mathbf{x}) > f(\mathbf{x}^*)$ but that the implication in (14.2) does not follow: that is, $(\mathbf{x}-\mathbf{x}^*)\,\mathbf{f}'(\mathbf{x}^*) \leqslant 0$. We derive a contradiction. Define $\hat{\mathbf{x}}$ by: $\hat{x}_1 = x_1 - \epsilon$, $\hat{x}_i = x_i$, $i = 2, \ldots, n$ where $\epsilon > 0$ and 'small'. For $\epsilon > 0$ and sufficiently small, we still have $f(\hat{\mathbf{x}}) > f(\mathbf{x}^*)$. But $(\hat{x}_1 - x_1^*) f_1'(\mathbf{x}^*) = (x_1 - x_1^*) f_1'(\mathbf{x}^*) - \epsilon f_1'(\mathbf{x}^*) < (x_1 - x_1^*) f_1'(\mathbf{x}^*)$ since $\epsilon > 0$ and $f_1'(\mathbf{x}^*) > 0$. For $i = 2, \ldots, n$, $(\hat{x}_i - x_i^*) f_i'(\mathbf{x}^*) = (x_i - x_i^*) f_i'(\mathbf{x}^*)$, trivially since then $\hat{x}_i = x_i$. Hence

$$(\hat{\mathbf{x}}-\mathbf{x}^*)\,\mathbf{f}'(\mathbf{x}^*) < (\mathbf{x}-\mathbf{x}^*)\,\mathbf{f}'(\mathbf{x}^*) \leqslant 0$$

Therefore we have

$$f(\hat{\mathbf{x}}) > f(\mathbf{x}^*) \quad \text{and} \quad (\hat{\mathbf{x}}-\mathbf{x}^*)\,\mathbf{f}'(\mathbf{x}^*) < 0$$

which contradicts (14.1). So the implication in (14.2) must indeed follow and non-stationary quasi-concavity implies (14.1) and (14.2). Of course (14.1) and (14.2) imply quasi-concavity.

Theorem 14.1 Suppose $D \subset R^n$ is convex and open and suppose $f: D \to R$ is C^1 and non-stationary. Then f is quasi-concave if and only if

(a) $\mathbf{x}, \mathbf{x}^* \in D$ and $f(\mathbf{x}) \geqslant f(\mathbf{x}^*) \Rightarrow (\mathbf{x}-\mathbf{x}^*)\,\mathbf{f}'(\mathbf{x}^*) \geqslant 0$

(b) $\mathbf{x}, \mathbf{x}^* \in D$ and $f(\mathbf{x}) > f(\mathbf{x}^*) \Rightarrow (\mathbf{x}-\mathbf{x}^*)\,\mathbf{f}'(\mathbf{x}^*) > 0$

Actually, as is easily seen using the C^1, non-stationarity of f, (a) is redundant in this statement since (b) ⇒ (a); we state both for ease of reference. The non-stationarity assumption also helps us arrive at the following characterization of strict quasi-concavity, which had no analogue without non-stationarity in chapter 13.

Theorem 14.2 Suppose $D \subset R^n$ is convex and open and suppose $f: D \to R$ is C^1 and non-stationary. Then f is strictly quasi-concave if and only if

$$\mathbf{x}, \mathbf{x}^* \in D,\ \mathbf{x} \neq \mathbf{x}^* \text{ and } f(\mathbf{x}) \geqslant f(\mathbf{x}^*) \Rightarrow (\mathbf{x}-\mathbf{x}^*)\,\mathbf{f}'(\mathbf{x}^*) > 0$$

A proof is given at the end of this chapter.

Corresponding results for quasi-convexity are found by reversing the sense of all inequalities in theorems 14.1 and 14.2.

14.3 Quasi-concave programming

The problem is:

$$\max_{\mathbf{x}\in D} f(\mathbf{x}) \text{ subject to } g(\mathbf{x}) \geqslant 0 \tag{14.3}$$

We assume that D is convex and open, $f:D\rightarrow R$ and $g:D\rightarrow R$ are quasi-concave and that the feasible set, $\{\mathbf{x}\in D \mid g(\mathbf{x})\geqslant 0\}$ is non-empty. As indicated in the Introduction, we simplify the analysis considerably by assuming also that f and g are non-stationary. In fact it follows from the non-emptiness of the feasible set and the non-stationarity of g that there exists $\mathbf{x}\in D$ where $g(\mathbf{x})>0$; that is, the usual constraint qualification is satisfied. To see why, suppose without loss of generality, since g is non-stationary, that $\hat{\mathbf{x}}\in D$ and $g_1'(\hat{\mathbf{x}})>0$. Define $x_1=\hat{x}_1+\epsilon$, $x_i=\hat{x}_i$, $i=2,\ldots,n$. For $\epsilon>0$ and small enough $\mathbf{x}$ thus defined will have the properties required: $\mathbf{x}\in D$, since D is open and $g(\mathbf{x})>0$. So the constraint qualification (CQ) which appeared throughout the earlier concave programming development will be missing from the ensuing quasi-concave results quite simply because it is implied by other assumptions we are making. Given all these assumptions, we would like, as usual, a characterization of solutions to (14.3). Happily the usual Kuhn–Tucker conditions still provide this: moreover with f non-stationary, λ^* cannot be zero and the conditions take on their simpler form:

Theorem 14.3 Suppose $D\subset R^n$ is convex and open and suppose $f:D\rightarrow R$ and $g:D\rightarrow R$ are C^1, non-stationary and quasi-concave. Assuming the feasible set for (14.3) is non-empty then $\mathbf{x}^*$ solves (14.3) if and only if there is a λ^* such that

(I) $\dfrac{\partial L}{\partial x_i}(\mathbf{x}^*,\lambda^*)=0,\ i=1,\ldots,n$

(II) $\lambda^*>0$

(III) $g(\mathbf{x}^*)=0$ and $\mathbf{x}^*\in D$

where $L(\mathbf{x},\lambda)=f(\mathbf{x})+\lambda g(\mathbf{x})$.

Proof A proof of 'only if' is given at the end of the chapter.

'if' Suppose (I)–(III) are satisfied by $\mathbf{x}^*, \lambda^*$ and suppose $\mathbf{x}^*$ does not solve (14.3): we derive a contradiction. Since $\mathbf{x}^*$ does not solve (14.3), there exists $\mathbf{x} \in D$ such that $g(\mathbf{x}) \geqslant 0$ (so $\mathbf{x}$ is feasible) and $f(\mathbf{x}) > f(\mathbf{x}^*)$. Since $f(\mathbf{x}) > f(\mathbf{x}^*)$ it follows from theorem 14.1 that

$$(\mathbf{x}-\mathbf{x}^*)\,\mathbf{f}'(\mathbf{x}^*) > 0 \tag{14.4}$$

Since $g(\mathbf{x}^*) = 0$ from (III) we also have $g(\mathbf{x}) \geqslant g(\mathbf{x}^*)$, and since g is quasi-concave:

$$(\mathbf{x}-\mathbf{x}^*)\,\mathbf{g}'(\mathbf{x}^*) \geqslant 0 \tag{14.5}$$

Now $\lambda^* > 0$ from (II) so that (14.4) plus λ^* multiplied by (14.5) gives

$$(\mathbf{x}-\mathbf{x}^*)\,(\mathbf{f}'(\mathbf{x}^*) + \lambda^*\mathbf{g}'(\mathbf{x}^*)) > 0$$

But (I) implies $(\mathbf{x}-\mathbf{x}^*)\,\{f'(\mathbf{x}^*) + \lambda^* g'(\mathbf{x}^*)\} = 0$, a contradiction.

Q.E.D.

The mechanics of solving quasi-concave programming problems are as before. Here is a simple example:

Example 14.1

$$\max_{\mathbf{x} \in R^2_{++}} \; x_1 x_2 \quad \text{subject to } x_1 + x_2 \leqslant 1$$

$f(\mathbf{x}) = x_1 x_2$ and is Cobb–Douglas and so quasi-concave and non-stationary; $g(\mathbf{x}) = 1 - x_1 - x_2$ and is linear and so quasi-concave and non-stationary; taking $\mathbf{x} = (\frac{1}{4}, \frac{1}{4})$ shows that the feasible set is not empty. The Lagrangean and K–T conditions are

$$L(\mathbf{x}, \lambda) = x_1 x_2 + \lambda(1 - x_1 - x_2)$$

(I) $x_2 - \lambda = 0,\ x_1 - \lambda = 0$

(II) $\lambda > 0$

(III) $\mathbf{x} \in R^2_{++},\ 1 = x_1 + x_2$

From (I) $x_1 = x_2 = \lambda$. From (III) $x_1 = x_2 = \lambda = \frac{1}{2}$. (II) is satisfied and so $\mathbf{x}^* = (\frac{1}{2}, \frac{1}{2})$ is the solution. The feasible set, typical contours of f and the solution are sketched in fig. 14.1. In this example there was exactly one solution to the quasi-concave programming problem. However, as in concave programming, there can in general be zero, one or more than one solution to a quasi-concave programming problem. Also, as in concave programming and easily shown (details omitted), if there is more than one solution to a quasi-concave programming problem, then there are an infinite number corre-

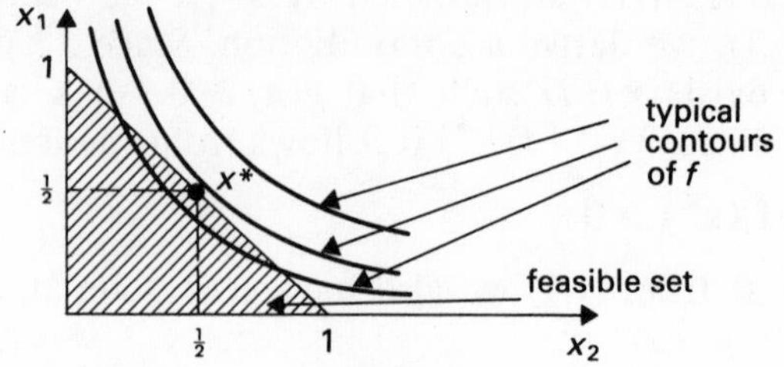

Figure 14.1

sponding to a convex set. The strict quasi-concavity assumption rules out such multiple solutions:

Corollary 1 to theorem 14.3 If in addition to the suppositions of theorem 14.3, f is strictly quasi-concave, then there is at most one solution to the problem (14.3).

Proof Suppose not so that $\mathbf{x}^1 \neq \mathbf{x}^2$ are two solutions to (14.3). Then

(a) $\mathbf{x}^1, \mathbf{x}^2 \in D$, $g(\mathbf{x}^1) \geqslant 0$ and $g(\mathbf{x}^2) \geqslant 0$ and

(b) $f(\mathbf{x}^1) = f(\mathbf{x}^2)$ otherwise both $\mathbf{x}^1$ and $\mathbf{x}^2$ are not solutions.

From (b), since f is strictly quasi-concave

$$f[\lambda \mathbf{x}^1 + (1-\lambda)\mathbf{x}^2] > f(\mathbf{x}^1) = f(\mathbf{x}^2) \quad \forall \lambda \in (0, 1)$$

Since D is convex and g is quasi-concave, $UC_g(0)$ is convex and hence from (a)

$$g[\lambda \mathbf{x}^1 + (1-\lambda)\mathbf{x}^2] \geqslant 0 \quad \text{and} \quad \lambda \mathbf{x}^1 + (1-\lambda)\mathbf{x}^2 \in D, \lambda \in [0, 1]$$

Therefore, for $\lambda \in (0, 1)$, $\lambda \mathbf{x}^1 + (1-\lambda)\mathbf{x}^2$ is feasible for (14.3) and gives a higher f value than $f(\mathbf{x}^1)$ or $f(\mathbf{x}^2)$. Hence $\mathbf{x}^1, \mathbf{x}^2$ are not solutions; a contradiction. *Q.E.D.*

Finally consider parameterized quasi-concave programming problems:

$$\max f(\mathbf{x}; \boldsymbol{\alpha}) \quad \text{subject to } g(\mathbf{x}; \boldsymbol{\alpha}) \geqslant 0, \text{ where } \boldsymbol{\alpha} \in A \tag{14.6}$$

We make the expected assumptions:

1. A and D are convex and open.
2. f and g are C^2.

3. For each $\boldsymbol{\alpha} \in A$, f and g are quasi-concave and non-stationary functions of $\mathbf{x}$.
4. For each $\boldsymbol{\alpha} \in A$ the feasible set for (14.6) is non-empty.
5. For each $\boldsymbol{\alpha} \in A$ there is exactly one solution to (14.6).

These five assumptions ensure that to each $\boldsymbol{\alpha} \in A$ there corresponds exactly one solution to (14.6) and this is characterized by the Kuhn–Tucker conditions from theorem 14.3. In particular, the solutions, Lagrange multipliers and optimal values give rise to functions, $x_i^*: A \to R$, $i = 1, \ldots, n$, $\lambda^*: A \to R$ and $V: A \to R$. We assume also:

6. For $i = 1, \ldots, n$, x_i^* is C^1; λ^* is C^1; V is C^2.

Now the envelope theorem for parameterized concave programming problems followed from the analogue of (6) and the Kuhn–Tucker conditions (see p. 106). Hence we now have enough to apply the reasoning for the envelope theorem to the current quasi-concave case.

Corollary 2 to theorem 14.3 For the parameterized quasi-concave programming problem (14.6) in which (1)–(6) are satisfied, the partial derivative of the Lagrangean with respect to a parameter evaluated at the solution to (14.6) equals the partial derivative of the optimal value function with respect to that parameter.

In other words, the concave programming result continues to apply in the quasi-concave setting.

Example 14.2

$$\max_{\mathbf{x} \in R^2_{++}} x_1 x_2 \quad \text{subject to } \alpha_1 x_1 + \alpha_2 x_2 \leqslant \alpha_3, \ \boldsymbol{\alpha} \in R^3_{++}$$

It is easy to check that (1)–(5) are satisfied. The Lagrangean is

$$L(\mathbf{x}, \lambda; \boldsymbol{\alpha}) = x_1 x_2 + \lambda[\alpha_3 - \alpha_1 x_1 - \alpha_2 x_2]$$

The K–T conditions are

(I) $x_2 - \lambda\alpha_1 = 0, x_1 - \lambda\alpha_2 = 0$

(II) $\lambda > 0$

(III) $\mathbf{x} \in R^2_{++}$ and $\alpha_3 = \alpha_1 x_1 + \alpha_2 x_2$

(I) $\Rightarrow \alpha_1 x_1 = \alpha_2 x_2$ and (III) $\Rightarrow x_1 = \alpha_3/2\alpha_1$, $x_2 = \alpha_3/2\alpha_2 : \mathbf{x} \in R^2_{++}$ since $\boldsymbol{\alpha} \in R^3_{++}$. Thus (I) $\Rightarrow \lambda = x_2/\alpha_1 = \alpha_3/2\alpha_1\alpha_2 > 0$ and (II) is satisfied.

The optimal value is $\alpha_3^2/4\alpha_1\alpha_2$ and the solution functions (etc.) are:

$$x_1^*(\alpha) = \frac{\alpha_3}{2\alpha_1},\ x_2^*(\alpha) = \frac{\alpha_3}{2\alpha_2},\ \lambda^*(\alpha) = \frac{\alpha_3}{2\alpha_1\alpha_2},\ V(\alpha) = \frac{\alpha_3^2}{4\alpha_1\alpha_2}$$

From the envelope theorem we should have

$$\frac{\partial V}{\partial \alpha_i} = \frac{\partial L}{\partial \alpha_i} \text{ evaluated at } \mathbf{x}^*(\alpha), \lambda^*(\alpha), \quad i = 1, 2, 3$$

That is

$$\frac{\partial V}{\partial \alpha_2} = -\frac{\alpha_3^2}{4\alpha_1^2\alpha_2} = -\lambda^*(\alpha)\, x_1^*(\alpha) = -\frac{\alpha_3^2}{4\alpha_1^2\alpha_2}$$

$$\frac{\partial V}{\partial \alpha_2} = -\frac{\alpha_3^2}{4\alpha_1\alpha_2^2} = -\lambda^*(\alpha)\, x_2^*(\alpha) = -\frac{\alpha_3^2}{4\alpha_1\alpha_2^2}$$

and

$$\frac{\partial V}{\partial \alpha_3} = \frac{\alpha_3}{2\alpha_1\alpha_2} = \lambda^*(\alpha) = \frac{\alpha_3}{2\alpha_1\alpha_2}$$

The results are confirmed.

14.4 Second derivatives and quasi-concavity

Second derivative characterizations of quasi-concavity are complicated. Since we need them only at a specific point later, we narrow discussion down to the bare essentials needed at this specific point. In particular we concentrate exclusively on second derivative results for *strictly* quasi-concave functions on the domain R^n_{++} which are C^2 and *monotone increasing*; i.e. $\forall \mathbf{x} \in R^n_{++}, f_i'(\mathbf{x}) > 0, i = 1, \ldots, n$. And like the second derivative results for strict concavity, what we provide is not quite a characterization of these functions. In other words, we provide a set of necessary conditions for strict quasi-concavity and a set of sufficient conditions for strict quasi-concavity (both under the simplifying assumptions) but these conditions are not quite the same. We start with the necessary conditions.

Suppose, then, that $f: R^n_{++} \to R$ is C^2, monotone increasing and strictly quasi-concave. From theorem 14.2

$$\mathbf{x}, \mathbf{x}^* \in R^n_{++}, \mathbf{x} \neq \mathbf{x}^* \text{ and } f(\mathbf{x}) \geqslant f(\mathbf{x}^*) \Rightarrow (\mathbf{x} - \mathbf{x}^*)\, \mathbf{f}'(x^*) > 0$$

$$\therefore\ \mathbf{x}, \mathbf{x}^* \in R^n_{++}, \mathbf{x} \neq \mathbf{x}^* \text{ and } (\mathbf{x} - \mathbf{x}^*)\, \mathbf{f}'(\mathbf{x}^*) \leqslant 0 \Rightarrow f(\mathbf{x}) < f(\mathbf{x}^*)$$

This means that $\mathbf{x}^*$ solves the following problem (uniquely):

$$\max_{\mathbf{x}\in R^n_{++}} f(\mathbf{x}) \quad \text{subject to } (\mathbf{x}-\mathbf{x}^*)\,\mathbf{f}'(\mathbf{x}^*) \leqslant 0$$

Since $\mathbf{x}^*$ satisfies the constraint with equality, $\mathbf{x}^*$ solves also:

$$\max_{\mathbf{x}\in R^n_{++}} f(\mathbf{x}) \quad \text{subject to } (\mathbf{x}-\mathbf{x}^*)\,\mathbf{f}'(\mathbf{x}^*) = 0$$

The constraint requires

$$x_1 = x_1^* - \sum_{i=2}^{n} (x_i - x_i^*)\frac{f_i'(\mathbf{x}^*)}{f_1'(\mathbf{x}^*)}$$

Hence $(x_2^*, \ldots, x_n^*)$ solves

$$\max_{(x_2,\ldots,x_n)\in A} f\left[x_1^* - \sum_{i=2}^{n} (x_i - x_i^*)\frac{f_i'(\mathbf{x}^*)}{f_1'(\mathbf{x}^*)}, x_2, \ldots, x_n\right]$$

where

$$A = \left\{(x_2, \ldots, x_n) \in R^{n-1}_{++} \,|\, x_1^* - \sum_{i=2}^{n} (x_i - x_i^*)\frac{f_i'(\mathbf{x}^*)}{f_1'(\mathbf{x}^*)} > 0\right\}$$

Define $g: A \to R$ by

$$g(x_2, \ldots, x_n) = f\left[x_1^* - \sum_{i=2}^{n} (x_i - x_i^*)\frac{f_i'(\mathbf{x}^*)}{f_1'(\mathbf{x}^*)}, x_2, \ldots, x_n\right]$$

$$= f(Z), \text{ say, for notational convenience.}$$

Then $(x_2^*, \ldots, x_n^*)$ solves:

$$\max_{(x_2,\ldots,x_n)\in A} g(x_2, \ldots, x_n)$$

In particular, therefore, $(x_2^*, \ldots, x_n^*)$ satisfies the necessary conditions for a local unconstrained maximum of g and the Hessian of g at $\mathbf{x}^*$ must be negative semidefinite. To evaluate this Hessian, we start with

$$g_i'(x_2, \ldots, x_n) = -\frac{f_i'(\mathbf{x}^*)}{f_1'(\mathbf{x}^*)} f_1'(Z) + f_i'(Z), i = 2, \ldots, n$$

and

$$g_{ij}''(x_2, \ldots, x_n) = -\frac{f_i'(\mathbf{x}^*)}{f_1'(\mathbf{x}^*)}\left\{-\frac{f_j'(\mathbf{x}^*)}{f_1'(\mathbf{x}^*)} f_{11}''(Z) + f_{1j}''(Z)\right\}$$

$$+\left\{-\frac{f_j'(\mathbf{x}^*)}{f_1'(\mathbf{x}^*)} f_{i1}''(Z) + f_{ij}''(Z)\right\}$$

for $i, j = 2, \ldots, n$. At $x_2^*, \ldots, x_n^*$, Z becomes $\mathbf{x}^*$ and rearranging we get

$$g''_{ij}(x_2^*, \ldots, x_n^*) = \frac{1}{(f'_1)^2}\{f'_i f'_j f''_{11} - f'_i f'_1 f''_{1j} - f'_1 f'_j f''_{i1} + (f'_1)^2 f''_{ij}\}$$

all derivatives of f being evaluated at $\mathbf{x}^*$. But the right-hand side is easily seen to correspond to

$$g''_{ij}(x_2^*, \ldots, x_n^*) = -\frac{1}{(f'_1)^2}\begin{vmatrix} f''_{11} & f''_{1j} & f'_1 \\ f''_{i1} & f''_{ij} & f'_i \\ f'_1 & f'_j & 0 \end{vmatrix}$$

again all derivatives being calculated at $\mathbf{x}^*$.

When $n = 2$, the requirement that the Hessian of g be negative semidefinite reduces to the scalar condition $g''(x_2^*) \leqslant 0$, or from the last formula:

$$\begin{vmatrix} f''_{11}(\mathbf{x}^*) & f''_{12}(\mathbf{x}^*) & f'_1(\mathbf{x}^*) \\ f''_{21}(x^*) & f''_{22}(x^*) & f'_2(\mathbf{x}^*) \\ f'_1(\mathbf{x}^*) & f'_2(\mathbf{x}^*) & 0 \end{vmatrix} \geqslant 0$$

This matrix is the 2×2 Hessian of f 'bordered' with a row and column of $(f'_1(\mathbf{x}^*) \quad f'_2(\mathbf{x}^*) \quad 0)$: it is known as the *bordered Hessian* of f. Hence in the two-variable case we have the necessary second derivative property for strict quasi-concavity: the bordered Hessian of f must be non-negative.

We now explain how the negative semidefiniteness of g translates into a condition on f when $n > 2$. In general the bordered Hessian of f at $\mathbf{x}^*$ is the $(n+1) \times (n+1)$ matrix

$$\begin{vmatrix} f''_{11}(\mathbf{x}^*) \ldots f''_{1n}(\mathbf{x}^*) & f'_1(\mathbf{x}^*) \\ \cdots\cdots\cdots\cdots & \\ f''_{n1}(\mathbf{x}^*) \ldots f''_{nn}(\mathbf{x}^*) & f'_n(\mathbf{x}^*) \\ f'_1(\mathbf{x}^*) \ \ldots f'_n(\mathbf{x}^*) & 0 \end{vmatrix}$$

The kth-order bordered leading principal minor of f at $\mathbf{x}^*$, $k = 2, \ldots, n$

$$\begin{vmatrix} f''_{11}(\mathbf{x}^*) \ldots f''_{1k}(\mathbf{x}^*) & f'_1(\mathbf{x}^*) \\ \cdots\cdots\cdots\cdots & \\ f''_{k1}(\mathbf{x}^*) \ldots f''_{kk}(\mathbf{x}^*) & f'_k(\mathbf{x}^*) \\ f'_1(\mathbf{x}^*) \ \ldots f'_k(\mathbf{x}^*) & 0 \end{vmatrix}$$

Correspondingly, define the kth leading principal minor of g (of order $(k-1) \times (k-1)$, note), at $\mathbf{x}^*$ as follows for $k = 2, \ldots, n$:

$$\begin{vmatrix} g''_{22}(\mathbf{x}^*) & \ldots & g''_{2k}(\mathbf{x}^*) \\ g''_{k2}(\mathbf{x}^*) & \ldots & g''_{kk}(\mathbf{x}^*) \end{vmatrix}$$

We prove the following at the end of the chapter.

Lemma 14.1 For $k = 2, \ldots, n$, the kth-order bordered leading principal minor of f at $\mathbf{x}^*$ has opposite sign to the kth leading principal minor of g at $\mathbf{x}^*$.

For instance, when $k = 2$, this says that

$$g''_{22}(\mathbf{x}^*) \leqslant 0 \Leftrightarrow \begin{vmatrix} f''_{11}(\mathbf{x}^*) & f''_{12}(\mathbf{x}^*) & f'_1(\mathbf{x}^*) \\ f''_{21}(\mathbf{x}^*) & f''_{22}(\mathbf{x}^*) & f'_2(\mathbf{x}^*) \\ f'_1(\mathbf{x}^*) & f'_2(\mathbf{x}^*) & 0 \end{vmatrix} \geqslant 0$$

which we had earlier.

Now since $g''(\mathbf{x}^*)$ is negative semidefinite, the kth leading principal minor of g at $\mathbf{x}^*$ has sign 0 or $(-1)^{k-1}$. Hence the kth-order bordered leading principal minor of f at $\mathbf{x}^*$ has sign 0 or $(-1)^k$ from lemma 14.1. This is the desired necessary condition:

Theorem 14.4 Suppose $f: R^n_{++} \to R$ is C^2, monotone increasing and strictly quasi-concave. Then for all $\mathbf{x}^* \in R^n_{++}$, and for $k = 2, \ldots, n$, the kth-order bordered leading principal minor of f at $\mathbf{x}^*$ has sign 0 or $(-1)^k$.

If we rule out zero values for bordered minors, the necessary condition in theorem 14.4 becomes sufficient. A proof of this is given at the end of the chapter.

Theorem 14.5 Suppose $f: R^2_{++} \to R$ is C^2, monotone increasing and suppose that, for all $x^* \in R^n_{++}$ and for $k = 2, \ldots, n$, the kth-order bordered leading principal minor of f at $\mathbf{x}^*$ has sign $(-1)^k$. Then f is strictly quasi-concave.

The situation is somewhat similar to the second derivative properties of strictly concave functions: a sufficient condition for strict concavity is that the leading principal minors have a certain (non-zero) sign. This condition is not quite necessary since some minors of strictly concave functions may be zero: allowing zero values produces a necessary condition, however. Similarly here for the strictly quasi-concave case (except the leading principal minors are now bordered).

Theorem 14.5 provides a mechanical procedure for identifying strictly quasi-concave functions. Here are a couple of simple examples:

Examples 14.3

(a) $f:R^2_{++}\to R$ where $f(\mathbf{x})=x_1^2x_2$. When $n=2$ there is only the second-order bordered leading principal minor (= bordered Hessian) to consider. This is

$$\begin{vmatrix} 2x_2 & 2x_1 & 2x_1x_2 \\ 2x_1 & 0 & x_1^2 \\ 2x_1x_2 & x_1^2 & 0 \end{vmatrix} = -2x_2x_1^4+4x_1^4x_2+4x_1^4x_2$$

$$=6x_1^4x_2>0 \quad \forall \mathbf{x}\in R^2_{++}$$

Hence f is strictly quasi-concave.

(b) $f:R^3_{++}\to R$ where $f(\mathbf{x})=x_1x_2x_3$. The second-order bordered leading principal minor is

$$\begin{vmatrix} 0 & x_3 & x_2x_3 \\ x_3 & 0 & x_1x_3 \\ x_2x_3 & x_1x_3 & 0 \end{vmatrix} = x_3^3x_1x_2+x_3^3x_1x_2>0 \quad \forall \mathbf{x}\in R^3_{++}$$

and the bordered Hessian itself is

$$\begin{vmatrix} 0 & x_3 & x_2 & x_2x_3 \\ x_3 & 0 & x_1 & x_1x_3 \\ x_2 & x_1 & 0 & x_1x_2 \\ x_2x_3 & x_1x_3 & x_1x_2 & 0 \end{vmatrix} = -3x_1^2x_2^2x_3^2<0 \quad \forall \mathbf{x}\in R^3_{++}$$

and so f is strictly quasi-concave. (Both (a) and (b) are Cobb–Douglas functions so the answers here in fact follow from chapter 13.)

For monotone decreasing strictly quasi-convex functions, positive semidefiniteness of the Hessian of g is the necessary condition, which means that the leading principal minors of this Hessian are all non-negative, equivalent to the non-positivity of all the bordered leading principal minors of f; strict negativity of the latter is then sufficient for f to be strictly quasi-convex.

Example 14.4 $f:R^2_{++}\to R$ where $f(\mathbf{x})=-x_1^2x_2$. From (a) in the last examples the bordered Hessian is

$$\begin{vmatrix} -2x_2 & -2x_1 & -2x_1x_2 \\ -2x_1 & 0 & -x_1^2 \\ -2x_1x_2 & -x_1^2 & 0 \end{vmatrix} = -6x_1^4x_2<0 \quad \forall \mathbf{x}\in R^2_{++}$$

and f is strictly quasi-convex.

14.5 Proof of theorem 14.2

'Only if' Suppose f is C^1, non-stationary and strictly quasi-concave. Then f is quasi-concave and from theorem 14.1

$$\mathbf{x}, \mathbf{x}^* \in D, f(\mathbf{x}) > f(\mathbf{x}^*) \Rightarrow (\mathbf{x}-\mathbf{x}^*)\,\mathbf{f}'(\mathbf{x}^*) > 0$$

So what is left to show is

$$\mathbf{x}, \mathbf{x}^* \in D, \mathbf{x} \neq \mathbf{x}^* \text{ and } f(\mathbf{x}) = f(\mathbf{x}^*) \Rightarrow (\mathbf{x}-\mathbf{x}^*)\,\mathbf{f}'(\mathbf{x}^*) > 0$$

Suppose this is false and $f(\mathbf{x}) = f(\mathbf{x}^*)$, $\mathbf{x} \neq \mathbf{x}^*$ but $(\mathbf{x}-\mathbf{x}^*)\,f'(\mathbf{x}^*) = 0$ (we cannot have <0 from (a) of theorem 14.1). Let $\hat{\mathbf{x}} = \lambda\mathbf{x} + (1-\lambda)\,\mathbf{x}^*$, $\lambda \in (0, 1)$. Then $(\hat{\mathbf{x}} - \mathbf{x}^*)\,\mathbf{f}'(\mathbf{x}^*) = (\lambda\mathbf{x} + (1-\lambda)\,\mathbf{x}^* - \mathbf{x}^*)\,\mathbf{f}'(\mathbf{x}^*) = \lambda(\mathbf{x}-\mathbf{x}^*)\,\mathbf{f}'(\mathbf{x}^*) = 0$. But as f is strictly quasi-concave, $f(\hat{\mathbf{x}}) > \mathbf{f}(\mathbf{x}^*)$ and so $(\hat{\mathbf{x}}-\mathbf{x}^*)\,\mathbf{f}'(\mathbf{x}^*) > 0$ from (b) of theorem 14.1, a contradiction.

'if' Suppose f satisfies

$$\mathbf{x}, \mathbf{x}^* \in D, \mathbf{x} \neq \mathbf{x}^* \text{ and } f(\mathbf{x}) \geqslant f(\mathbf{x}^*) \Rightarrow (\mathbf{x}-\mathbf{x}^*)\,\mathbf{f}'(\mathbf{x}^*) > 0$$

Then (a) and (b) of theorem 14.1 are satisfied and f is certainly quasi-concave. Suppose f is not strictly quasi-concave. Then for some $\mathbf{x}, \mathbf{x}^* \in D$, $\mathbf{x} \neq \mathbf{x}^*$, $f(\mathbf{x}) \geqslant f(\mathbf{x}^*)$, $\lambda \in (0, 1)$ and $\hat{\mathbf{x}} = \lambda\mathbf{x} + (1-\lambda)\,\mathbf{x}^*$, we have $f(\hat{\mathbf{x}}) = f(\mathbf{x}^*)$. But then

$$f(\mathbf{x}) \geqslant f(\hat{x}) \Rightarrow (\mathbf{x}-\hat{\mathbf{x}})\,\mathbf{f}'(\mathbf{x}) > 0 \Rightarrow (\mathbf{x}-\mathbf{x}^*)\,\mathbf{f}'(\hat{\mathbf{x}}) > 0$$

and

$$f(\mathbf{x}^*) \geqslant f(\hat{x}) \Rightarrow (\mathbf{x}^*-\hat{\mathbf{x}})\,\mathbf{f}'(\hat{\mathbf{x}}) > 0 \Rightarrow (\mathbf{x}^*-\mathbf{x})\,\mathbf{f}'(\hat{\mathbf{x}}) > 0$$

a contradiction. *Q.E.D.*

14.6 Proof of 'only if' in theorem 14.3

Suppose $\mathbf{x}^*$ solves (14.3) which of course requires $\mathbf{x}^* \in D$. We first show that $g(\mathbf{x}^*) = 0$. Suppose not: then $g(\mathbf{x}^*) > 0$ and small enough movements from $\mathbf{x}^*$ to $\mathbf{x}$ will maintain $g(\mathbf{x}) > 0$ and $\mathbf{x} \in D$. Since f is non-stationary we may suppose, without loss of generality, that $f_1'(\mathbf{x}^*) > 0$. Define $\mathbf{x}$ by $x_1 = x_1^* + \epsilon$, $x_i = x_i^*$, $i = 2, \ldots, n$. For $\epsilon > 0$ and sufficiently small, $\mathbf{x} \in D$, $g(\mathbf{x}) > 0$ and, since $f_1'(\mathbf{x}^*) > 0$, $f(\mathbf{x}) > f(\mathbf{x}^*)$. This means $\mathbf{x}^*$ does not solve (14.3)–a contradiction. Hence $g(\mathbf{x}^*) = 0$ and (III) is satisfied. To show that (I) and (II) are satisfied, define the following two sets:

$$A = \{\mathbf{x} \in D \mid f(\mathbf{x}) > f(\mathbf{x}^*)\}$$

$$B = \{\mathbf{x} \in D \mid g(\mathbf{x}) \geqslant 0 = g(\mathbf{x}^*)\}$$

In fact $B = UC_g(0)$, which is convex since g is quasi-concave; B is non-empty by assumption. A is also non-empty (as above we may assume $f_1'(\mathbf{x}^*) > 0$, $\mathbf{x}$ as defined above will belong to A for ϵ sufficiently small and $f(\mathbf{x}) > f(\mathbf{x}^*)$). A is convex: let $\mathbf{x}^1, \mathbf{x}^2 \in A$ so that $f(\mathbf{x}^1) > f(\mathbf{x}^*)$ and $f(\mathbf{x}^2) > f(\mathbf{x}^*)$; without loss of generality suppose $f(\mathbf{x}^1) \geqslant f(\mathbf{x}^2)$; since f is quasi-concave $f[\lambda\mathbf{x}^1 + (1-\lambda)\mathbf{x}^2] \geqslant f(\mathbf{x}^2)$, $\forall\lambda \in [0, 1]$; hence, $\forall\lambda \in [0, 1]$, $f[\lambda\mathbf{x}^1 + (1-\lambda)\mathbf{x}^2] > f(\mathbf{x}^*)$ and $\lambda\mathbf{x}^1 + (1-\lambda)\mathbf{x}^2 \in A$; so A is convex. Thus A and B are both non-empty convex sets in R^n. Moreover they are disjoint since $\mathbf{x}^*$ solves (14.3). Hence by the separating hyperplane theorem there is a hyperplane

$$H = \left\{\mathbf{x} \in R^n \mid \sum_{i=1}^{n} \alpha_i x_i = \beta\right\} \text{ say, such that}$$

$$\mathbf{x} \in D, f(\mathbf{x}) > f(\mathbf{x}^*) \Rightarrow \Sigma\alpha_i x_i \geqslant \beta \text{ or } \mathbf{x} \in H^+ \tag{1}$$

$$\mathbf{x} \in D, g(\mathbf{x}) \geqslant g(\mathbf{x}^*) = 0 \Rightarrow \Sigma\alpha_i x_i \leqslant \beta \text{ or } \mathbf{x} \in H^- \tag{2}$$

We first show that the strict inequality in the first implication can be made weak. Suppose $\mathbf{x} \in D$ and $f(\mathbf{x}) = f(\mathbf{x}^*)$. Since f is non-stationary we may, as usual, assume without loss of generality that $f_1'(\mathbf{x}) > 0$; let $\hat{x}_1 = x_1 + \epsilon$, $\hat{x}_i = x_i$, $i = 2, \ldots, n$. For $\epsilon > 0$ and sufficiently small, $\hat{\mathbf{x}} \in D$ and $f(\hat{\mathbf{x}}) > f(\mathbf{x}^*)$. Hence $\Sigma\alpha_i\hat{x}_i \geqslant \beta$. Letting $\epsilon \to 0$ we get $\Sigma\alpha_i x_i \geqslant \beta$ also. Thus,

$$\mathbf{x} \in D,\ f(\mathbf{x}) \geqslant f(\mathbf{x}^*) \Rightarrow \Sigma\alpha_i x_i \geqslant \beta \tag{3}$$

Putting $\mathbf{x} = \mathbf{x}^*$ in (2) and (3) gives $\beta \geqslant \Sigma\alpha_i x_i^* \geqslant \beta$ so that $\Sigma\alpha_i x_i^* = \beta$ or $\mathbf{x}^* \in H$. The hyperplane H goes through $\mathbf{x}^*$ and from (2) has all of $UC_g(0)$ on one side of it. Since g is C^1 and non-stationary, H must be the unique tangent hyperplane to $UC_g(0)$ at $\mathbf{x}^*$; i.e.

$$H = \{\mathbf{x} \in R^n \mid (\mathbf{x} - \mathbf{x}^*)\,\mathbf{g}'(\mathbf{x}^*) = 0\} \tag{4}$$

From (2), H^- is the half-space containing $UC_g(0)$. Since g is quasi-concave

$$\mathbf{x} \in D, g(\mathbf{x}) \geqslant g(\mathbf{x}^*) \Rightarrow (\mathbf{x} - \mathbf{x}^*)\,\mathbf{g}'(\mathbf{x}^*) \geqslant 0$$

and $\{\mathbf{x} \in R^n \mid (\mathbf{x} - \mathbf{x}^*)\,\mathbf{g}'(\mathbf{x}^*) \geqslant 0\}$ is the half space of

$$\{\mathbf{x} \in R^n \mid (\mathbf{x} - \mathbf{x}^*)\,\mathbf{g}'(\mathbf{x}^*) = 0\}$$

containing $UC_g(0)$. Hence

$$H^- = \{\mathbf{x} \in R^n \mid (\mathbf{x} - \mathbf{x}^*)\,\mathbf{g}'(\mathbf{x}^*) \geqslant 0\} \tag{5}$$

Applying similar reasoning to f and (3) gives

$$H = \{\mathbf{x} \in R^n \mid (\mathbf{x} - \mathbf{x}^*)\,\mathbf{f}'(\mathbf{x}^*) = 0\} \tag{6}$$

$$H^+ = \{\mathbf{x} \in R^n \mid (\mathbf{x} - \mathbf{x}^*)\,\mathbf{f}'(\mathbf{x}^*) \geqslant 0\} \tag{7}$$

Next we use these results to show:

(a) $f_i'(\mathbf{x}^*) = 0$ if and only if $g_i'(\mathbf{x}^*) = 0$

(b) $f_i'(\mathbf{x}^*) > 0$ if and only if $g_i'(\mathbf{x}^*) < 0$

(c) $f_i'(\mathbf{x}^*) < 0$ if and only if $g_i'(\mathbf{x}^*) > 0$

Take $i = 1$ for convenience and without loss of generality and define $\mathbf{x}$ by $x_1 = x_1^* + \epsilon$, $x_i = x_i^*$, $i = 2, \ldots, n$ where $\epsilon > 0$. Suppose $f_1'(\mathbf{x}^*) = 0$. Then $(\mathbf{x} - \mathbf{x}^*)\mathbf{f}'(\mathbf{x}^*) = 0$ and $\mathbf{x} \in H$ from (6). But $(\mathbf{x} - \mathbf{x}^*)\mathbf{g}'(\mathbf{x}^*) = \epsilon g_1'(\mathbf{x}^*) = 0$ since $\mathbf{x} \in H$, from (4). As $\epsilon > 0$ it follows that $g_1'(\mathbf{x}^*) = 0$. The reverse implication follows similarly, establishing (a). For (b) suppose $f_1'(\mathbf{x}^*) > 0$. Then $(\mathbf{x} - \mathbf{x}^*)\mathbf{f}'(\mathbf{x}^*) > 0$ and $\mathbf{x} \notin H$ but $\mathbf{x} \in H^+$ from (6) and (7). $(\mathbf{x} - \mathbf{x}^*)\mathbf{g}'(\mathbf{x}^*) = \epsilon g_1'(\mathbf{x}^*)$ which cannot be $\geqslant 0$ as then $\mathbf{x}$ would belong to H or H^- from (4) and (5). As $\epsilon > 0$ we must have $g_1'(\mathbf{x}^*) < 0$; the reverse implication for (b) and the result in (c) are established similarly.

Finally from (4) and (6)

$$(\mathbf{x} - \mathbf{x}^*)\,\mathbf{g}'(\mathbf{x}^*) = 0 \text{ if and only if } (\mathbf{x} - \mathbf{x}^*)\,\mathbf{f}'(\mathbf{x}^*) = 0 \tag{8}$$

Since f is non-stationary assume, without loss of generality, that $f_1'(\mathbf{x}^*) > 0$; from (b), $g_1'(\mathbf{x}^*) < 0$. Define

$$\lambda^* = -\frac{f_1'(\mathbf{x}^*)}{g_1'(\mathbf{x}^*)}$$

Then $\lambda^* > 0$ satisfies (II), and by construction (I) is satisfied for $i = 1$. For i such that $f_i'(\mathbf{x}^*) = 0$, $g_i'(\mathbf{x}^*) = 0$ from (a) and (I) follows trivially for these i. Suppose $f_i'(\mathbf{x}^*) \neq 0$ some $i > 1$. Define $\mathbf{x}$ so that $x_j = x_j^*, j \neq 1$ or i and $x_1 - x_1^* \neq 0$, $x_i - x_i^* \neq 0$. From (8)

$$(x_1 - x_1^*)\,g_1'(\mathbf{x}^*) + (x_i - x_i^*)\,g_i'(\mathbf{x}^*) = 0 \text{ if and only if}$$
$$(x_1 - x_1^*)\,f_1'(\mathbf{x}^*) + (x_i - x_i^*)\,f_i'(\mathbf{x}^*) = 0$$

Hence,

$$\frac{x_1 - x_1^*}{x_i - x_i^*} = -\frac{g_i'(\mathbf{x}^*)}{g_1'(\mathbf{x}^*)} \quad \text{iff} \quad \frac{x_1 - x_1^*}{x_i - x_i^*} = -\frac{f_i'(\mathbf{x}^*)}{f_1'(\mathbf{x}^*)}$$

and

$$-\frac{g_i'(\mathbf{x}^*)}{g_1'(\mathbf{x}^*)} = -\frac{f_i'(\mathbf{x}^*)}{f_1'(\mathbf{x}^*)} \quad \text{or} \quad -\frac{f_i'(\mathbf{x}^*)}{g_i'(\mathbf{x}^*)} = -\frac{f_1'(\mathbf{x}^*)}{g_1'(\mathbf{x}^*)} = \lambda^*$$

satisfying (I) for these i also. *Q.E.D.*

14.7 Proof of lemma 14.1

Write f_{ij} for $f_{ij}''(\mathbf{x}^*)$ and α_i for $f_i'(\mathbf{x}^*)/f_1'(\mathbf{x}^*)$ for short. Then the kth leading principal minor of g is the $(k-1) \times (k-1)$ determinant

$$\begin{vmatrix} \alpha_2^2 f_{11} - \alpha_2 f_{12} - \alpha_2 f_{21} + f_{22} & \dots & \alpha_2 \alpha_k f_{11} - \alpha_2 f_{1k} - \alpha_k f_{21} + f_{2k} \\ \dots & \dots & \dots \\ \alpha_k \alpha_2 f_{11} - \alpha_k f_{12} - \alpha_2 f_{k1} + f_{k2} & \dots & \alpha_k^2 f_{11} - \alpha_k f_{1k} - \alpha_k f_{k1} + f_{kk} \end{vmatrix}$$

Adding on a new first row and last column, this equals

$$(-1)^k \begin{vmatrix} -\alpha_2 f_{11} + f_{12} & \dots & -\alpha_k f_{11} + f_{1k} & 1 \\ \alpha_2^2 f_{11} - \alpha_2 f_{12} - \alpha_2 f_{21} + f_{22} & \dots & \alpha_2 \alpha_k f_{11} - \alpha_2 f_{1k} - \alpha_k f_{21} + f_{2k} & 0 \\ \dots & \dots & \dots & \dots \\ \alpha_k \alpha_2 f_{11} - \alpha_k f_{12} - \alpha_2 f_{k1} + f_{k2} & \dots & \alpha_k^2 f_{11} - \alpha_k f_{1k} - \alpha_k f_{k1} + f_{kk} & 0 \end{vmatrix}$$

Adding $\alpha_i \times$ row 1 to row i, this in turn equals

$$(-1)^k \begin{vmatrix} f_{12} - \alpha_2 f_{11} & \dots & f_{1k} - \alpha_k f_{11} & 1 \\ f_{22} - \alpha_2 f_{21} & \dots & f_{2k} - \alpha_k f_{21} & \alpha_2 \\ \dots & \dots & \dots & \dots \\ f_{k2} - \alpha_2 f_{k1} & \dots & f_{kk} - \alpha_k f_{k1} & \alpha_k \end{vmatrix}$$

$$= (-1)^{2k+1} \begin{vmatrix} 0 & f_{12} - \alpha_2 f_{11} & \dots & f_{1k} - \alpha_k f_{11} & 1 \\ 0 & f_{22} - \alpha_2 f_{21} & \dots & f_{2k} - \alpha_k f_{21} & \alpha_2 \\ \dots & \dots & \dots & \dots & \dots \\ 0 & f_{k2} - \alpha_2 f_{k1} & \dots & f_{kk} - \alpha_k f_{k1} & \alpha_k \\ 1 & \alpha_2 & & \alpha_k & 0 \end{vmatrix}$$

adding a new first column and last row.

Now $2k+1$ is odd, so $(-1)^{2k+1} = -1$. Adding $f_{i1} \times$ last row to row i in last determinant shows that this equals

$$(-1)\begin{vmatrix} f_{11} & f_{12}\cdots f_{1k} & 1 \\ f_{21} & f_{22}\cdots f_{2k} & \alpha_2 \\ \cdots & \cdots & \cdots \\ f_{k1} & f_{k2}\cdots f_{kk} & \alpha_k \\ 1 & \alpha_2 \;\cdots\; \alpha_k & 0 \end{vmatrix}$$

Inserting $\alpha_i = f_i'(\mathbf{x}^*)/f_1'(\mathbf{x}^*)$ in the last row and column, and taking out $1/f_1'(\mathbf{x}^*)$ from each reduces the last expression to

$$-\frac{1}{[f_1'(\mathbf{x}^*)]^2}\begin{vmatrix} f_{11}''(\mathbf{x}^*)\ldots f_{1k}''(\mathbf{x}^*) & f_1'(\mathbf{x}^*) \\ \cdots & \cdots \\ f_{k1}''(\mathbf{x}^*)\ldots f_{kk}'' & f_k'(\mathbf{x}^*) \\ f_1'(\mathbf{x}^*)\ \ldots f_k'(\mathbf{x}^*) & 0 \end{vmatrix}$$

from which the lemma follows.

14.8 Proof of theorem 14.5

Suppose f is C^2 and monotone increasing and that the kth-order bordered leading principal minors of f have sign $(-1)^k$ at $\mathbf{x}^*$ for all $\mathbf{x}^* \in R^n_{++}$ and for $k = 2, \ldots, n$. Choose any $\mathbf{x}^* \in R^n_{++}$ and define A and $g: A \to R$ as in the necessity proof in the text. From lemma 14.1 it follows that the Hessian of g at $(x_2^*, \ldots, x_n^*)$ is negative definite. By construction of g, $(x_2^*, \ldots, x_n^*)$ is a stationary point of g; hence from the negative definiteness, $(x_2^*, \ldots, x_n^*)$ is a strict local maximum of g. It follows that $\mathbf{x}^*$ is a strict local solution of

$$\max_{\mathbf{x}\in R^n_{++}} f(\mathbf{x}) \quad \text{subject to } (\mathbf{x}-\mathbf{x}^*)\,\mathbf{f}'(\mathbf{x}^*) = 0 \tag{1}$$

We first show that $\mathbf{x}^*$ is also a strict global solution of (1). Suppose not. Then there exists $\tilde{\mathbf{x}} \in R^n_{++}$ such that $(\tilde{\mathbf{x}}-\mathbf{x}^*)\,\mathbf{f}'(\mathbf{x}^*) = 0$ and $f(\tilde{\mathbf{x}}) \geqslant f(\mathbf{x}^*)$. Define $\phi: [0, 1] \to R$ by $\phi(\lambda) = f[\lambda\tilde{\mathbf{x}} + (1-\lambda)\,\mathbf{x}^*] = f(\mathbf{x}(\lambda))$, say, so that $\phi(0) = f(\mathbf{x}^*), \phi(1) = f(\tilde{\mathbf{x}})$ and $\phi(1) \geqslant \phi(0)$. Now $[\mathbf{x}(\lambda)-\mathbf{x}^*]\,\mathbf{f}'(\mathbf{x}^*) = [(\lambda\tilde{\mathbf{x}} + (1-\lambda)\mathbf{x}^*) - \mathbf{x}^*]\mathbf{f}'(\mathbf{x}^*) = \lambda(\tilde{\mathbf{x}}-\mathbf{x}^*)\mathbf{f}'(\mathbf{x}^*) = 0$ so $\mathbf{x}(\lambda) = \lambda\tilde{\mathbf{x}} + (1-\lambda)\,\mathbf{x}^*$ is feasible for (1). For $\lambda > 0$ but sufficiently close to zero, it follows that $f(\mathbf{x}^*) > f[\lambda\tilde{\mathbf{x}} + (1-\lambda)\,\mathbf{x}^*] = f(\mathbf{x}(\lambda))$ since $\mathbf{x}^*$ is a strict local solution of (1); that is $\phi(0) > \phi(\lambda)$ for $\lambda > 0$ but sufficiently close to 0. Since $\phi(1) \geqslant \phi(0)$, ϕ must have a local minimum somewhere in (0, 1), say at $\hat{\lambda}$; i.e.

$$\phi(\hat{\lambda}) \leqslant \phi(\lambda) \text{ for all } \lambda \text{ sufficiently close to } \hat{\lambda} \tag{2}$$

$\phi'(\hat{\lambda}) = 0$ as $\hat{\lambda}$ is a local minimum: so $\phi'(\hat{\lambda}) = (\tilde{\mathbf{x}} - \mathbf{x}^*) f'[\mathbf{x}(\hat{\lambda})] = 0$ and $[\mathbf{x}(\lambda) - \mathbf{x}(\hat{\lambda})]\mathbf{f}'(\mathbf{x}(\hat{\lambda})) = (\lambda - \hat{\lambda})(\tilde{\mathbf{x}} - \mathbf{x}^*)\mathbf{f}'(x(\hat{\lambda})) = 0$, for $\lambda \in (0, 1)$. Substituting $\mathbf{x}(\hat{\lambda})$ for $\mathbf{x}^*$ in (1) we see that

$$f(\mathbf{x}(\hat{\lambda})) > f(\mathbf{x}),\ \forall \mathbf{x} \in R^n_{++} \text{ sufficiently close to } \mathbf{x}(\hat{\lambda})$$
$$\text{where } (\mathbf{x} - \mathbf{x}(\hat{\lambda}))\,\mathbf{f}'(\mathbf{x}(\hat{\lambda})) = 0$$

In particular for λ sufficiently close to $\hat{\lambda}$, since $[\mathbf{x}(\lambda) - \mathbf{x}(\hat{\lambda})]\mathbf{f}'(\mathbf{x}(\hat{\lambda})) = 0$

$$f(\mathbf{x}(\hat{\lambda})) > f(\mathbf{x}(\lambda))$$

Hence

$$\phi(\hat{\lambda}) > \phi(\lambda) \text{ for all } \lambda \text{ sufficiently close to } \hat{\lambda} \tag{3}$$

But (3) contradicts (2). So the supposition is wrong and $\mathbf{x}^*$ is a strict global solution of

$$\max_{\mathbf{x} \in R^n_{++}} f(x) \quad \text{subject to } (\mathbf{x} - \mathbf{x}^*)\,\mathbf{f}'(\mathbf{x}^*) = 0$$

We now show that $\mathbf{x}^*$ is also a strict global solution to

$$\max_{\mathbf{x} \in R^n_{++}} f(\mathbf{x}) \quad \text{subject to } (\mathbf{x} - \mathbf{x}^*)\,\mathbf{f}'(\mathbf{x}^*) \leqslant 0$$

Suppose $\mathbf{x} \in R^n_{++}$, $\mathbf{x} \neq \mathbf{x}^*$ and $(\mathbf{x} - \mathbf{x}^*)\mathbf{f}'(\mathbf{x}^*) < 0$. Define ϵ by

$$(\mathbf{x} - \mathbf{x}^*)\,\mathbf{f}'(\mathbf{x}^*) + \epsilon f_1'(\mathbf{x}^*) = 0 \tag{4}$$

$\epsilon > 0$ since $f_1'(\mathbf{x}^*) > 0$ and $(\mathbf{x} - \mathbf{x}^*)\,\mathbf{f}'(\mathbf{x}^*) < 0$. Define $\hat{\mathbf{x}} \in R^n_{++}$ by $\hat{x}_1 = x_1 + \epsilon$, $\hat{x}_i = x_i$, $i = 2, \ldots, n$. Since $f_1' > 0$ everywhere, $f(\hat{\mathbf{x}}) > f(\mathbf{x})$. Also from (4), $(\hat{\mathbf{x}} - \mathbf{x}^*)\mathbf{f}'(\mathbf{x}^*) = 0$. Since $\mathbf{x}^*$ is a strict global solution to (1) it follows that $f(\mathbf{x}^*) \geqslant f(\hat{\mathbf{x}})$ ($\hat{\mathbf{x}}$ could equal $\mathbf{x}^*$) and so $f(\mathbf{x}^*) > f(x)$. Hence

$$f(\mathbf{x}^*) > f(\mathbf{x}) \text{ for any } \mathbf{x} \in R^n_{++} \text{ such that } \mathbf{x} \neq \mathbf{x}^*$$
$$\text{and } (\mathbf{x} - \mathbf{x}^*)\,\mathbf{f}'(\mathbf{x}^*) < 0$$

Moreover since $\mathbf{x}^*$ is a strict global solution to (1),

$$f(\mathbf{x}^*) > f(\mathbf{x}) \text{ for any } \mathbf{x} \in R^n_{++} \text{ such that } \mathbf{x} \neq \mathbf{x}^*$$
$$\text{and } (\mathbf{x} - \mathbf{x}^*)\,\mathbf{f}'(\mathbf{x}^*) \leqslant 0$$

That is

$$\mathbf{x}, \mathbf{x}^* \in R^n_{++},\ \mathbf{x} \neq \mathbf{x}^* \text{ and } f(\mathbf{x}) \geqslant f(\mathbf{x}^*)$$
$$\Rightarrow (\mathbf{x} - \mathbf{x}^*)\,\mathbf{f}'(\mathbf{x}^*) > 0$$

From theorem 14.2, f is strictly quasi-concave. *Q.E.D.*

Exercise 14

1. (a) By evaluating the bordered Hessian show that $f:R^2_{++} \to R$ defined by $f(\mathbf{x}) = x_1 x_2$ is strictly quasi-concave.

   (b) Find the solution functions and optimal value functions for

   $$\max_{\mathbf{x} \in R^2_{++}} x_1 x_2 \quad \text{subject to } p_1 x_1 + p_2 x_2 \leqslant m$$
   $$\text{where } (\mathbf{p}, m) \in R^3_{++}$$

   (c) Show that the optimal value function in (b) is quasi-convex in $\mathbf{p}$ for fixed $m > 0$.

   (d) Replace $x_1 x_2$ in (b) by $f(x_1, x_2)$ where f is strictly quasi-concave. Find consequences of the envelope theorem applied to this problem.

2. Consider a C^2 function $f:R^2_{++} \to R$ for which $f_i'(\mathbf{x}) > 0$, $\forall \mathbf{x} \in R^2_{++}$, $i = 1, 2$. The absolute value of the slope of the contour through $\mathbf{x}^* \in R^2_{++}$ of this function is

   $$+\frac{f_2'(x_1^*, x_2^*)}{f_1'(x_1^*, x_2^*)}$$

   Or, writing $x_1 = h(x_2)$ as the equation of the contour for $\mathbf{x}$ near $\mathbf{x}^*$, the absolute value of the slope of the contour through $\mathbf{x}$ is

   $$+\frac{f_2'[h(x_2), x_2]}{f_1'[h(x_2), x_2]}$$

   By differentiating with respect to x_2 show that the rate of change of this slope with respect to x_2 is negative at x_2^* if and only if the bordered Hessian of f at $\mathbf{x}^*$ is positive.

15 Quasi-concavity in the theories of the consumer and firm

15.1 Introduction

The developments of the theories of the consumer and firm in this book have so far rested on the assumptions of concave utility and production functions. It is generally desirable in mathematical economics, indeed in mathematics as a whole, that models or theories should rest upon as weak a set of assumptions as possible. In the current context this principle implies the desirability of relaxing the earlier concavity assumption on utility and production functions to quasi-concavity. Of course there is no guarantee that this relaxation will be possible, and this chapter is devoted to a discussion of the theories of the consumer and firm under the weaker quasi-concavity assumption. With respect to the consumer we will find that there are additional reasons for the substitution of quasi-concavity for concavity, over and above the desire for minimal assumptions. Moreover, the desired substitution will turn out to be possible leaving intact more or less all of the previous consumer theory results. However, with respect to the firm, substitution of quasi-concave instead of concave production functions leads to new difficulties and the behaviour of the quasi-concave firm is considerably different from that of the concave firm.

15.2 Quasi-concavity in the theory of the consumer

A basic assumption of the consumer model was that the consumer has preferences between vectors of goods in the consumption set which can be represented by a utility function. That is, if X is the consumer's consumption set, then there exists a function $U:X \to R$ such that for $\mathbf{x}^1, \mathbf{x}^2 \in X$:

(a) $U(\mathbf{x}^1) > U(\mathbf{x}^2)$ if and only if $\mathbf{x}^1$ is strictly preferred by the consumer to $\mathbf{x}^2$.

(b) $U(\mathbf{x}^1) = U(\mathbf{x}^2)$ if and only if the consumer is indifferent between $\mathbf{x}^1$ and $\mathbf{x}^2$.

Suppose now that there is another function, $W: X \to R$ with the following properties for $\mathbf{x}^1, \mathbf{x}^2 \in X$:

(i) $W(\mathbf{x}^1) > W(\mathbf{x}^2)$ if and only if $U(\mathbf{x}^1) > U(\mathbf{x}^2)$

(ii) $W(\mathbf{x}^1) = W(\mathbf{x}^2)$ if and only if $U(\mathbf{x}^1) = U(\mathbf{x}^2)$.

This requires that W has the same contours, upper contours and hence lower contours as U; we say that W is a *contour-preserving transformation of U*. In particular if W is a monotone increasing transformation of U it will be contour-preserving. Clearly any contour-preserving transformation of U will also represent the consumer's preferences if U is such a representation. Consequently, if our basic assumption is to be that the consumer has preferences over X and no more than that, we should admit only that these preferences can be represented by a utility function *or* any contour-preserving transformation of it. The assumption of concavity does not satisfy this requirement since, for instance, monotone increasing transformations of concave functions need not be concave. However, contour-preserving transformations of quasi-concave functions are quasi-concave and the replacement of concavity with quasi-concavity in consumer theory is doubly desirable. To execute this replacement refer back to chapter 12 and replace the assumption that U is strictly concave (i.e. (A12.3) with the following

U is strictly quasi-concave on R^n_{++}

With this change, but leaving all other assumptions intact, analysis of the expenditure minimization and utility maximization problems proceeds as in chapter 12 with the obvious change that these parameterized concave programming problems now become parameterized quasi-concave programming problems. However, the K–T characterizations of solutions and all subsequent analysis of comparative statics etc. remain the same as before. In particular the expenditure minimization problem gives rise to Hicksian demand functions and an expenditure function with the following properties:

(15.1) For fixed $\bar{u} \in A$, $e: R^n_{++} \times A \to R$ is a concave, linearly homogeneous function of $\mathbf{p}$.

(15.2) For fixed $\bar{u} \in A$, and for $i = 1, \ldots, n$, $x_i^H : R^n_{++} \times A \to R$ is a homogeneous of degree zero function of $\mathbf{p}$.

(15.3) For $i = 1, \ldots, n$, and for all $(\mathbf{p}, \bar{u}) \in R^n_{++} \times A$, $\partial e/\partial p_i(\mathbf{p}, \bar{u}) = x_i^H(\mathbf{p}, \bar{u})$ and the Slutsky matrix $\mathbf{S}(\mathbf{p}, \bar{u})$ is symmetric and negative semidefinite.

The utility maximization problem produces Marshallian demand functions and an indirect utility function with all the earlier properties. However, to complete this picture we can now report:

Theorem 15.1 For fixed $m \in R_{++}$, the indirect utility function $\psi : R^{n+1}_{++} \to R$ is quasi-convex in $\mathbf{p}$.

Proof Fix $m \in R_{++}$ and delete it as an argument of ψ for convenience. We have to show

$$\mathbf{p}^1, \mathbf{p}^2 \in R^n_{++} \text{ and } \psi(\mathbf{p}^1) \leqslant \psi(\mathbf{p}^2) \Rightarrow \psi[\lambda \mathbf{p}^1 + (1-\lambda)\mathbf{p}^2] \leqslant \psi(\mathbf{p}^2), \quad \forall \lambda \in [0, 1]$$

which is the 'algebraic' definition of quasi-convexity. Choose any $\mathbf{p}^1, \mathbf{p}^2 \in R^n_{++}$ and suppose $\mathbf{x}^1$ solves (UM) at $(\mathbf{p}^1, m)$, $\mathbf{x}^2$ solves (UM) at $(\mathbf{p}^2, m)$ and $\mathbf{x}$ solves (UM) at $(\lambda \mathbf{p}^1 + (1-\lambda)\mathbf{p}^2, m)$ where $\lambda \in [0, 1]$. Then:

(i) $\psi(\mathbf{p}^1) = U(\mathbf{x}^1)$, $\psi(\mathbf{p}^2) = U(\mathbf{x}^2)$, $\psi[\lambda \mathbf{p}^1 + (1-\lambda)\mathbf{p}^2] = U(\mathbf{x})$, and

(ii) $\sum_i p_i^1 x_i^1 \leqslant m$, $\sum_i p_i^2 x_i^2 \leqslant m$, $\sum_i [\lambda p_i^1 + (1-\lambda) p_i^2]\, x_i \leqslant m$

It follows that either (a) $\Sigma p_i^1 x_i \leqslant m$ or (b) $\Sigma p_i^2 x_i \leqslant m$: if not, we have $\Sigma p_i^1 x_i > m$ and $\Sigma p_i^2 x_i > m$ so that $\Sigma [\lambda p_i^1 + (1-\lambda) p_i^2]\, x_i > m$, contradicting (ii). So either (a) $\mathbf{x}$ is feasible for (UM) at $(\mathbf{p}^1, m)$ or (b) $\mathbf{x}$ is feasible for (UM) at $(\mathbf{p}^2, m)$. In case (a) we have $U(\mathbf{x}) \leqslant U(\mathbf{x}^1)$ since $\mathbf{x}^1$ solves (UM) at $(\mathbf{p}^1, m)$. Hence using (i), $\psi[\lambda \mathbf{p}^1 + (1-\lambda)\mathbf{p}^2] \leqslant \psi(\mathbf{p}^1)$ and so

$$\psi(\mathbf{p}^1) \leqslant \psi(\mathbf{p}^2) \Rightarrow \psi[\lambda \mathbf{p}^1 + (1-\lambda)\mathbf{p}^2] \leqslant \psi(\mathbf{p}^2)$$

In case (b), $U(\mathbf{x}) \leqslant U(\mathbf{x}^2)$ and $\psi[\lambda \mathbf{p}^1 + (1-\lambda) p^2] \leqslant \psi(\mathbf{p}^2)$. In particular

$$\psi(\mathbf{p}^1) \leqslant \psi(\mathbf{p}^2) \Rightarrow \psi[\lambda \mathbf{p}^1 + (1-\lambda)\mathbf{p}^2] \leqslant \psi(\mathbf{p}^2)$$

Hence the desired implication follows in all cases and ψ is quasi-convex. *Q.E.D.*

The 'duality' links of chapter 12 between expenditure minimization and utility maximization remain intact, the Slutsky equation follows and the earlier comparative static analysis of (UM) continues to apply. In particular we have for (UM) under quasi-concavity:

(15.4) For any $(\mathbf{p}, m) \in R^{n+1}_{++}$, $\psi: R^{n+1}_{++} \to R$ is homogeneous of degree zero in $(\mathbf{p}, m)$; and for fixed $m \in R_{++}$, ψ is a quasi-convex function of $\mathbf{p}$.

(15.5) For any $(\mathbf{p}, m) \in R^{n+1}_{++}$ and for $i = 1, \ldots, n$, $x_i^M: R^{n+1}_{++} \to R$ is homogeneous of degree zero in $(\mathbf{p}, m)$.

(15.6) For any $(\mathbf{p}, m) \in R^{n+1}_{++}$ and for $i = 1, \ldots, n$, $x_i^M(\mathbf{p}, m) = -\partial\psi/\partial p_i / \partial\psi/\partial m$ and from the Slutsky equation the following matrix is symmetric and negative semidefinite, for all $(\mathbf{p}, m) \in R^{n+1}_{++}$:

$$\begin{bmatrix} \dfrac{\partial x_1^M}{\partial p_1} + x_1^M \dfrac{\partial x_1^M}{\partial m} & \cdots & \dfrac{\partial x_1^M}{\partial p_n} + x_n^M \dfrac{\partial x_1^M}{\partial m} \\ \cdots & \cdots & \cdots \\ \dfrac{\partial x_n^M}{\partial p_1} + x_1^M \dfrac{\partial x_n^M}{\partial m} & \cdots & \dfrac{\partial x_n^M}{\partial p_n} + x_n^M \dfrac{\partial x_n^M}{\partial m} \end{bmatrix}$$

the matrix being evaluated at $(\mathbf{p}, m)$.

15.3 Quasi-concavity in the theory of the firm

In the study of profit maximization and cost minimization in chapters 10 and 11, concavity of the production function was assumed. In the interests of parsimony of assumptions, relaxation of concavity to quasi-concavity is desirable. As we have just seen, a similar relaxation is possible for the consumer model and leaves the earlier concave consumer theory results more or less intact. However, the profit maximization model of the firm runs into difficulties under the weaker assumption of a quasi-concave production function. Technically the problem is as follows. The profit maximization problem is:

$$\text{(FP)} \qquad \max_{(x_0, \mathbf{x}) \in R^{n+1}_{+}} p_0 x_0 - \sum_{i=1}^{n} p_i x_i \text{ s.t. } f(\mathbf{x}) - x_0 \geqslant 0, \qquad (p_0, \mathbf{p}) \in R^{n+1}_{++}$$

The constraint function is, say, $g: R^{n+1}_{+} \to R$ with values $g(x_0, \mathbf{x}) = f(\mathbf{x}) - x_0$. Now if f is *concave* then g is the sum of concave functions

(x_0 is linear) and so is concave. However, if f is *quasi-concave* then from the composition discussion of chapter 13 it is *not* necessarily true that g is quasi-concave. For instance if $n = 1$ and $f(x_1) = x_1^2$, f is quasi-concave as it is monotone increasing: but $g(x_0, x_1) = x_1^2 - x_0$ is not quasi-concave as its bordered Hessian is

$$\begin{vmatrix} 0 & 0 & 1 \\ 0 & 2 & 2x_1 \\ 1 & 2x_1 & 0 \end{vmatrix} = -2 < 0$$

The lack of quasi-concavity in g means that we cannot apply our earlier procedures. Profit maximizing firms with merely quasi-concave production functions do indeed behave quite differently from profit maximizing concave firms. For instance in our example of $f(x_1) = x_1^2$ we have 'increasing returns' throughout and in fact (FP) cannot have a solution (see fig. 15.1). By increasing x_1 the firm can forever attain higher-valued contours of $p_0x_0 - p_1x_1$ and so no profit maximum exists. For some quasi-concave production functions, solutions to (FM) do exist but then a different problem emerges. For instance fig. 15.2 shows a production function with $n = 1$ again where in fact a solution to (FP) does exist, for all $(p_0, \mathbf{p}) \in R^{n+1}_{++}$. Here the production function exhibits increasing returns up to output level $\hat{x}_0$ (or input level $\hat{x}_1$) and decreasing returns thereafter. For prices giving the contour of $p_0x_0 - p_1x_1$ as shown in fig. 15.2 there are two solutions to (FP), namely $(0, 0)$ and $(\hat{x}_0, \hat{x}_1)$. Keeping p_0 fixed and raising p_1 produces steeper contours and $(0, 0)$ becomes the only solution while lowering p_1 produces flatter contours and a unique solution on the production function graphs to the right of $(\hat{\hat{x}}_0, \hat{\hat{x}}_1)$.

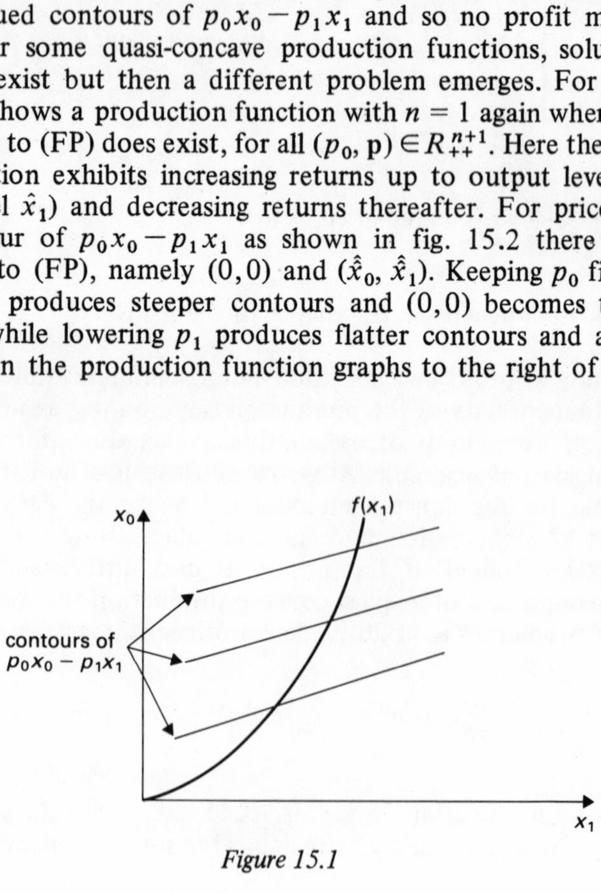

Figure 15.1

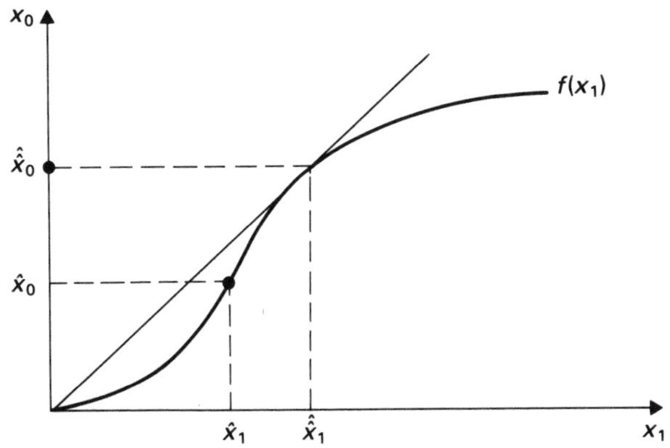

Figure 15.2

Multiple solutions, non-interior solutions and discontinuous solutions thus emerge.

It follows that we cannot analyse profit maximizing firms facing quasi-concave production functions in the manner of chapter 10 for the concave case. As we see shortly, however, various special cases can be analysed, although of course the firm behaviour differs from that of chapter 10.

On the other hand there is no difficulty in extending the analysis of cost minimization to the quasi-concave. The problem is:

$$\text{(CM)} \quad \min_{\mathbf{x}\in R_+^n} \sum_{i=1}^{n} p_i x_i \text{ s.t. } f(\mathbf{x}) \geqslant \bar{x}_0 \quad \text{where } (\mathbf{p}, \bar{x}_0) \in R_{++}^n \times A$$

Now $\bar{x}_0$ is a constant and the constraint function is $f(\mathbf{x}) - \bar{x}_0$ which is quasi-concave if f is quasi-concave. Following the (EM) story in the last section we can replace the concavity assumption of chapter 11 (A11.3), by

f is strictly quasi-concave on R_{++}^n

and we get the following results:

(15.7) For fixed $\bar{x}_0 \in A$, $C: R_{++}^n \times A \to R$ is a concave linearly homogeneous function of $\mathbf{p}$.

(15.8) For fixed $\bar{x}_0 \in A$ and for $i = 1, \ldots, n$, $x_i^c : R_{++}^n \times A \to R$ is a homogeneous of degree zero function of $\mathbf{p}$.

(15.9) For $i = 1, \ldots, n$ and for all $(\mathbf{p}, \bar{x}_0) \in R_{++}^n \times A$, $\partial C / \partial p_i (\mathbf{p}, \bar{x}_0) = x_i^c(\mathbf{p}, \bar{x}_0)$ and the firm's Slutsky matrix is symmetric and negative semidefinite.

So the comparative static results for (CM) with respect to price changes remain the same for quasi-concave firms as for the concave case. Consider, however, the relation between C and $\bar{x}_0$, for fixed **p**. Under the concave assumption this 'cost curve' was a convex, increasing function of $\bar{x}_0$. In the quasi-concave case the cost curve must still be increasing but need not be convex. For instance when $n = 1$ and as in chapter 11 we get that $C(p_1, \bar{x}_0) = p_1 f^{-1}(\bar{x}_0)$. Figure 15.3 shows a quasi-concave (but not concave) production function and its cost curve for fixed p_1. The production function exhibits increasing returns up to output $\hat{x}_0$ and decreasing returns thereafter. The cost curve has the inverse properties to this. Phrasing this argument more precisely $f''(x_1)>0$ for $x_1 \in (0, \hat{x}_1)$ and $f''(x_1)<0$ for $x_1 \in (\hat{x}_1, +\infty)$, a point of inflexion occurring at $x_1 = \hat{x}_1$. Using the formulae for derivatives of inverse functions (see section 11.6) we get:

$$\frac{\partial C}{\partial \bar{x}_0} = \frac{p_1}{f'[f^{-1}(\bar{x}_0)]} \quad \text{and} \quad \frac{\partial^2 C}{\partial \bar{x}_0^2} = -p_1 \frac{f''[f^{-1}(\bar{x}_0)]}{\{f'[f^{-1}(\bar{x}_0)]\}^3}$$

Hence the cost curve has *negative* second derivative between 0 and $\hat{x}_0$ $(= f(\hat{x}_1))$ and positive second derivative thereafter.

The particular example chosen in fig. 15.3 is an important one since it corresponds to a common 'microeconomics 1' set of assumptions about the production function–increasing returns up to a point and decreasing returns thereafter. The cost curve of fig. 15.3 is therefore the corresponding total cost curve, and it is useful to investigate the form of the marginal and average cost curves. Marginal cost is $MC(\bar{x}_0) = \partial C/\partial \bar{x}_0$–remember **p** is being held constant and the slope of the marginal cost curve $\partial^2 C/\partial \bar{x}_0^2$ is negative up to $\hat{x}_0$ and positive thereafter. The marginal cost curve is 'U-shaped' under these assumptions–see fig. 15.4. On the other hand average cost is $AC(\bar{x}_0) =$

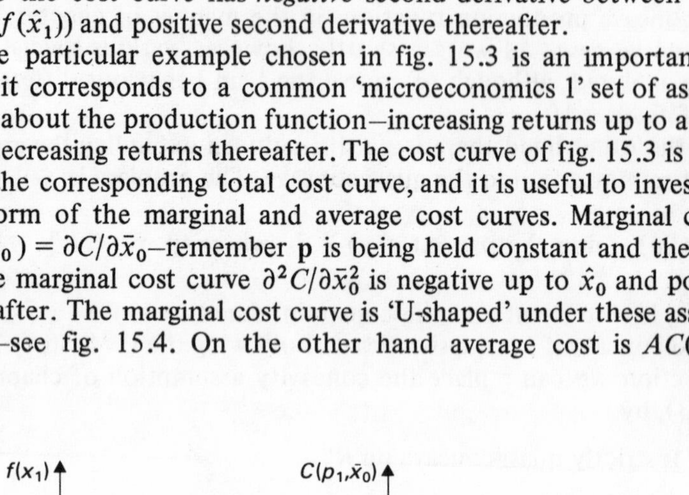

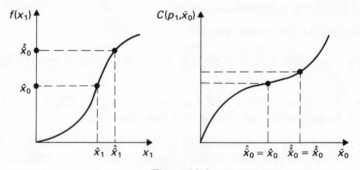

Figure 15.3

$[C(\mathbf{p}, x_0)]/\bar{x}_0$–remember again $\mathbf{p}$ is fixed and the slope of the average cost curve is

$$\frac{\partial AC}{\partial \bar{x}_0} = \frac{\dfrac{\partial C}{\partial \bar{x}_0} \cdot \bar{x}_0 - C(\mathbf{p}, x_0)}{\bar{x}_0^2} = \frac{1}{\bar{x}_0}\left[\frac{\partial C}{\partial \bar{x}_0} - \frac{C(\mathbf{p}, \bar{x}_0)}{x_0}\right]$$

$$= \frac{1}{\bar{x}_0}[MC(\bar{x}_0) - AC(\bar{x}_0)]$$

$$= \frac{1}{\bar{x}_0}\left[\frac{p_1}{f'} - \frac{p_1 f^{-1}(\bar{x}_0)}{\bar{x}_0}\right]$$

where f' is evaluated at $[f^{-1}(\bar{x}_0)]$.

Inspecting fig. 15.3, you see that $MC(\hat{\hat{\bar{x}}}_0) = AC(\hat{\hat{\bar{x}}}_0)$ and that average cost is decreasing up to $\hat{\hat{\bar{x}}}_0$ and increasing thereafter. Hence the average cost curve is also 'U-shaped' attaining a minimum at $\hat{\hat{\bar{x}}}_0$ where marginal equals average cost. Figure 15.4 brings together these observations about average and marginal cost curves in a probably familiar diagram. Figure 15.4 has emerged from the assumption that the firm produces one output from one input according to a production function which is quasi-concave and exhibits increasing returns up to a certain output level ($\hat{\bar{x}}_0$ in fig. 15.4) and decreasing returns thereafter. Similar configurations to fig. 15.4 can emerge for firms using n inputs. To investigate this it is useful first to digress into a brief study of *homothetic functions*.

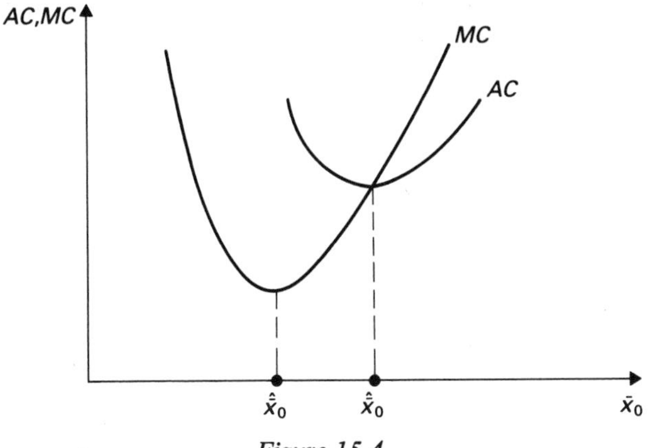

Figure 15.4

15.4 Homothetic functions

In chapter 9 we studied homogeneous functions in some detail; $f:R^n_{++} \to R$ is homogeneous of degree r if $f(t\mathbf{x}) = t^r f(\mathbf{x})$, $\forall t > 0$, $\forall \mathbf{x} \in R^n_{++}$. Homothetic functions are a generalization of the class of homogeneous functions:

Definition 15.1 $f:R^n_{++} \to R$ is *homothetic* if f is a monotone increasing transformation of some homogeneous function; or, f is homothetic if $f(x) = h[g(\mathbf{x})]$ where h is monotone increasing and g is homogeneous.

For instance consider $f:R^2_{++} \to R$ where $f(\mathbf{x}) = \ln(x_1^2 + x_2^2)$. $f(t\mathbf{x}) = \ln(t^2x_1^2 + t^2x_2^2) = 2\ln t + \ln(x_1^2 + x_2^2) \neq t^r f(\mathbf{x})$ for any r and so f is *not* homogeneous. However, with $g(\mathbf{x}) = x_1^2 + x_2^2$ and $h(g) = \ln(g)$, $f(\mathbf{x}) = h[g(\mathbf{x})]$, g is homogeneous (of degree 2), h is monotone increasing and so f is homothetic as a monotone increasing transformation of a homogeneous function. Of course any homogeneous function is homothetic–put $h(g) = g$, $g(\mathbf{x}) = f(\mathbf{x})$–but not vice-versa. Homothetic functions are a generalization of the class of homogeneous functions.

From the discussion of monotone increasing transformations in chapter 13 we know that only the numbering or labelling, and not the shape, of contours is affected by a monotone increasing transformation. Now when $n = 2$ the contours of a homogeneous function are parallel displacements of each other. It follows therefore that homothetic functions will also have this property since the contour map of a homothetic function is merely a re-labelling of the contour map of some homogeneous function. Alternatively if $f(\mathbf{x}) = h[g(\mathbf{x})]$ is homothetic (h monotone increasing, g homogeneous of degree r say) then the absolute value of the slope of the contour of f through $t\mathbf{x}^*$, at $t\mathbf{x}^*$, is

$$\frac{f_2'(t\mathbf{x}^*)}{f_1'(t\mathbf{x}^*)} = -\frac{h'[g(t\mathbf{x}^*)]\,g_2'(t\mathbf{x}^*)}{h'[g(t\mathbf{x}^*)]\,g_1'(t\mathbf{x}^*)} = -\frac{g_2'(t\mathbf{x}^*)}{g_1'(t\mathbf{x}^*)}$$

$$= -\frac{t^{r-1}g_2'(\mathbf{x}^*)}{t^{r-1}g_1'(\mathbf{x}^*)} \quad \text{(since } g_i' \text{ is homogeneous of degree } r-1\text{)}$$

$$= -\frac{g_2'(\mathbf{x}^*)}{g_1'(\mathbf{x}^*)} = -\frac{h'[g(\mathbf{x}^*)]\,g_2'(\mathbf{x}^*)}{h'[g(\mathbf{x}^*)]\,g_1'(\mathbf{x}^*)} = -\frac{f_2'(\mathbf{x}^*)}{f_1'(\mathbf{x}^*)}$$

Hence the slope at $t\mathbf{x}^*$ is the same as at $\mathbf{x}^*$ and homothetic functions have the same parallel contour property as homogeneous functions.

15.5 Homothetic production functions and the cost minimizing firm

In this section we are interested in the relation between costs and output (input prices fixed) when there are n inputs and when the production function is homothetic, as well as quasi-concave, etc.

It is helpful to consider first the case where the production function is homogeneous of degree r. The firm's conditional input demands at $(\mathbf{p}, \bar{x}_0)$ are characterized by two conditions:

(a) $\dfrac{f_i'(\mathbf{x})}{f_j'(\mathbf{x})} = \dfrac{p_i}{p_j}, \quad \forall i, j = 1, \ldots, n$

(b) $f(\mathbf{x}) = \bar{x}_0$.

Now suppose prices are fixed at $\mathbf{p}$ but $\bar{x}_0$ changes to $t\bar{x}_0$ where $t > 0$. Consider the input vector $t^{1/r}\mathbf{x}$. This input vector solves the cost minimization problem at $(\mathbf{p}, t\bar{x}_0)$ since, using the homogeneity of f:

(c) $\dfrac{f_i'(t^{1/r}\mathbf{x})}{f_j'(t^{1/r}\mathbf{x})} = \dfrac{f_i'(\mathbf{x})}{f_j'(\mathbf{x})} = \dfrac{p_i}{p_j}, \quad \forall i, j = 1, \ldots, n$ from (a)

(d) $f(t^{1/r}\mathbf{x}) = tf(x) = t\bar{x}_0$ from (b)

Hence

$$x_i^c(\mathbf{p}, t\bar{x}_0) = t^{1/r} x_i^c(\mathbf{p}, \bar{x}_0), \ \forall t > 0, \ \forall i$$

Consequently

$$C(\mathbf{p}, t\bar{x}_0) = \sum_{i=1}^{n} p_i x_i^c(\mathbf{p}, t\bar{x}_0) = t^{1/r} \Sigma p_i x_i^c(\mathbf{p}, \bar{x}_0) = t^{1/r} C(\mathbf{p}, \bar{x}_0)$$

When the production function is homogeneous of degree r, conditional input demand functions and the cost function are homogeneous of degree $1/r$ in $\bar{x}_0$, for fixed $\mathbf{p}$. It follows that we can write the cost function (in particular) in the following way

$$C(\mathbf{p}, \bar{x}_0) = \bar{x}_0^{1/r} h(\mathbf{p})$$

or, since $C(\mathbf{p}, 1) = h(\mathbf{p})$, we can write

(15.10) $\quad C(\mathbf{p}, \bar{x}_0) = C(\mathbf{p}, 1)\, \bar{x}_0^{1/r}$

If $r \geqslant 1$ then cost is a concave function of $\bar{x}_0$ for fixed **p** whilst for $r \leqslant 1$, cost is a convex function of $\bar{x}_0$ for fixed **p**. In particular we cannot generate the 'concave then convex' total cost curve of fig. 15.3 with a homogeneous production function. The reason for this is that a homogeneous of degree r production function either has increasing returns *everywhere* (when $r > 1$), constant returns everywhere ($r = 1$) or decreasing returns everywhere ($r < 1$), thus ruling out the production function of fig. 15.3.

Let us now consider a more general homothetic case. We assume that the production function can be written as $f(\mathbf{x}) = h[g(\mathbf{x})]$ where

(i) g is linearly homogeneous and quasi-concave (= concave);

(ii) h is monotone increasing, C^2 and $h''(g) > 0$ for $g \in (0, \hat{g})$, $h''(\hat{g}) = 0, h''(g) < 0$ for $g > \hat{g}$;

(iii) $g(0) = 0$ and $h(0) = 0$.

Figure 15.5 illustrates the graph of h under these assumptions. With $n = 1$ and $g(x) = x_1$, we generate the production function of fig. 15.3 as a special case. Generally under (i)–(iii) the production function is homothetic, quasi-concave, etc. and the conditions (a) and (b) continue to characterize the conditional input demands at $\mathbf{p}, \bar{x}_0$. Using (i)–(iii) these conditions become:

$$\frac{g_i'(\mathbf{x})}{g_j'(\mathbf{x})} = \frac{p_i}{p_j}, \quad \forall i, j = 1, \ldots, n$$

$$g(\mathbf{x}) = h^{-1}(\bar{x}_0)$$

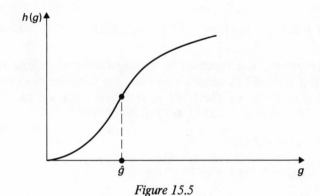

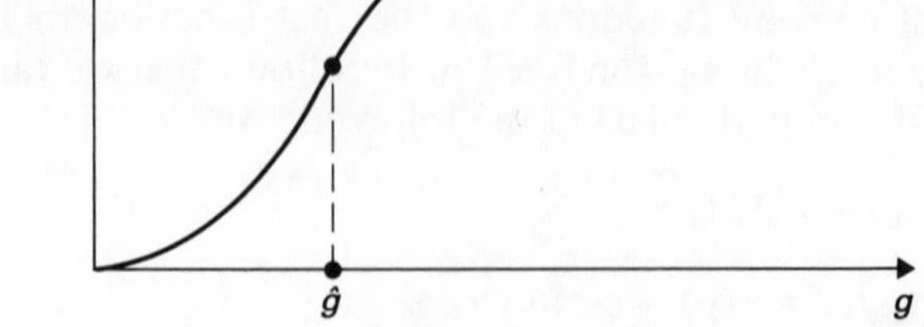

Figure 15.5

Keeping $\mathbf{p}$ fixed change $\bar{x}_0$ to $t\bar{x}_0$, $t > 0$. Consider $\alpha\mathbf{x}$ where $\alpha = h^{-1}(t\bar{x}_0)/h^{-1}(\bar{x}_0)$. Then

$$\frac{g_i'(\alpha\mathbf{x})}{g_j'(\alpha\mathbf{x})} = \frac{p_i}{p_j}, \quad \forall i, j = 1, \ldots, n$$

and $g(\alpha\mathbf{x}) = h^{-1}(t\bar{x}_0)$ since $g(\alpha\mathbf{x}) = \alpha g(\mathbf{x}) = \alpha h^{-1}(\bar{x}_0) = h^{-1}(t\bar{x}_0)$ from the definition of α. Hence

$$\forall i, x_i^c(\mathbf{p}, t\bar{x}_0) = \frac{h^{-1}(t\bar{x}_0)}{h^{-1}(\bar{x}_0)} x_i^c(\mathbf{p}, \bar{x}_0)$$

and

$$C(\mathbf{p}, t\bar{x}_0) = \frac{h^{-1}(t\bar{x}_0)}{h^{-1}(\bar{x}_0)} C(\mathbf{p}, \bar{x}_0)$$

With $\bar{x}_0 = 1$, we get

$$C(\mathbf{p}, t) = \frac{h^{-1}(t)}{h^{-1}(1)} C(\mathbf{p}, 1)$$

Hence the homothetic generalization of (15.10) is

$$C(\mathbf{p}, \bar{x}_0) = \left[\frac{C(\mathbf{p}, 1)}{h^{-1}(1)}\right] h^{-1}(\bar{x}_0)$$

Now the square bracket here is some constant, k say, since $\mathbf{p}$ is fixed; so that the relation between cost and output, deleting the fixed $\mathbf{p}$, is

$$C(\bar{x}_0) = kh^{-1}(\bar{x}_0)$$

It follows from the discussion in section 15.3 that the graph of this relation has the same qualitative features as the total cost curve of fig. 15.3; in particular $C(0) = 0$, $C''(\bar{x}_0) < 0$ for $\bar{x}_0 \in (0, \hat{g})$, $C''(\hat{g}) = 0$, $C''(\bar{x}_0) > 0$, $\bar{x}_0 > \hat{g}$. Hence the U-shaped average and marginal cost curve configuration of fig. 15.4 emerges also for n-input firms facing homothetic production functions satisfying (i)–(iii).

Exercise 15

1. In the Cobb–Douglas and Stone–Geary utility exercise 12, questions 1 and 7, we assumed that $\Sigma\alpha_i < 1$ to ensure strict concavity. Now we only need strict quasi-concavity and so this restriction is unnecessary. However, it is common to assume $\Sigma\alpha_i = 1$ so as to simplify algebra.

(a) Write down the formulae for the Stone–Geary (linear expenditure system) indirect utility, expenditure, Marshallian demand and Hicksian demand functions when $\Sigma\alpha_i = 1$.

(b) By putting $\gamma = 0$ in (a), write down the corresponding formulae for the Cobb–Douglas case when $\Sigma\alpha_i = 1$.

(c) Show that the indirect utility function found in (a) is quasi-convex in $\mathbf{p}$ for fixed m.

2. The Gorman polar form of the expenditure function is

$$e(p, \bar{u}) = a(\mathbf{p}) + \bar{u}b(\mathbf{p})$$

where $a(\mathbf{p})$, $b(\mathbf{p})$ are concave, linearly homogeneous functions.

(a) Show that the expenditure function of question 1(a) above is a special case of this Gorman polar form.

(b) For the Gorman polar form:

(i) find formulae for the Hicksian demands, the indirect utility function and the Marshallian demands;

(ii) show that expenditure $p_k x_k^M(\mathbf{p}, m)$ is a linear function of m (but not necessarily of $\mathbf{p}$).

3. The production function of a two-input firm is

$$f(\mathbf{x}) = h[g(\mathbf{x})]$$

where $g(\mathbf{x}) = x_1^{1/2}x_2^{1/2}$ and $h^{-1}(\bar{x}_0) = \bar{x}_0^3 - \bar{x}_0^2 + \bar{x}_0$

(a) Show that this production function is quasi-concave and homothetic.

(b) Show that the firm's cost function is:

$$C(\mathbf{p}, \bar{x}_0) = 2p_1^{1/2}p_2^{1/2}(\bar{x}_0^3 - \bar{x}_0^2 + \bar{x}_0)$$

(c) Assuming input prices are fixed at $p_1 = p_2 = 1$ derive and sketch the firm's total cost curve, average cost curve and marginal cost curve.

16 Closed and open sets and supporting hyperplanes

16.1 Introduction

In various earlier chapters we have attempted to provide insights into the elementary microeconomic theory of the firm and the consumer, based on the developments of the theory of concave and quasi-concave functions and (parameterized) concave and quasi-concave programming. The exposition of the microeconomics has left a number of gaps. To fill these gaps we now turn back to mathematics in this chapter to provide a further base for the later extensions of the economics discussion. This chapter is devoted to a more precise account of the notion of an open set and the related concept of a closed set, discussed in an informal manner earlier; we are led into some treatment of supporting hyperplane theorems, and these are related to the separating hyperplane theorem of chapter 1. Chapter 17 then discusses existence and differentiability of solutions to parameterized programming problems, drawing in particular on the notion of a closed set, while chapter 18 makes use of supporting hyperplanes to introduce the reader to so-called duality features of microeconomic models.

16.2 Closed and open sets in R

Suppose $S \subset R$ and suppose $x \in S$. Suppose that all points 'immediately to the right' of x and all points 'immediately to the left' of x are also in S. Then x is said to be an *interior point* of S (relative to R). This is a bit imprecise. More exactly:

Definition 16.1 $x \in S \subset R$ is an *interior point* of S (relative to R) if, and only if, for some $\epsilon > 0$, $(x - \epsilon, x + \epsilon) \subset S$.

Figure 16.1 illustrates the set $(x - \epsilon, x + \epsilon)$. It is merely the set of points in R whose distance from x is less than ϵ and is known as an

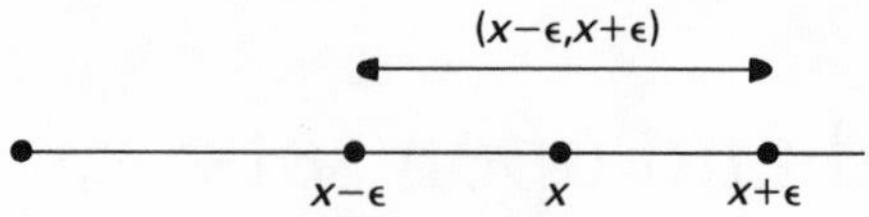

Figure 16.1

ϵ-neighbourhood of x (relative to R); remember $\epsilon > 0$. So for x to be an interior point of S (omitting the 'relative to R' qualification for brevity) requires that we be able to put *some* (may be very small) ϵ-neighbourhood around $x \in S$ so that this whole neighbourhood is contained in S. To illustrate, consider $S_1 = [0, 1]$ as in chapter 1. Suppose $x \in S_1$. Is x an interior point? Suppose first that in fact $x \in (0, 1)$. Fairly obviously such an x is an interior point of S_1. To be precise we need to find an $\epsilon > 0$ to satisfy definition 16.1 for any such x. Here is one way. Take first the case where $x \geqslant \frac{1}{2}$ (and $x < 1$ of course) and let $\epsilon = (1-x)/2$. Then $\epsilon > 0$ since $x < 1$ and $x - \epsilon = x - \frac{1}{2} + \frac{1}{2}x \geqslant 0$ since $x \geqslant \frac{1}{2}$. Moreover $x + \epsilon = \frac{1}{2}x + \frac{1}{2} \leqslant 1$ since $x < 1$. So $(x-\epsilon, x+\epsilon) \subset [0, 1]$, as required. For the case $x \leqslant \frac{1}{2}$ (and $x > 0$), $\epsilon = x/2$ allows a similar demonstration. Hence any point in $(0, 1)$ is indeed an interior point of $[0, 1]$. However, the 'end points' 0 and 1 are not interior points (as you would expect!) since for every $\epsilon > 0$, $0 - \epsilon < 0$ and $1 + \epsilon > 1$ precluding the construction of the neighbourhood required in definition 16.1. So the set of interior points of S_1 is $(0, 1)$: we write $\text{int}\, S_1 = (0, 1)$ to denote this. The 'end points' 0 and 1 are not interior points.

Definition 16.2 x (not *necessarily* in S) is a boundary point of $S \subset R$ (relative to R) if and only if every ϵ-neighbourhood of x (relative to R) contains some points in S *and* some points not in S.

Interior points cannot be boundary points since they possess an ϵ-neighbourhood containing *only* points of the set. Conversely boundary points cannot be interior points. For the S_1 example, any $x \in (0, 1)$ is not a boundary point, therefore. However, 0 is a boundary point, as you would expect. For any ϵ-neighbourhood of 0 contains points in S_1 (just to the right of 0) and points not in S_1 (just to the left of 0). Similarly 1 is a boundary point of S_1. Finally there are no boundary points outside $[0, 1]$ since if $x < 0$ then with $\epsilon = \frac{1}{2}x$, $(x-\epsilon, x+\epsilon)$ is an ϵ-neighbourhood of x containing *no* points in S_1; similarly $x > 1$ cannot be a boundary point. In general ∂S denotes the set of boundary points S; we have shown that $\partial S_1 = \{0, 1\}$.

Before we announce the crucial distinction of this section consider in its own right the set $(0, 1)$ (i.e. $\text{int}\, S_1$). Running through the previous arguments applied directly to $(0, 1)$ the reader will find, with minor amendments, that (i) all points of $(0, 1)$ are interior points of $(0, 1)$, and (ii) 0 and 1 are also the boundary points of $(0, 1)$ even though they do not belong to the set itself.

Two distinctions between $[0, 1]$ and $(0, 1)$ emerge. The boundary points of $[0, 1]$ are a subset of $[0, 1]$, but this is not true of $(0, 1)$; second, all points of $(0, 1)$ are interior points but this is not true of $[0, 1]$.

Definition 16.3 A set $S \subset R$ is *closed* (relative to R) if and only if the set of boundary points of S (relative to R) is a subset of S.

Definition 16.4 A set $S \subset R$ is *open* (relative to R) if and only if all points in S are interior points of S (relative to R).

Hence $[0, 1]$ is closed (and not open) while $(0, 1)$ is open (and not closed). Clearly the numbers 0 and 1 are arbitrary in the previous discussion and in fact any interval of the form $[a, b]$ is closed while the corresponding interval (a, b) is open. The open/closed properties of other intervals of R are listed below. The reader can check the arguments supporting the list.

Set, S	*Interior, int S*	*Boundary, ∂S*	*S closed*	*S open*
$[a, b)$	(a, b)	$\{a, b\}$	No	No
$(a, b]$	(a, b)	$\{a, b\}$	No	No
$[a, +\infty)$	$(a, +\infty)$	$\{a\}$	Yes	No
$(-\infty, b]$	$(-\infty, b)$	$\{b\}$	Yes	No
$(a, +\infty)$	$(a, +\infty)$	$\{a\}$	No	Yes
$(-\infty, b)$	$(-\infty, b)$	$\{b\}$	No	Yes
$(-\infty, +\infty)$	$(-\infty, +\infty)$	$\emptyset$	Yes	Yes

Notice that the first two sets listed are neither closed nor open since they contain some but not all of their boundary points. More mysterious is the last entry for R itself. Here all points are interior (so R is open) but R has no boundary points; so $\emptyset$ is its set of boundary points and since $\emptyset \subset R$, R is closed as well!

More easily and referring back to chapter 1, the reader can also check that S_2, S_6 and S_7 are closed, S_3, S_4 and S_8 are open while S_5 is neither open nor closed.

16.3 Closed and open sets in R^n

The ideas of the last section generalize easily to higher dimensions once we define *the distance between two points* $\mathbf{x}^1$ *and* $\mathbf{x}^2$ *in* R^n,

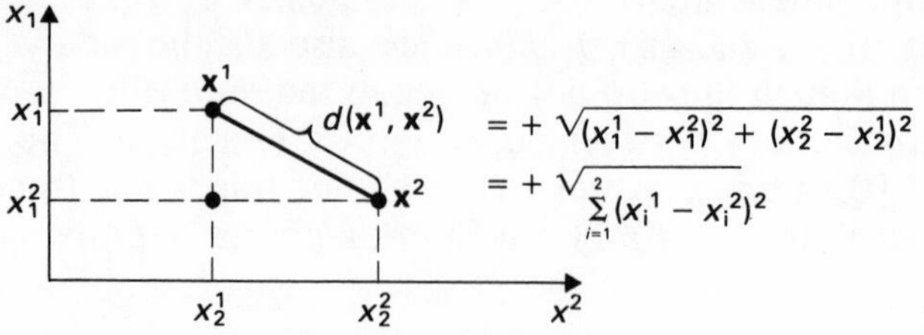

Figure 16.2

denoted $d(\mathbf{x}^1, \mathbf{x}^2)$. This is:

$$d(\mathbf{x}^1, \mathbf{x}^2) = + \sqrt{\sum_{i=1}^{n} (x_i^1 - x_i^2)^2}$$

When $n = 2$ this reduces to the well-known Pythagoras formula for the length of the hypotenuse of a right-angled triangle; see fig. 16.2.

Now when $\epsilon > 0$, an ϵ-neighbourhood of $\mathbf{x} \in R^n$ (relative to R^n) written $N_\epsilon(\mathbf{x})$, is defined as the set of points in R^n whose distance from $\mathbf{x}$ is less than ϵ; i.e. if $\epsilon > 0$

$$N_\epsilon(\mathbf{x}) = \{\mathbf{y} \in R^n \mid d(\mathbf{x}, \mathbf{y}) < \epsilon\}$$

Definition 16.5 $\mathbf{x} \in S \subset R^n$ is an interior point of S (relative to R^n) if and only if there is some ϵ-neighbourhood of $\mathbf{x}$ (relative to R^n) which is contained in S.

When $n = 2$ for instance, $N_\epsilon(\mathbf{x})$ is the inside of a circle, centre $\mathbf{x}$ and radius ϵ. So for $\mathbf{x}$ to an interior point of $S \subset R^2$ (relative to R^2) requires that there be some (perhaps very small) circle centre $\mathbf{x}$ and of non-zero radius whose interior is wholly contained in S.

Definition 16.6 $\mathbf{x} \in R^n$ is a boundary point of $S \subset R^n$ (relative to R^n) if and only if every ϵ-neighbourhood of $\mathbf{x}$ (relative to R^n) contains some points in S *and* some points not in S.

'int S' and '∂S' will continue to denote the sets of interior points and the set of boundary points of $S \subset R^n$ (relative to R^n).

Definition 16.7 A set $S \subset R^n$ is open (relative to R^n) if and only if all points in S are interior points (relative to R^n).

Definition 16.8 A set $S \subset R^n$ is closed (relative to R^n) if and only if the set of boundary points of S (relative to R^n) is a subset of S.

It is rather tedious to carry round the qualification 'relative to R^n' through what follows. Consequently, and as we did in the earlier discussion of the $n=1$ case, we often omit this qualification when the context makes clear the dimension n which is relevant.

As examples of the concepts introduced so far in this section we offer the following few remarks (relative to R^2) about the sets shown in fig. 1.2 in chapter 1:

S_9 open since a small circle can be drawn round any point of S_9 to lie totally within S_9 and so $\text{int}\, S_9 = S_9$;

S_{10} closed since a circle round any point of S_{10} contains points in and not in S_{10} and so $\partial S \subset S$ (in fact $\partial S = S$);

S_{11} closed since the perimeter of the circle is ∂S and is contained in S;

S_{12} neither open nor closed.

Furthermore, and more importantly, notice that, for any n:

(i) R^n is both closed and open since, like R, $\partial R^n = \emptyset$ and $\text{int}\, R^n = R^n$;

(ii) R^n_+ is closed but not open since $\partial R^n_+ = \{\mathbf{x} \in R^n_+ | x_i = 0, \text{ some } i\} \subset R^n_+$ and no point in ∂R^n_+ is an interior point;

(iii) R^n_{++} is open but not closed since $\text{int}\, R^n_{++} = R^n_{++}$ but $\partial R^n_{++} = \partial R^n_+$ and contains points not in R^n_{++}.

Finally we report without proof the following results.

Theorem 16.1 If $D \subset R^n$ is closed and $f{:}D \to R$ is continuous then $\{\mathbf{x} \in D | f(\mathbf{x}) \geqslant y\} = UC_f(y)$ is a closed set for all y in the range of f.

Theorem 16.2 If $D \subset R^n$ is open and $f{:}D \to R$ is continuous then $\{\mathbf{x} \in D | f(\mathbf{x}) > y\}$ is an open set for all y in the range of f.

Theorem 16.3 The intersection of two closed (open) sets is closed (open). In particular:

(a) The production set of a typical firm, $\{(x_0, \mathbf{x}) \in R^{n+1}_+ | f(\mathbf{x}) - x_0 \geqslant 0\}$, is a *closed* set if the production function f is continuous, since the function $f(\mathbf{x}) - x_0$ is also then continuous.

(b) The budget set of a typical consumer is

$$\left\{\mathbf{x} \in R^n_+ | m - \sum_{i=1}^{n} p_i x_i \geqslant 0\right\}$$

where $(\mathbf{p}, m) \in R^n_{++}$ and is a *closed* set since for fixed

$$(\mathbf{p}, m) \in R^n_{++}, m - \sum_{i=1}^{n} p_i x_i$$

is a continuous function of **x**.

16.4 Support hyperplanes

Suppose $S \subset R^2$ is a convex set and suppose that **x** is a boundary point of S; fig. 16.3 shows two possibilities. In each case it is clear that you can draw a line (i.e. a hyperplane in R^2) through **x** such that all of S lies on one side of this line (hyperplane); in the two cases shown, H constitutes such a hyperplane. Such a hyperplane is called a *support hyperplane* to S at the boundary point **x**. In fig. 16.3(a) H is the only such hyperplane to S at **x** whereas in fig. 16.3(b) there are many support hyperplanes to S at **x** (H is just one of them); in both cases there is at least one such support hyperplane. This is true in general.

Theorem 16.4: The support hyperplane theorem Suppose $S \subset R^n$ is convex and let $\mathbf{x} \in \partial S$, the boundary of S relative to R^n. Then there exists a hyperplane $H \subset R^n$ which contains **x** (i.e. $\mathbf{x} \in H$) and which 'supports' S (i.e. $S \subset H^+$ or $S \subset H^-$).

If H is a support hyperplane to the convex set S at **x** such that $S \subset H^+$ (say), then H^+ is said to be a *supporting half-space* to S at **x**; in fig. 16.3(a) the set of points on or 'above' H is such a supporting half-space while in fig. 16.3(b) the points on or 'below' H form a supporting half-space. Consider now what happens to the supporting

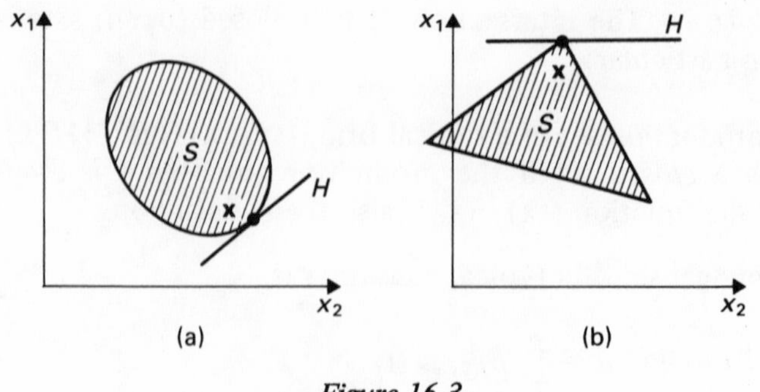

Figure 16.3

hyperplanes H and the associated supporting half-spaces as $\mathbf{x}$ moves around the boundary of S in fig. 16.3. After a little thought in both cases (a) and (b) you should find the following result not too surprising.

Theorem 16.5: The Minkowski theorem Suppose $S \subset R^n$ is convex and closed relative to R^n. Then S equals the intersection of its supporting half-spaces.

In other words, if we go right round the boundary of S in fig. 16.3(a) or 16.3(b), constructing supporting half-spaces for each boundary point then the intersection of (the infinite number) of all these half-spaces will be S itself. Theorem 16.5 shows that a closed convex set can be characterized as the intersection of its supporting half-spaces: this characterization lies at the heart of the duality discussion in chapter 18.

Exercise 16

1. S and T are two closed convex sets in R^n such that $\text{int}\, S \neq \emptyset$ (relative to R^n) and $\text{int}\, S \cap \text{int}\, T = \emptyset$. Suppose $\mathbf{x} \in \partial S \cap \partial T$. Show that there is a hyperplane which separates S from T.

2. (a) Suppose $f{:}R \to R$ is a concave (and hence continuous) function but f is not necessarily differentiable, at x^* say. By considering $(f(x^*), x^*)$ as a point of HG_f show that there is at least one value of σ such that

$$f(x^*) + (x - x^*)\,\sigma \geqslant f(x),\ \forall x$$

σ is known as a subgradient of f (see chapter 19).

(b) What difference does it make in (a) if f is differentiable at x^*?

(c) Find the set of subgradients at $x^* = 0$ for $f(x) = -|x|$.

17 Existence and differentiability of solutions to programming problems

17.1 Introduction

The various microeconomic models we have met so far have been based on a variety of assumptions. In all cases the models have resulted in parameterized programming problems, and in all cases, either explicitly or implicitly, we have made the following two assumptions:

(a) for all admissible values of the parameters there is at least one solution to the programming problem;

(b) the solution, multiplier and optimal value functions for the problem are suitably differentiable.

The objective of this chapter is to refine the earlier models by providing results which ensure properties (a) and (b). Thus we address two issues in this chapter. First given a programming problem are there theorems which yield sufficient conditions to ensure the existence of at least one solution to the problem? Secondly, given a set of solution, multiplier and optimal value functions for a parameterized programming problem, are there results which give sufficient conditions to ensure that these functions have the required differentiability properties? Once we have provided answers to these questions we apply the results to the earlier consumer and firm models.

17.2 Existence of solutions

Consider the problem:

$$\max_{\mathbf{x}\in D} f(\mathbf{x}) \text{ subject to } g(\mathbf{x}) \geqslant 0 \tag{17.1}$$

It is very easy to find examples of simple and apparently innocuous problems of this form which do not have a solution; e.g.

$$\max_{x \in R} x \text{ s.t. } x \geqslant 0$$

has no solution although it certainly satisfies all our earlier assumptions for a concave programming problem. There is, however, a celebrated theorem which gives conditions under which (17.1) has at least one solution. The feasible set for (17.1) is $\{\mathbf{x} \in D \mid g(\mathbf{x}) \geqslant 0\}$. *If* this set is *closed and bounded* and if f is a *continous* function then (17.1) has at least one solution. A set is said to be *compact* if it is closed and bounded. Hence we assert, without proof;

Theorem 17.1 If f is continuous and the feasible set for (17.1) is non-empty and compact then (17.1) has at least one solution.

To remind the reader, a set $S \subset R^n$ is bounded if there exists a number M such that

$$\mathbf{x} \in S \text{ implies } -M < x_i < +M, \forall i$$

Although this condition is satisfied in some of our earlier micro-economic models it is not satisfied in all of them; for instance the feasible set of the firm's profit maximization problem is not bounded in this way. Consequently we need more than theorem 17.1 to cover all earlier cases. We introduce one alternative via a definition. A set $S \subset R^n$ is *bounded above* if there exists a number M such that

$$\mathbf{x} \in S \text{ implies } x_i < +M, \forall i$$

and is *bounded below* if there exists M such that

$$\mathbf{x} \in S \text{ implies } -M < x_i, \forall i$$

The condition we want is a 'mixture' of these two notions. Partition the set $\{1, 2, \ldots, n\}$ into two subsets, I and J say; i.e. $I \cup J = \{1, 2, \ldots, n\}$ and $I \cap J = \emptyset$. S is *bounded above with respect to I and bounded below with respect to J* if there exists a number M such that

$$\mathbf{x} \in S \text{ implies } \begin{cases} x_i < +M, & \forall i \in I \\ -M < x_i, & \forall i \in J \end{cases}$$

If $I = \{1, \ldots, n\}$ so that $J = \emptyset$ this is equivalent to the 'bounded above' definition whilst if $I = \emptyset$, $J = \{1, \ldots, n\}$ it reduces to the 'bounded below' definition. Figure 17.1 illustrates three sets in R^2. In case (a), S is bounded above, in (b) it is bounded below and in (c) S is bounded above with respect to $\{1\}$ and bounded below with respect to $\{2\}$; none of three sets are bounded, however.

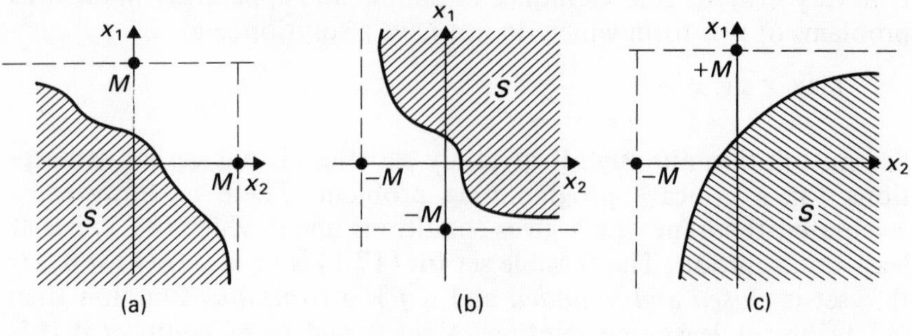

Figure 17.1

A useful alternative to theorem 17.1 is:

Theorem 17.2 Suppose f is C^1 and concave and

(i) $f_i'(\mathbf{x}) > 0$, $\forall \mathbf{x} \in D$ for $i \in I$

(ii) $f_i'(\mathbf{x}) < 0$, $\forall \mathbf{x} \in D$ for $i \in J$

where $I \cup J = \{1, 2, \ldots, n\}$ and $I \cap J = \emptyset$. Suppose further that the feasible set for (17.1) is closed, non-empty, convex and bounded above with respect to I and bounded below with respect to J. Then (17.1) has at least one solution.

For instance if f is C^1, concave and monotone increasing ($f_i'(\mathbf{x}) > 0$, $\forall \mathbf{x} \in D$, $\forall i$ so that $I = \{1, \ldots, n\}$, $J = \emptyset$) and if the feasible set is closed, convex and bounded above then (17.1) has at least one solution.

17.3 Differentiability of solutions

Consider the following parameterized programming problem:

$$\max_{\mathbf{x} \in D} f(\mathbf{x}; \alpha) \text{ subject to } g(\mathbf{x}; \alpha) \geqslant 0 \text{ where } \alpha \in A \tag{17.2}$$

Suppose we know that the solutions to (17.2) give rise to solution functions, multiplier functions and an optimal value function characterized by the Kuhn–Tucker conditions where $\lambda^*(\alpha) > 0$, $\forall \alpha \in A$. That is $\mathbf{x} = \mathbf{x}^*(\alpha)$, $\lambda = \lambda^*(\alpha)$ if and only if

$$\frac{\partial f}{\partial x_1}(\mathbf{x};\alpha)+\lambda\frac{\partial g}{\partial x_1}(\mathbf{x};\alpha)=0$$

$$\cdots\cdots\cdots\cdots\cdots\cdots\cdots$$

$$\frac{\partial f}{\partial x_n}(\mathbf{x};\alpha)+\lambda\frac{\partial g}{\partial x_n}(\mathbf{x};\alpha)=0$$

$$g(\mathbf{x};\alpha)=0$$

where $\lambda > 0$. Then first of all we would like to know conditions which ensure that $\mathbf{x}^*(\alpha)$ and $\lambda^*(\alpha)$ are all C^1 functions.

To uncover a general procedure to answer this question, consider the system:

$$F_1(\mathbf{y};\alpha)=0$$

$$\cdots\cdots\cdots\cdots$$

$$F_m(\mathbf{y};\alpha)=0$$

where $\mathbf{y}\in R^m$ and each F_i is C^1. Suppose we know that we can solve this system of equations uniquely for y in terms of any $\alpha\in A$, giving functions $y_i^*: A\to R$ with values $y_i^*(\alpha)$, $i=1,\ldots,m$ as the 'solution functions'. Then it follows from the implicit function theorem that the y_i^* functions will be C^1 *provided that*

$$\begin{vmatrix} \dfrac{\partial F_1}{\partial y_1} & \cdots & \dfrac{\partial F_1}{\partial y_m} \\ \cdots & \cdots & \cdots \\ \dfrac{\partial F_m}{\partial y_1} & \cdots & \dfrac{\partial F_m}{\partial y_m} \end{vmatrix} \neq 0,\ \forall\alpha\in A$$

where the derivatives are evaluated at $(\mathbf{y}^*(\alpha),\alpha)$.

Applying this result to our Kuhn–Tucker conditions, with $m = n+1$ and $\mathbf{y}=(\mathbf{x},\lambda)$, the condition for $\mathbf{x}^*(\alpha)$ and $\lambda^*(\alpha)$ to be C^1 becomes

$$\begin{vmatrix} \dfrac{\partial^2 f}{\partial x_1^2}+\lambda\dfrac{\partial^2 g}{\partial x_1^2} & \cdots & \dfrac{\partial^2 f}{\partial x_1\,\partial x_m}+\lambda\dfrac{\partial^2 g}{\partial x_1\,\partial x_m} & \dfrac{\partial g}{\partial x_1} \\ \cdots & \cdots & \cdots & \cdots \\ \dfrac{\partial^2 f}{\partial x_n\,\partial x_1}+\lambda\dfrac{\partial^2 g}{\partial x_n\,\partial x_1} & \cdots & \dfrac{\partial^2 f}{\partial x_n^2}+\lambda\dfrac{\partial^2 g}{\partial x_n^2} & \dfrac{\partial g}{\partial x_n} \\ \dfrac{\partial g}{\partial x_1} & \cdots & \dfrac{\partial g}{\partial x_n} & 0 \end{vmatrix} \neq 0,\ \forall\alpha\in A$$

derivatives being evaluated at $\mathbf{x}^*(\alpha)$, $\lambda^*(\alpha)$. As a general expression this is not too informative. However, when we apply it to our specific microeconomic models it becomes a much neater and more transparent condition.

17.4 The utility maximization problem

We now apply the existence and differentiability discussions to the theories of the consumer and firm, starting with the consumer's utility maximization problem;

$$\text{(UM)} \quad \max_{\mathbf{x} \in R^n_+} U(\mathbf{x}) \text{ subject to } m - \sum_{i=1}^{n} p_i x_i \geqslant 0$$

$$\text{where } (\mathbf{p}, m) \in R^{n+1}_{++}$$

Now for any $(\mathbf{p}, m) \in R^{n+1}_{++}$ the feasible set for (UM)

$$\{\mathbf{x} \in R^n_+ \mid m - \Sigma p_i x_i \geqslant 0\}$$

is a closed set. Moreover this feasible set is bounded since if $\mathbf{x}$ is in the set then $0 \leqslant x_i \leqslant m/p_i, \forall i$; choosing $M > \max_i (m/p_i)$ ensures the boundedness. Hence the feasible set is compact for any $(\mathbf{p}, m) \in R^{n+1}_{++}$ and if $U = R^n_+ \to R$ is continuous it follows by theorem 17.1 that there exists at least one solution to (UM).

Now assume that for every $(\mathbf{p}, m) \in R^{n+1}_{++}$ any solution to (UM) belongs to R^n_{++}; and assume further that U is strictly quasi-concave on R^n_{++}. Then it follows that there is at most one solution to (UM) and hence from the existence result there is exactly one solution to (UM) for any $(\mathbf{p}, m) \in R^{n+1}_{++}$. Thus (UM) defines solution functions and multiplier functions $\mathbf{x}^M : R^{n+1}_{++} \to R$, $\lambda^M : R^{n+1}_{++} \to R$ which are characterized by the following K–T conditions: $\mathbf{x} = \mathbf{x}^M(\mathbf{p}, m)$, $\lambda = \lambda^M(\mathbf{p}, m)$ iff

$$U_1'(\mathbf{x}) - \lambda p_1 = 0$$

$$\cdots\cdots\cdots\cdots\cdots$$

$$U_n'(\mathbf{x}) - \lambda p_n = 0$$

$$m - \sum_{i=1}^{n} p_i x_i = 0$$

It follows that $\lambda^M(\mathbf{p}, m) > 0$, for all $(\mathbf{p}, m) \in R^{n+1}_{++}$ assuming $U_i'(\mathbf{x}) > 0$. Assuming that U is C^2 on R^n_{++} we can apply the earlier differentiability discussion and $\mathbf{x}^M$ and λ^M will be C^1 if

$$\begin{vmatrix} U''_{11} & \dots & U''_{1n} & -p_1 \\ \dots & \dots & \dots & \dots \\ U''_{n1} & \dots & U''_{nn} & -p_n \\ -p_1 & \dots & -p_n & 0 \end{vmatrix} \neq 0, \forall (\mathbf{p}, m) \in R^{n+1}_{++}$$

derivatives being evaluated at $\mathbf{x}^M(p, m)$, $\lambda^M(p, m)$. From K–T, $-p_1 = U'_i(\mathbf{x})/\lambda$ and since $\lambda > 0$ this condition is equivalent to

$$\begin{vmatrix} U''_{11} & \dots & U''_{1n} & U'_1 \\ \dots & \dots & \dots & \dots \\ U''_{n1} & \dots & U''_{nn} & U'_n \\ U'_1 & \dots & U'_n & 0 \end{vmatrix} \neq 0, \forall (\mathbf{p}, m) \in R^{n+1}_{++}$$

derivatives being evaluated at $\mathbf{x}^M(p, m)$. In particular this condition is satisfied if $\forall \mathbf{x} \in R^n_{++}$

$$\begin{vmatrix} U''_{11}(\mathbf{x}) & \dots & U''_{1n}(\mathbf{x}) & U'_1(\mathbf{x}) \\ \dots & \dots & \dots & \dots \\ U''_{n1}(\mathbf{x}) & \dots & U''_{nn}(\mathbf{x}) & U'_n(\mathbf{x}) \\ U'_n(\mathbf{x}) & \dots & U'_n(\mathbf{x}) & 0 \end{vmatrix} \neq 0$$

That is, the solution and multiplier functions for (UM) will be C^1 if the bordered Hessian of U is non-singular on R^n_{++}. Since U is strictly quasi-concave we know that the sign of this bordered Hessian is $(-1)^n$ *or* 0; unfortunately we cannot rule out the possibility of 0 and consequently non-singularity of the bordered Hessian is needed as an extra assumption, but one which is sufficient to ensure that $\mathbf{x}^M$ and λ^M are C^1.

Turning to the indirect utility, ψ and assuming $\mathbf{x}^M$, λ^M are C^1, it follows immediately that ψ is C^1 since $\psi(\mathbf{p}, m) = U[\mathbf{x}^M(\mathbf{p}, m)]$ and is a C^1 function of a C^1 function. Applying the envelope theorem

$$\frac{\partial \psi}{\partial m} = \lambda^M(\mathbf{p}, m)$$

and

$$\frac{\partial \psi}{\partial p_i} = -\lambda^M(\mathbf{p}, m)\, x_i^M(\mathbf{p}, m)$$

Since $\mathbf{x}^M$, λ^M are C^1 it follows that the first partial derivatives of ψ are C^1, i.e. ψ is C^2. To sum up we need only make the following assumptions about (UM):

(a) $U: R^n_+ \to R$ is continuous on R^n_+ and C^2 on R^n_{++};

(b) $\forall \mathbf{x} \in R^n_{++}$, $U_i'(\mathbf{x}) > 0$, $\forall i$;

(c) U is strictly quasi-concave on R^n_{++};

(d) the bordered Hessian of U is non-singular on R^n_{++};

(e) $\forall (\mathbf{p}, m) \in R^{n+1}_{++}$, any solution to (UM) belongs to R^n_{++}.

Then (UM) defines C^1 solution and multiplier functions, $\mathbf{x}^M$, λ^M and a C^2 optimal value function ψ, and all our earlier analysis of these functions (comparative statics etc) rests merely on these five assumptions.

17.5 The expenditure minimization and cost minimization problems

The consumer's expenditure minimization problem is

$$\text{(EM)} \quad \min_{\mathbf{x} \in R^n_+} \Sigma p_i x_i \text{ s.t. } U(\mathbf{x}) \geqslant \bar{u} \text{ where } (\mathbf{p}, \bar{u}) \in R^n_{++} \times A$$

This problem has the same set of solutions as

$$\max_{\mathbf{x} \in R^n_+} -\Sigma p_i x_i \text{ s.t. } U(\mathbf{x}) \geqslant \bar{u} \text{ where } (\mathbf{p}, \bar{u}) \in R^n_{++} \times A \qquad (17.3)$$

Assume that $U: R^n_+ \to R$ is continuous on R^n_+ and strictly quasi-concave on R^n_{++}: then U is also quasi-concave on R^n_+ and the feasible set for (17.3) is $UC_u(\bar{u})$ and is a closed, convex set. Also this feasible set is bounded below since it is a subset of R^n_+. The objective function in (17.3) is C^1 and concave with negative first partial derivatives everywhere. Hence from theorem 17.2 there exists at least one solution to (17.3), and hence to (EM), for any $(\mathbf{p}, \bar{u}) \in R^n_{++} \times A$.

Assume now that for every $(\mathbf{p}, \bar{u}) \in R^n_{++} \times A$ any solution to (EM) must belong to R^n_{++}. Then from strict quasi-concavity there is at most one solution to (EM) and hence exactly one solution to (EM) for any $(\mathbf{p}, \bar{u}) \in R^n_{++} \times A$. Thus (EM) defines solution and multiplier functions, $\mathbf{x}^H: R^n_{++} \times A \to R$, $\lambda^H: R^n_{++} \times A \to R$ characterized by K–T; $\mathbf{x} = \mathbf{x}^H(\mathbf{p}, \bar{u})$, $\lambda = \lambda^H(\mathbf{p}, \bar{u})$ if and only if

$$-p_1 + \lambda U_1'(\mathbf{x}) = 0$$

$$\cdots\cdots\cdots\cdots\cdots$$

$$-p_n + \lambda U_n'(\mathbf{x}) = 0$$

$$U(\mathbf{x}) - \bar{u} \qquad = 0$$

Assuming $U_i'(\mathbf{x}) > 0$, $\lambda^H(\mathbf{p}, \bar{u}) > 0$, for all $(\mathbf{p}, \bar{u}) \in R^n_{++} \times A$ and assuming U is C^2 on R^n_{++}, the differentiability condition is

$$\begin{vmatrix} \lambda U''_{11} & \dots & \lambda U''_{1n} & U'_1 \\ \dots & \dots & \dots & \dots \\ \lambda U''_{n1} & \dots & \lambda U''_{nn} & U'_n \\ U'_1 & \dots & U'_n & 0 \end{vmatrix} \neq 0, \forall (\mathbf{p}, \bar{u}) \in R^n_{++} \times A$$

the determinant being evaluated at $\mathbf{x}^H(\mathbf{p}, \bar{u})$, $\lambda^H(\mathbf{p}, \bar{u})$. Since $\lambda > 0$ this is again equivalent to the non-singularity of the bordered Hessian of U. Under this condition, $\mathbf{x}^H$, λ^H and e are C^1. From the envelope theorem

$$\frac{\partial e}{\partial \bar{u}} = \lambda^H(\mathbf{p}, \bar{u})$$

and

$$\frac{\partial e}{\partial p_i} = x_i^H(\mathbf{p}, \bar{u}), \ i = 1, \dots, n$$

and e is in fact C^2. Hence our earlier analysis of (EM) rests merely on properties (a)–(e) of the last section (with (EM) replacing (UM) in (e), of course).

Since the firm's cost minimization problem is formally equivalent to (EM) the above reasoning can be applied directly and we find that the assumptions supporting the (CM) model can be pared down to;

(a) $f: R^n_+ \to R$ is continuous on R^n_+, C^2 on R^n_{++} and $f(0) = 0$;

(b) for all $\mathbf{x} \in R^n_{++}$, $f'_i(\mathbf{x}) > 0, i = 1, \dots, n$;

(c) f is strictly concave on R^n_{++};

(d) the bordered Hessian of f is non-singular on R^n_{++};

(e) for all $(\mathbf{p}, \bar{x}_0) \in R^n_{++} \times A$, any solution to (CM) belongs to R^n_{++}.

17.6 The profit maximization problem

This is:

$$\text{(FP)} \qquad \max_{(x_0, \mathbf{x}) \in R^{n+1}_+} p_0 x_0 - \sum_{i=1}^{n} p_i x_i \ \text{ subject to } \ x_0 \leqslant f(\mathbf{x})$$

where $(p_0, \mathbf{p}) \in R^{n+1}_{++}$.

The feasible set is $\{(x_0, \mathbf{x}) \in R^{n+1}_+ \mid f(\mathbf{x}) - x_0 \geqslant 0\}$ and is bounded below since it is a subset of R^{n+1}_+. The objective function in (FP) is decreasing with respect to $J = \{1, \ldots, n\}$ but increasing with respect to $I = \{0\}$. Hence to invoke theorem 17.2 we assume that in addition the feasible set is bounded above with respect to x_0; that is, there is some level of output, M say, such that $f(\mathbf{x}) < M$, $\forall \mathbf{x} \in R^n_+$. We refer to this assumption for simplicity as 'finite maximum output'. Assuming also that f is continuous on R^n_+ and strictly concave on R^n_{++}, f will be concave on R^n_+ and the feasible set is a closed convex set. From theorem 17.2 there exists at least one solution. Assuming interior solutions, strict concavity ensures at most one solution and hence exactly one solution, giving rise to solution functions and multiplier functions characterized by K–T: $x_0 = x_0^*(p_0, \mathbf{p})$, $\mathbf{x} = \mathbf{x}^*(p_0, p)$ and $\lambda = \lambda^*(p_0, \mathbf{p})$ if and only if

$$\begin{aligned}
&p_0 - \lambda = 0\\
&-p_1 + \lambda f_1'(\mathbf{x}) = 0\\
&\cdots\cdots\cdots\cdots\cdots\\
&-p_n + f_n'(\mathbf{x}) = 0\\
&f(\mathbf{x}) - x_0 = 0
\end{aligned}$$

$\lambda = p_0 > 0$ is ensured and assuming f is C^2 on R^n_{++}, the solution and multiplier functions will be C^1 provided that

$$\begin{vmatrix}
0 & 0 & 0 & \ldots & 0 & -1\\
0 & \lambda f_{11}'' & \lambda f_{12}'' & \ldots & \lambda f_{1n}'' & f_1'\\
\cdots & \cdots & \cdots & \cdots & \cdots & \cdots\\
0 & \lambda f_{n1}'' & \lambda f_{n2}'' & \ldots & \lambda f_{nn}'' & f_n'\\
-1 & f_1' & f_2' & \ldots & f_n' & 0
\end{vmatrix} \neq 0$$

for all $(p_0, \mathbf{p}) \in R^{n+1}_{++}$, the determinant being evaluated at $\mathbf{x}^*(p_0, \mathbf{p})$, $\lambda^*(p_0, \mathbf{p})$. Expanding this determinant by the first row and then by the first column reduces the condition (since $\lambda > 0$) to:

$$\begin{vmatrix}
f_{11}'' & \ldots & f_{1n}''\\
\cdots & \cdots & \cdots\\
f_{n1}'' & \ldots & f_{nn}''
\end{vmatrix} \neq 0$$

and if the Hessian of f is non-singular on R^n_{++} this condition will be satisfied and the solution and multiplier functions will be C^1. The profit function is then certainly C^1 and in fact is C^2 from Hotelling's lemma. Hence the analysis of (FP) rests merely on the following assumptions:

(a) $f: R^n_+ \to R$ is continuous on R^n_+, C^2 on R^n_{++} and $f(0) = 0$;

(b) for all $\mathbf{x} \in R^n_{++}$, $f_i'(\mathbf{x}) > 0$, $i = 1, \ldots, n$;

(c) f is strictly concave on R^n_{++};

(d) there is a finite maximum output;

(e) the Hessian of f is non-singular on R^n_{++};

(f) for all $(p_0, \mathbf{p}) \in R^{n+1}_{++}$, any solution to (FP) belongs to R^{n+1}_{++}.

Notice that (e) has to be a separate assumption since (c) implies merely that the Hessian of f has sign $(-1)^n$ or 0; some strictly concave functions do have singular Hessians.

17.7 The implicit function theorem: a brief introduction

Suppose we have a system of m equations:

$$\begin{aligned} F_1(\mathbf{y}; \alpha) &= 0 \\ F_2(\mathbf{y}; \alpha) &= 0 \\ \cdots&\cdots \\ F_m(\mathbf{y}; \alpha) &= 0 \end{aligned}$$

where $\mathbf{y} \in R^m$ and $\alpha \in R^n$. Suppose the equations are satisfied simultaneously at (say), $\mathbf{y}^* \in R^m$ and $\alpha^* \in R^n$ and suppose further that for each $i = 1, \ldots, m$, F_i is a C^1 function, at least in some neighbourhood of $(\mathbf{y}^*, \alpha^*)$, say $N_\epsilon(\mathbf{y}^*, \alpha^*)$. Finally suppose that

$$\begin{vmatrix} \dfrac{\partial F_1}{\partial y_1} & \cdots & \dfrac{\partial F_1}{\partial y_m} \\ \cdots & \cdots & \cdots \\ \dfrac{\partial F_m}{\partial y_1} & \cdots & \dfrac{\partial F_m}{\partial y_m} \end{vmatrix} \neq 0, \text{ the derivatives being evaluated at } (\mathbf{y}^*, \alpha^*)$$

Then the implicit function theorem states that there exists

(i) a neighbourhood of α^*, $N_\delta(\alpha^*)$, say, where $\delta < \epsilon$, and

(ii) m C^1 functions, $h_i : N_\delta(\alpha^*) \to R$, $i = 1, \ldots, m$ such that if $\alpha \in N_\delta(\alpha^*)$ then for $i = 1, \ldots, m$, $y_i = h_i(\alpha) \Leftrightarrow F_i(\mathbf{y}; \alpha) = 0$

More loosely the theorem gives conditions under which the original system $F_i(\mathbf{y}; \alpha) = 0$, $i = 1, \ldots, m$, which defines $\mathbf{y}$ implicitly in terms of α and is assumed to be satisfied at $(\mathbf{y}^*, \alpha^*)$, can be solved for the vector $\mathbf{y}$ as C^1 *functions* of α at least for α near α^*.

For instance in chapter 4 (p. 51) we had the 'system' of one equation,

$$f(x_1, x_2) - y = 0 \quad \text{where } y \text{ is a constant}$$

which we supposed was satisfied at x_1^*, x_2^*. With $x_1 = y$ and $x_2 = \alpha$ and assuming f is C^1 near $\mathbf{x}^*$ we can find a C^1 function $h : N_\delta(x_2^*) \to R$ such that for $x_2 \in N_\delta(x_2^*)$

$$f(x_1, x_2) - y = 0 \Leftrightarrow x_1 = h(x_2)$$

provided

$$\frac{\partial}{\partial x_1}[f(x_1, x_2) - y] \neq 0 \text{ at } \mathbf{x}^*$$

i.e. provided $f_1'(\mathbf{x}^*) \neq 0$, as asserted on p. 51. The implicit function theorem was also used in the last section of chapter 7. In the present chapter, however, we are effectively using only half the implicit function theorem which tells us that we can solve for $\mathbf{y}$ as *functions* of α near α^* *and* that these functions are C^1. We already know (from strict concavity, uniqueness, etc.) that we can solve the relevant equations for 'y' as functions of 'α' throughout the domain of α and we invoke the implicit function theorem only to establish the C^1 nature of these functions.

The reader who wishes to pursue the implicit function theorem in more detail is referred to the bibliographical notes.

Exercise 17

1. The production function of a one input firm is

$$f(x_1) = \begin{cases} 2x_1^{1/2}, & 0 \leqslant x_1 \leqslant 1 \\ 1 + x_1, & x_1 \geqslant 1 \end{cases}$$

(a) Sketch the graph of this production function and of its first derivative: hence observe that f is C^1.

(b) By sketching the graph of $f(x_1) - (p_1/p_0)x_1$ for the three cases (i) $p_1/p_0 > 1$, (ii) $p_1/p_0 = 1$ and (iii) $p_1/p_0 < 1$ show that the input demands for this firm are described by:

$$\frac{p_1}{p_0} > 1 \text{ implies } x_1 = \frac{p_0^2}{p_1^2};$$

$\frac{p_1}{p_0} = 1$ implies $x_1 \in [1, \infty)$; and

$\frac{p_1}{p_0} < 1$ implies that no solution exists to the profit maximization problem

(c) The input demands in (b) have two unusual features: when $p_1/p_0 = 1$ there are multiple solutions to the profit maximization problem and when $p_1/p_0 < 1$ there is no solution to this problem. Which aspects of the production function cause this firm to violate the existence and uniqueness results of the text?

2. Using the assumption $U_i'(\mathbf{x}) > 0$, $\forall i$, $\forall \mathbf{x} \in R^n_{++}$ show that there is no solution to the consumer's utility maximization problem when $m > 0$, $\mathbf{p} \in R^n_+$ and $p_i = 0$ some i. What feature of this problem prevents the use of theorem 17.1?

18 Introduction to duality theory

18.1 Introduction

Up to this point a firm has been defined or characterized by its production function and from this we have derived profit functions, cost functions, output supply and input demand functions and conditional input demand functions, giving us five classes of functions associated with a firm. The question we pose in this chapter is: given *any* one of these classes of functions can we find the other four? Similarly for the consumer, where the classes are utility functions, indirect utility functions, expenditure functions, Marshallian demand functions and Hicksian demand functions.

To be more precise, suppose for instance that we know a firm's profit function and that this function satisfies our earlier properties of profit functions (C^2, convex, linearly homogeneous, etc.). Ideally we would like:

(1) procedures for deriving the other four classes of functions (production functions, etc.) from this function;

(2) to know that (for instance) the derived production function when plugged into the profit maximization problem produces the original profit function so that the procedures in (1) are consistent;

(3) to know also that (for instance) the derived production function has all the earlier properties expected of a production function (C^2, concave, etc.).

This is a tall order and in fact we will only go so far as (1) and provide a complete catalogue of 'procedures' without going into the associated questions in (2) and (3). Of course when these procedures in (1) are applied to any particular example the reader can check mechanically that the requirements in (2) and (3) are satisfied. Nonetheless our omission of the general theory relating to (2) and (3) is a gap which would take up too many pages to fill, so that the interested reader should pursue this matter elsewhere (see bibliographical notes). Let us merely assert that 'usually' there is no problem with (2) and (3).

The term 'duality' is much overworked. There is a precise mathematical usage of the term, which we come to in the next chapter, concerning the dual of a concave program: it turns out that the 'dual of the dual' is the original program. Since when (2) is satisfied we have a similar 'coming back on itself' property for the procedures of this chapter we stretch the term duality to describe the current material. In fact economists have tended towards an even more liberal usage of the term duality to include Shephard's lemma, Roy's identity, etc. and much of the material already developed in this book beyond Kuhn–Tucker. The reader should be aware that the term has come to be used in these various ways.

18.2 Duality in the theory of the firm

The preceding discussions of the theory of the firm have led us to consider the following five classes of functions associated with a firm:

(a) the production function, $f(\mathbf{x})$;

(b) the profit function, $\Pi(p_0, \mathbf{p})$;

(c) the cost function, $C(\mathbf{p}, \bar{x}_0)$;

(d) the output supply function, $x_0^*(p_0, \mathbf{p})$ and the input demand functions, $x_i^*(p_0, \mathbf{p})$, $i = 1, \ldots, n$;

(e) the conditional input demand functions, $x_i^c(\mathbf{p}, \bar{x}_0)$, $i = 1, \ldots, n$.

Under the concave production function assumptions of chapters 10 and 11 we know how to derive (b)–(e) from knowledge of (a). In a sense the production function characterizes the firm since it contains enough information for us to derive all the other economically useful information about the firm, *viz.*: (b)–(e). The broad issue to be addressed in this section is then: does (b), (c), (d) or (e) also characterize a firm in this sense? For instance does knowledge of the profit function allow us to find (a), (c), (d) and (e)? Similarly for (c), (d), (e).

It is perhaps as well to warn the reader at the outset that this book will provide only an incomplete answer to these questions. In par-

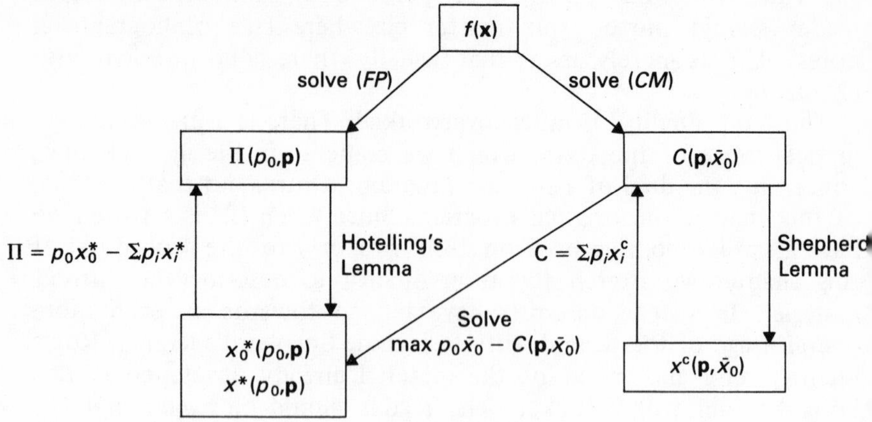

Figure 18.1

ticular we shall assume (and not derive) throughout that the firm has a production function which satisfies all assumptions of chapters 10 and 11.

A useful starting point for the discussion is fig. 18.1, which indicates the links between (a)–(e) which we have uncovered in our earlier discussions.

Clearly we have an immediate gap with respect to our objective: in fig. 18.1 there are no arrows going into the $f(\mathbf{x})$ box; at least as yet, we have no way of recovering the firm's production function from knowledge of (b), (c), (d), (e). Therefore we provide first a method for deriving a production function from knowledge of the profit function: since we can derive (b) from (c), (d) or (e) this will allow us to reach $f(\mathbf{x})$ starting from knowledge of any one of (b), (c), (d) and (e).

Consider the case where $n=1$: fig. 18.2 illustrates the solutions to the firm's profit maximization problem at two different prices, (p_0^1, p_1^1), (p_0^2, p_1^2). Here Y denotes the firm's production set; i.e. $Y=\{(x_0, x_1)\in R_+^2 | x_0 \leqslant f(x_1)\}$. Our starting point, however, is that we know Π but do not know f or Y. A procedure for finding f (and Y) from Π emerges as follows. Figure 18.2 shows us that the line $p_0^1x_0 - p_1^1x_1 = \Pi(p_0^1, p_1^1)$ is a support hyperplane to the convex set Y; similarly $p_0^2x_0 - p_1^2x_1 = \Pi(p_0^2, p_1^2)$ is also such a support hyperplane. Indeed as (p_0, p_1) varies through R_{++}^2, the lines $p_0x_0 - p_1x_1 = \Pi(p_0, p_1)$ constitute the set of support hyperplanes to the upper boundary of Y. Indeed in the mathematics literature Π is known as the support function for Y. Now it is clear that if $(x_0, x_1)\in Y$

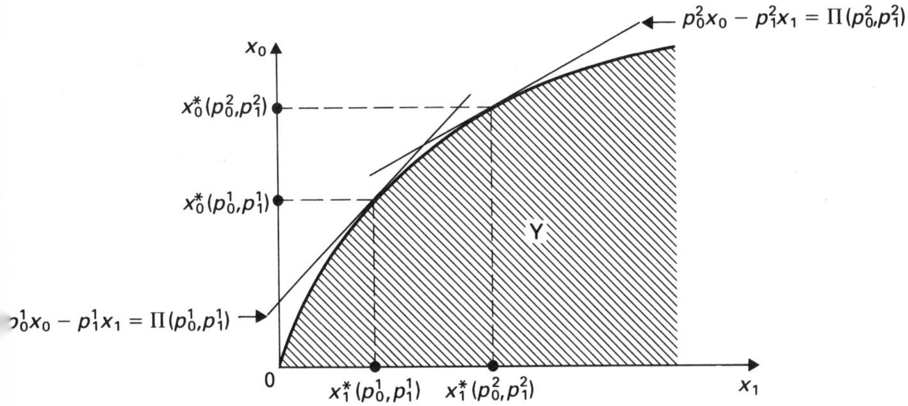

Figure 18.2

then it must lie on or below every one of these support hyperplanes—if not (x_0, x_1) would be feasible and give higher profits than $\Pi(p_0, p_1)$ at some (p_0, p_1), a contradiction. Conversely if $(x_0, x_1) \in R_+^2$ and lies on or below every one of these support hyperplanes then (x_0, x_1) belongs to the intersection of the half-spaces supporting Y. But by the Minkowski theorem of chapter 16, Y equals the intersection of its supporting half-spaces and so $(x_0, x_1) \in Y$. Hence

$$Y = \{(x_0, x_1) \in R_+^2 \mid p_0 x_0 - p_1 x_1 \leqslant \Pi(p_0, p_1),\ \forall (p_0, p_1) \in R_{++}^2\}$$

We now assert that, via the Minkowski theorem, we have generally (and not just for $n = 1$)

$$Y = \{(x_0, \mathbf{x}) \in R_+^{n+1} \mid p_0 x_0 - \Sigma p_i x_i \leqslant \Pi(p_0, \mathbf{p}),\ \forall (p_0, \mathbf{p}) \in R_{++}^{n+1}\} \quad (18.1)$$

(18.1) essentially characterizes the convex production set as the intersection of its supporting half-spaces and allows us to find Y and f as follows. Since Π is linearly homogeneous,

$$\pi(p_0, \mathbf{p}) = p_0 \Pi\left(1, \frac{\mathbf{p}}{p_0}\right)$$

and (18.1) can be written

$$Y = \{(x_0, \mathbf{x}) \in R_+^{n+1} \mid x_0 - \Sigma \frac{p_i}{p_0} x_i \leqslant \Pi\left(1, \frac{\mathbf{p}}{p_0}\right), \forall (p_0, \mathbf{p}) \in R_{++}^{n+1}\}$$
$$= \{(x_0, \mathbf{x}) \in R_+^{n+1} \mid x_0 \leqslant \Sigma r_i x_i + \Pi(1, \mathbf{r}),\ \forall \mathbf{r} \in R_{++}^n\}$$

(writing $r_i = p_i/p_0$, $i = 1, \ldots, n$)

$$= \left\{(x_0, \mathbf{x}) \in R_+^{n+1} \,|\, x_0 \leqslant \min_{\mathbf{r} \in R_{++}^n} [\Sigma r_i x_i + \Pi(1, \mathbf{r})]\right\}$$

where $\min_{\mathbf{r} \in R_{++}^n} [\cdot]$ denotes the minimum value of $[\cdot]$ for $\mathbf{r} \in R_{++}^n$. But $\Sigma r_i x_i + \Pi(1, \mathbf{r})$ is a convex function and its minimum value therefore occurs where

$$x_1 + \frac{\partial \Pi}{\partial r_1}(1, \mathbf{r}) = 0$$

$$\ldots\ldots\ldots\ldots\ldots\ldots$$

$$x_n + \frac{\partial \Pi}{\partial r_n}(1, \mathbf{r}) = 0$$

From Hotelling's lemma, $\partial \Pi / \partial r_i \, (1, \mathbf{r}) = -x_i^*(1, \mathbf{r})$; therefore we want a value of $\mathbf{r}$ which solves

$$\left.\begin{aligned} x_1 &= x_1^*(1, \mathbf{r}) \\ &\ldots\ldots\ldots\ldots \\ x_n &= x_n^*(1, \mathbf{r}) \end{aligned}\right\} \tag{18.2}$$

Hence the required minimum value is

$$\begin{aligned} &\Sigma r_i x_i + \Pi(1, \mathbf{r}) \quad \text{at } \mathbf{r} \text{ which solves (18.2)} \\ &= x_0^*(1, \mathbf{r}) \qquad\qquad \text{at } \mathbf{r} \text{ which solves (18.2), since} \\ &\Pi(1, \mathbf{r}) = x_0^*(1, \mathbf{r}) - \Sigma r_i x_i^*(1, \mathbf{r}) \end{aligned}$$

Hence:

$$Y = \{(x_0, \mathbf{x}) \in R_+^{n+1} \,|\, x_0 \leqslant x_0^*(1, \mathbf{r}) \text{ where } \mathbf{r} \text{ solves (18.2)}\}$$

But

$$Y = \{(x_0, \mathbf{x}) \in R_+^{n+1} \,|\, x_0 \leqslant f(\mathbf{x})\} \text{ and so}$$

$$f(\mathbf{x}) = x_0^*(1, \mathbf{r}) \text{ where } \mathbf{r} \text{ solves (18.2).}$$

So we arrive at the production function by solving (18.2) for $\mathbf{r}$ in terms of $\mathbf{x}$ and substituting this value into $x_0^*(1, \mathbf{r})$. Alternatively we write down 'normalized' ($p_0 = 1$) output supply and input demand functions

$$\left.\begin{aligned} x_0 &= x_0^*(1, \mathbf{r}) \\ x_1 &= x_1^*(1, \mathbf{r}) \\ &\ldots\ldots\ldots\ldots \\ x_n &= x_n^*(1, \mathbf{r}) \end{aligned}\right\} \tag{18.3}$$

and solve the last n of these for $\mathbf{r}$ in terms of $\mathbf{x}$; then we substitute into the right-hand side of the first equation to give the production function.

Examples 18.1

(a) $n = 1$ and $\Pi(p_0, p_1) = p_0^2/4p_1$. By Hotelling's lemma (18.3) becomes

$$x_0 = \frac{p_0}{2p_1} = \frac{1}{2r_1}$$

$$x_1 = \frac{p_0^2}{4p_1^2} = \frac{1}{4r_1^2} \Rightarrow r_1 = \frac{1}{2x_1^{1/2}}$$

Hence

$$x_0 = \frac{1}{2(1/2x_1^{1/2})} = x_1^{1/2} = f(x_1)$$

(b) $n = 2$ and $\Pi(p_0, \mathbf{p}) = p_0^2(1/4p_1 + 1/p_2)$. By Hotelling's lemma (18.3) is

$$x_0 = 2p_0\left(\frac{1}{4p_1} + \frac{1}{p_2}\right) = \frac{1}{2r_1} + \frac{2}{r_2}$$

$$x_1 = \frac{p_0^2}{4p_1^2} = \frac{1}{4r_1^2} \Rightarrow r_1 = \frac{1}{2x_1^{1/2}}$$

$$x_2 = \frac{p_0^2}{p_2^2} = \frac{1}{r_2^2} \Rightarrow r_2 = \frac{1}{x_2^{1/2}}$$

Hence

$$f(\mathbf{x}) = \frac{1}{2(1/2x_1^{1/2})} + \frac{2}{1/x_2^{1/2}} = x_1^{1/2} + 2x_2^{1/2}$$

So we now have a procedure which takes us from a firm's profit function back to the production function. Hence, starting at any box in fig. 18.1 we can now 'follow arrows' and (eventually) end up at any other box; starting from any one of (a)–(e) we can find the others.

18.3 Duality in the theory of the consumer

Our discussion of the consumer has uncovered five classes of functions:

(a) the utility function, $U(\mathbf{x})$;

(b) the indirect utility function, $\psi(\mathbf{p}, m)$;

(c) the expenditure function, $e(\mathbf{p}, \bar{u})$;

(d) the Marshallian demand functions, $x_i^M(\mathbf{p}, m), i = 1, \ldots, n$;

(e) the Hicksian demand functions, $x_i^H(\mathbf{p}, \bar{u}), i = 1, \ldots, n$.

Broadly speaking these parallel (a) to (e) of section 18.2 on the firm. Figure 18.3 illustrates the links between these five concepts which we know so far. In this figure, (D1)–(D4) refer to the duality properties announced earlier in chapter 12. We have two problems: first, there is no way as yet of recovering U from any of the other four classes of functions; secondly, careful inspection of fig. 18.2 reveals that knowledge of the Marshallian demand functions *alone* does not allow inference of any of the other functions. Resolution of the second problem, known as the ***integrability*** problem, is more difficult than the first, and we offer only a few brief remarks on it. On the other hand there is a relatively straightforward way of recovering U from knowledge of ψ (and hence from knowledge of $\mathbf{x}^H$ or e) to which we now turn. We assume that the consumer has a quasi-concave utility function satisfying all the other assumptions of chapter 12: we want to find this function, given ψ.

As in section 18.2 it is convenient to define 'normalized prices', $r_i = p_i/m$, $i = 1, \ldots, n$. Since ψ is homogeneous of degree zero in

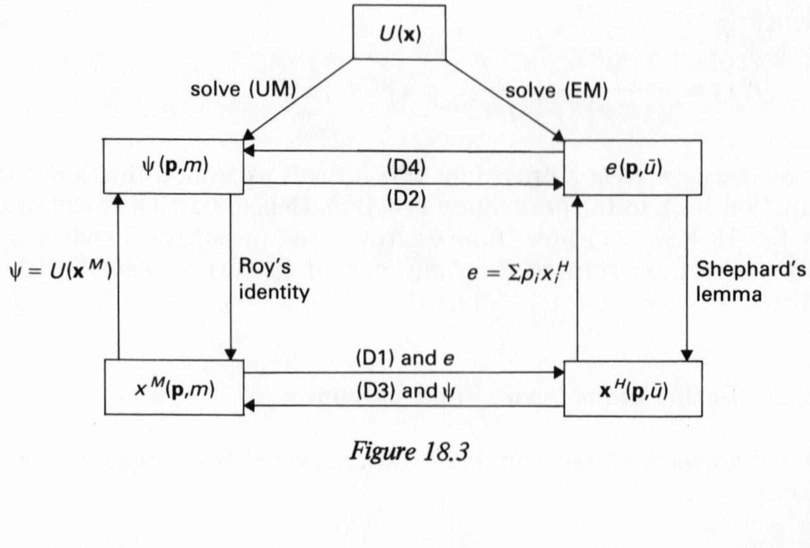

Figure 18.3

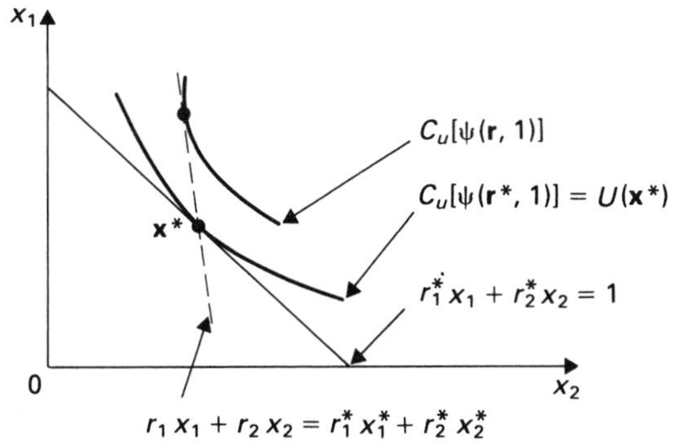

Figure 18.4

$\mathbf{p}, m$ it follows that $\psi(\mathbf{p}, m) = \psi(\mathbf{p}/m, 1) = \psi(\mathbf{r}, 1)$ in this new notation. Of course $\psi(\mathbf{r}, 1)$ measures the level of utility at the solution to (UM) when prices are $\mathbf{r}$ and income is 1. Figure 18.4 illustrates this typical solution when $n = 2$: prices are $\mathbf{r}^*$ at the point $\mathbf{x}^* \in R^2_{++}$. Now consider any other set of prices $\mathbf{r} \in R^2_{++}$ such that $\Sigma r_i x_i^* \leqslant 1$. The dotted line in fig. 18.4 shows the budget line for one such set of prices where in fact $\Sigma r_i x_i^* = 1$. The higher indifference curve is then the highest attainable and you see that $\psi(\mathbf{r}, 1) \geqslant \psi(\mathbf{r}^*, 1)$. It should also be clear that whenever $\Sigma r_i x_i^* \leqslant 1$ we will have $\psi(\mathbf{r}, 1) \geqslant \psi(\mathbf{r}^*, 1)$; i.e.

$$\Sigma r_i x_i^* \leqslant 1 \Rightarrow \psi(\mathbf{r}, 1) \geqslant \psi(\mathbf{r}^*, 1)$$

or

$$\psi(\mathbf{r}^*, 1) = \min_{\mathbf{r} \in R^n_{++}} \{\psi(\mathbf{r}, 1) \text{ subject to } \Sigma r_i x_i^* \leqslant 1\}$$

where min{ } denotes the minimum value of ψ subject to $\Sigma r_i x_i^* \leqslant 1$ and $\mathbf{r} \in R^n_{++}$. But $\psi(\mathbf{r}^*, 1) = U(\mathbf{x}^*)$–see fig. 18.4 again. Hence

$$U(\mathbf{x}^*) = \min_{\mathbf{r} \in R^n_{++}} \{\psi(\mathbf{r}, 1) \text{ subject to } \Sigma r_i x_i^* \leqslant 1\}$$

This is generally true even when $n > 2$ provided U is quasi-concave (etc.) and provides a method of deriving U from ψ, as follows. First solve for $\mathbf{r}$ in terms of $\mathbf{x}^*$

$$\min_{\mathbf{r} \in R^n_{++}} \psi(\mathbf{r}, 1) \text{ subject to } \Sigma r_i x_i^* \leqslant 1$$

Substituting the outcome into $\psi(\mathbf{r}, 1)$ gives the utility function.

Example 18.2 $n = 2$ and

$$\psi(\mathbf{p}, m) = \frac{m^2}{4p_1 p_2} = \frac{1}{4(p_1/m)(p_2/m)} = \frac{1}{4r_1 r_2}$$

Consider

$$\min_{\mathbf{r} \in R^2_{++}} \frac{1}{4r_1 r_2} \text{ subject to } r_1 x_1^* + r_2 x_2^* \leqslant 1$$

this becomes a standard quasi-concave programming problem with Lagrangean and K–T conditions:

$$L(r_1, r_2, \lambda; x_1^*, x_2^*) = -\frac{1}{4r_1 r_2} + \lambda[1 - r_1 x_1^* - r_2 x_2^*]$$

(I) $\dfrac{1}{4r_1^2 r_2} - \lambda x_1^* = 0, \quad \dfrac{1}{4r_1 r_2^2} - \lambda x_2^* = 0$

(II) $\lambda > 0$

(III) $r_1 > 0, r_2 > 0$ and $r_1 x_1^* + r_2 x_2^* = 1$

From (I)

$$r_2 = r_1 \frac{x_1^*}{x_2^*}$$

and from (III)

$$r_1 x_1^* + r_1 x_1^* = 1 \text{ and } r_1 = \frac{1}{2x_1^*}$$

Similarly

$$r_2 = \frac{1}{2x_2^*} \text{ and so } U(\mathbf{x}^*) = \frac{1}{4(1/2x_1^*)(1/2x_2^*)} = x_1^* x_2^*$$

Thus $U(\mathbf{x}) = x_1 x_2$ is the consumer's utility function.

Thus given information on any one of the five classes of functions associated with a consumer *except* the Marshallian demand functions we can uncover the other four types of function. At the moment, however, we have no way of deriving any of the other four classes from the Marshallian demands. If we could recover U (for instance) from $\mathbf{x}^M$ then of course we could find the rest: recovery of U from $\mathbf{x}^M$ is known as the *integrability problem*. One aspect of this integrability problem is that there is not going to be a unique U associated with $\mathbf{x}^M$. For instance if U gives rise to $\mathbf{x}^M$ then we know that any monotone increasing transformation of U also represents the consumer's preferences and gives rise to the same Marshallian demands. Hence from $\mathbf{x}^M$ the best we can hope for is determination of U up to a monotonic transformation; i.e. given $\mathbf{x}^M$ we can only hope to find either U or a monotonic transformation of U and we will have no way of identifying U definitely. More substantially it turns out the only methods known for getting out of the $\mathbf{x}^M$ box involve solutions of systems of partial differential equations, and since the mathematics here goes beyond the remit of this book we refer the reader elsewhere for pursuit of the integrability business (see bibliographical notes).

Exercise 18

1. A two-input firm's cost function is

$$C(\mathbf{p}, \bar{x}_0) = \bar{x}_0^2 \frac{p_1 p_2}{p_1 + p_2}$$

Calculate the firm's

(a) profit function;
(b) production function;
(c) output supply and input demand functions;
(d) conditional input demand functions.

2. A firm's profit function is

$$\pi(p_0, \mathbf{p}) = \frac{p_0^2}{4} \sum_{i=1}^{n} \frac{\alpha_i^2}{p_i}$$

Find the firm's production function.

3. A consumer's indirect utility function in an economy where there are three goods is:

$$\psi(\mathbf{p}, m) = \frac{m(p_1 + p_3)^{1/2}}{2p_1^{1/2} p_2^{1/2} p_3^{1/2}}$$

(a) Find the expenditure function and the Hicksian and Marshallian demand functions.

(b) Show that the consumer's direct utility function is:

$$U(\mathbf{x}) = x_2^{1/2}(x_1^{1/2} + x_3^{1/2})$$

4. A consumer's indirect utility function is:

$$\psi(\mathbf{p}, m) = \ln m - \sum_{j=1}^{n} \alpha_j \ln\left(\frac{p_j}{\alpha_j}\right)$$

where $\alpha_j > 0$, $\forall j$ and $\Sigma_{j=1}^{n} \alpha_j = 1$. Find the consumer's direct utility function.

19 Multiple constraint concave programming and linear programming

19.1 Introduction

Thus far all our programming problems have involved exactly one constraint. The objective of this chapter is to generalize some of our earlier results to the many-constraint setting, at least with respect to concave programming. We also take this opportunity to provide a brief introduction to a special class of multiple-constraint concave programming problems, namely the class of linear programming problems. Linear programming is a vast subject mainly because new techniques for solution (other than Kuhn–Tucker) become available. We suggest the source of these but refer the reader elsewhere for fuller coverage.

19.2 Multiple constraint concave programming

We generalize the problem of chapter 6 in the following way

$$\max_{\mathbf{x}\in D} f(\mathbf{x}) \text{ subject to } g_i(\mathbf{x}) \geqslant 0,\ i = 1, \ldots, m \tag{19.1}$$

We assume that D is convex and open and $f: D \to R$, $g_i : D \to R$, $i = 1, \ldots, m$ are all concave functions. The feasible set is

$$D \cap \left[\bigcap_{i=1}^{m} UC_{g_i}(0) \right]$$

and is convex as it is the intersection of convex sets. The constraint qualification is:

(CQ) $\exists\, \mathbf{x} \in D$ where $g_i(\mathbf{x}) > 0,\ i = 1, \ldots, m$

The Lagrangean for (19.1) involves a multiplier λ_i for each constraint function, $i = 1, \ldots, m$ as follows (where $\boldsymbol{\lambda} = (\lambda_1, \ldots, \lambda_m)$)

$$L(\mathbf{x}, \boldsymbol{\lambda}) = f(\mathbf{x}) + \sum_{i=1}^{m} \lambda_i g_i(\mathbf{x})$$

By a straightforward extension of the arguments of chapter 6 (details omitted) we get:

Theorem 19.1 Suppose D is convex and open and $f, g_i, i = 1, \ldots, m$, are all concave functions. Then $\mathbf{x}^*$ solves (19.1) if and only if there exists a vector $\boldsymbol{\lambda}^*$ such that the following Kuhn–Tucker conditions are satisfied:

(A) $L(\mathbf{x}^*, \boldsymbol{\lambda}^*) \geqslant L(\mathbf{x}, \boldsymbol{\lambda}^*), \forall \mathbf{x} \in D$;

(B) $\lambda_i^* \geqslant 0, i = 1, \ldots, m$;

(C) for $i = 1, \ldots, m, \lambda_i^* g_i(\mathbf{x}^*) = 0$;

(D) for $i = 1, \ldots, m, g_i(\mathbf{x}^*) \geqslant 0$ and $\mathbf{x}^* \in D$.

If in addition f and g_i, $i = 1, \ldots, m$, are C^1 then (A) can be replaced with either

(1) $\dfrac{\partial L}{\partial x_i}(\mathbf{x}^*, \boldsymbol{\lambda}^*) = 0, i = 1, \ldots, n$ or

(2) $f_i'(\mathbf{x}^*) + \sum_{k=1}^{m} \lambda_k g_{ki}'(\mathbf{x}^*) = 0, i = 1, \ldots, n$

where g_{ki}' means $\partial g_k / \partial x_i$.

Example 19.1 $\max_{x \in R} x$ subject to $1 - x^2 \geqslant 0, x \leqslant 0$. This is a one-variable, two-constraint problem. $f(x) = x$ is linear and so concave; $g_1(x) = 1 - x^2$ and is concave; $g_2(x) = -x$ is linear and so concave. For (CQ) set $x = -\frac{1}{2}$; then $g_1(x) = \frac{3}{4}$, $g_2(x) = \frac{1}{2}$ and both are positive. Hence (CQ) is satisfied (the feasible set is in fact $[-1, 0]$ – see fig. 19.1). The Lagrangean and the K–T conditions are

$$L = x + \lambda_1(1 - x^2) - \lambda_2 x$$

(A) $\dfrac{\partial L}{\partial x} = 1 - 2x\lambda_1 - \lambda_2 = 0$;

(B) $\lambda_1 \geqslant 0, \lambda_2 \geqslant 0$;

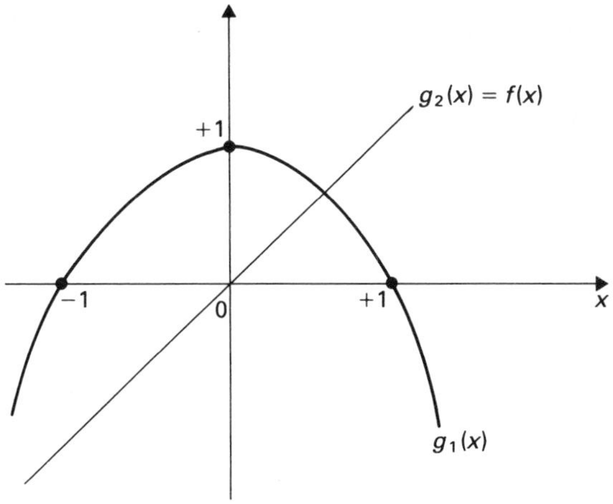

Figure 19.1

(C) either $\lambda_1 = 0$ or $1-x^2 = 0$ *and* either $\lambda_2 = 0$ or $x = 0$;

(D) $1-x^2 \geqslant 0$ *and* $x \leqslant 0$

To solve we follow the pattern of the single-constraint case and take the various possibilities in (C) in turn. But there are four possibilities here ($\lambda_1^* = \lambda_2^* = 0$; $\lambda_1^* = 0$, $g_2(\mathbf{x}) = 0$; $g_1(\mathbf{x}) = 0$, $\lambda_2^* = 0$; $g_1(\mathbf{x}) = g_2(\mathbf{x}) = 0$). As an inspired guess (see fig. 19.1) we try $g_2(x) = 0$ and $\lambda_1 = 0$ first. Then $x = 0$ satisfies (C) with $\lambda_1 = 0$. From (A) $\lambda_2 = 1 > 0$. So $x = 0$, $\lambda_1 = 0$ satisfies (A), (B) and (C); (D) is satisfied at $x = 0$. So $x = 0$ is the solution. (The reader can check that there are no others.)

For minimization we change the sign of the objective and solve the equivalent maximum problem, as usual.

You might notice that the sort of calculations involved in solving (A)–(D) above would become very involved as the number of constraints increases: in (C), with m constraints, there are 2^m different possibilities to try (with $m = 5$ this means 32 possibilities!). In the special case where all functions (f and g_i, $i = 1, \ldots, m$) are linear, computational efficiencies become available, as we shall see shortly.

Very often in economics (as indeed in example 19.1) some of the multiple constraints are non-negativity constraints on the variables in the problem. Consider for instance:

$$\max_{\mathbf{x} \in D} f(\mathbf{x}) \text{ subject to } g_i(\mathbf{x}) \geqslant 0,\ i = 1, \ldots, m$$

$$\text{and } x_i \geqslant 0,\ i = 1, \ldots, n \qquad (19.2)$$

Of course (19.2) is covered by theorem 19.1 assuming f and g_i, $i = 1, \ldots, m$ are concave (and C^1) since (19.2) then has $m + n$ concave and C^1 constraint functions. Writing $\boldsymbol{\mu}$ for the n-vector of multipliers associated with the non-negativity constraint functions the Lagrangean for (19.2) is

$$L(\mathbf{x}, \boldsymbol{\lambda}, \boldsymbol{\mu}) = f(\mathbf{x}) + \sum_{i=1}^{m} \lambda_i g_i(\mathbf{x}) + \sum_{i=1}^{n} \mu_i x_i$$

and the (K–T) conditions are:

(A) $f_i'(\mathbf{x}^*) + \sum_{k=1}^{m} \lambda_k^* g_{ki}'(\mathbf{x}^*) + \mu_i^* = 0, i = 1, \ldots, n;$

(B) $\lambda_i^* \geqslant 0, i = 1, \ldots, m$ and $\mu_i^* \geqslant 0, i = 1, \ldots, n;$

(C) for $i = 1, \ldots, m, \lambda_i^* g_i(\mathbf{x}^*) = 0$ and for $i = 1, \ldots, n, \mu_i^* x_i^* = 0;$

(D) for $i = 1, \ldots, m, g_i(\mathbf{x}^*) \geqslant 0;$ for $i = 1, \ldots, n, x_i^* \geqslant 0; \mathbf{x}^* \in D.$

$\boldsymbol{\mu}^*$ can be removed from these conditions since the following are equivalent to (A)–(D) (as the reader can easily check):

(a) $f_i'(\mathbf{x}^*) + \sum_{k=1}^{m} \lambda_k^* g_{ki}'(\mathbf{x}^*) \leqslant 0$ and $x_i^* [f_i'(\mathbf{x}^*) + \sum_{k=1}^{m} \lambda_k^* g_{ki}'(\mathbf{x}^*)] = 0,$
$i = 1, \ldots, n;$

(b) $\lambda_i^* \geqslant 0, i = 1, \ldots, m;$

(c) for $i = 1, \ldots, m, \lambda_i^* g_i(\mathbf{x}^*) = 0;$

(d) as (D) above—so defining a new Lagrangean for (19.2) as:

$$\hat{L}(\mathbf{x}, \boldsymbol{\lambda}) = f(\mathbf{x}) + \sum_{i=1}^{m} \lambda_i g_i(\mathbf{x})$$

which effectively ignores the non-negativity constraints in (19.2) in the Lagrangean construction, the conditions (a)–(d) become

(i) $\dfrac{\partial \hat{L}}{\partial x_i}(\mathbf{x}^*, \boldsymbol{\lambda}^*) \leqslant 0$ and either $\dfrac{\partial \hat{L}}{\partial x_i}(\mathbf{x}^*, \boldsymbol{\lambda}^*) = 0$ or $x_i^* = 0;$

(ii) $\lambda_i^* \geqslant 0, i = 1, \ldots, m;$

(iii) for $i = 1, \ldots, m, \lambda_i^* g_i(\mathbf{x}^*) = 0;$

(iv) for $i = 1, \ldots, m, g_i(\mathbf{x}^*) \geqslant 0;$ for $i = 1, \ldots, n, x_i^* \geqslant 0; \mathbf{x}^* \in D$

Often the Kuhn–Tucker conditions for a problem with non-negativity constraints are written as (i)–(iv) with $\hat{L}$ as the Lagrangean.

19.3 The profit maximizing firm revisited

Our analysis of the firm in chapter 10 started with the following profit maximization problem:

$$\text{(FP)} \qquad \max_{(x_0, \mathbf{x}) \in R_+^{n+1}} p_0 x_0 - \sum_{i=1}^{n} p_i x_i \text{ subject to } x_0 \leqslant f(\mathbf{x})$$

We removed the non-negativity constraint $(x_0, \mathbf{x}) \in R_+^{n+1}$ by assuming that only an 'interior' solution was possible. Now instead we assume that f can be defined on some open set D containing R_+^n and is C^1 there. Then we can re-write (FP) as:

$$\max_{(x_0, \mathbf{x}) \in R \times D} p_0 x_0 - \Sigma p_i x_i \text{ subject to } x_0 \leqslant f(\mathbf{x}), x_i \geqslant 0, \qquad i = 0, \ldots, n \qquad (19.3)$$

Here the non-negativity constraint of (FP) is explicit and we have extended the domain to an open set, $R \times D$, containing the original domain. Assuming f is concave we have exactly a problem of the (19.2) variety. The 'modified' Lagrangean is

$$L(x_0, \mathbf{x}, \lambda) = p_0 x_0 - \Sigma p_i x_i + \lambda[f(\mathbf{x}) - x_0]$$

and the K–T conditions are, much as before:

(i) $p_0 - \lambda \leqslant 0$ and either $p_0 - \lambda = 0$ or $x_0 = 0$; for $i = 1, \ldots, n$, $-p_i + \lambda f_i'(\mathbf{x}) \leqslant 0$ and either $-p_i + \lambda f_i'(\mathbf{x}) = 0$ or $x_i = 0$;

(ii) $\lambda \geqslant 0$;

(iii) either $\lambda = 0$ or $f(\mathbf{x}) - x_0 = 0$;

(iv) $f(\mathbf{x}) - x_0 \geqslant 0$ and $x_i \geqslant 0, i = 0, \ldots, n$.

Now (ii) is ensured by (i) since $\lambda \geqslant p_0 > 0$; hence $\lambda > 0$ and (iii) becomes $f(\mathbf{x}) = x_0$. Summarizing this the profit maximizing plan for a firm, at prices $(p_0, \mathbf{p})$, is characterized by the following four conditions:

(α) $p_0 \leqslant \lambda$ and either $p_0 = \lambda$ or $x_0 = 0$;

(β) for $i = 1, \ldots, n$, $p_i \geqslant \lambda f_i'(\mathbf{x})$ and either $p_i = \lambda f_i'(\mathbf{x})$ or $x_i = 0$;

(γ) $f(\mathbf{x}) = x_0$;

(δ) $x_i \geqslant 0, i = 0, \ldots, n$.

We can identify three possible solution types depending on which non-negativity constraints are 'binding':

(1) *Inaction* In this case $x_i = 0, i = 0, \ldots, n$.

(2) *Corner solution* $x_0 > 0$ but $x_i = 0, i = 1, \ldots, n$.

(3) *Interior solution* $x_i > 0, i = 0, \ldots, n$.

In chapter 10 we assumed that the production function was such that at all prices only interior solutions were possible; however, many production functions allow corner and inaction solutions.

Example 19.2 $n = 1$ and $f(x_1) = \ln(x_1 + 1)$. $f(0) = 0$, f is C^2 on R_+, $f'(x_1) > 0$, $\forall x_1 \in R_+$, $f''(x_1) < 0$, $\forall x_1 \in R_+$ so that (A10.1)–(A10.3) are certainly satisfied. Moreover f can be 'extended' to domain $(-1, +\infty)$ which is open and so allows the (α)–(δ) characterization (given above):

(α) $p_0 \leqslant \lambda$ and either $p_0 = \lambda$ or $x_0 = 0$;

(β) $p_1 \geqslant \lambda \dfrac{1}{x_1 + 1}$ and either $p_1 = \lambda \dfrac{1}{x_1 + 1}$ or $x_1 = 0$;

(γ) $x_0 = \ln(x_1 + 1)$;

(δ) $x_0, x_1 \geqslant 0$.

We search through the solution types in turn to see if they can be generated at some prices:

(1) Inaction. $x_0 = 0$ requires $p_0 \leqslant \lambda$ and $x_1 = 0$ requires $p_1 \geqslant \lambda$. Hence if $p_1 \geqslant p_0$ we get an inaction solution with $(x_0, x_1) = 0$. If $x_1 = 0$ then $x_0 = 0$ and 'corner' solutions cannot arise when $n = 1$.

(2) Interior. $x_0 > 0$ requires $p_0 = \lambda$. $x_1 > 0$ requires

$$p_1 = \lambda \frac{1}{x_1 + 1} = \frac{p_0}{x_1 + 1}$$

and hence $p_1 < p_0$. So if $p_0 > p_1$ we get an interior solution with $x_1 = p_0/p_1 - 1$ and $x_0 = \ln p_0/p_1$.

Because of the strict concavity of f in this example there is a unique solution at each (p_0, p_1), giving the following output supply and input demand *functions*:

$$x_0^*(p_0, p_1) = \begin{cases} 0 & \text{if } \dfrac{p_0}{p_1} \leqslant 1 \\ \ln \dfrac{p_0}{p_1} & \text{if } \dfrac{p_0}{p_1} > 1 \end{cases}$$

$$x_1^*(p_0, p_1) = \begin{cases} 0 & \text{if } \dfrac{p_0}{p_1} \leqslant 1 \\ \dfrac{p_0}{p_1} - 1 & \text{if } \dfrac{p_0}{p_1} > 1 \end{cases}$$

Notice, however, that these functions cease to be C^1 when $p_0 = p_1$: for instance when $p_1 = 2$

$$\frac{\partial x_1^*}{\partial p_0} = \begin{cases} -\frac{1}{2} \text{ if } p_0 > 2 \\ 0 \text{ if } p_0 < 2 \end{cases}$$

a discontinuous jump occurring at $p_0 = p_1 = 2$. One of the nice features of the 'interior solutions only' assumption earlier is that everywhere C^1 solution functions can emerge, allowing the earlier calculus-based comparative static conclusions. However, without the interior assumption, it is possible to generalize our comparative static analysis by replacing derivatives with subgradients (see next section): the interested reader is referred to the bibliographical notes.

With $n = 2$ (instead of $n = 1$ in the example), inaction solutions, corner solutions with only input 1 used, corner solutions with only input 2 used and interior solutions are all possible—see exercise 19, question 1. Perhaps more interesting than this corner solution analysis is the possibility of analysing input shortages using the multiple-constraint setting—see exercise 19, question 2, and bibliographical notes.

19.4 Subgradients and Lagrange multipliers as shadow values

In the one-constraint setting, we saw earlier (chapter 8) that if we 'perturbed' the constraint in a concave programming problem, by an amount α say, then the derivative of the optimal value as a function of α (the perturbation function) with respect to α gave us the Lagrange multiplier and justified the use of the term 'shadow value of the constraint' for this multiplier. Of course this observation depended on the differentiability of the perturbation function which, as observed in chapter 8, is not a problem provided the constraint does not switch from being 'binding' to 'non-binding' for some α. To pursue this matter satisfactorily in the many-constraint setting, however, we do have to admit the possibility of 'switches' in the set of binding constraints and face up to the lack of differentiability of the perturbation function. First we define the 'perturbed' version of (19.1):

$$\max_{\mathbf{x}\in D} f(\mathbf{x}) \text{ subject to } g_i(\mathbf{x}) + \alpha_i \geqslant 0,\ i = 1, \ldots, m \text{ where } \boldsymbol{\alpha}\in A \qquad (19.4)$$

Here $A \subset R^m$ is the admissible set for the perturbation parameter vector α and $0 \in A$. We assume also:

(A19.1) A is convex and open: D is convex and open.

(A19.2) f and g_i are concave, $i = 1, \ldots, m$.

(A19.3) For each $\boldsymbol{\alpha}\in A$, $\exists \mathbf{x}\in D$ such that $g_i(\mathbf{x}) + \alpha_i > 0, i = 1, \ldots, m$.

(A19.4) For each $\boldsymbol{\alpha}\in A$, there exists at least one solution to (19.4).

As compared with chapter 8, we are generalizing in several ways. Not only do we allow multiple constraints; but also we do not require differentiability of f and g_i, $i = 1, \ldots, m$ nor do we demand a unique solution but only 'at least one solution'. If there is at least one solution for any $\boldsymbol{\alpha}\in A$, the optimal value of all solutions at this $\boldsymbol{\alpha}\in A$ will be the same–otherwise they are not all solutions. Hence (A19.4) is sufficient to ensure the existence of an optimal value *function* known again as the *perturbation function* for (19.1), denoted $V: A \to R$ with values $V(\alpha)$.

It is now left to the reader to re-work theorem 8.2 to produce:

Theorem 19.2 Under assumptions (A19.1)–(A19.4) the perturbation function V is concave.

However, even when f and g_i, $i = 1, \ldots, m$, are C^2, suitable differentiability of V everywhere is unlikely.

Example 19.3 This is the perturbed version of example 19.1

$$\max_{x\in R} x \text{ subject to } 1 - x^2 + \alpha_1 \geqslant 0, -x + \alpha_2 \geqslant 0$$

With $A = \{\alpha \in R^2 | \alpha_1 > -1 \text{ and } \alpha_2 > -\sqrt{1+\alpha_1}\}$, (A19.1)–(A19.4) are satisfied. For ease we solve this perturbed problem by graphical inspection. The feasible set is

$$[-\sqrt{1+\alpha_1},\ +\sqrt{1+\alpha_1}] \cap (-\infty, \alpha_2]$$

and the largest value of x on this set occurs when

$$x = \min[+\sqrt{1+\alpha_1}, \alpha_2] = V(\alpha_1, \alpha_2)$$

V is concave as the 'min' of two concave functions (see exercise 7, question 5). But V is not differentiable when $\alpha_2 = +\sqrt{1+\alpha_1}$. For instance with $\alpha_1 = 3$

$$V(3, \alpha_2) = \begin{cases} \alpha_2 \text{ if } \alpha_2 \leqslant 2 \\ 2 \ \text{ if } \alpha_2 \geqslant 2 \end{cases}$$

and clearly $\partial V/\partial \alpha_2$ does not exist at (3.2).

To progress from here we need the notion of a *subgradient* of a concave function, and we digress to introduce this before returning to our perturbation theme. Consider a concave function $f: R \to R$ which is continuous but not differentiable everywhere: for instance fig. 19.2 sketches the graph of such a function, not differentiable at x^*, but C^1 everywhere else. For any point $\hat{x} \neq x^*$ there is a unique tangent line to G_f at $(f(\hat{x}), \hat{x})$ which has the property that the tangent line lies everywhere on or above the graph. Algebraically

$$f(\hat{x}) + (x - \hat{x}) f'(\hat{x}) \geqslant f(x), \ \forall x$$

where, of course, $f'(x)$ is the slope of the tangent line. However, at x^*, where f is not differentiable, there is no longer a unique tangent line with this property. Rather there are many (more than one) such

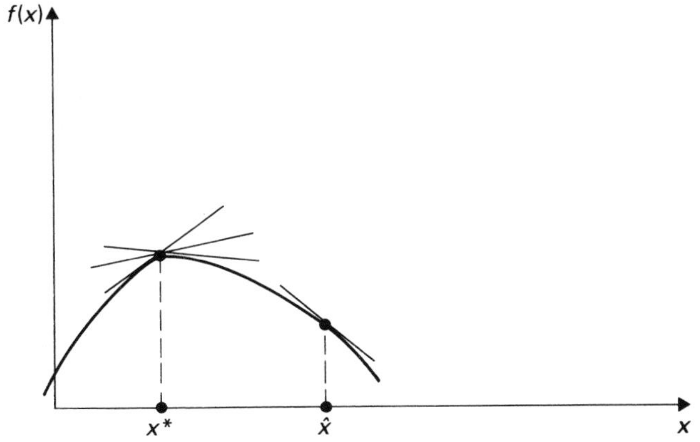

Figure 19.2

lines–three are drawn. Hence there is at least one value of σ (the slope of such a line) where

$$f(x^*) + (x - x^*)\,\sigma \geqslant f(x), \;\; \forall x$$

A value of σ satisfying this inequality is known as a *subgradient of f at x^**. It should be reasonably clear from fig. 19.2 that concave functions possess subgradients even at points where they are not differentiable, and that where they are differentiable the subgradient is unique and equals the derivative (at $\hat{x}$, $\sigma = f'(\hat{x})$). Generally ($n > 1$) the hypograph of a concave function is a convex set, a point on the graph is in the boundary of this convex set, and so there is a supporting hyperplane to the hypograph through each point on the graph. The slopes of these hyperplanes are the subgradients of the function at the respective points. Formally:

Definition 19.1 $\sigma \in R^n$ is a subgradient of $f: D \to R$, $D \subset R^n$ at $\mathbf{x}^* \in D$ if and only if

$$f(\mathbf{x}^*) + (\mathbf{x} - \mathbf{x}^*)\,\sigma \geqslant f(\mathbf{x}), \;\; \forall \mathbf{x} \in D$$

Without formal proof, but following the above discussion, we assert:

(1) if f is concave and D is convex and open, then f has at least one subgradient at $\mathbf{x}^*$, $\forall \mathbf{x}^* \in D$;

(2) if in addition f is differentiable at $\mathbf{x}^* \in D$ then $\mathbf{f}'(\mathbf{x}^*)$ is the unique subgradient of f at $\mathbf{x}^*$.

Hence the notion of subgradients generalizes the notion of a gradient or derivative for concave functions and provides information on the 'rate of change' of such functions even when they are not 'smooth'.

Returning to our perturbation theme we now state, again without proof, the crucial result.

Theorem 19.3 Under assumptions (A19.1)–(A19.4) and for $\boldsymbol{\alpha}^* \in A$, the set of subgradients of V at $\boldsymbol{\alpha}^*$ equals the set of Lagrange multipliers which satisfy the (K–T) conditions for (19.4) at $\boldsymbol{\alpha}^*$.

In particular with $\boldsymbol{\alpha}^* = 0$ we find that the set of Lagrange multipliers satisfying the K–T conditions for (19.1) are equal to the set of subgradients of the perturbation function for (19.1) at $\boldsymbol{\alpha}^* = 0$, and we have a nice generalization of the interpretation of Lagrange multipliers initiated in chapter 8.

Even more particularly, if the perturbation function for (19.1) is differentiable at $\boldsymbol{\alpha}^* = 0$ we have that:

$$\lambda_i^* = V_i'(0),\; i = 1, \ldots, m$$

so that the ith Lagrange multiplier measures exactly the rate of change of optimal value in (19.1) as the ith constraint is relaxed a little. When $m = 1$ this is exactly the chapter 8 result.

Overall the value λ_i^* at the solution to (19.1) gives us information on the rate of change of optimal value as the ith constraint is relaxed. This is so whether λ_i^* is unique or not.

Lagrange multipliers are shadow values of constraints.

19.5 Linear programming

If we take the multiple-constraint concave programming problem with non-negativity constraints (19.2) and impose the extra assumption that f and g_i, $i = 1, \ldots, m$ are all *linear* (and so concave) functions, we have the classical linear programming problem. Specifically suppose:

$$f(\mathbf{x}) = \sum_{j=1}^{n} c_j x_j$$

and

$$g_i(\mathbf{x}) = r_i - \sum_{j=1}^{n} a_{ij} x_j, \; i = 1, \ldots, m$$

Then the general linear programming problem is

$$\text{(LP)} \quad \begin{cases} \max\limits_{\mathbf{x} \in R^n} \sum\limits_{j=1}^{n} c_j x_j \\ \text{subject to } r_i - \sum\limits_{j=1}^{n} a_{ij} x_j \geqslant 0, \quad i = 1, \ldots, m \\ \text{and } x_j \geqslant 0, \qquad\qquad\qquad i = 1, \ldots, n \end{cases}$$

Alternatively, writing $\mathbf{c} = \begin{bmatrix} c_1 \\ \vdots \\ c_n \end{bmatrix}$, $\mathbf{r} = \begin{bmatrix} r_1 \\ \vdots \\ r_m \end{bmatrix}$, $\mathbf{x} = \begin{bmatrix} x_1 \\ \vdots \\ x_n \end{bmatrix}$

$$\mathbf{A} = \begin{bmatrix} a_{11} & \ldots & a_{1n} \\ \ldots & \ldots & \ldots \\ a_{m1} & \ldots & a_{mn} \end{bmatrix}$$

and $\mathbf{c}^T$ as the transpose of $\mathbf{c}$, the problem (LP) becomes

$$\text{(LP)} \quad \begin{cases} \max\limits_{\mathbf{x} \in R^n} \ \mathbf{c}^T\mathbf{x} \\ \text{subject to } \mathbf{A}\mathbf{x} \leqslant \mathbf{r} \\ \text{and} \qquad \mathbf{x} \geqslant 0 \end{cases}$$

Assuming (CQ) is satisfied (i.e. that there exists an $\mathbf{x} > 0$ such that $\mathbf{A}\mathbf{x} < \mathbf{r}$) (LP) becomes a problem whose solutions are characterized by theorem 19.1 (or its non-negativity constraint version): and any such (LP) problem can be solved in principle using the K–T conditions. However, the linearity opens up new solution possibilities. In particular we now demonstrate by example that any one- or two-variable (LP) can be solved *graphically*.

Example 19.4 $\max_{x \in R} 4x+1$ subject to $1+3x \geqslant 0$, $2-x \geqslant 0$, $x \geqslant 0$. Figure 19.3 shows the graphs of the constraint functions, $g_1(x) = 1+3x$, $g_2(x) = 2-x$. The feasible set is $[0, 2]$ and clearly the maximum of $4x+1$ on this set occurs at $x^* = 2$, which is the solution.

Example 19.5 $\max_{\mathbf{x} \in R^2} x_1 + x_2$ subject to $x_1 + 2x_2 \leqslant 1$, $2x_1 + x_2 \leqslant 1$, $x_1 \geqslant 0$, $x_2 \geqslant 0$, i.e. $\max x_1 + x_2$ subject to $1 - x_1 - 2x_2 \geqslant 0$, $1 - 2x_1 - x_2 \geqslant 0$, $x_1 \geqslant 0$, $x_2 \geqslant 0$.

Write $g_1(\mathbf{x}) = 1 - x_1 - 2x_2$ and $g_2(\mathbf{x}) = 1 - 2x_1 - x_2$; we draw the relevant *contours* of g_1, g_2 in fig. 19.4. The feasible set can now be

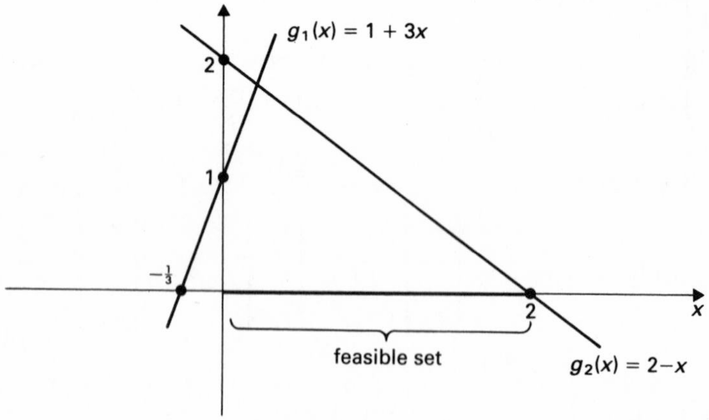

Figure 19.3

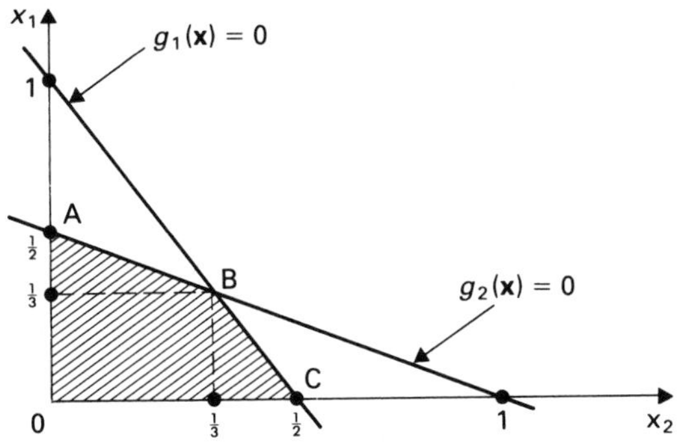

Figure 19.4

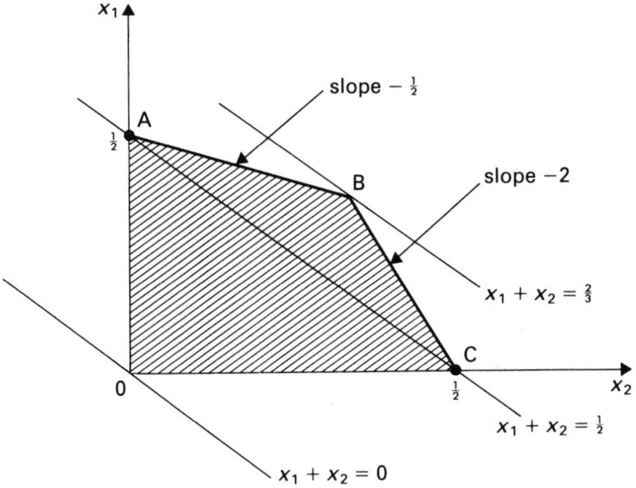

Figure 19.5

seen as the shaded region OABC. The co-ordinates of B are given by $1 = 2x_1 + x_2$ and $1 = x_1 + 2x_2$ whence $(x_1, x_2) = (\frac{1}{3}, \frac{1}{3})$. The slope of AB (from $g_2(x)$) is $-\frac{1}{2}$ and that of BC is -2. Now impose contours of objective function: their equation is $x_1 + x_2 = k$. These are lines of slope -1 and k increases as we move to the north-east. Clearly the highest contour we can get on to is $x_1 + x_2 = \frac{2}{3}$ and we get there at B, with $x_1 = x_2 = \frac{1}{3}$. So $x_1 = x_2 = \frac{1}{3}$ is the solution. Notice that if the objective function were $x_1 + 4x_2$, instead the contour slope would be $-\frac{1}{4}$ and these contours would be flatter than both AB and BC. So the solution would then be at A, with $x_1 = \frac{1}{2}, x_2 = 0$ as in fig. 19.6.

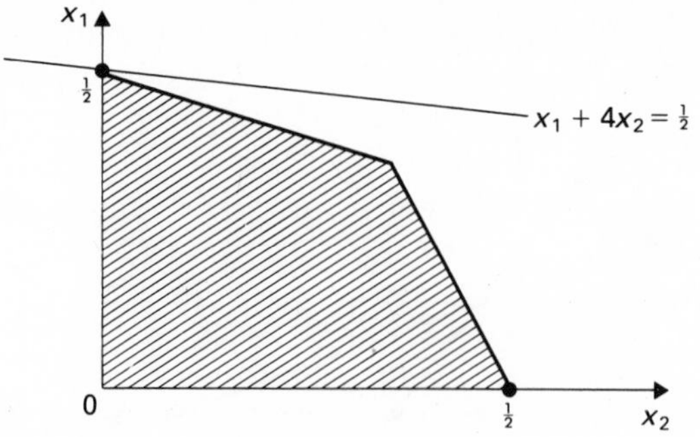

Figure 19.6

The graphs used in example 19.5 illustrate a potential solution method for linear programs. The feasible set is the convex shaded region with boundary OABC. On this boundary *either* (a) two of the constraints are satisfied with equality (*at* O, A, B and C), *or* (b) just one of the constraints is satisfied with equality (everywhere else on OABC).

We refer to points where two of the constraints are satisfied with equality as *vertices*: so O, A, B and C are the vertices in our example. Suppose we can identify vertices and hence evaluate $f(\mathbf{x})$ at each of them. Then it is easy to show that

(i) If at a given vertex the value of the objective function exceeds that at any other vertex, then the solution occurs at the given vertex.

(ii) if a number of vertices yield an identical value of the objective function, larger than that at any other vertex, then there are an infinite number of solutions. These occur at all convex combinations of these vertices. (For example, if in example 19.5 the objective had been $x_1 + 2x_2$ the solution would have been given by all points between C and B.)

For the general (LP) problem these ideas extend as follows. A *vertex* is a value of $\mathbf{x}$ in the feasible set where n of the $m + n$ constraints are satisfied with equality. There are a finite number of vertices. If (i) above is true of a given vertex then this vertex is the solution. If (ii) is true then the solution occurs at all convex combinations of those vertices yielding the largest value of the objective function.

This suggests a general computational procedure for solving (LP) problems: (a) identify the vertices of the feasible set, (b) evaluate the objective function $f(\mathbf{x})$ at each of them and then (c) determine which of (i) and (ii) is true and thus find the solution.

For instance in example 19.5: (a) the vertices are $0 = (0, 0)$, $A = (\frac{1}{2}\ 0)$, $B = (\frac{1}{3}, \frac{1}{3})$, $C = (0, \frac{1}{2})$ and (b) $f(\mathbf{x}) = 0$ at 0, $\frac{1}{2}$ at A, $\frac{2}{3}$ at B, $\frac{1}{2}$ at C and so (c) B is the solution.

For the general (LP) problem there are computational procedures based on (a), (b), (c). The most well-known is the *Simplex* method, which allows you to identify and search through vertices for the largest $f(\mathbf{x})$ in a computationally efficient manner. So for linear programming there are practicable alternatives to the Kuhn–Tucker approach. We do not go into these any further here; see bibliographical notes.

19.6 Saddlepoints and duality

Suppose we start with a multiple (but not necessarily linear) constraint concave programming problem (19.1) which satisfies the requirements of theorem 19.1 except possibly differentiability. Suppose further that this problem has at least one solution, $\mathbf{x}^*$ say. Then we know that there is a vector $\boldsymbol{\lambda}^* \in R_+^m$ such that

$$L(\mathbf{x}^*, \boldsymbol{\lambda}^*) \geqslant L(\mathbf{x}, \boldsymbol{\lambda}^*), \quad \forall \mathbf{x} \in D$$

We also know:

(i) $L(\mathbf{x}^*, \boldsymbol{\lambda}^*) = f(\mathbf{x}^*) + \Sigma_{i=1}^m \lambda_i^* g_i(\mathbf{x}^*) = f(\mathbf{x}^*)$ from (C) of the K–T conditions;

(ii) for $\boldsymbol{\lambda} \in R_+^m$, $L(\mathbf{x}^*, \boldsymbol{\lambda}) = f(\mathbf{x}^*) + \Sigma_{i=1}^m \lambda_i g_i(\mathbf{x}^*) \leqslant f(\mathbf{x}^*) = L(\mathbf{x}^*, \boldsymbol{\lambda}^*)$ since $g_i(\mathbf{x}^*) \geqslant 0$ from (D) of the K–T conditions. Hence we have

$$\max_{\mathbf{x} \in D} L(\mathbf{x}, \boldsymbol{\lambda}^*) = L(\mathbf{x}^*, \boldsymbol{\lambda}^*) = \min_{\lambda \in R_+^m} L(\mathbf{x}^*, \boldsymbol{\lambda}) \qquad (19.5)$$

Thus a solution to (19.1), $\mathbf{x}^*$ say, with an associated multiplier $\boldsymbol{\lambda}^*$, constitutes a *saddlepoint* of the Lagrangean. From (19.5) it defines the minimum value of L with respect to variations of $\boldsymbol{\lambda} \in R_+^m$ and the maximum value of L with respect to variations of $\mathbf{x} \in D$. In particular, we refer to the original program (19.1) as the *primal* program, with optimal value $f(\mathbf{x}^*)$, and (19.5) leads us to consider the so-called *dual* program:

$$\min_{\lambda \in R_+^m} \left[\max_{\mathbf{x} \in D} f(\mathbf{x}) + \Sigma \lambda_i g_i(\mathbf{x}) \right] \qquad (19.6)$$

This dual program has a number of nice properties, even in the general non-linear setting. In particular, under our earlier assumptions on the primal program, the dual has a solution; its optimal value is $f(\mathbf{x}^*)$, the same as the primal; and $\boldsymbol{\lambda}^*$ solves (19.6) if and only if $\boldsymbol{\lambda}^*$ is a solution value of the multiplier in the primal. However, the most useful result comes from the dual formulation in the linear context. For the (LP) problem (19.6) becomes:

$$\min_{\substack{\lambda \in R_+^m \\ \mu \in R_+^n}} \left[\max_{\mathbf{x} \in R^n} \mathbf{c}^T\mathbf{x} + \boldsymbol{\lambda}(\mathbf{r} - \mathbf{A}\mathbf{x}) + \boldsymbol{\mu}\mathbf{x} \right] \tag{19.7}$$

where $\boldsymbol{\lambda}$ and $\boldsymbol{\mu}$ are row vectors of multipliers, $\boldsymbol{\mu}$ associated with the non-negativity constraints and $\boldsymbol{\lambda}$ with the other constraints. Rearranging, (19.7) becomes

$$\min_{\substack{\lambda \in R_+^m \\ \mu \in R_+^n}} \left[\boldsymbol{\lambda}\mathbf{r} + \max_{\mathbf{x} \in R^n} (\mathbf{c}^T - \boldsymbol{\lambda}\mathbf{A} + \boldsymbol{\mu})\,\mathbf{x} \right] \tag{19.8}$$

Since (19.8) has a solution (under our assumptions) it must be that the solution value of $\boldsymbol{\mu}$ satisfies $\boldsymbol{\mu} = \boldsymbol{\lambda}\mathbf{A} - \mathbf{c}^T$ so that

$$\max_{\mathbf{x} \in R^n} (\mathbf{c}^T - \lambda\mathbf{A} + \boldsymbol{\mu})\,\mathbf{x} = 0$$

If not some element of the row vector $\mathbf{c}^T - \boldsymbol{\lambda}\mathbf{A} + \boldsymbol{\mu}$ is not zero and some choice of $\mathbf{x}$ and $\boldsymbol{\lambda}$ allows unbounded values and no solution can be attained in (19.8). So, given that $\boldsymbol{\mu} = \boldsymbol{\lambda}\mathbf{A} - \mathbf{c}^T$, the solution value of $\boldsymbol{\lambda}$ must minimize $\boldsymbol{\lambda}\mathbf{r}$ subject to the constraint $\boldsymbol{\lambda}\mathbf{A} - \mathbf{c}^T = \boldsymbol{\mu} \geqslant 0$. Hence (19.8) becomes

$$\min_{\lambda \in R_+^m} \boldsymbol{\lambda}\mathbf{r} \text{ subject to } \boldsymbol{\lambda}\mathbf{A} - \mathbf{c}^T \geqslant 0$$

or

$$(\text{DLP}) \begin{cases} \min_{\lambda \in R^m} \boldsymbol{\lambda}\mathbf{r} \\ \text{subject to } \boldsymbol{\lambda}\mathbf{A} \geqslant \mathbf{c}^T \\ \text{and} \qquad \boldsymbol{\lambda} \geqslant 0 \end{cases}$$

This is the dual problem to (LP) and is also a linear program whose variables are the multipliers $\boldsymbol{\lambda}$ of the primal. A simple mechanical procedure leads to (DLP) from (LP):

(1) Introduce new variables $\boldsymbol{\lambda}$ equal in number to m in (LP).

(2) The objective function becomes $\boldsymbol{\lambda}\mathbf{r}$, $\mathbf{r}$ as in (LP).

(3) The dual constraints are $\boldsymbol{\lambda} \geqslant 0$ and $\boldsymbol{\lambda}\mathbf{A} \geqslant \mathbf{c}^T$, $\mathbf{A}$ and $\mathbf{c}^T$ as in (LP).

If you now apply this procedure *to (DLP)* itself and let the new variables be **x** you end up back at (LP)–the dual of the dual is the primal.

One of the nice features of (DLP) is that it is linear, and so amenable to graphical/computational solution. It gives us the shadow values of the primal constraints which graphical/computational solution of the primal does not. Notice symmetrically that the solutions $\mathbf{x}^*$ of the primal give us shadow values of the dual constraints.

Example 19.6 The dual of example 19.5. The primal was:

$$\max_{\mathbf{x}\in R^2} (1 \quad 1)\begin{bmatrix} x_1 \\ x_2 \end{bmatrix}$$

subject to

$$\begin{bmatrix} 1 & 2 \\ 2 & 1 \end{bmatrix}\begin{bmatrix} x_1 \\ x_2 \end{bmatrix} \leqslant \begin{bmatrix} 1 \\ 1 \end{bmatrix}$$

and $x_1, x_2 \geqslant 0$

with solution $x_1 = x_2 = \frac{1}{3}$. Mechanical formulation of the dual gives

$$\min_{\lambda\in R^2} (1 \quad 1)\begin{bmatrix} \lambda_1 \\ \lambda_2 \end{bmatrix}$$

subject to

$$\begin{bmatrix} 1 & 2 \\ 2 & 1 \end{bmatrix}\begin{bmatrix} \lambda_1 \\ \lambda_2 \end{bmatrix} \geqslant \begin{bmatrix} 1 \\ 1 \end{bmatrix}$$

and $\lambda_1, \lambda_2 \geqslant 0$.

Graphical solution (details omitted) gives $\lambda_1 = \lambda_2 = \frac{1}{3}$. So the shadow values of the primal constraints are $\lambda_1 = \lambda_2 = \frac{1}{3}$ and shadow values of the dual constraints are $x_1 = x_2 = \frac{1}{3}$.

Notice that the requirement for graphical solution of the primal is two primal variables, while that for the dual is two primal constraints. In example 19.5 there were two primal variables and two primal constraints so that both primal and dual problems were accessible graphically. With three variables and two constraints in a primal program, for instance, the dual (but not the primal) remains solvable by graphical methods.

Exercise 19

1. The production function of a two-input firm is

$$f(\mathbf{x}) = \ln(x_1 + 1) + \ln(x_2 + 1)$$

Inaction, interior and corner solution to the profit maximization problem are all possible. Find the firm's output supply and input demand functions.

2. A cost maximizing firm uses two inputs with production function $f(\mathbf{x})$. Because inputs are in short supply the quantities of the two inputs are further constrained by:

$$x_1 \leqslant \bar{x}_1, \; x_2 \leqslant \bar{x}_2$$

where $\bar{x}_1, \bar{x}_2 > 0$ are upper bounds on the input quantities available to the firm. The firm's restricted (or 'quantity constrained') cost minimization problem is

$$\min_{\mathbf{x} \in R^2_+} p_1 x_1 + p_2 x_2 \text{ subject to } f(\mathbf{x}) \geqslant \bar{x}_0, \; x_i \leqslant \bar{x}_i, \; i = 1, 2$$

where $(\mathbf{p}, \bar{x}_0, \bar{x}_1, \bar{x}_2) \in R^5_{++}$ and $f(\bar{x}_1, \bar{x}_2) > \bar{x}_0$ (so that the firm can at least achieve the pre-assigned output from available input). Assuming that only 'interior' solutions are possible (that is, R^2_+ can be replaced by R^2_{++} in the minimization problem) and that f is concave (etc.):

(a) write down the K–T conditions characterizing the solution to the restricted cost minimization problem;

(b) for the case where $f(\mathbf{x}) = x_1^{1/4} x_2^{1/4}$ show that the solutions to the restricted cost minimization problem are

$$x_1 = \begin{cases} \bar{x}_0^2 \dfrac{p_2^{1/2}}{p_1^{1/2}} & \text{if } \bar{x}_1 \geqslant \bar{x}_0^2 \dfrac{p_2^{1/2}}{p_1^{1/2}} \text{ and } \bar{x}_2 \geqslant \bar{x}_0^2 \dfrac{p_1^{1/2}}{p_2^{1/2}} \\[2ex] \bar{x}_1 & \text{if } \bar{x}_1 < \bar{x}_0^2 \dfrac{p_2^{1/2}}{p_1^{1/2}} \\[2ex] \dfrac{\bar{x}_0^4}{\bar{x}_2} & \text{if } \bar{x}_2 < \bar{x}_0^2 \dfrac{p_1^{1/2}}{p_2^{1/2}} \end{cases}$$

$$x_2 = \begin{cases} \bar{x}_0^2 \dfrac{p_1^{1/2}}{p_2^{1/2}} & \text{if } \bar{x}_1 \geqslant \bar{x}_0^2 \dfrac{p_2^{1/2}}{p_1^{1/2}} \text{ and } \bar{x}_2 \geqslant \bar{x}_0^2 \dfrac{p_1^{1/2}}{p_2^{1/2}} \\[2ex] \dfrac{\bar{x}_0^4}{\bar{x}_1} & \text{if } \bar{x}_1 < \bar{x}_0^2 \dfrac{p_2^{1/2}}{p_1^{1/2}} \\[2ex] \bar{x}_2 & \text{if } \bar{x}_2 < \bar{x}_0^2 \dfrac{p_1^{1/2}}{p_2^{1/2}} \end{cases}$$

These functions are known as the restricted conditional input demand functions. The resulting optimal value function for the restricted cost minimization problem is known as the restricted cost function. Evaluate the restricted cost function for this example.

3. The production function of a two-input firm is:

$$f(\mathbf{x}) = \min[x_1 + 2x_2,\ 2x_1 + x_2]$$

(a) By considering $UC_f(y)$, or otherwise, show that f is quasi-concave.

(b) Show that f is linearly homogeneous and hence, from (a), concave.

(c) The firm's cost minimization problem can be written as a linear programming problem:

$$\min p_1 x_1 + p_2 x_2$$

$$\text{subject to } x_1 + 2x_2 \geqslant \bar{x}_0$$

$$2x_1 + x_2 \geqslant \bar{x}_0$$

$$x_1, x_2 \geqslant 0$$

Solving this program graphically, show that the firm's conditional input demands are

$$x_1^c(\mathbf{p}, \bar{x}_0) = \begin{cases} 0 & \text{if } \frac{1}{2} > \frac{p_2}{p_1} \\ [0, \frac{1}{3}\bar{x}_0] & \text{if } \frac{1}{2} = \frac{p_2}{p_1} \\ \frac{1}{3}\bar{x}_0 & \text{if } 2 > \frac{p_2}{p_1} > \frac{1}{2} \\ [\frac{1}{3}\bar{x}_0, \bar{x}_0] & \text{if } \frac{p_2}{p_1} = 2 \\ \bar{x}_0 & \text{if } \frac{p_2}{p_1} > 2 \end{cases}$$

and

$$x_2^c(\mathbf{p}, \bar{x}_0) = \begin{cases} 0 & \text{if } \dfrac{1}{2} > \dfrac{p_1}{p_2} \\ [0, \tfrac{1}{3}\bar{x}_0] & \text{if } \dfrac{1}{2} = \dfrac{p_1}{p_2} \\ \tfrac{1}{3}\bar{x}_0 & \text{if } 2 > \dfrac{p_1}{p_2} > \dfrac{1}{2} \\ [\tfrac{1}{3}\bar{x}_0, \bar{x}_0] & \text{if } \dfrac{p_1}{p_2} = 2 \\ \bar{x}_0 & \text{if } \dfrac{p_1}{p_2} > 2 \end{cases}$$

4. (a) Formulate and solve graphically the dual of the following linear program:

$$\max x_1 + x_2 + x_3$$
$$\text{subject to } 2x_1 + 4x_2 + x_3 \leqslant 5$$
$$x_1 + 5x_2 + 2x_3 \leqslant 15$$
$$x_1, x_2, x_3 \geqslant 0$$

(b) Observing that only one dual variable is non-zero at the solution, it follows that only one constraint has non-zero shadow value (i.e. is 'binding') at the solution to the primal. Furthermore only one dual constraint is binding at the solution, so that only one primal variable is non-zero. Hence show that the primal solution is $x_1 = x_2 = 0$, $x_3 = 5$.

20 Concavifiability and quasi-concave programming with multiple constraints

20.1 Introduction

In chapter 19 we discussed concave programming with many constraints. At least as far as Kuhn–Tucker is concerned the many-constraint results could be demonstrated via straightforward extensions of the single-constraint results. Although the transition is somewhat more difficult the same is roughly true of quasi-concave programming. However, instead of pursuing this route we now offer a different approach to quasi-concave programming. A quasi-concave function is *concavifiable* if there exists a monotone increasing transformation of the function which is concave. It turns out that if the quasi-concave functions in a programming problem (with many constraints) are all concavifiable then the problem can be reduced to a concave programming problem and chapter 19 produces the desired Kuhn–Tucker characterization. We show this in section 20.2. In section 20.3 we then describe conditions under which quasi-concave functions are concavifiable. The overall outcome allows us to address quasi-concave consumer theory with many constraints.

The reason for the change in direction is simply to allow us to introduce the reader to the concavifiability issue.

20.2 Concavifiability and multiple-constraint quasi-concave programming

Consider a quasi-concave function $f{:}D \rightarrow R$, where $D \subset R^n$ and is convex, with range $E \subset R$. Let $h: E \rightarrow R$ be a C^1 monotone increasing function so that $g{:}D \rightarrow R$, with values $g(\mathbf{x}) = h[f(\mathbf{x})]$, is a monotone increasing transformation of f. From the discussions of chapter 13 we can be sure that g is also quasi-concave; even if h is concave all we can be *sure* of is that g is quasi-concave. The concavifiability issue emerges in answer to the question: is there *some* monotone increasing (concave) transformation h such that $h[f(\mathbf{x})]$ is concave if f is quasi-concave?

Definition 20.1 The quasi-concave function $f: D \to R$ where $D \subset R^n$ is open and convex, is said to be *concavifiable* if there exists a monotone increasing C^1 transformation $h: E \to R$, where E is the range of f, such that the function $g: D \to R$ with values $g(\mathbf{x}) = h[f(\mathbf{x})]$ is *concave*.

In other words a quasi-concave function is concavifiable if it can be monotonically transformed into a concave function. The natural question is: are all quasi-concave functions concavifiable? In the next section we address this complex issue briefly. To say that the answer is usually, but not always, 'yes' conveys enough truth for us to move on immediately and address quasi-concave programming with multiple constraints where all the quasi-concave functions are concavifiable. Consider then

$$\max_{\mathbf{x} \in D} f(\mathbf{x}) \text{ subject to } g_i(\mathbf{x}) \geqslant 0, \ i = 1, \ldots, m \tag{20.1}$$

The feasible set for (20.1) is

$$\{\mathbf{x} \in D \mid g_i(\mathbf{x}) \geqslant 0, \ i = 1, \ldots, m\} = S, \text{ say}$$

We assume D is convex and open and that $f: D \to R$ and $g_i: D \to R$, $i = 1, \ldots, m$ are all C^1 quasi-concave functions. Since the behaviour of f, g_i outside the feasible set is not relevant to the solution of (20.1) all we add to these assumptions is that $f: S \to R$ and $g_i: S \to R$ are concavifiable. Hence there exist $m + 1$ monotone increasing functions, $h, h_1, \ldots, h_m$ such that

$$\begin{aligned} h[f(\mathbf{x})] &= F(\mathbf{x}), & \forall \mathbf{x} \in S \\ h_1[g_1(\mathbf{x})] &= G_1(\mathbf{x}), & \forall \mathbf{x} \in S \\ &\cdots\cdots\cdots\cdots & \\ h_m[g_m(\mathbf{x})] &= G_m(\mathbf{x}), & \forall \mathbf{x} \in S \end{aligned}$$

where $F: S \to R$ and $G_i: S \to R, i = 1, \ldots, m$, are all concave functions.

Now the solutions to (20.1) are $\mathbf{x}^*$ such that

$$\mathbf{x}^* \in S \text{ and } f(\mathbf{x}^*) \geqslant f(\mathbf{x}), \ \forall \mathbf{x} \in S$$

Since h is monotone increasing this is equivalent to

$$\mathbf{x}^* \in S \text{ and } F(\mathbf{x}^*) \geqslant F(\mathbf{x}), \ \forall \mathbf{x} \in S$$

Moreover since $h_i, i = 1, \ldots, m$, are monotone increasing

$$S = \{\mathbf{x} \in D \mid G_i(\mathbf{x}) \geqslant h_i(0), \ i = 1, \ldots, m\}$$

Combining these two observations the set of solutions to (20.1) is the same as the set of solutions to:

$$\max_{\mathbf{x} \in D} F(\mathbf{x}) \text{ subject to } G_i(\mathbf{x}) \geqslant h_i(0), \ i = 1, \ldots, m \tag{20.2}$$

But here we have a multiple-constraint *concave* programming problem where solutions can be characterized using chapter 19. We need (CQ) for (20.2). That is, we require the existence of $\mathbf{x} \in D$ such that $G_i(\mathbf{x}) > h_i(0), i = 1, \ldots, m$, which is equivalent to:

(CQ) $\exists\, \mathbf{x} \in D$ such that $g_i(\mathbf{x}) > 0, \ i = 1, \ldots, m$

With this assumption $\mathbf{x}^*$ solves (20.2) and hence (20.1) if and only if:

(A) $F_i'(\mathbf{x}^*) + \sum_{k=1}^{m} \lambda_k^* G_{ki}'(\mathbf{x}^*) = 0, \ i = 1, \ldots, n;$

(B) $\lambda_k^* \geqslant 0, \ k = 1, \ldots, m;$

(C) for all $k = 1, \ldots, m, \ \lambda_k^* = 0$ or $G_k(\mathbf{x}^*) = h_k(0);$

(D) for all $k = 1, \ldots, m, \ G_k(\mathbf{x}^*) \geqslant h_k(0)$ and $\mathbf{x}^* \in D$.

Now $F_i'(\mathbf{x}^*) = h' f_i'(\mathbf{x}^*)$ and $G_{ki}(\mathbf{x}^*) = h_k' g_{ki}'(\mathbf{x}^*)$. Defining $\mu_k^* = \lambda_k^*(h_k'/h'), \ k = 1, \ldots, m$, we see that μ_k^* has the same sign as λ_k^* since h_k' and $h' > 0$. (A)–(D) thus become:

(1) $f_i'(\mathbf{x}^*) + \sum_{k=1}^{m} \mu_k^* g_{ki}'(\mathbf{x}^*) = 0;$

(2) $\mu_k^* \geqslant 0, \ k = 1, \ldots, m;$

(3) for all $k = 1, \ldots, m, \ \mu_k^* = 0$ or $g_k(\mathbf{x}^*) = 0;$

(4) for all $k = 1, \ldots, m, \ g_k(\mathbf{x}^*) \geqslant 0$ and $\mathbf{x}^* \in D$.

Writing the Lagrangean for (20.1) as

$$L(\mathbf{x}, \boldsymbol{\mu}) = f(\mathbf{x}) + \sum_{k=1}^{m} \mu_k g_k(\mathbf{x})$$

(1)–(4) are merely the usual K–T conditions and we have therefore shown that these conditions characterize the solutions to multiple-constraint, *concavifiable quasi-concave* programming problems.

Theorem 20.1 Assume D is convex and open and $f = D \to R$ and $g_i = D \to R$ are all C^1 quasi-concave functions. Assume also that $f = S \to R$ and $g_i = S \to R$, $i = 1, \ldots, m$ are concavifiable functions, where S is the feasible set for (20.1). Then $\mathbf{x}^*$ solves (20.1) if and only if the K–T conditions (1)–(4) are satisfied.

This is very nice, but focuses on the unanswered question of whether quasi-concave functions are in general concavifiable.

20.3 Conditions for concavifiability

Consider a one-variable quasi-concave function $f = D \to R$ where $D \subset R$ is convex and open. Suppose in fact that f is C^2 and monotone increasing. Then f is concavifiable since f^{-1} exists, is monotone increasing and

$$f^{-1}[f(x)] = x = g(x) \text{ which is concave}$$

However, this 'trick' is to no avail in discussions of concavifiability of monotone increasing, quasi-concave functions of more than one variable.

Consider instead a different argument applied to the same f as above. Define:

$$g(x) = -e^{-rf(x)}$$

where r is some positive constant to be specified soon. Straightforward differentiation gives, for $x \in D$

$$g''(x) = re^{-rf(x)}[f''(x) - r\{f'(x)\}^2]$$

Since $f'(\mathbf{x}) > 0$ for $x \in D$ we get

$$g''(x) = re^{-rf(x)} f'(x)^2 \left\{ \frac{f''(x)}{[f'(x)]^2} - r \right\}, \quad \forall x \in D$$

For $\mathbf{x} \in D$ the term outside the right-hand side bracket is positive. Now let $C \subset D$ be any *compact* convex subset of D. Since f is C^2, by theorem 17.1 $f''(x)/[f'(x)]^2$ attains a maximum somewhere on C, with a value M say. Choosing r positive and greater than M ensures $g''(x) < 0$, $\forall \mathbf{x} \in C$ and the restriction of f to C is concavifiable with the monotone increasing transformation $h(f) = -e^{-rf}$ for some positive r. This argument does generalize (details omitted).

Theorem 20.2 Suppose $D \subset R^n$ is convex and open and let C be any compact convex subset of D. Suppose $f: D \to R$ is C^2, quasi-concave and that $f_i'(\mathbf{x}) > 0$, $\forall \mathbf{x} \in D$. Then the restriction of f to C is concavifiable. More precisely there exists $r > 0$ such that $g: C \to R$ defined by $g(\mathbf{x}) = -e^{-rf(\mathbf{x})}$ is concave.

References are found in the bibliographical notes.

20.4 Applications to consumer theory

We analyse the consumer's utility maximization problem without the interior solutions assumption. The problem is

$$\text{(UM)} \quad \max_{\mathbf{x} \in R^n_+} U(\mathbf{x}) \text{ subject to } \sum_{i=1}^{n} p_i x_i \leqslant m \text{ where } (\mathbf{p}, m) \in R^{n+1}_{++}$$

We now assume that there is an open convex set D containing R^n_+ such that U can be defined on D and $U: D \to R$ is C^2, quasi-concave and satisfies $U_i'(\mathbf{x}) > 0$, $\forall \mathbf{x} \in D$, $\forall i$. Fix $(\mathbf{p}, m) \in R^{n+1}_{++}$. The feasible set for (UM) can be written

$$\left\{\mathbf{x} \in D \,\middle|\, \sum_{i=1}^{n} p_i x_i \leqslant m \text{ and } x_i \geqslant 0,\ i = 1, \ldots, n \right\} = S$$

say, and is compact and convex since $(\mathbf{p}, m) \in R^{n+1}_{++}$. From theorem 20.2, $U: S \to R$ is concavifiable. Hence from theorem 20.1 the K–T conditions (1)–(4) characterize solutions to (UM). Writing (UM) in the (20.1) format:

$$\max_{\mathbf{x} \in D} U(\mathbf{x}) \text{ subject to } m - \sum_{i=1}^{n} p_i x_i \geqslant 0,\ x_i \geqslant 0,\ i = 1, \ldots, n$$

the Lagrangean is

$$L(\mathbf{x}, \lambda, \boldsymbol{\mu}) = U(\mathbf{x}) + \lambda\left(m - \sum_{i=1}^{n} p_i x_i\right) + \sum_{i=1}^{n} \mu_i x_i$$

and the relevant K–T conditions are:

(1) For $i = 1, \ldots, n$, $U_i'(\mathbf{x}) - \lambda p_i + \mu_i = 0$;

(2) $\lambda \geqslant 0$ and $\mu_i \geqslant 0$, $i = 1, \ldots, n$;

(3) $\lambda = 0$ or $m - \Sigma p_i x_i = 0$; for $i = 1, \ldots, n$, $\mu_i = 0$ or $x_i = 0$;

(4) $m - \Sigma p_i x_i \geqslant 0$ and $x_i \geqslant 0$, $i = 1, \ldots, n (\Rightarrow \mathbf{x} \in D)$

From (1) $\lambda = [U_i'(\mathbf{x}) + \mu_i]/p_i > 0$ and so $m - \Sigma p_i x_i = 0$ and the consumer buys something.

Two types of solution remain:

(1) *Interior solutions* where $x_i > 0$, $\forall i$ and so $\mu_i = 0$, $\forall i$ in which case (1)–(4) reduce to the K–T conditions of chapter 12.

(2) *Corner solutions* where $x_i > 0$ for at least one i and $x_i = 0$ for at least one i.

Example 20.1 $n = 2$ and $U(\mathbf{x}) = (x_1 + 1)^2(x_2 + 1)^2$. With $D = \{\mathbf{x} \in R^2 \mid x_1 > -1, x_2 > -1\}$, $R^2_+ \subset D$ and $U: D \to R$ is C^2 with $U'_i(\mathbf{x}) > 0$, $\forall \mathbf{x} \in D$, $i = 1, 2$. Moreover $\ln U = 2\ln(x_1 + 1) + 2\ln(x_2 + 1)$ and is concave on D so that U is quasi-concave on D. The K–T conditions chacterizing the (UM) solution are:

(1) $2(x_1 + 1)(x_2 + 1)^2 - \lambda p_1 + \mu_1 = 0$
$\quad 2(x_1 + 1)^2(x_2 + 1) - \lambda p_2 + \mu_2 = 0$

(2) $\mu_1 \geqslant 0, \mu_2 \geqslant 0$

(3) $m = p_1 x_1 + p_2 x_2$; $\mu_1 = 0$ or $x_1 = 0$; $\mu_2 = 0$ or $x_2 = 0$

(4) $x_1 \geqslant 0$, $x_2 \geqslant 0$

1. *Interior solutions.* Here $x_1 > 0, x_2 > 0$ so $\mu_1 = \mu_2 = 0$.

From (1) $\quad \dfrac{x_2 + 1}{x_1 + 1} = \dfrac{p_1}{p_2}$, which implies $p_2 x_2 = p_1 x_1 + p_1 - p_2$.

From (3) $\quad m = p_1 x_1 + p_1 x_1 + p_1 - p_2$

and $\quad x_1 = \dfrac{m + p_2 - p_1}{2p_1} > 0$ if $m > p_1 - p_2$.

Similarly $\quad x_2 = \dfrac{m + p_1 - p_2}{2p_2} > 0$ if $m > p_2 - p_1$.

Hence if $\quad 1 + \dfrac{p_2}{m} > \dfrac{p_1}{m} > \dfrac{p_2}{m} - 1$

we get a unique interior solution defined by the x_1, x_2 values above.

2. *Corner solution at which only good 1 is bought.* Here $x_1 > 0$ and $x_2 = 0$ so $\mu_1 = 0, \mu_2 \geqslant 0$.

From (3)

$$x_1 = \frac{m}{p_1}$$

and from (1)

$$\lambda = \frac{2[(m/p_1) + 1]}{p_1}$$

and

$$\mu_2 = 2\frac{p_2}{p_1}\left(\frac{m}{p_1} + 1\right) - 2\left(\frac{m}{p_1} + 1\right)^2$$

$$= 2\left(\frac{m}{p_1} + 1\right)\left[\frac{p_2}{p_1} - \frac{m}{p_1} - 1\right] = 2\left(\frac{m}{p_1} + 1\right)\left[\frac{p_2 - m - p_1}{p_1}\right]$$

$$\geqslant 0 \text{ if } p_2 - p_1 \geqslant m \text{ or if } \frac{p_2}{m} - 1 \geqslant \frac{p_1}{m}$$

So when

$$\frac{p_2}{m} - 1 \geqslant \frac{p_1}{m}, \quad x_1 = \frac{m}{p_1}, \quad x_2 = 0$$

is the solution.

3. *Corner solution at which only good 2 is bought.* This is symmetric with 2, giving

$$x_1 = 0, \; x_2 = \frac{m}{p_2} \text{ if } \frac{p_1}{m} \geqslant 1 + \frac{p_2}{m}$$

At each $(\mathbf{p}, m) \in R^3_{++}$ there is a unique solution and so this consumer's Marshallian demand functions are:

$$x_1^M(\mathbf{p}, m) = \begin{cases} 0 & \text{if } \dfrac{p_1}{m} \geqslant 1 + \dfrac{p_2}{m} \\[2ex] \dfrac{m + p_2 - p_1}{2p_1} & \text{if } 1 + \dfrac{p_2}{m} > \dfrac{p_1}{m} > \dfrac{p_2}{m} - 1 \\[2ex] \dfrac{m}{p_1} & \text{if } \dfrac{p_2}{m} - 1 \geqslant \dfrac{p_1}{m} \end{cases}$$

$$x_2^M(\mathbf{p}, m) = \begin{cases} \dfrac{m}{p_2} & \text{if } \dfrac{p_1}{m} \geqslant 1 + \dfrac{p_2}{m} \\[2ex] \dfrac{m + p_1 - p_2}{2p_2} & \text{if } 1 + \dfrac{p_2}{m} > \dfrac{p_1}{m} > \dfrac{p_2}{m} - 1 \\[2ex] 0 & \text{if } \dfrac{p_2}{m} - 1 \geqslant \dfrac{p_1}{m} \end{cases}$$

Again we do not have differentiability, and subgradients are needed to generalize our earlier differentiable story. Perhaps more interestingly we can now handle extra constraints on the consumer. For example, shortages of goods can be modelled by imposing extra constraints on (UM)–see bibliographical notes and exercise 20, question 2.

Exercise 20

1. Show that the quasi-concave function $f = R \to R$ where $f(x) = x^3$ is not concavifiable on any compact convex set C where $0 \in \operatorname{int} C$ (hence the stationarity assumption in theorem 20.2 cannot be removed).

2. The restricted expenditure minimization problem for a consumer in a two-good economy is

$$\min_{\mathbf{x} \in R_+^2} p_1 x_1 + p_2 x_2 \text{ subject to } U(\mathbf{x}) \geqslant \bar{u},\ x_i \geqslant \bar{x}_i,\ i = 1, 2$$

where $\bar{x}_1, \bar{x}_2$ are quantity constraints or 'rations'.

(a) Assuming $U(\mathbf{x}) = x_1^{1/4} x_2^{1/4}$, and using question 2 of exercise 19, write down the solution functions (the restricted Hicksian demands, denoted $x_i^{HR}(\mathbf{p}, \bar{u}, \bar{x}_1, \bar{x}_2)$, $i = 1, 2$) and the optimal value function (the restricted expenditure function, denoted $e^R(\mathbf{p}, \bar{u}, \bar{x}_1, \bar{x}_2)$) for this problem.

(b) The ration $\bar{x}_i$ is said to be binding at the solution to the rationed expenditure minimization problem if the corresponding multiplier is strictly positive. When $\bar{x}_i$ is binding, good j is said to be a disequilibrium substitute (complement) for i if $\partial x_j^{HR} \mid \partial \bar{x}_i < (>)\ 0$. Show that in the case considered in (a) both goods are disequilibrium substitutes.

Bibliographical notes

Chapters 1–7

There is a presumption in the text that the reader has some background in calculus and matrix algebra. Readers who do not have this and wish to recap are referred to Binmore (1984), Birchenhall and Grout (1984), Chiang (1974), Lambert (1985) and Silberberg (1978) for calculus. For matrix algebra the reader is referred to Chiang (1974), Hadley (1961) and Lambert (1985); all include coverage of basic matrix algebra, determinants and definite matrices although Hadley (1961) is the most sophisticated.

Birchenhall and Grout (1984) and Lambert (1985) also discuss, at some length, convex sets, concave functions and concave programming, while Binmore (1984), Chiang (1974) and Silberberg (1978) deal briefly with these subjects. Much more comprehensive and sophisticated treatments of concavity (etc.) are found in Avriel (1976), Eggleston (1958), Mangasarian (1969), Martos (1975), Nikaido (1968) and Rockafeller (1970) with, perhaps, Rockafeller (1970) as the ultimate reference and Avriel (1976) and Mangasarian (1969) as the most immediately useful; the reader will find proofs of most of the results of chapters 1–7 in most of these. In particular a straightforward proof of the continuity of concave functions on open convex domains, omitted from chapters 1–7, can be found in Mangasarian (1969, pp. 62–63). Proofs of the hyperplane theorems of chapter 1 can be found in Avriel (1976) and Mangasarian (1969).

The 'local' theory, discussed briefly in chapter 7, has much fuller coverage in Binmore (1984), Intriligator (1971) and Silberberg (1978) or in Avriel (1976) and Mangasarian (1969).

See also the surveys of Green and Heller (1981) and Intriligator (1981).

Chapter 8

Coverage of the envelope theorem is found in Birchenhall and Grout (1984), Dixit (1976), Lambert (1985) and Silberberg (1978); the differentiability assumptions needed for the theorem are too strong for the result to surface explicitly in the more sophisticated texts. Perturbation functions are implicitly discussed in Birchenhall and Grout (1984), Dixit (1976) and Silberberg (1978); Avriel (1976) and Geoffrion (1971) provide a detailed discussion minus differentiability assumptions and with a Kuhn–Tucker development from the perturbation theory.

Chapter 9

Most 'mathematics for economists' texts offer some coverage of homogeneous functions, including the Cobb–Douglas and C.E.S. cases; see e.g. Binmore (1984), Chiang (1974), Silberberg (1978).

Chapters 10–12

Derivation of comparative static results in consumer theory and the theory of the firm in a manner similar to chapters 10–12 can be found in Birchenhall and Grout (1984) and Varian (1984). The classical approach to comparative statics is found in most detail in Henderson and Quandt (1971), Silberberg (1978) or the original Samuelson (1947). For omitted subjects such as support functions, conjugate functions, distance functions (etc.) see Avriel (1976), Rockafeller (1970) and for applications, Deaton and Mullbauer (1980) and McFadden (1978). See also the surveys by Barten and Böhm (1981) and Nadiri (1981).

Chapters 13 and 14

Although many of the 'mathematics for economists' texts cited so far mention quasi-concavity, none offers any detailed development of the subject. For basic properties of quasi-concave functions and first derivative characterizations see Avriel (1976) and Mangasarian (1969). A more general version of the linearly homogeneous/quasi-concave function relation (theorem 13.3) can be found in Berge (1963). Detailed coverage of composition results is given by Martos

(1975). Our treatment of second derivative results and quasi-concave programming more or less follows that of the seminal paper in this area by Arrow and Enthoven (1961).

Chapter 15

Varian (1984) discusses both consumer theory and the theory of the firm under quasi-concavity. Deaton and Mullbauer (1980) provide extensive further coverage of the consumer model while Fuss and McFadden (1978) provide such coverage for the firm.

Chapter 16

Many of the mathematics books mentioned so far discuss open and closed sets and hyperplane theorems; e.g. see Avriel (1976), Berge (1963) and Mangasarian (1969).

Chapter 17

Theorem 17.1 is a fundamental result, a proof of which can be found in many books on mathematical analysis: see e.g. Apostol (1974, p. 73). With concave objective functions, other existence theorems follow from a study of 'directions of recession'; theorem 17.2 is implied by theorem 27.3 of Rockafeller (1970). Katzner (1970) provides a study of differentiability of Marshallian demands while Debreu (1972) offers a deeper coverage of this issue; note that we have omitted discussion of the fact that C^2 strictly concave functions have non-singular Hessians 'almost' everywhere, and of related issues. Apostol (1974) contains a proof and discussion of the implicit function theorem.

Chapter 18

The reader should start filling the gaps left by our coverage in chapter 18 by looking at Varian (1984), where, *inter alia*, an elementary discussion of integrability will be found: see also Birchenhall and Grout (1984). Thereafter Deaton and Mullbauer (1980), Diewert (1974), Fuss and McFadden (1978) and Shephard (1953, 1970) are recommended for deeper investigations: see also Diewert (1981).

Chapter 19

Multiple-constraint concave programming, subgradients, saddlepoints and duality are discussed in detail by Avriel (1976) and Geoffrion (1971). For a general (non-differentiable) discussion of comparative statics in the theory of the firm and for a discussion of input shortages (etc.) see McFadden (1978). Many elementary 'mathematics for economists' texts deal with linear programming; e.g. Chiang (1974) includes an elementary discussion of the Simplex method. See also Hadley (1962).

Chapter 20

Aumann (1975) provides a proof of theorem 20.1: see also Kannai (1977). A concavifiable quasi-concave function is referred to as an 'indirectly concave' function by Birchenhall and Grout (1984), who prove theorem 20.2, *inter alia*. Shortages of goods (i.e. rationing) receives a concise treatment from Neary and Roberts (1980); see also Deaton and Mullbauer (1980).

References

Apostol, T. M. (1974) *Mathematical Analysis*, 2nd edn. Reading, Massachusetts: Addison-Wesley Publishing Co.

Arrow, K. J. and Enthoven, A. C. (1961) Quasi-concave programming. *Econometrica*, **29**, 779–800.

Arrow, K. J. and Intriligator, M. (1981) *Handbook of Mathematical Economics*, vols. I and II. Amsterdam: North Holland.

Aumann, R. J. (1975) Values of markets with a continuum of traders. *Econometrica*, **43**, 611–645.

Avriel, M. (1976) *Non-linear Programming: analysis and methods*. Englewood Cliffs, New Jersey: Prentice Hall.

Barten, A. P. and Bohm, V. (1981) Consumer theory. In K. J. Arrow and M. Intriligator (eds), 1981, vol. II.

Berge, C. (1963) *Topological Spaces*. Edinburgh: Oliver and Boyd.

Binmore, K. (1984) *Calculus*. Cambridge: Cambridge University Press.

Birchenhall, C. and Grout, P. (1984) *Mathematics for Modern Economics*. Oxford: Philip Allan.

Chiang, A. C. (1974) *Fundamental Methods of Mathematical Economics*, 2nd edn. Tokyo: McGraw-Hill KogaKusha.

Deaton, A. and Mullbauer, J. (1980) *Economics and Consumer Behaviour*. Cambridge: Cambridge University Press.

Debreu, G. (1972) Smooth preferences. *Econometrica*, **40**, 603–616.

Diewert, E. (1974) Applications of duality theory. In M. Intriligator and D. Kendrick (eds), *Frontiers of Quantitative Economics*, vol. 2. Amsterdam: North Holland.

Diewert, E. (1981) Duality approaches to microeconomic theory. In K. J. Arrow and M. Intriligator (eds), 1981, vol. II.

Dixit, A. K. (1976) *Optimization in Economic Theory*. Oxford: Oxford University Press.

Eggleston, H. G. (1958) *Convexity*. Cambridge: Cambridge University Press.

Fuss, M. and McFadden, D. (1978) *Production Economics: a dual approach to theory and applications*, vol. 1. Amsterdam: North Holland.

Geoffrion, A. M. (1971) Duality in non-linear programming: a simplified applications oriented development. *SIAM Review*, **13**, 1–37.

Green, J. and Heller, W. P. (1981) Mathematical analysis and convexity with applications to economics. In K. J. Arrow and M. Intriligator (eds), 1981, vol. I.

Hadley, G. (1961) *Linear Algebra*. Reading, Massachusetts. Addison-Wesley Publishing Co.

Hadley, G. (1962) *Linear Programming*. Reading, Massachusetts. Addison-Wesley Publishing Co.

Henderson, J. and Quandt, R. E. (1971) *Microeconomic Theory: a mathematical approach*, 2nd edn. New York: McGraw-Hill Book Co.

Intriligator, M. (1971) *Mathematical Optimisation and Economic Theory*. Englewood Cliffs, New Jersey: Prentice Hall.

Intriligator, M. (1981) Mathematical programming with applications to economics. In K. J. Arrow and M. Intriligator (eds), 1981, vol. I.

Kannai, Y. (1977) Concavifiability and constructions of concave utility functions. *Journal of Mathematical Economics*, **4**, 1–56.

Katzner, D. W. (1970) *Static Demand Theory*. New York: Macmillan.

Lambert, P. (1985) *Advanced Mathematics for Economists: static and dynamic optimization*. Oxford: Basil Blackwell.

Mangasarian, O. L. (1969) *Non-linear Programming*. New York: McGraw-Hill Book Co.

Martos, B. (1975) *Non-linear Programming*. Amsterdam: North Holland.

McFadden, D. (1978) Cost, revenue and profit functions. In M. Fuss and D. McFadden (eds), 1978.

Nadiri, M. I. (1981) Producers theory. In K. J. Arrow and M. Intriligator (eds), 1981, vol. II.

Neary, J. D. and Roberts, K. W. S. (1980) The theory of household behaviour under rationing. *European Economic Review*, **13**, 25–42.

Nikaido, H. (1968) *Convex Structures and Economic Theory*. New York: Academic Press.

Rockafeller, R. T. (1970) *Convex Analysis*. Princeton, New Jersey: Princeton University Press.

Samuelson, P. A. (1947) *Foundations of Economic Analysis*. Cambridge, Mass.: Harvard University Press.

Silberberg, E. (1978) *The Structure of Economics: a mathematical analysis*. New York: McGraw-Hill Book Co.

Shephard, R. (1953) *Cost and Production Functions*. Princeton, New Jersey: Princeton University Press.

Shephard, R. (1970) *Theory of Cost and Production Functions*. Princeton, New Jersey: Princeton University Press.

Varian, H. (1984) *Microeconomic Analysis*, 2nd edn. New York: W. W. Norton and Co. Inc.

Index